Missions of Love

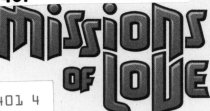

Volume 8

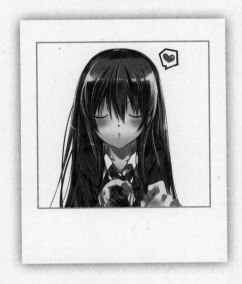

Ema Toyama

Missions of Love
Ema Toyama

Character

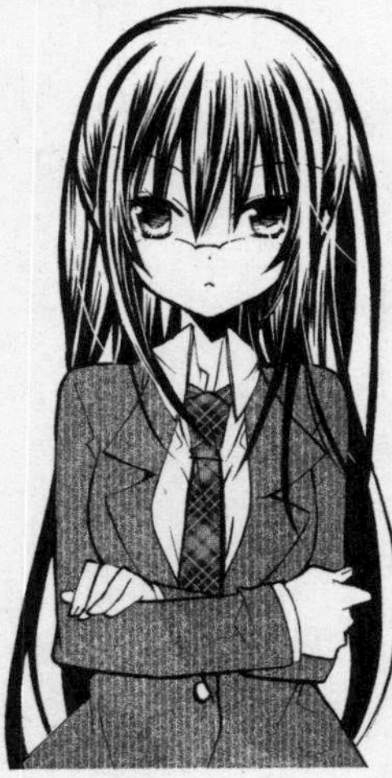

Shigure Kitami

The ever-popular, yet black-hearted, student body president. He made a game of charming all the girls and making them confess their love to him, then writing it all down in his student notebook, but Yukina discovered his secret!

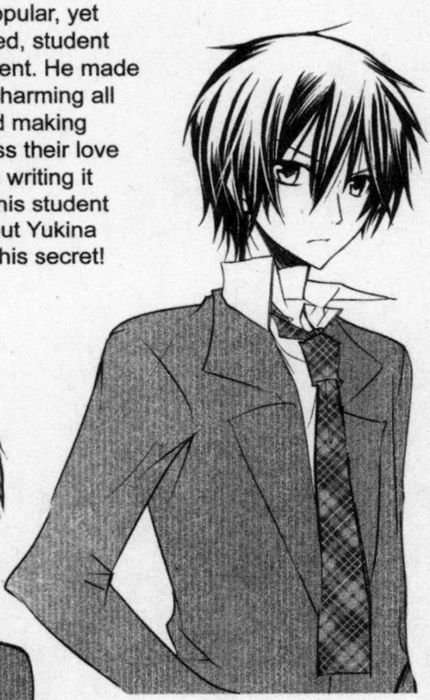

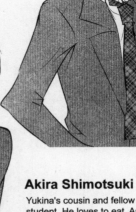

Yukina Himuro

A third-year junior high student who strikes terror in the hearts of all around her with her piercing gaze, feared as the “Absolute Zero Snow Woman.” Only Akira knows that she is also the popular cell phone novelist Yupina.

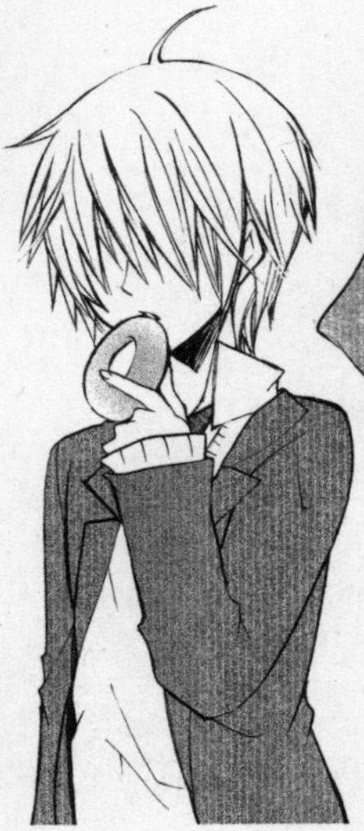

Akira Shimotsuki

Yukina's cousin and fellow student. He loves to eat. As Yukina's confidant, he can always be found nearby, watching over her. There's a good-looking face hiding behind that hair.

ne!

Mami Mizuno

A childhood friend of Shigure's. A sickly girl. The teachers love her, and she's very popular with the boys. She's a beautiful young girl who always wears a smile, but deep down, her heart is black. She has told Shigure how she feels about him, but...

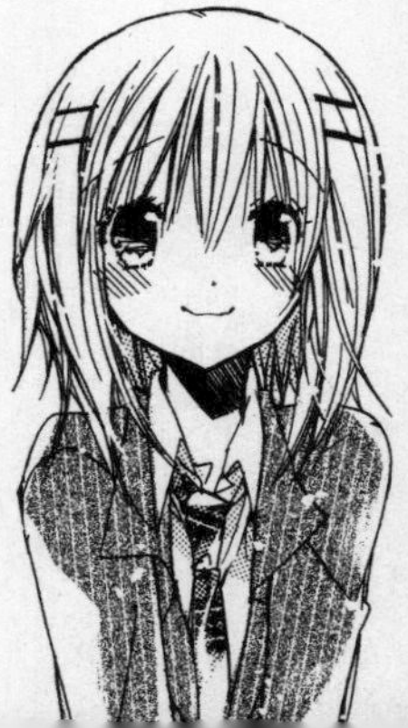

It is time for love.
Secret cell phone novelist vs. the most popular boy in school.
A mission of love for absolute servitude.

Story

Through her blackmail of Shigure, Yukina has been gaining more and more romantic experience. Their relationship was in constant flux, until Shigure promised to help her overcome her weakness—a promise that brought the two one step closer to each other. Meanwhile, Mami starts to have her suspicions about Yupina's cell phone novel....

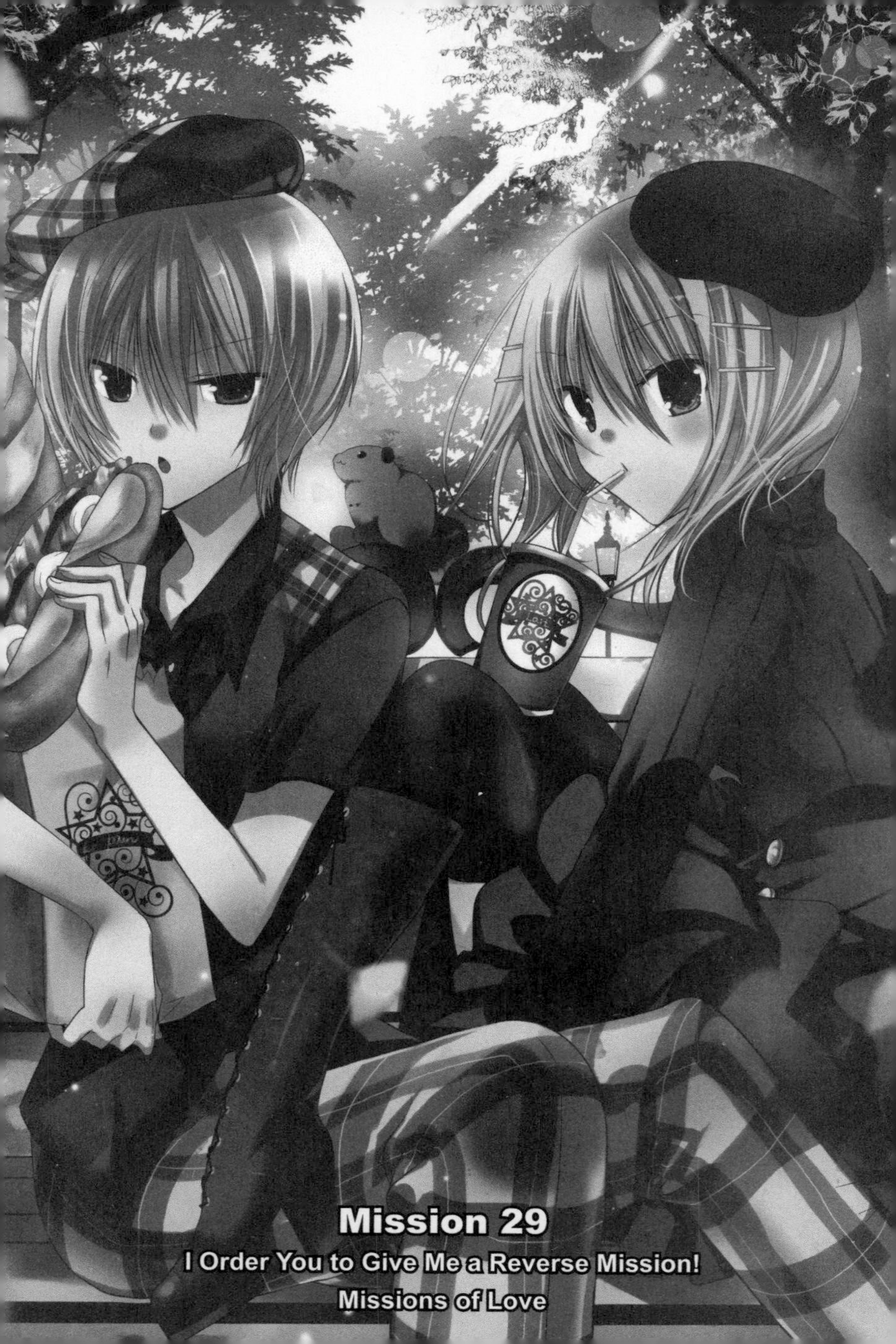

Mission 29

I Order You to Give Me a Reverse Mission!

Missions of Love

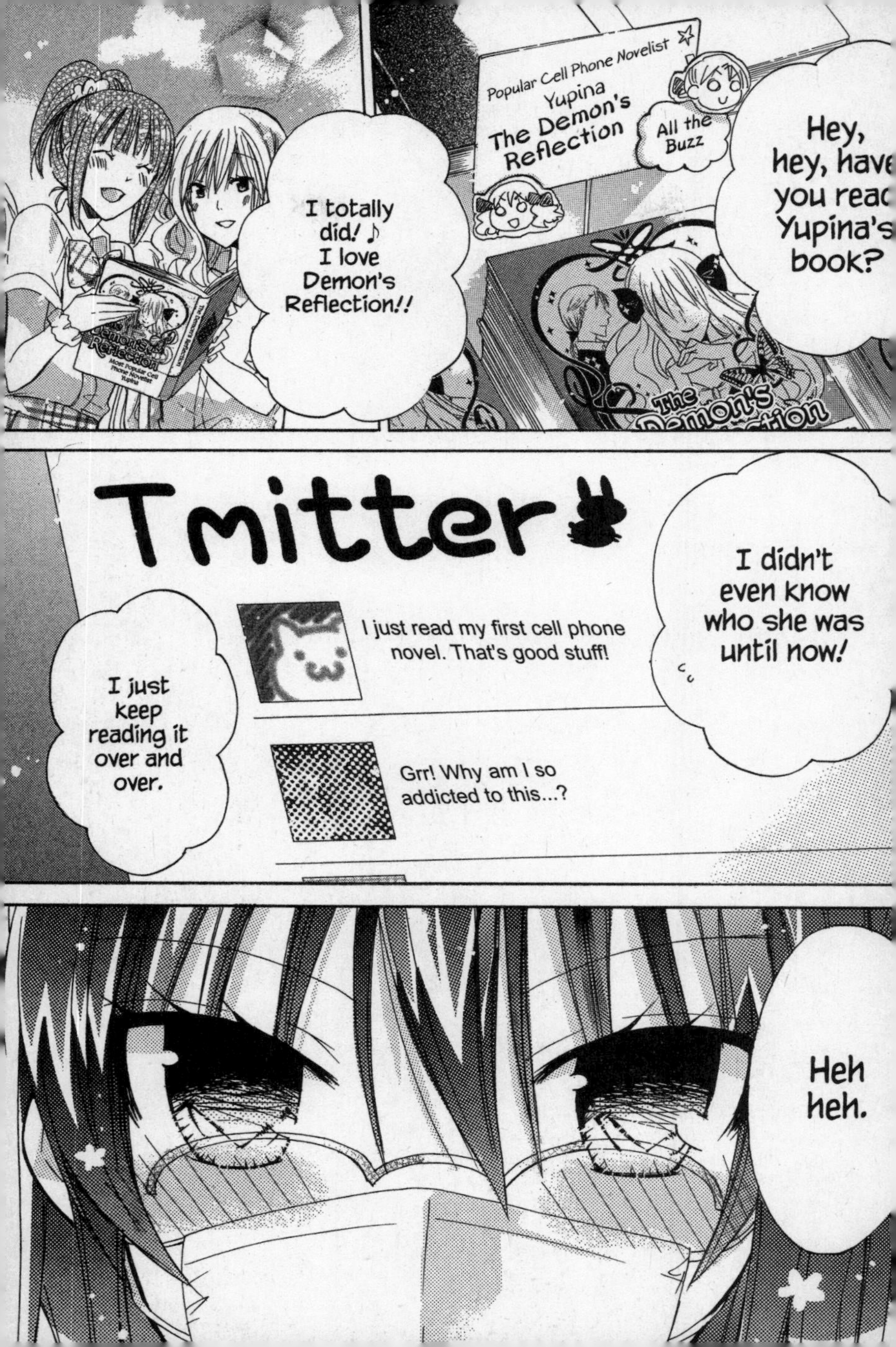

Hey, hey, have you read Yupina's book?
Popular Cell Phone Novelist Yupina The Demon's Reflection
All the Buzz
The Demon's Reflection
I totally did! ♪ I love Demon's Reflection!!
Demon's Reflection
Most Popular Cell Phone Novelist Yupina
Tmitter
I didn't even know who she was until now!
I just read my first cell phone novel. That's good stuff!
Grr! Why am I so addicted to this...?
I just keep reading it over and over.
Heh heh.

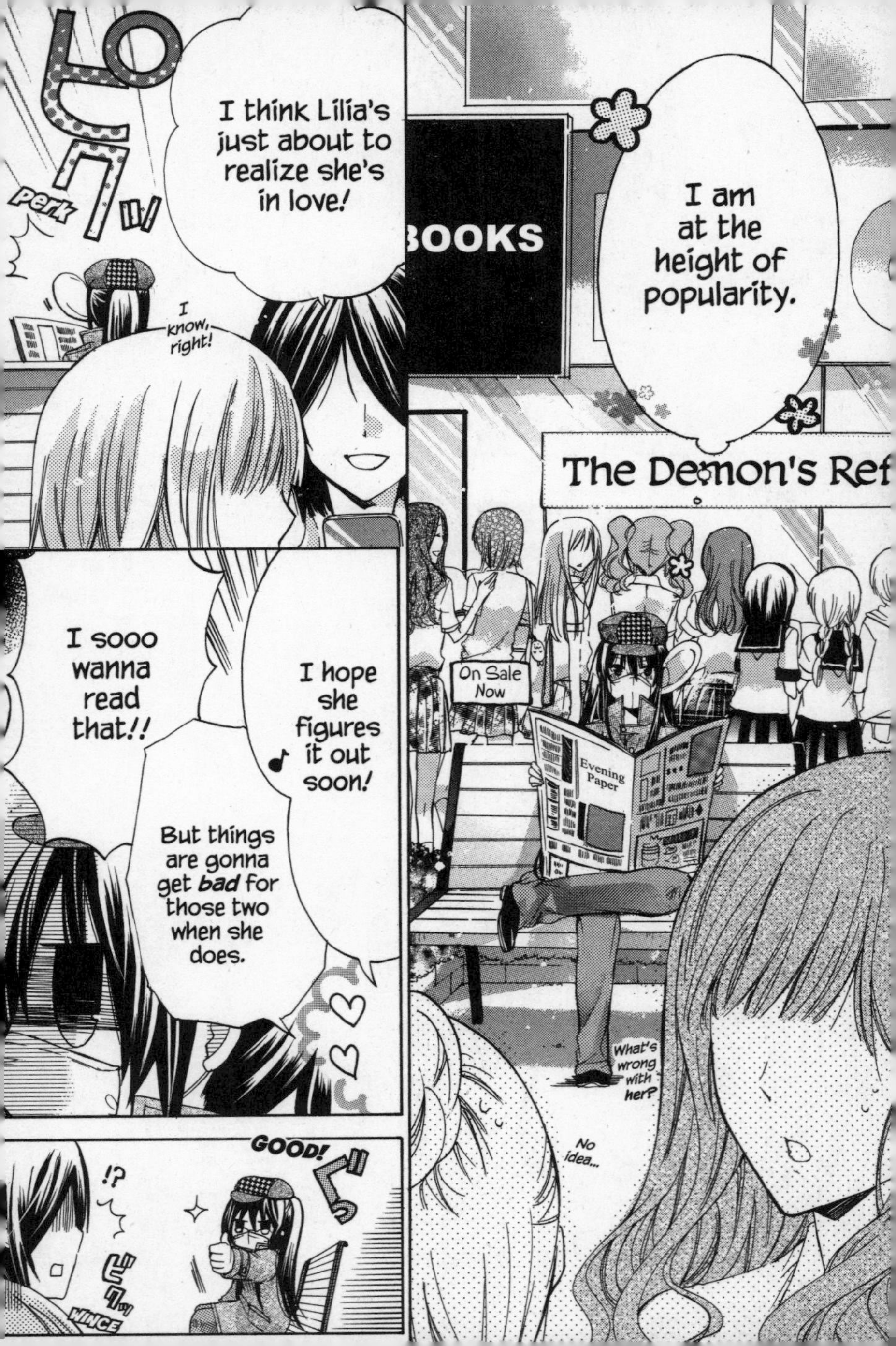
I am at the height of popularity.
BOOKS
The Demon's Ref
On Sale Now
Evening Paper
What's wrong with her?
No idea...
I think Lilia's just about to realize she's in love!
perk
I know, right!
I hope she figures it out soon!
I sooo wanna read that!!
But things are gonna get *bad* for those two when she does.
GOOD!
!?
WINCE

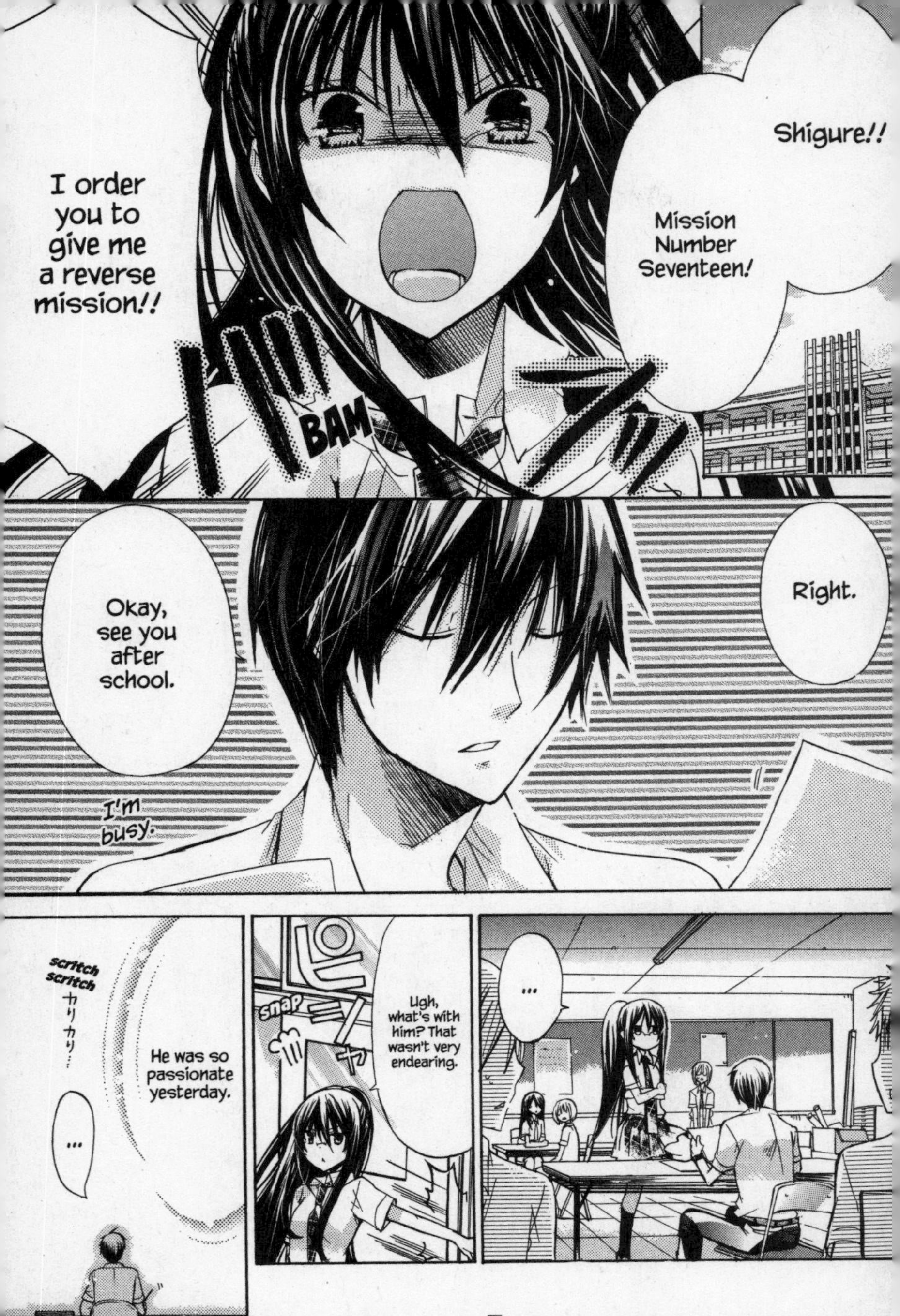
Shigure!!
Mission Number Seventeen!
BAM
I order you to give me a reverse mission!!
Right.
Okay, see you after school.
I'm busy.
...
snap
Ugh, what's with him? That wasn't very endearing.
He was so passionate yesterday.
scritch scritch
カリカリ…
...

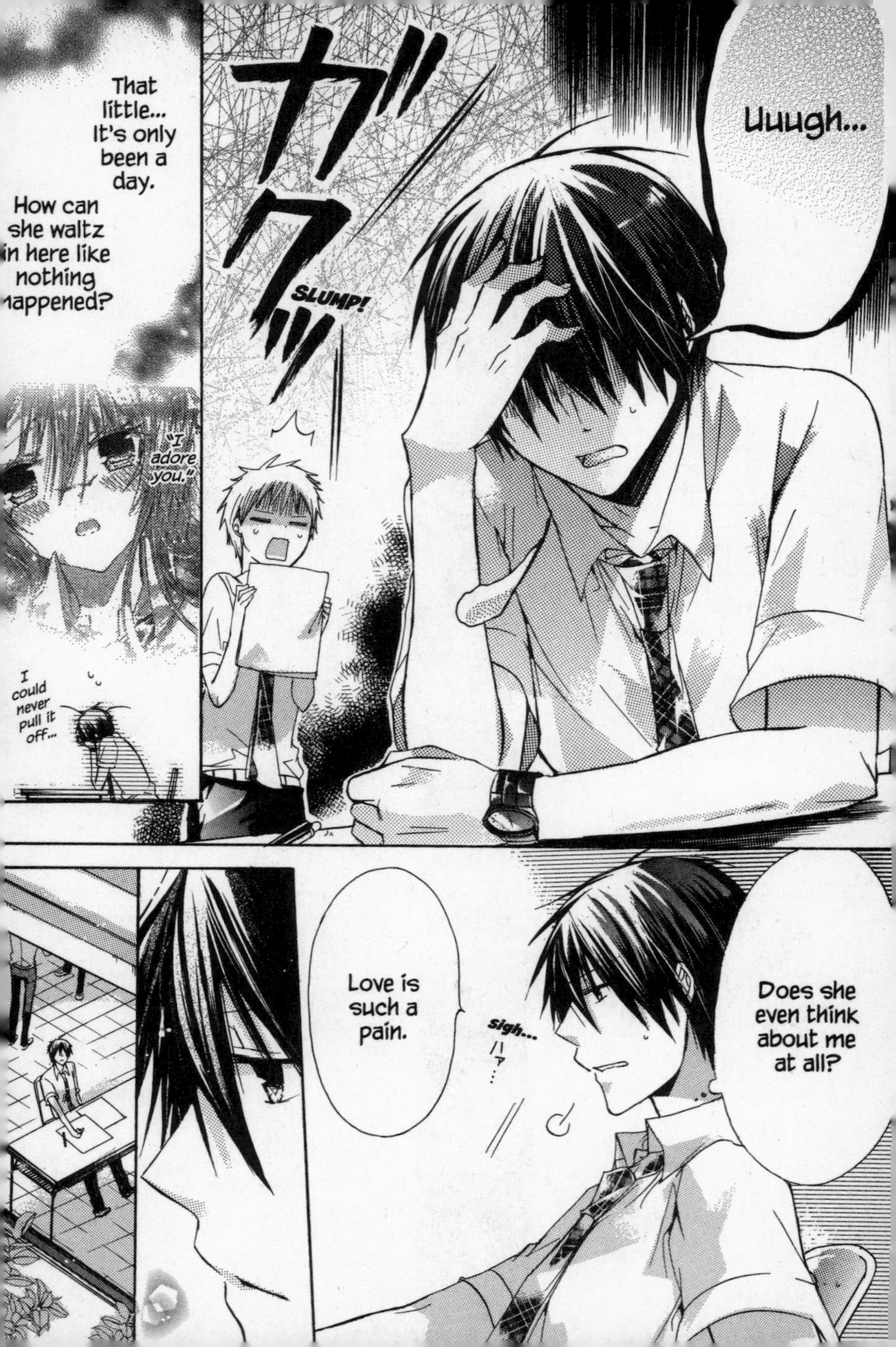
Uuugh...
ガクッ
SLUMP!
That little... It's only been a day.
How can she waltz in here like nothing happened?
"I adore you."
I could never pull it off...
Does she even think about me at all?
Sigh...
ハァ…
Love is such a pain.

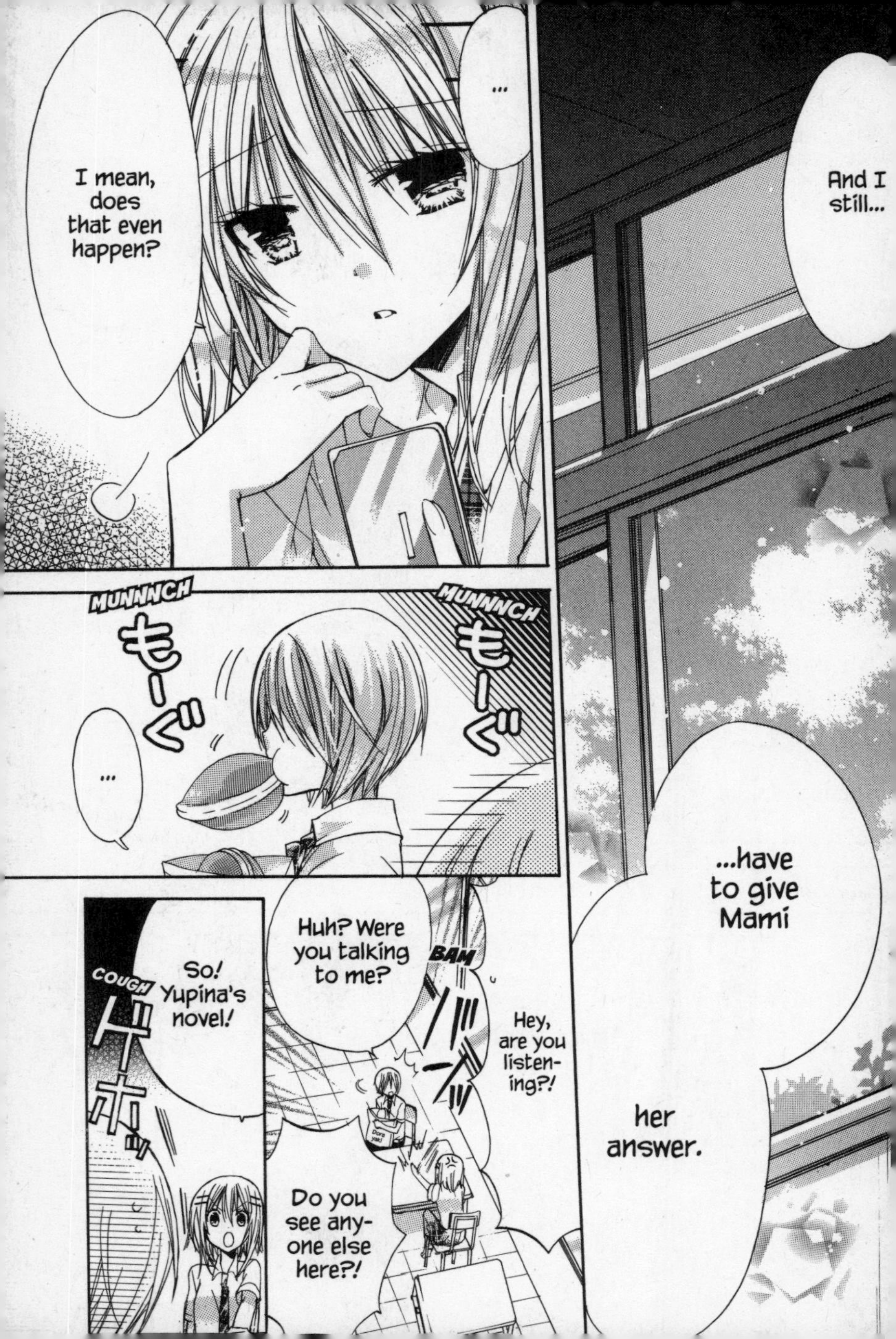

And I still...
...have to give Mami
her answer.
...
I mean, does that even happen?
MUNNNCH
もーぐ
MUNNNCH
もーぐ
...
Huh? Were you talking to me?
BAM
Hey, are you listen-ing?!
Do you see any-one else here?!
So! Yupina's novel!
COUGH
ゲホッ

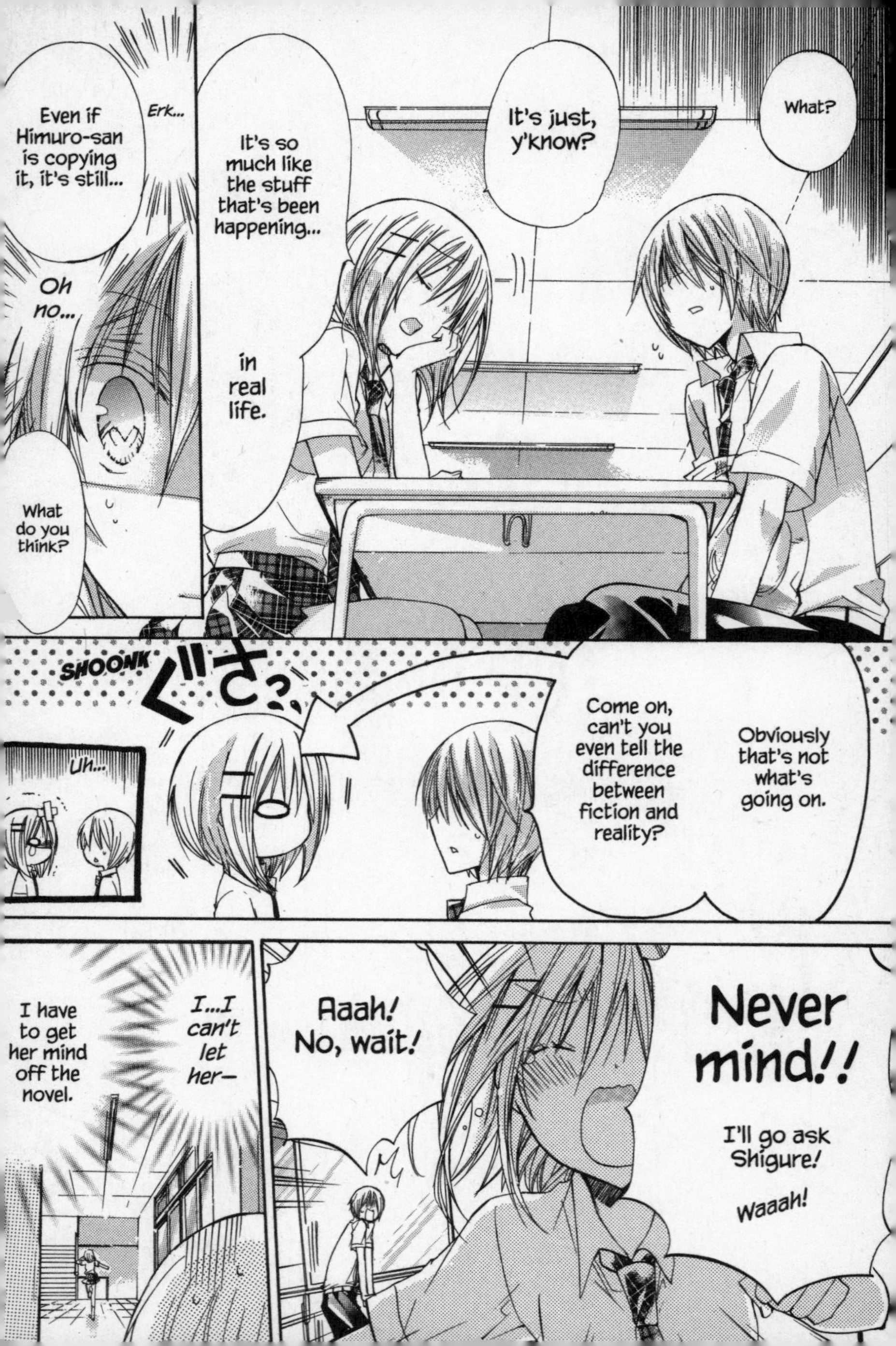
What?
It's just, y'know?
It's so much like the stuff that's been happening...
in real life.
Erk...
Even if Himuro-san is copying it, it's still...
Oh no...
What do you think?
Obviously that's not what's going on.
Come on, can't you even tell the difference between fiction and reality?
ぐさっ
SHOONK
Uh...
Never mind!!
I'll go ask Shigure!
Waaah!
Aaah! No, wait!
I...I can't let her—
I have to get her mind off the novel.

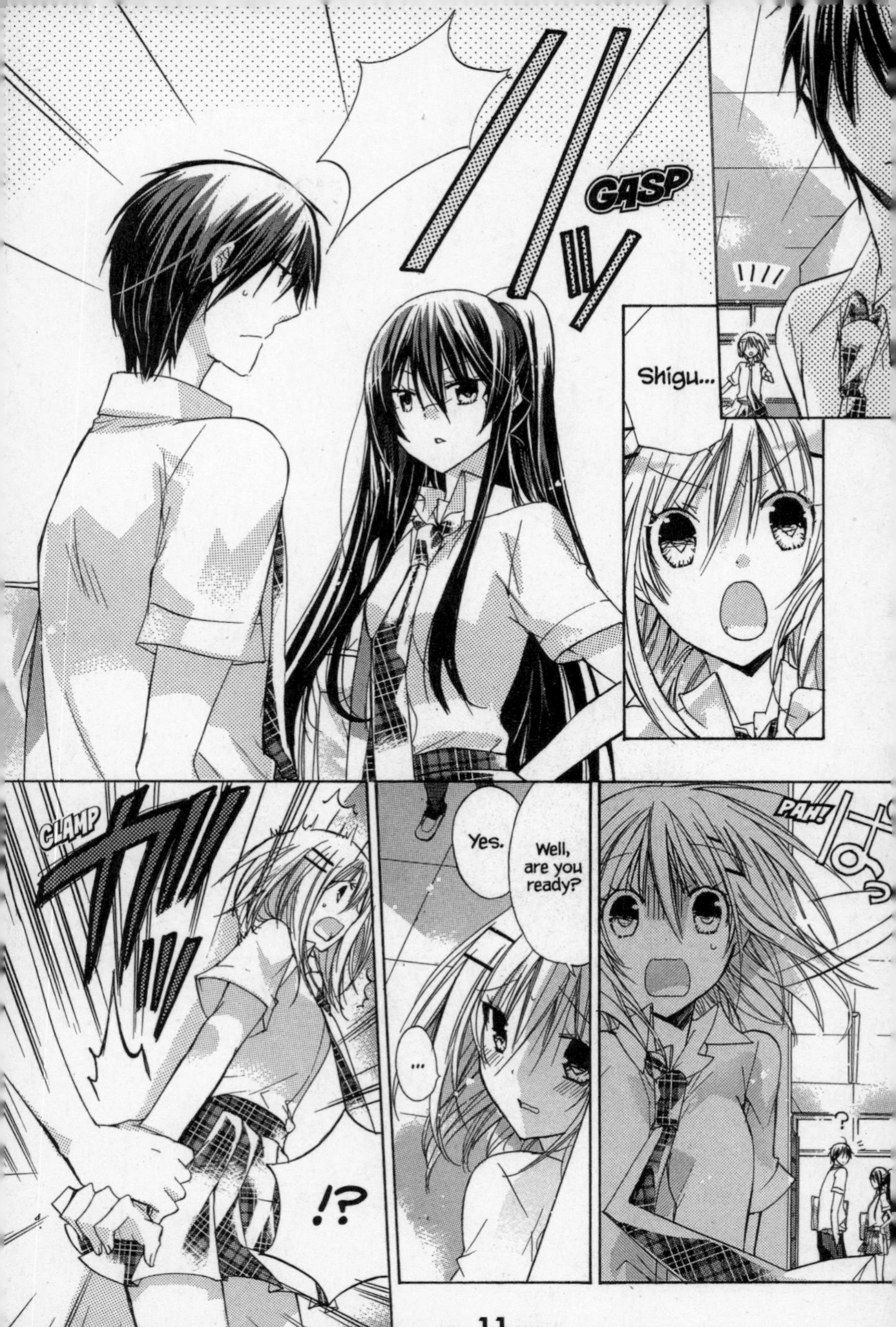
Shigu...
GASP
PAH!
Well, are you ready?
Yes.
...
CLAMP
!?

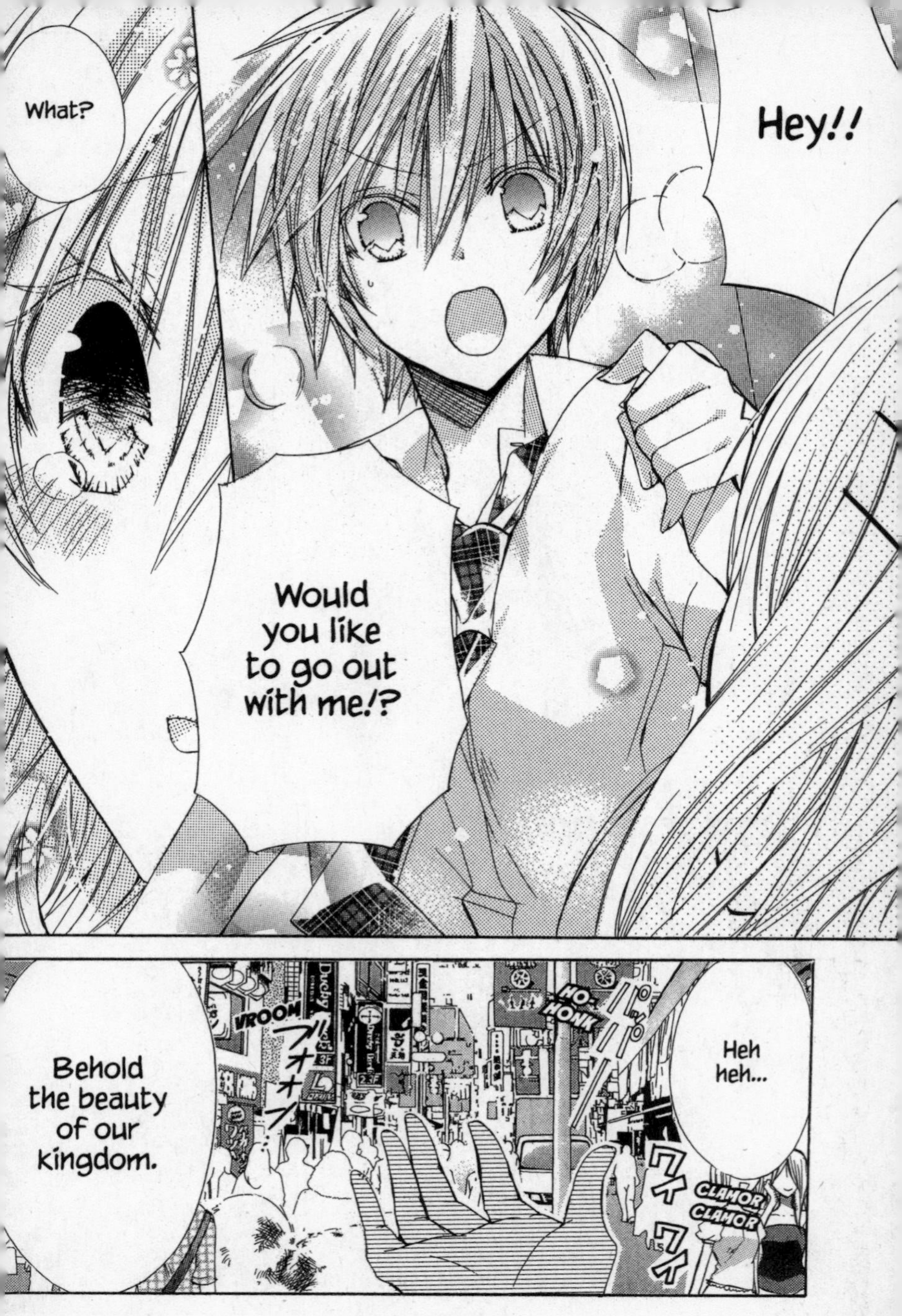
Hey!!
Would you like to go out with me!?
What?
Heh heh...
CLAMOR CLAMOR
HO-HONK
VROOM
Behold the beauty of our kingdom.

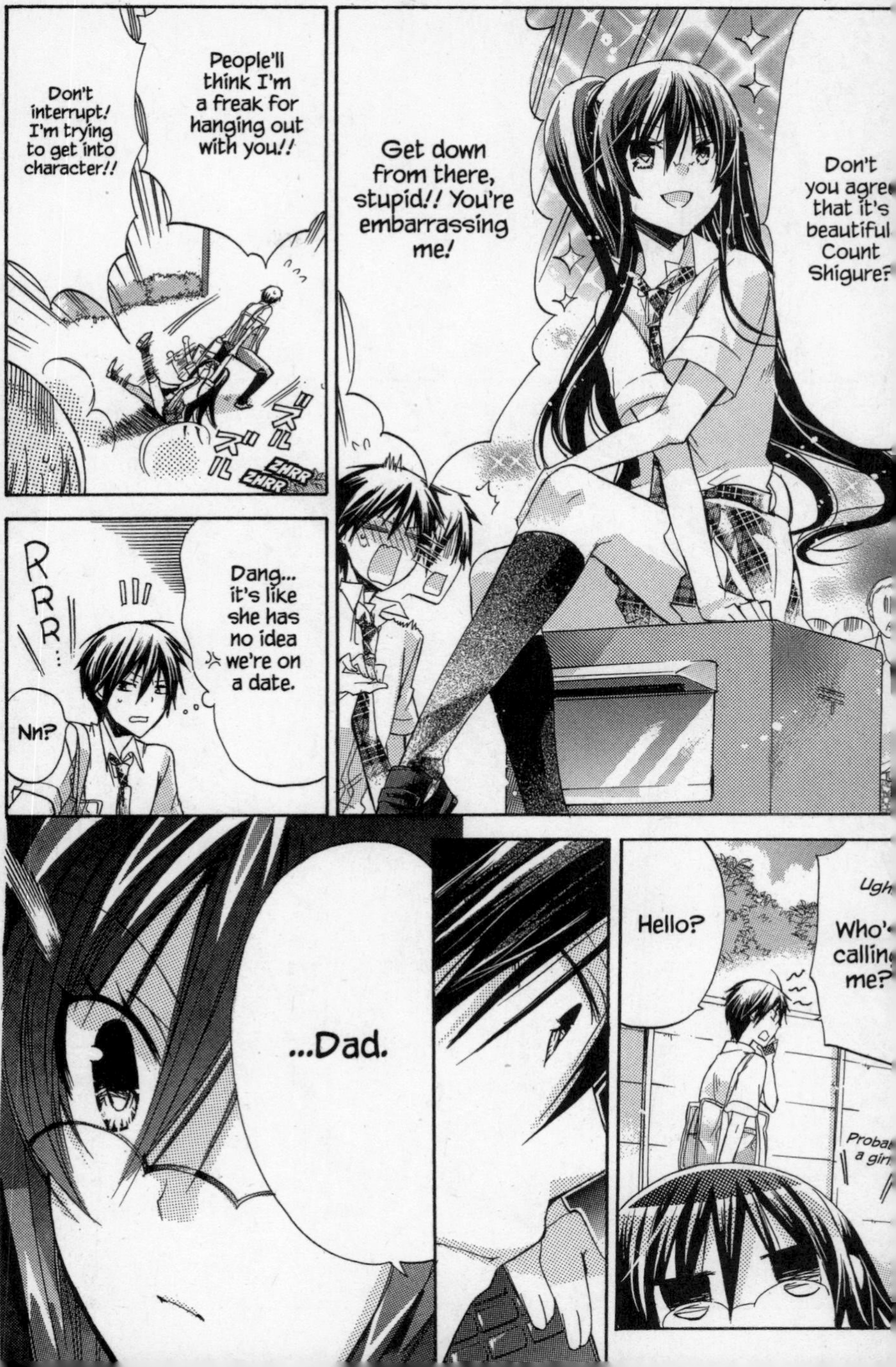
Don't you agre that it's beautiful Count Shigure?
Get down from there, stupid!! You're embarrassing me!
People'll think I'm a freak for hanging out with you!!
Don't interrupt! I'm trying to get into character!!
ズル ズル
ZHRR ZHRR
Dang... it's like she has no idea we're on a date.
RRR...
Nn?
Ugh
Who' callin me?
Hello?
Proba a gir
...Dad.

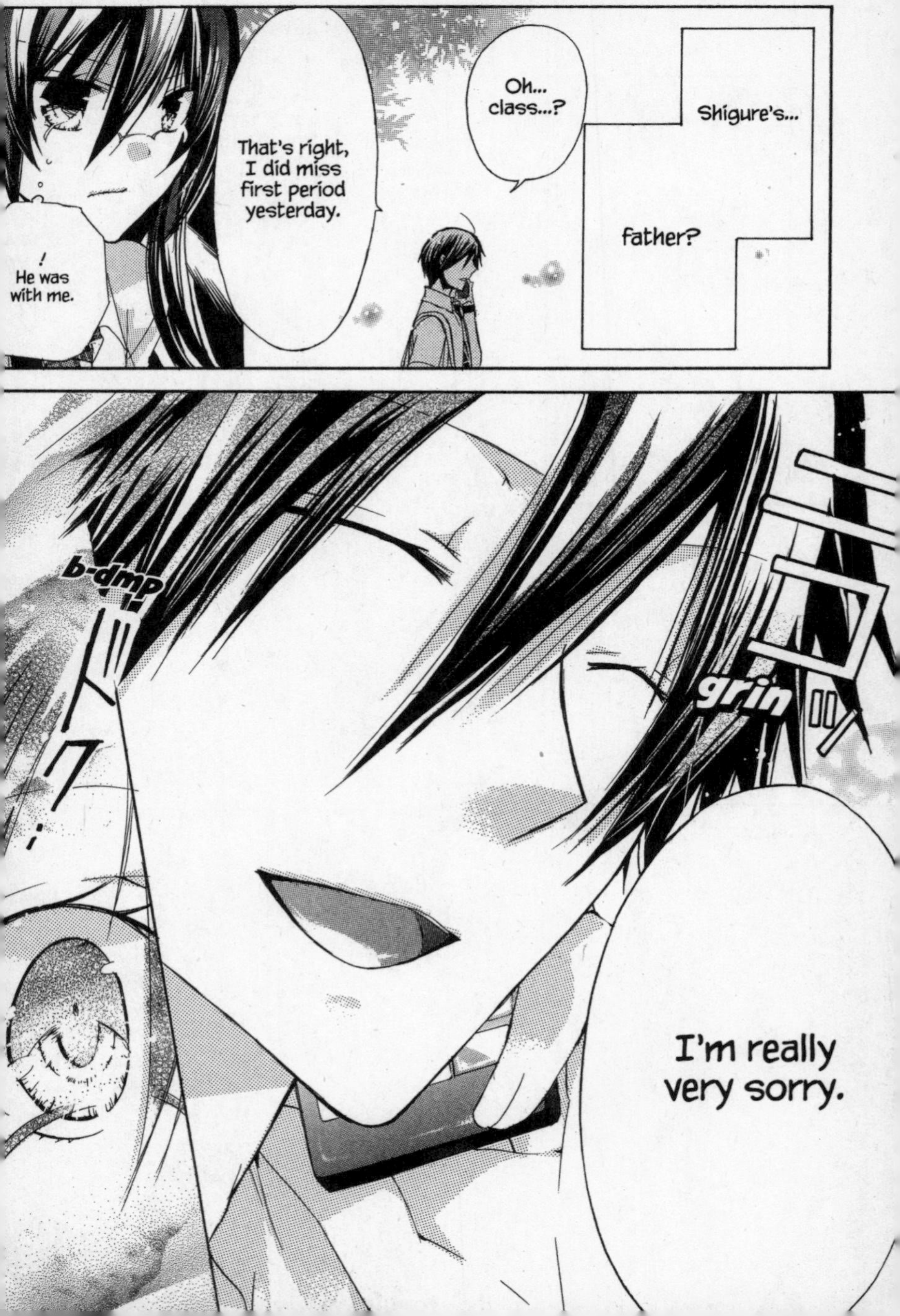
Shigure's...
father?
Oh... class...?
That's right, I did miss first period yesterday.
! He was with me.
grin
b-dmp
I'm really very sorry.

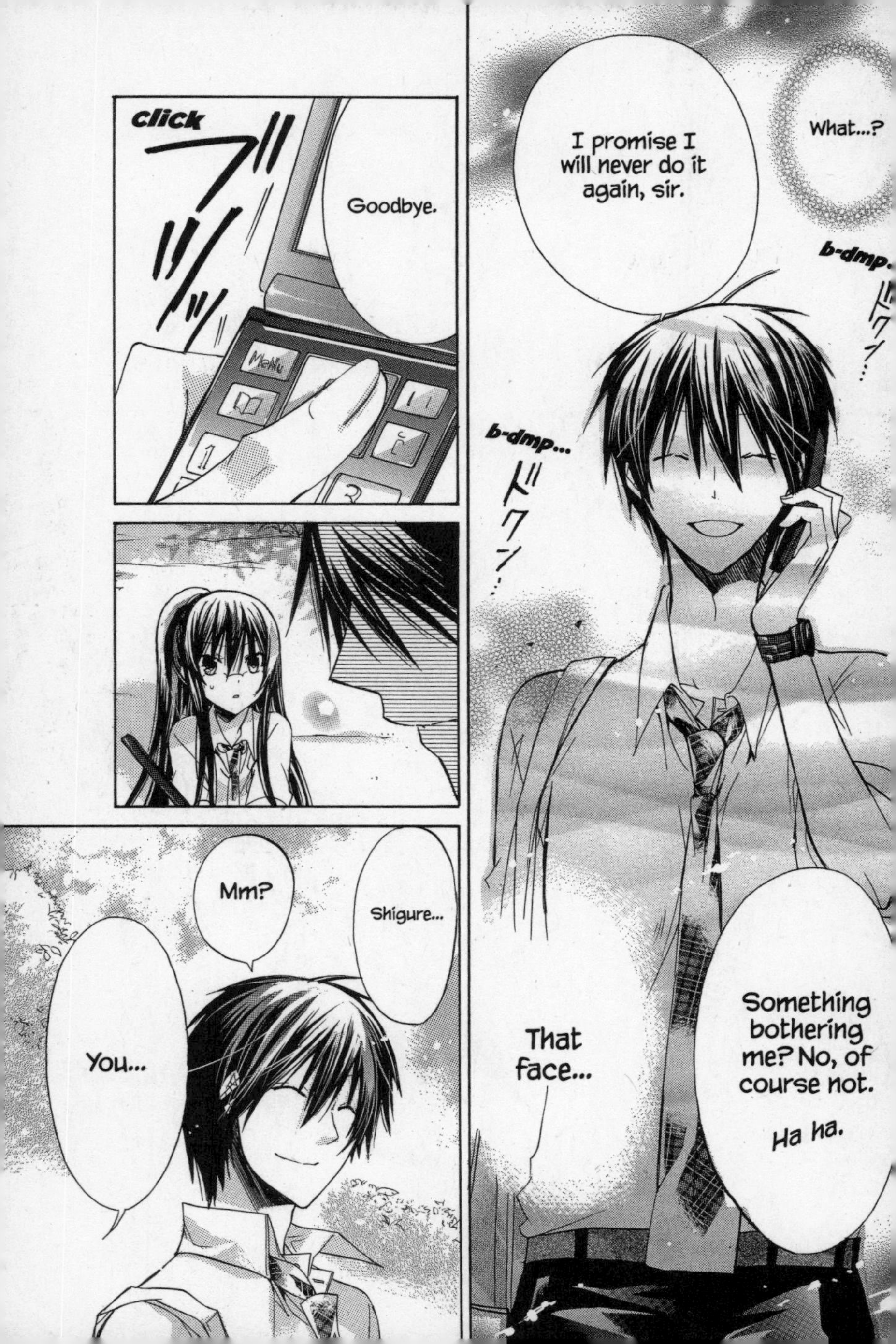
What...?
I promise I will never do it again, sir.
b-dmp.
b-dmp...
ドクン…
Something bothering me? No, of course not.
Ha ha.
That face...
click
Goodbye.
Shigure...
Mm?
You...

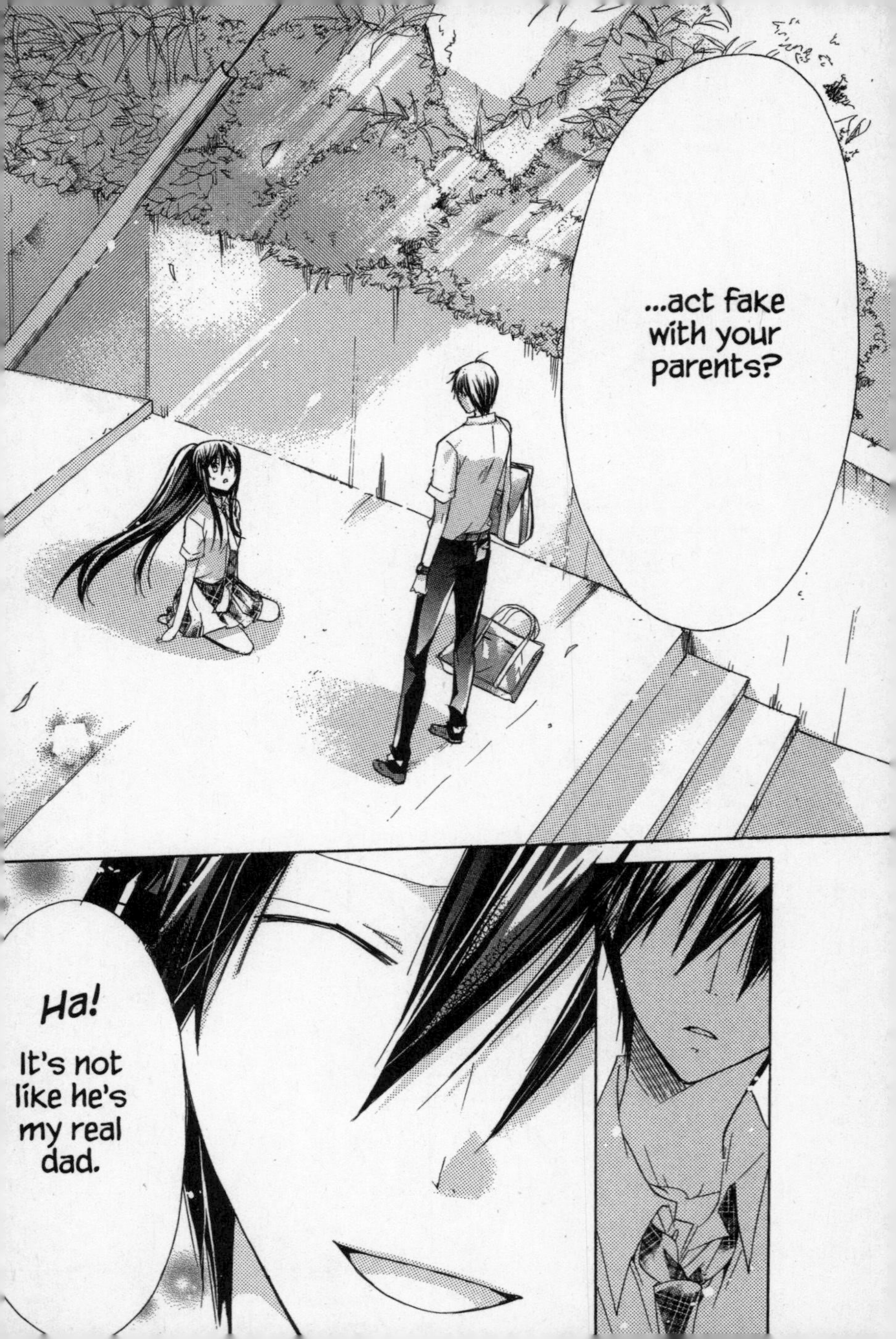
...act fake with your parents?
Ha!
It's not like he's my real dad.

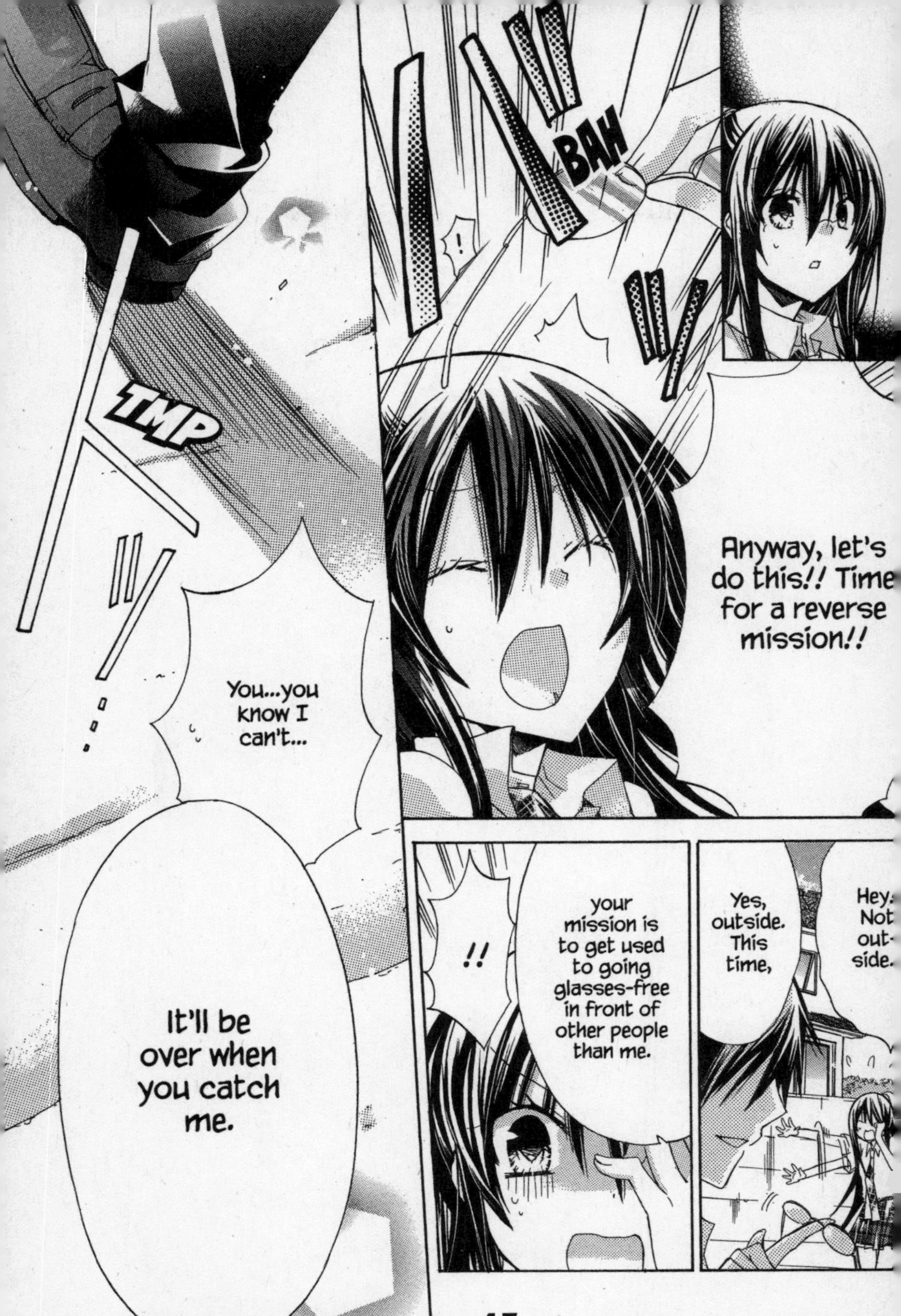
BAH
!
Anyway, let's do this!! Time for a reverse mission!!
Hey! Not outside.
Yes, outside. This time,
your mission is to get used to going glasses-free in front of other people than me.
!!
TMP
You...you know I can't...
It'll be over when you catch me.

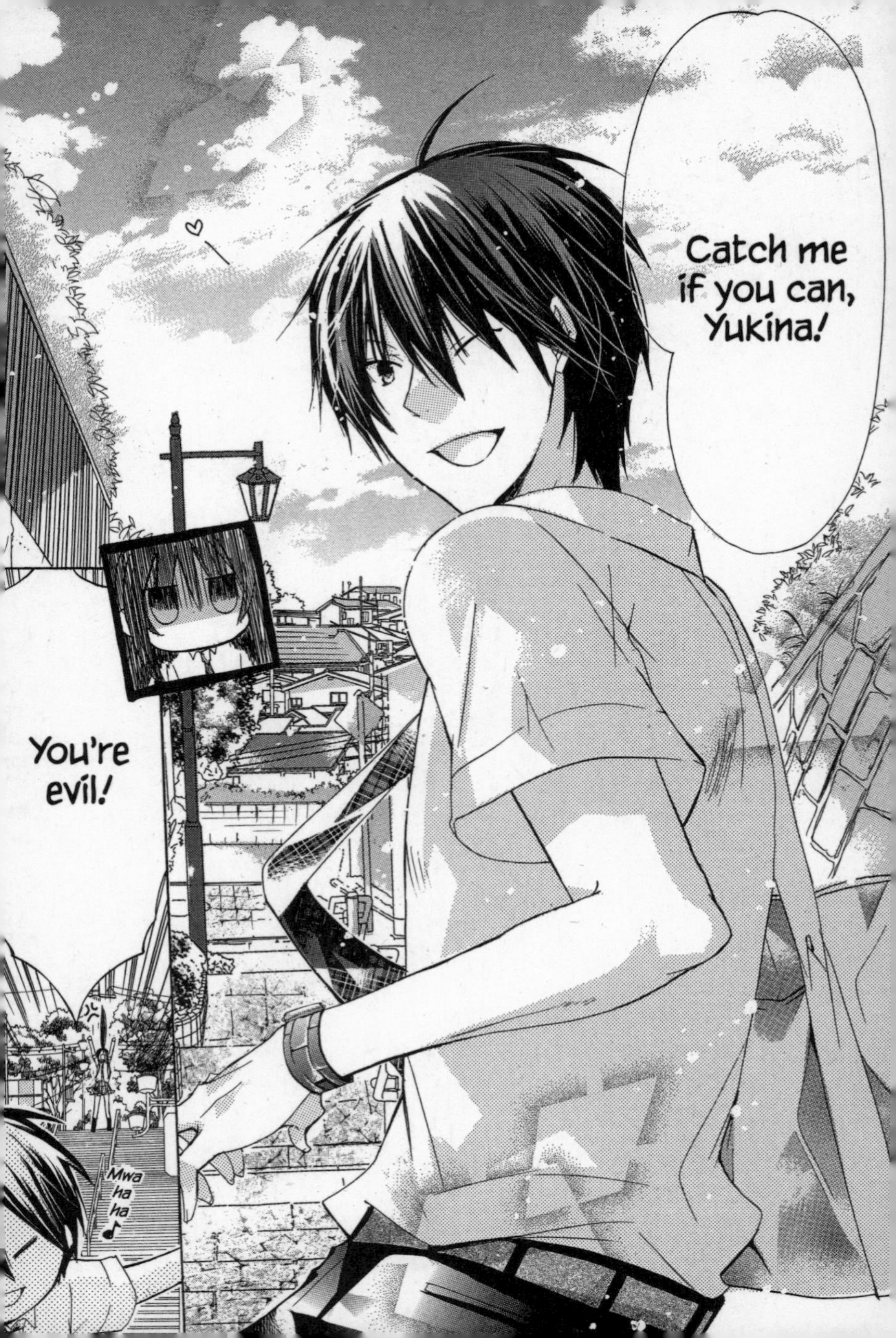

Catch me if you can, Yukina!
You're evil!
Mwa ha ha ♪

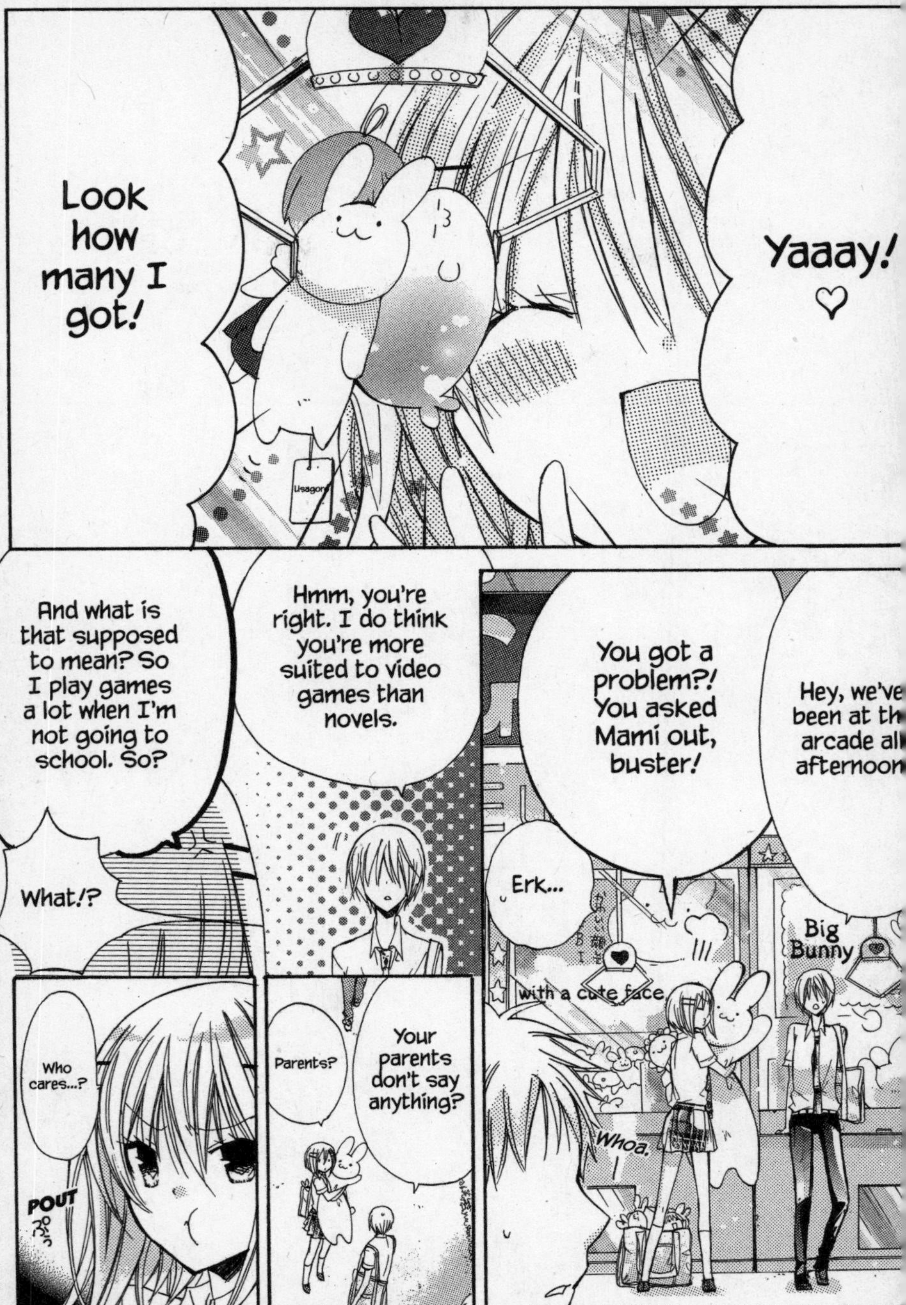
Yaaay! ♡
Look how many I got!
Hey, we've been at th arcade al afternoon
You got a problem?! You asked Mami out, buster!
Erk...
Big Bunny
with a cute face
Whoa.
Hmm, you're right. I do think you're more suited to video games than novels.
And what is that supposed to mean? So I play games a lot when I'm not going to school. So?
What!?
Your parents don't say anything?
Parents?
Who cares...?
POUT

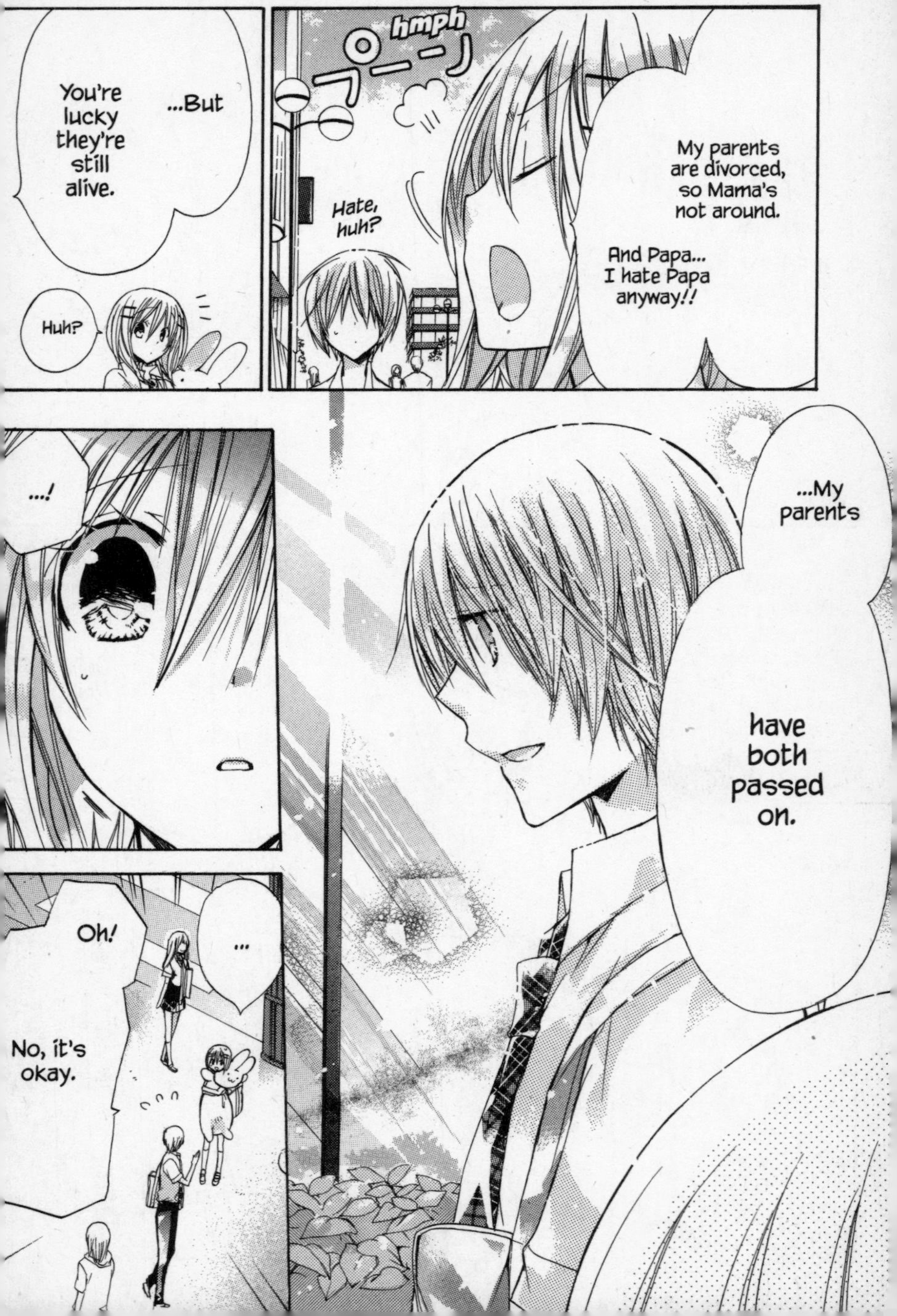
My parents are divorced, so Mama's not around.
And Papa... I hate Papa anyway!!
hmph
Hate, huh?
...But
You're lucky they're still alive.
Huh?
...My parents
have both passed on.
...!
...
Oh!
No, it's okay.

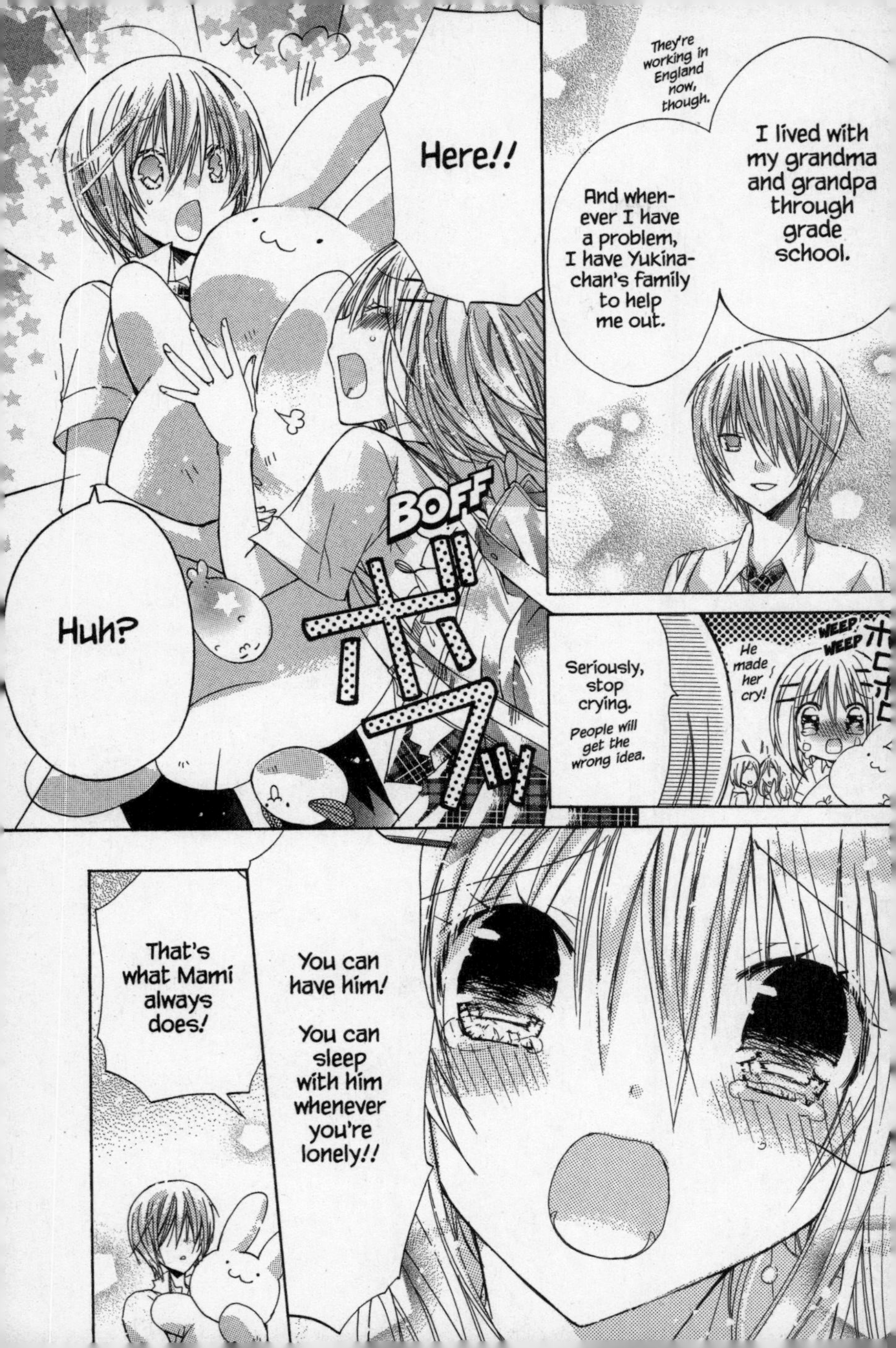

I lived with my grandma and grandpa through grade school.
They're working in England now, though.
And whenever I have a problem, I have Yukina-chan's family to help me out.
WEEP WEEP
He made her cry!
Seriously, stop crying.
People will get the wrong idea.
Here!!
BOFF
Huh?
You can have him!
You can sleep with him whenever you're lonely!!
That's what Mami always does!

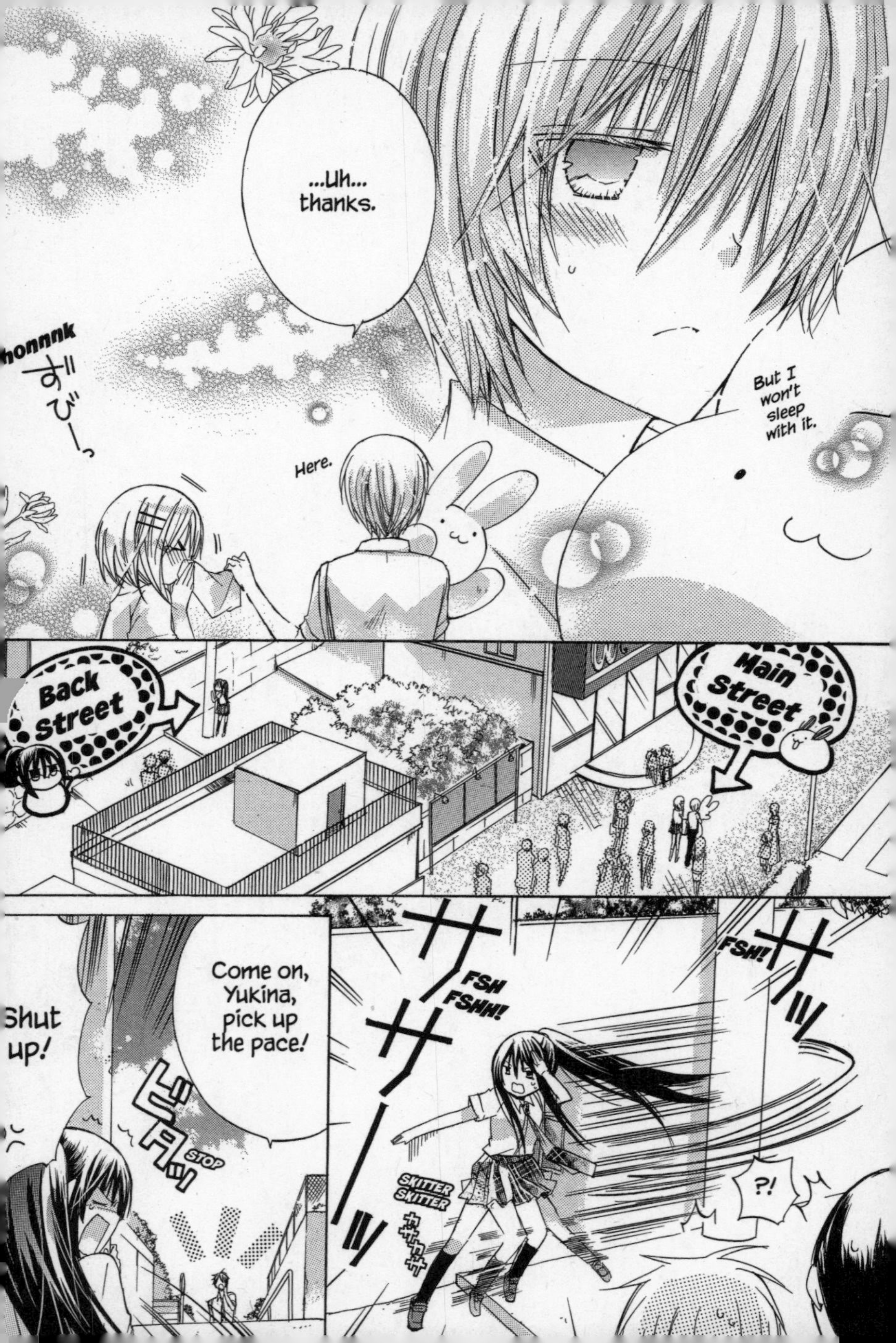
...uh... thanks.
But I won't sleep with it.
Here.
honnnk
ずび—っ
Main Street
Back Street
FSH!
ザ
FSH FSHH!
ザ
ザ
SKITTER SKITTER
カサカサ
?!
Come on, Yukina, pick up the pace!
STOP
ピタッ
Shut up!

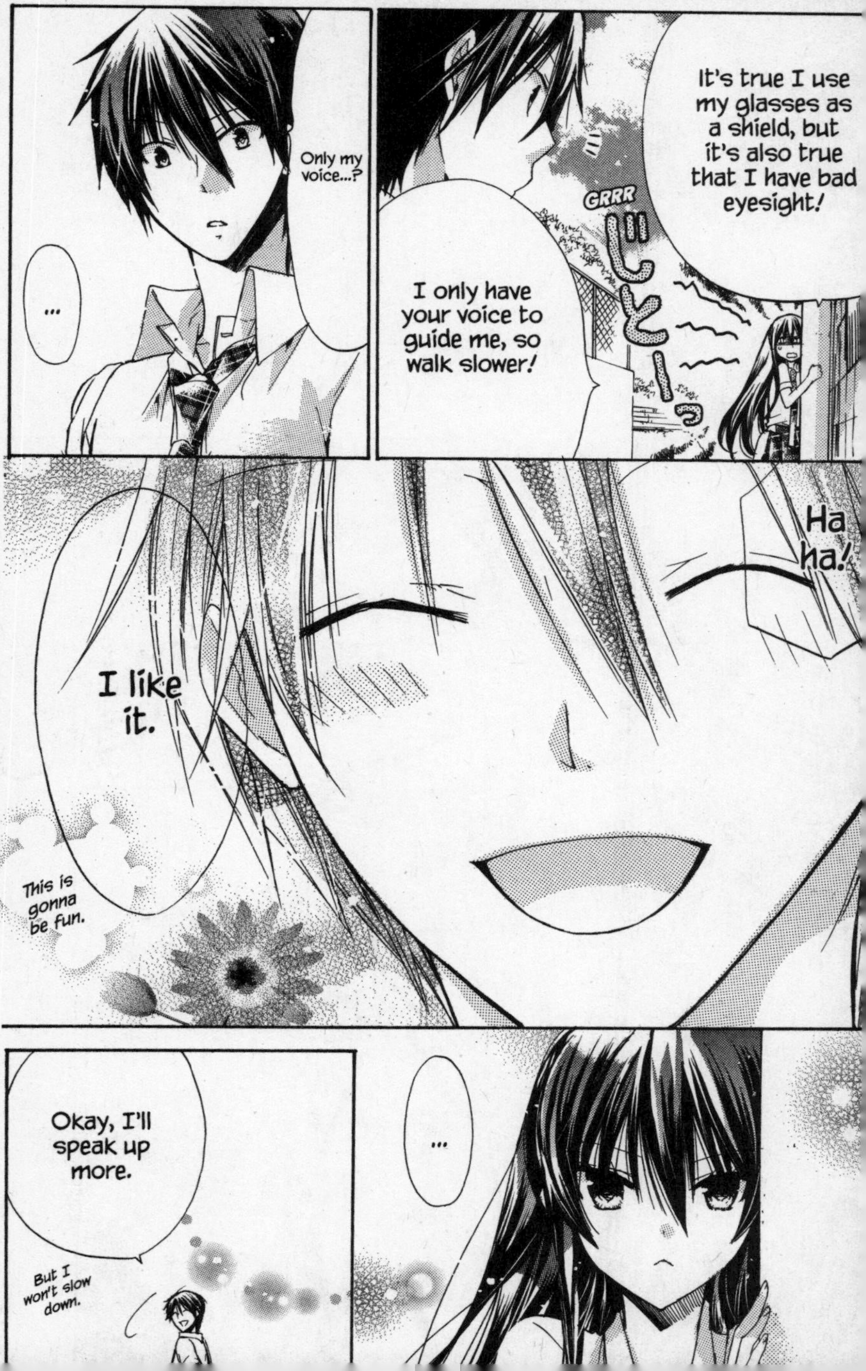
It's true I use my glasses as a shield, but it's also true that I have bad eyesight!
GRRR
じとーっ
I only have your voice to guide me, so walk slower!
Only my voice...?
...
Ha ha!
I like it.
This is gonna be fun.
...
Okay, I'll speak up more.
But I won't slow down.

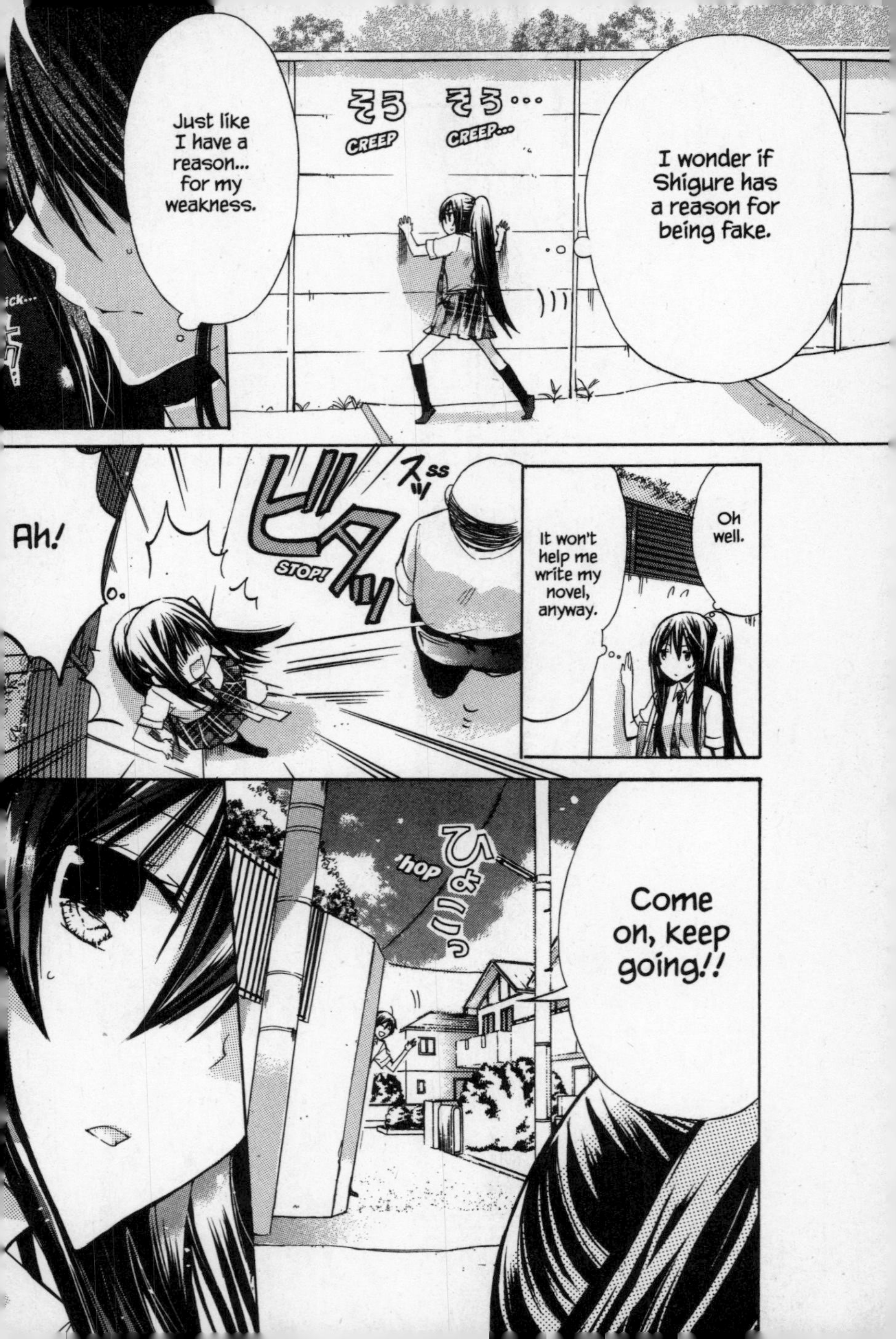
I wonder if Shigure has a reason for being fake.
そろ そろ…
CREEP CREEP...
Just like I have a reason... for my weakness.
Oh well.
It won't help me write my novel, anyway.
スッ
ss
ピタッ
STOP!
Ah!
Come on, keep going!!
ひょこっ
hop

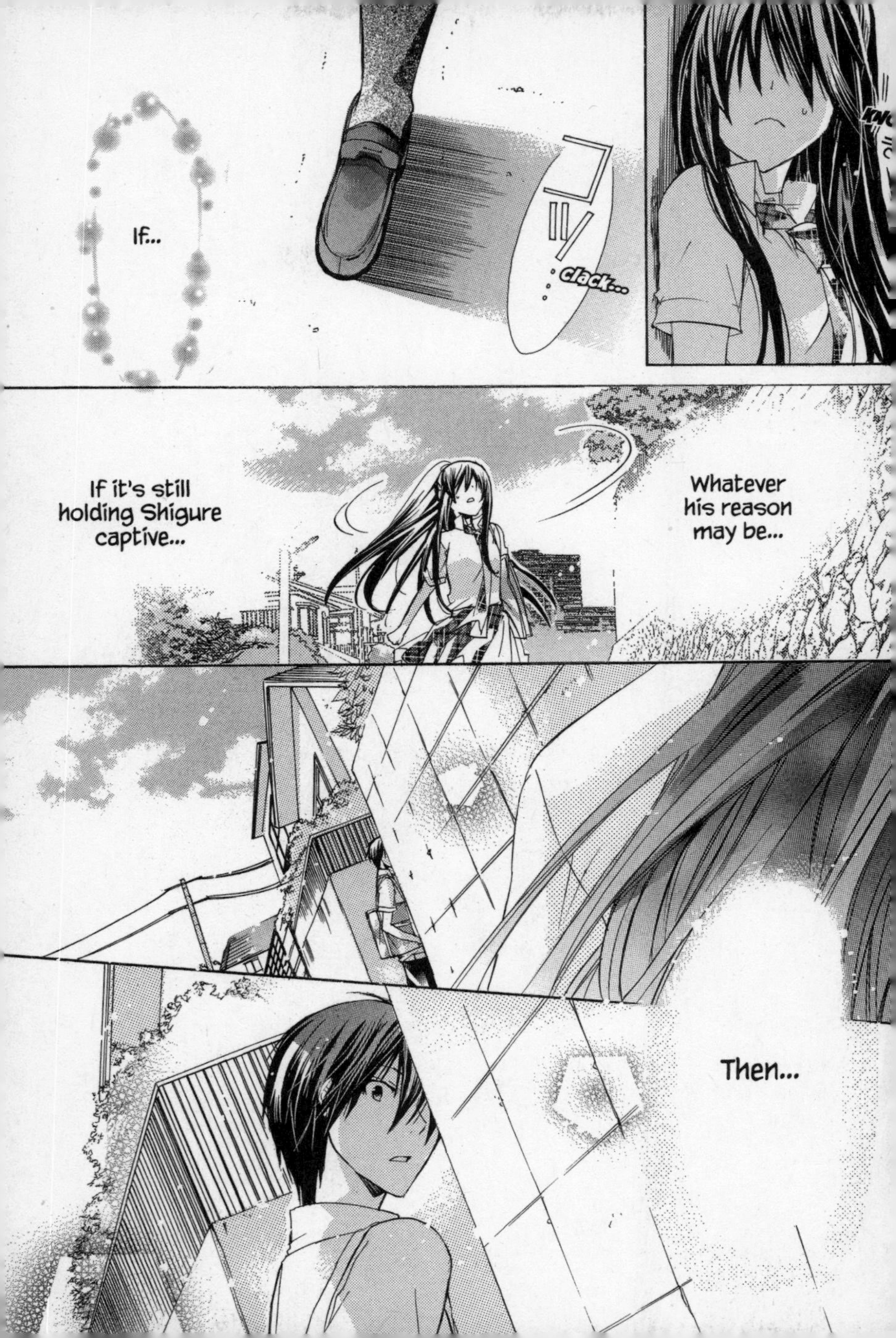
Clack...
If...
Whatever his reason may be...
If it's still holding Shigure captive...
Then...

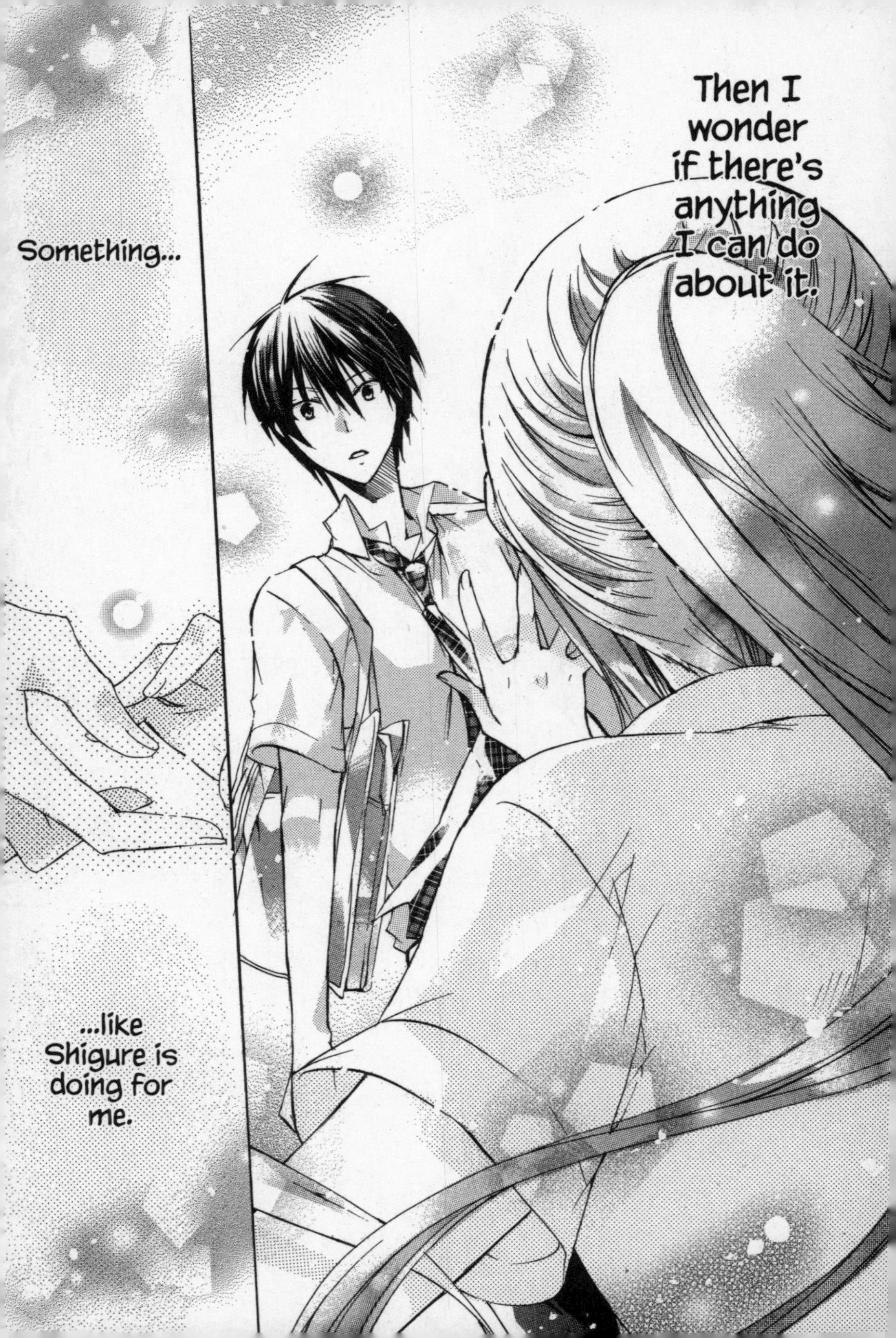
Then I wonder if there's anything I can do about it.
Something...
...like Shigure is doing for me.

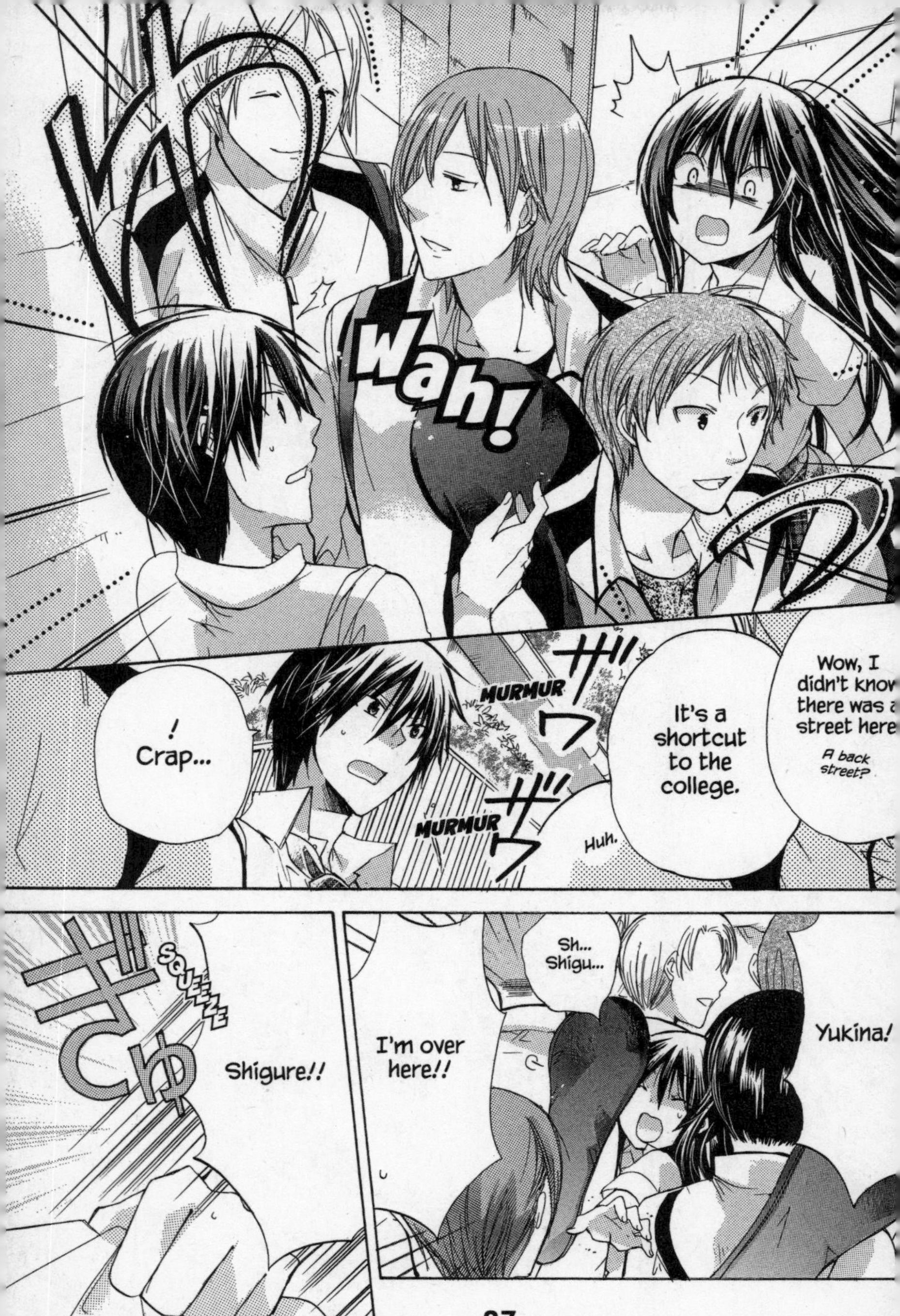
Wah!
Wow, I didn't know there was a street here
A back street?
It's a shortcut to the college.
Huh.
ザワ
MURMUR
ザワ
MURMUR
! Crap...
Yukina!
Sh... Shigu...
I'm over here!!
Shigure!!
ぎゅ
SQUEEZE

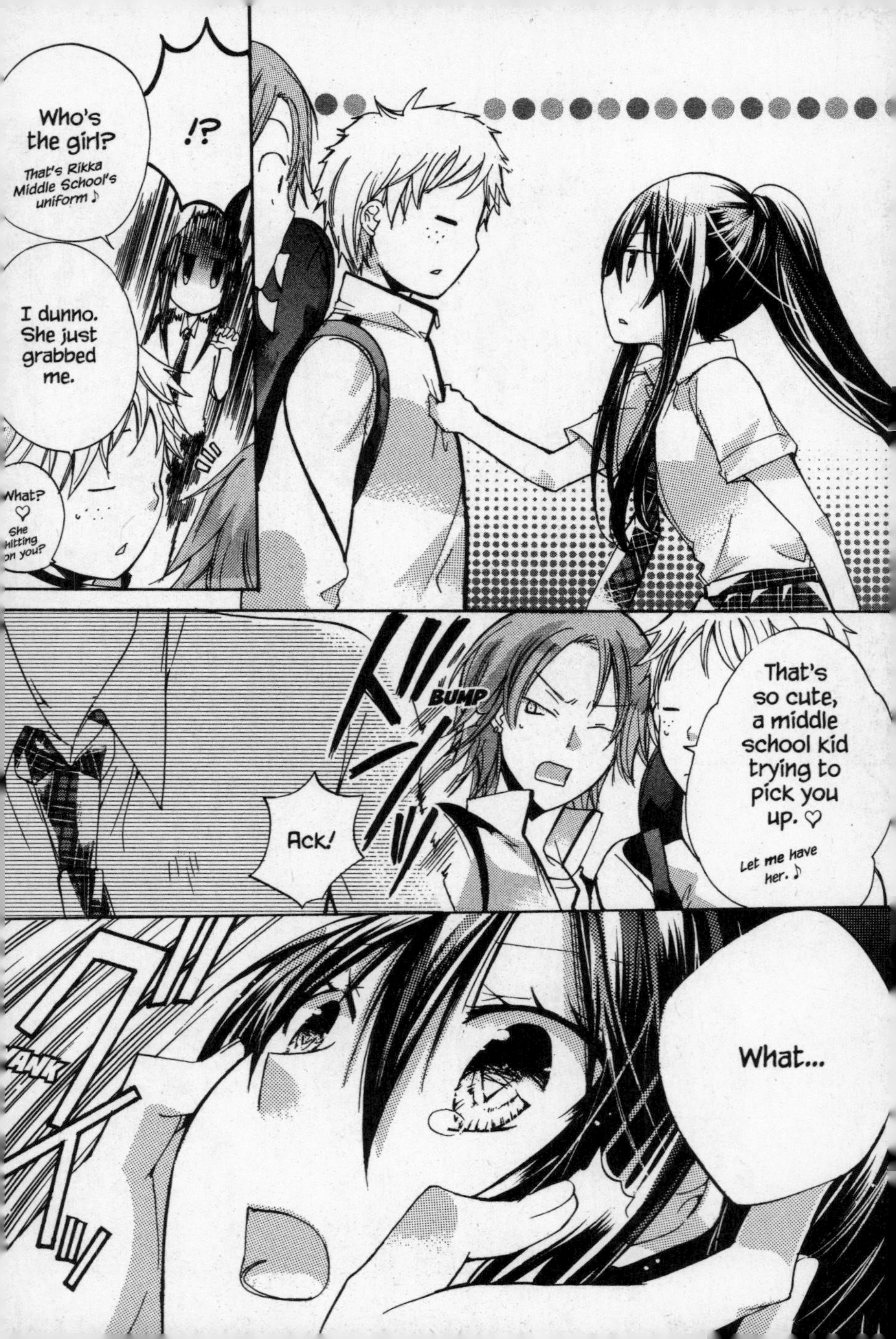
!?
Who's the girl?
That's Rikka Middle School's uniform ♪
I dunno. She just grabbed me.
What? ♡ She hitting on you?
That's so cute, a middle school kid trying to pick you up. ♡
Let me have her. ♪
BUMP
Ack!
What...

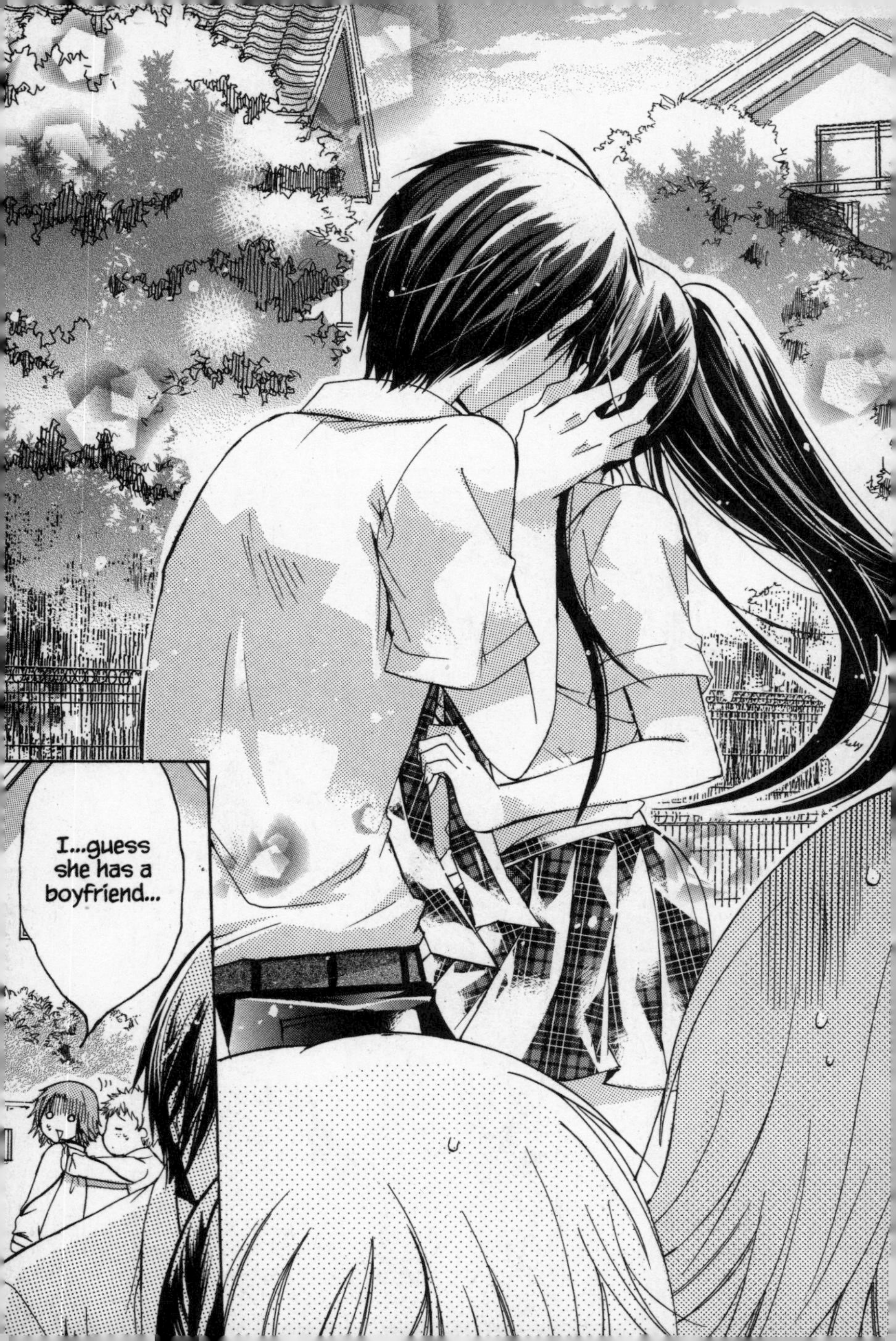
I...guess she has a boyfriend...

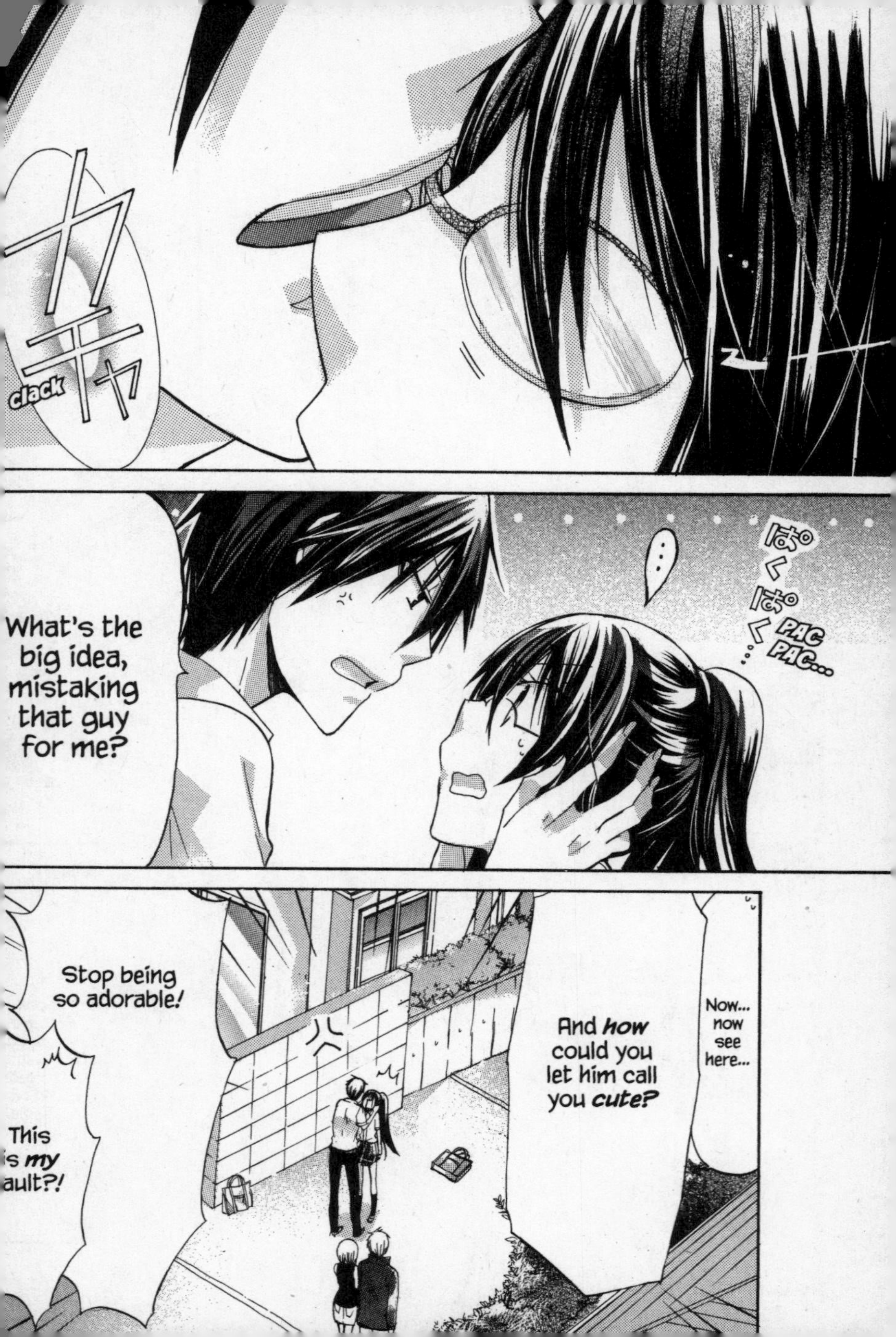
カチャ
clack
…
ぱくぱく…
PAC PAC…
What's the big idea, mistaking that guy for me?
Now… now see here…
And *how* could you let him call you *cute?*
Stop being so adorable!
This is *my* ault?!

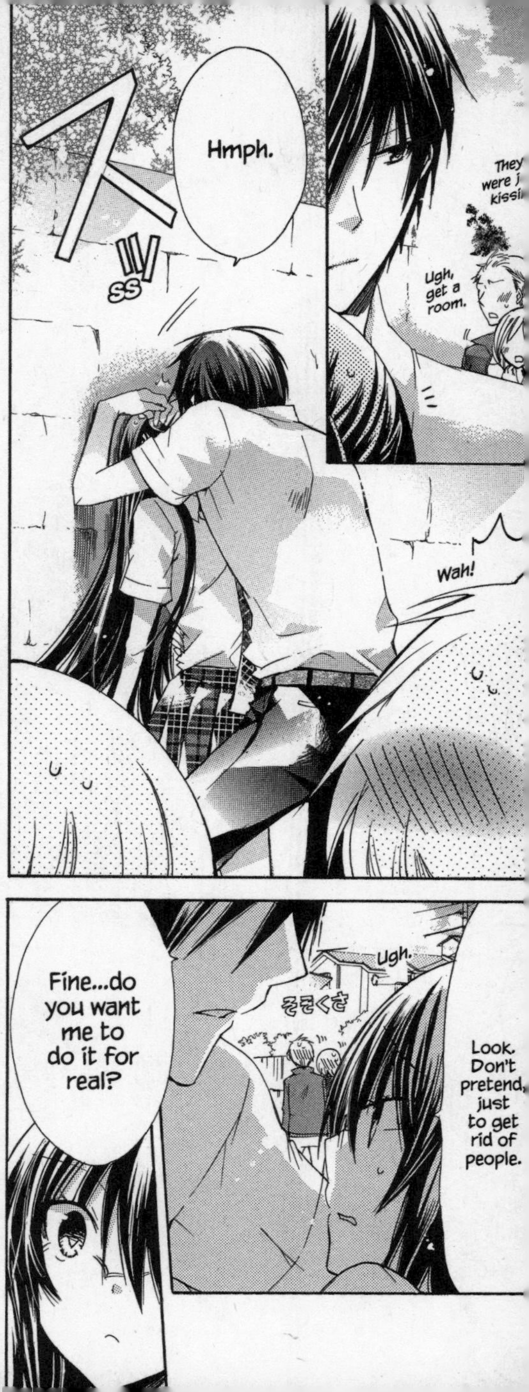
They
were j
kissi
Ugh, get a room.
Hmph.
ss
Wah!
Look. Don't pretend, just to get rid of people.
Ugh.
そそくさ
Fine...do you want me to do it for real?

The Secret to Staying Solid 1

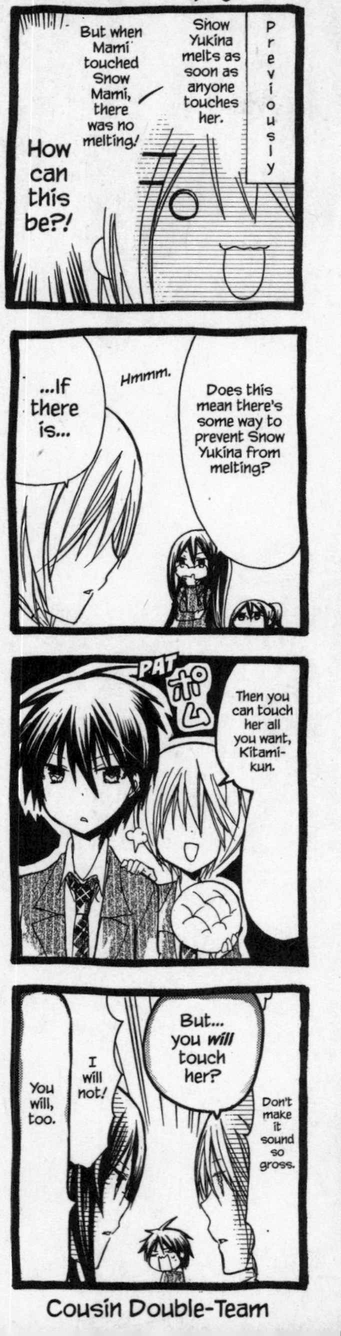
Previously
Snow Yukina melts as soon as anyone touches her.
But when Mami touched Snow Mami, there was no melting!
How can this be?!
Does this mean there's some way to prevent Snow Yukina from melting?
Hmmm.
...If there is...
PAT
ポム
Then you can touch her all you want, Kitami-kun.
But... you *will* touch her?
Don't make it sound so gross.
I will not!
You will, too.

Cousin Double-Team

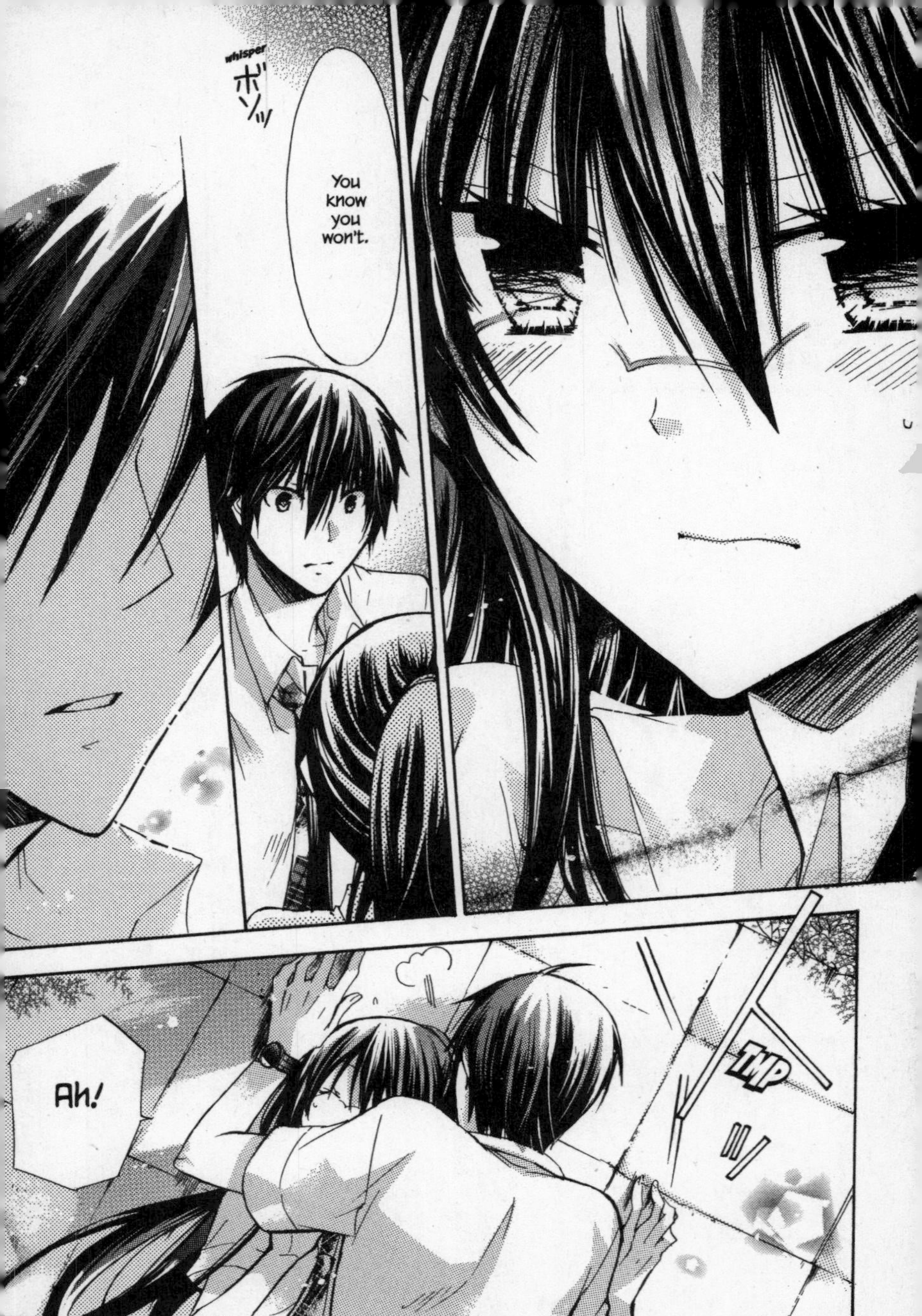
whisper
ボソッ
You know you won't.
TMP
Ah!

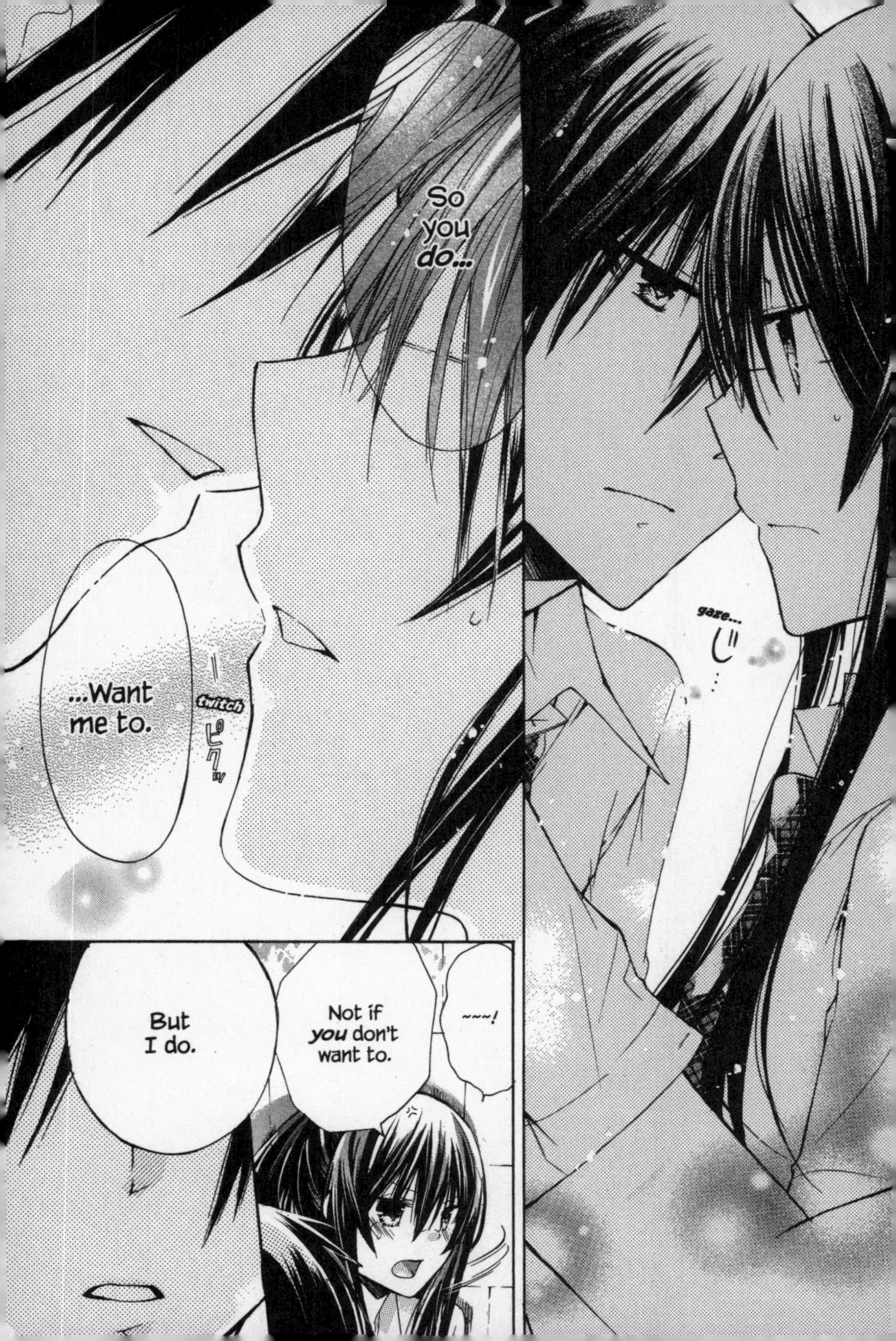
gaze...
じ…
So you do...
...Want me to.
twitch
~~~!
Not if *you* don't want to.
But I do.
~~~

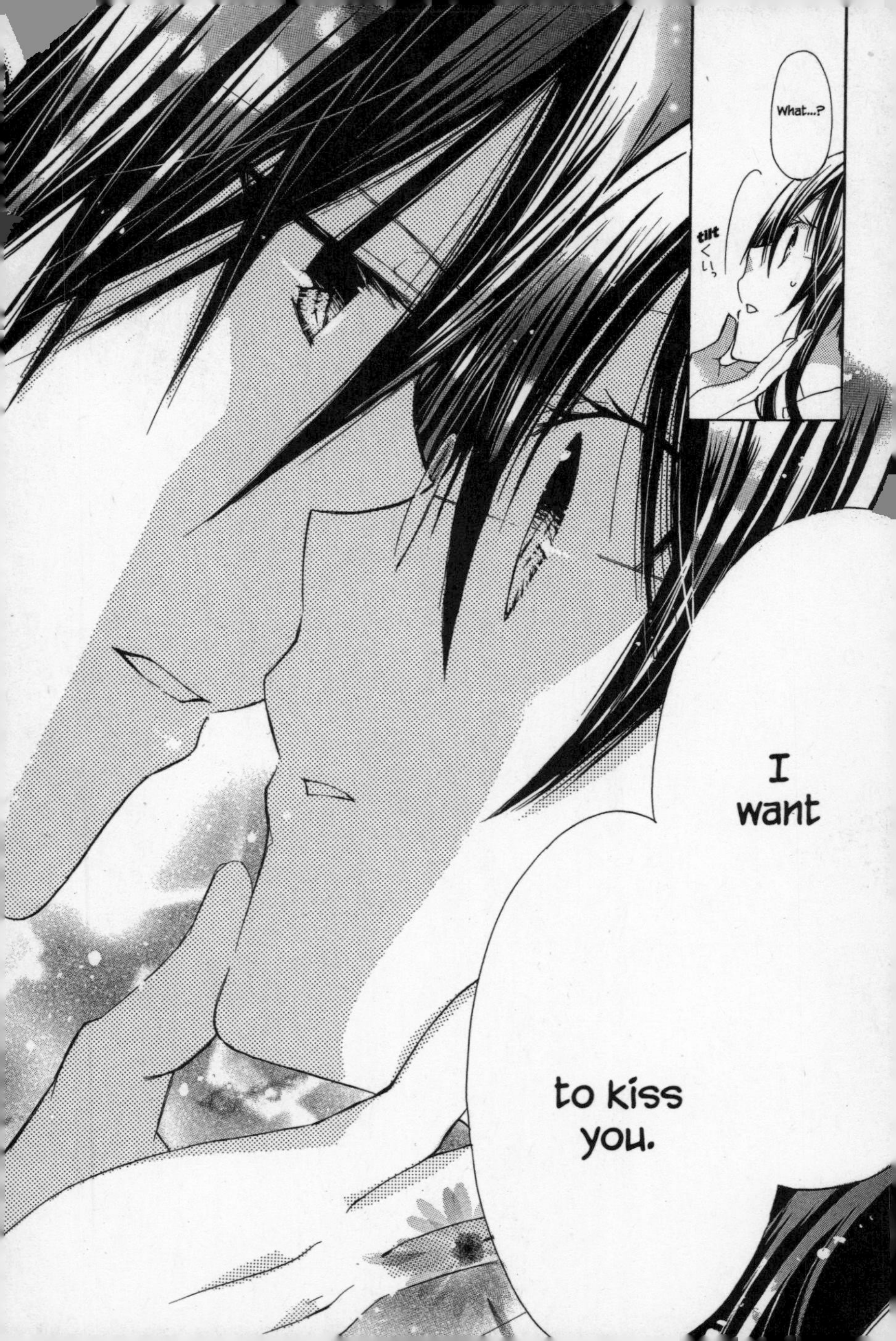
What...?
tilt くいっ
I want to kiss you.

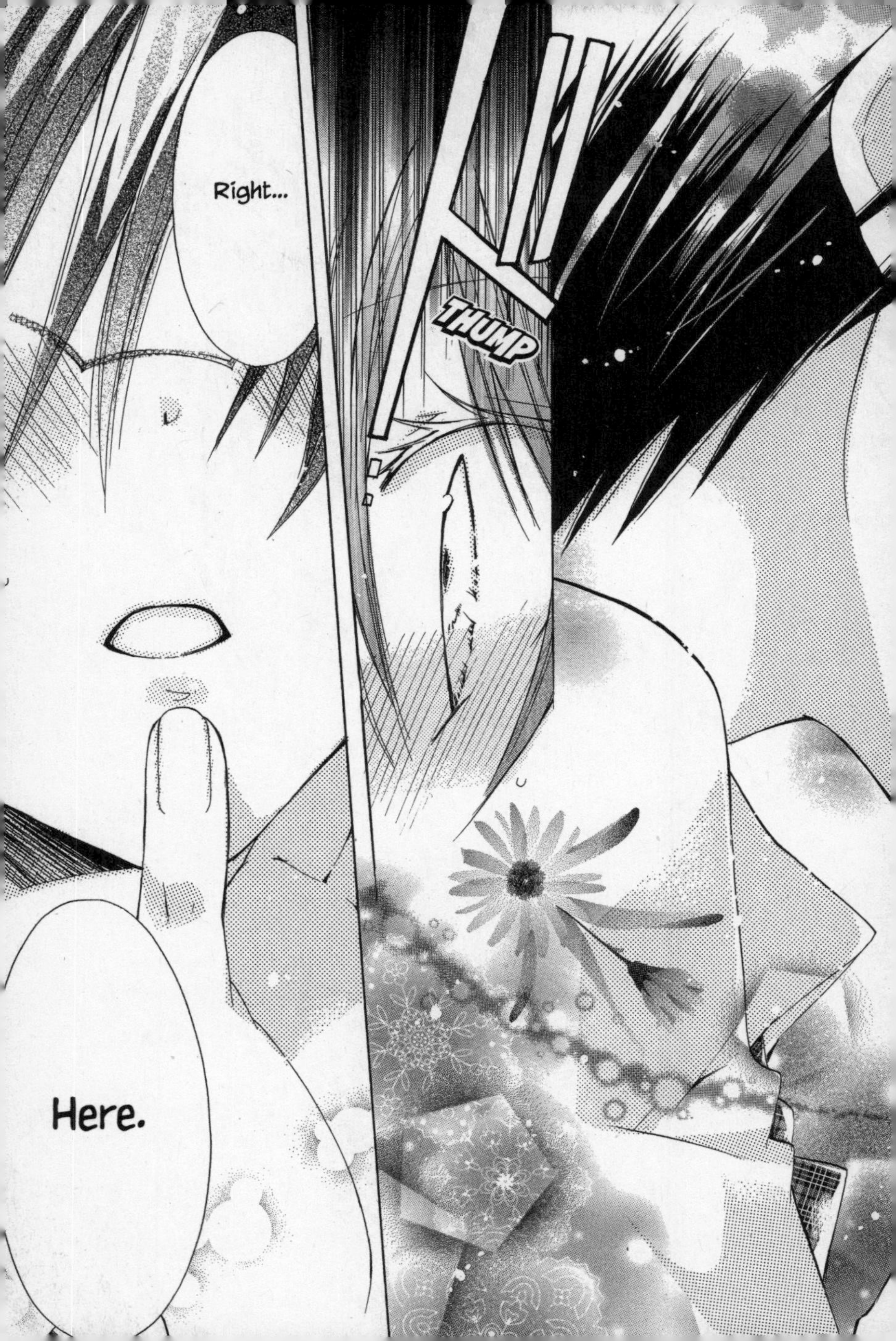
THUMP
Right...
Here.

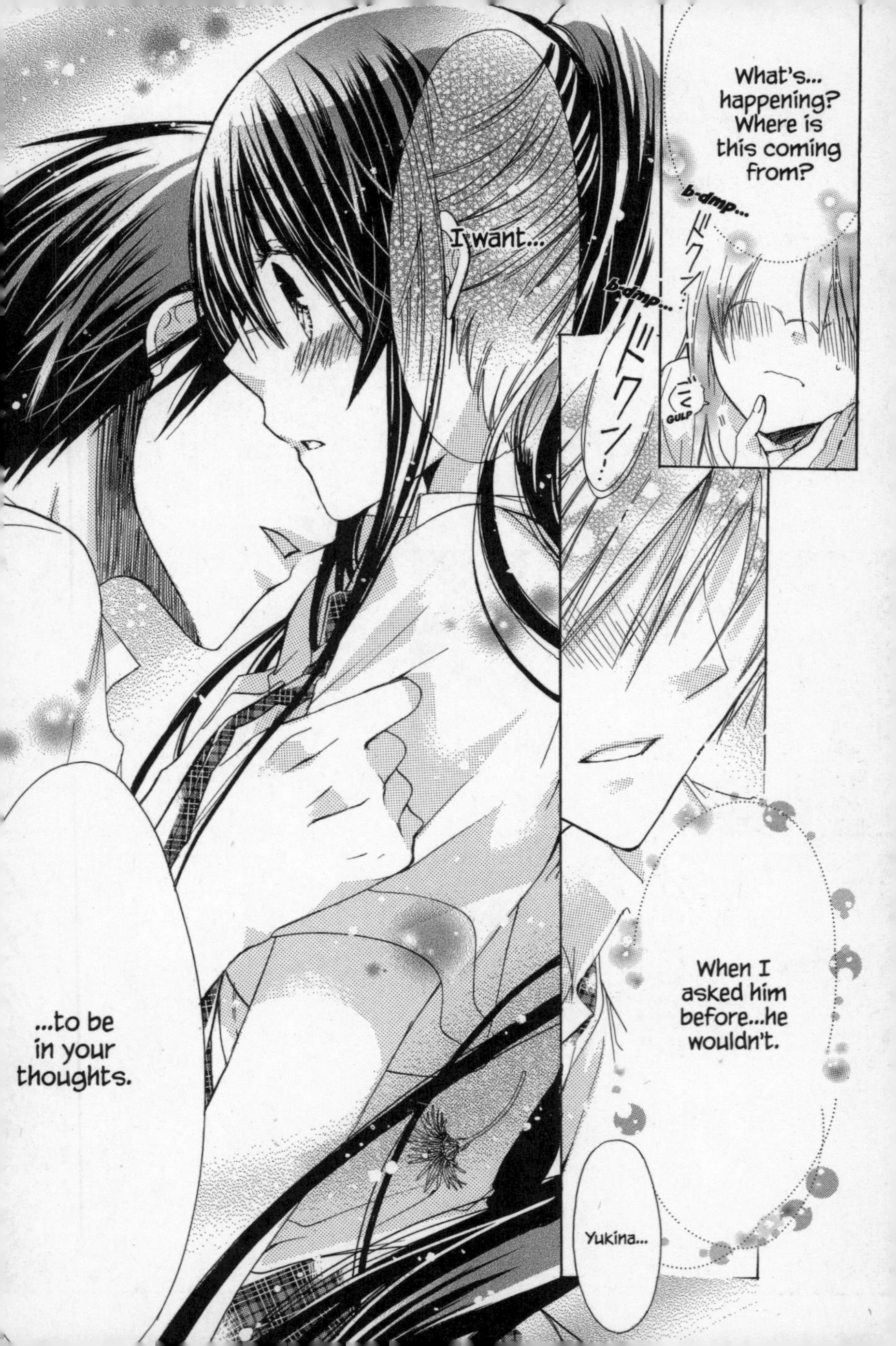
What's... happening? Where is this coming from?
b-dmp...
b-dmp...
GULP
When I asked him before...he wouldn't.
Yukina...
I want...
...to be in your thoughts.

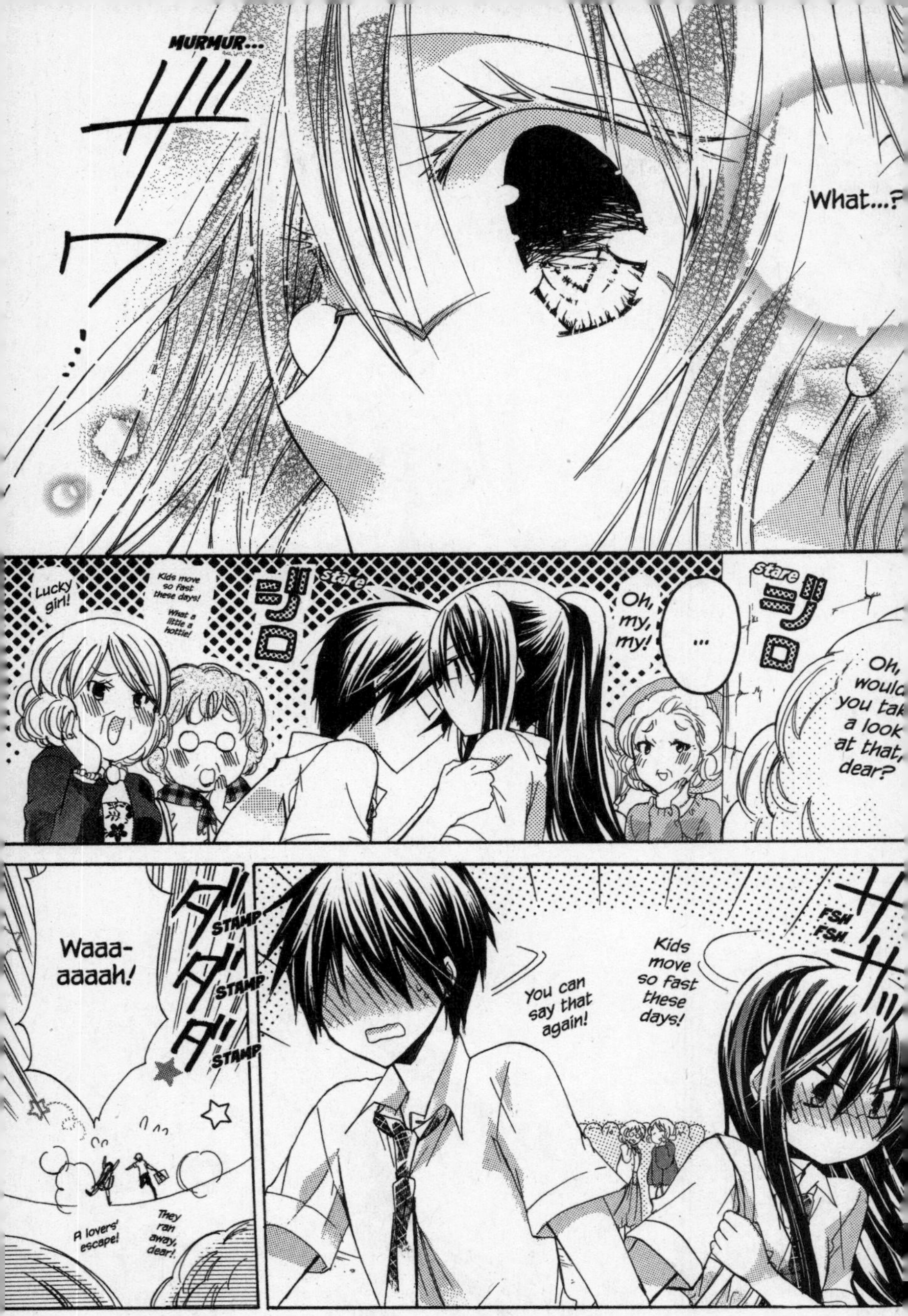
MURMUR...
What...?
stare
Oh, would you tak a look at that, dear?
...
Oh, my, my!
stare
Kids move so fast these days!
What a little a hottie!
Lucky girl!
FSH FSH
Kids move so fast these days!
You can say that again!
STAMP
STAMP
STAMP
Waaa-aaaah!
They ran away, dear!
A lovers' escape!

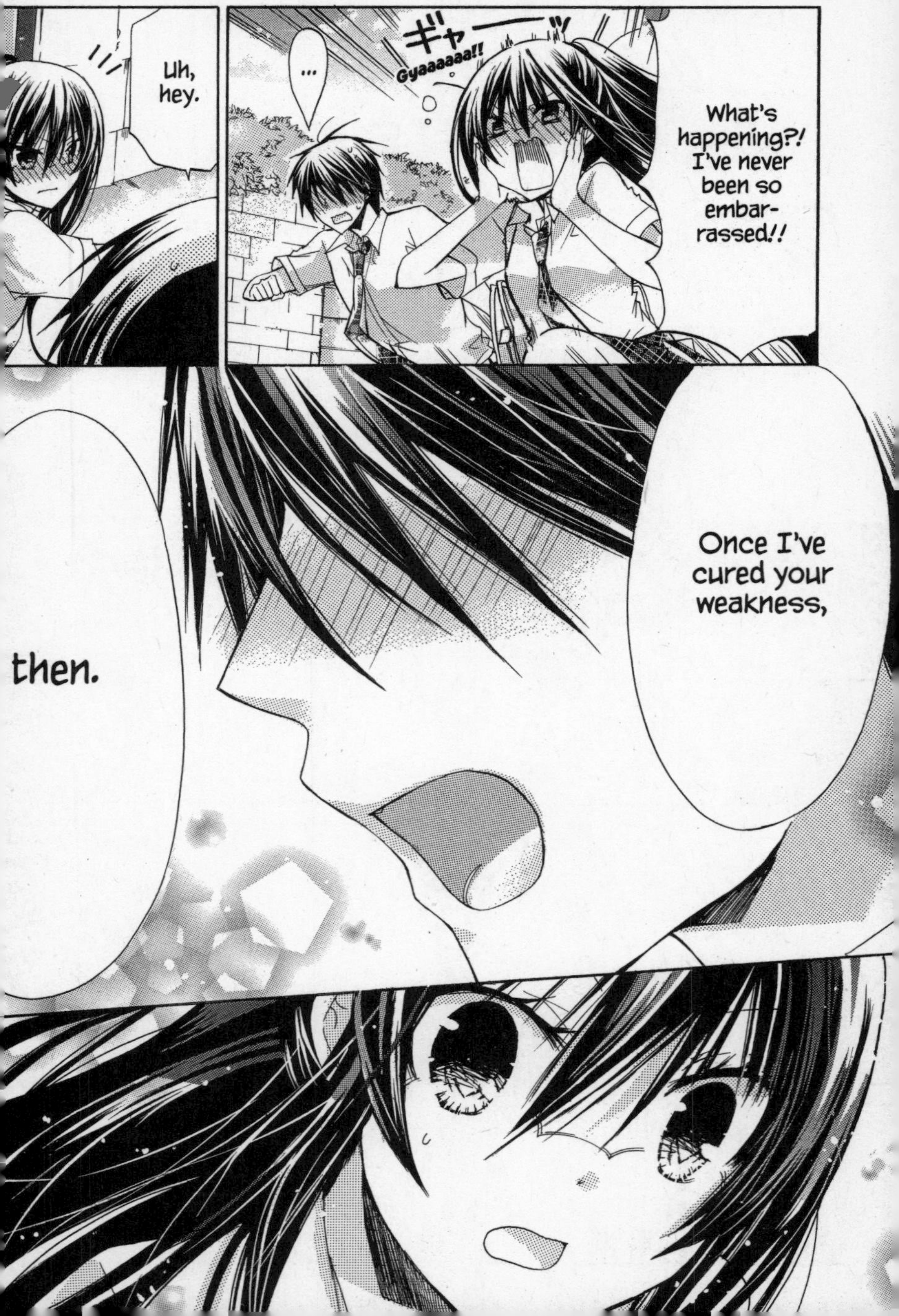
What's happening?! I've never been so embarrassed!!
ギャーーッ
Gyaaaaaa!!
...
uh, hey.
Once I've cured your weakness,
then.

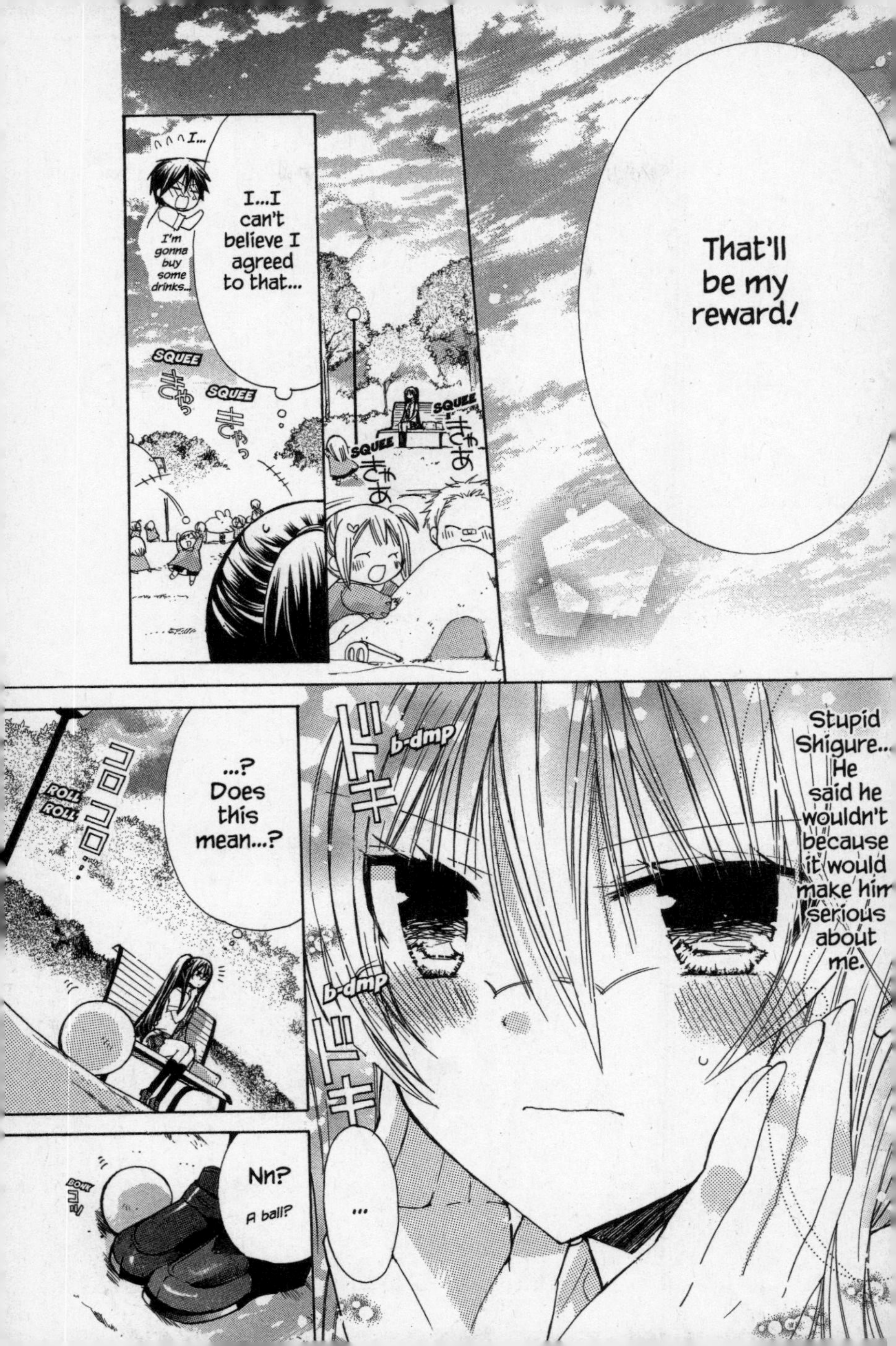
That'll be my reward!
SQUEE
きゃあ
SQUEE
きゃあ
I...
I...I can't believe I agreed to that...
I'm gonna buy some drinks...
SQUEE
きゃっ
SQUEE
きゃっ
Stupid Shigure... He said he wouldn't because it would make him serious about me.
b-dmp
b-dmp
...
...? Does this mean...?
ROLL ROLL
Nn?
A ball?
BONK

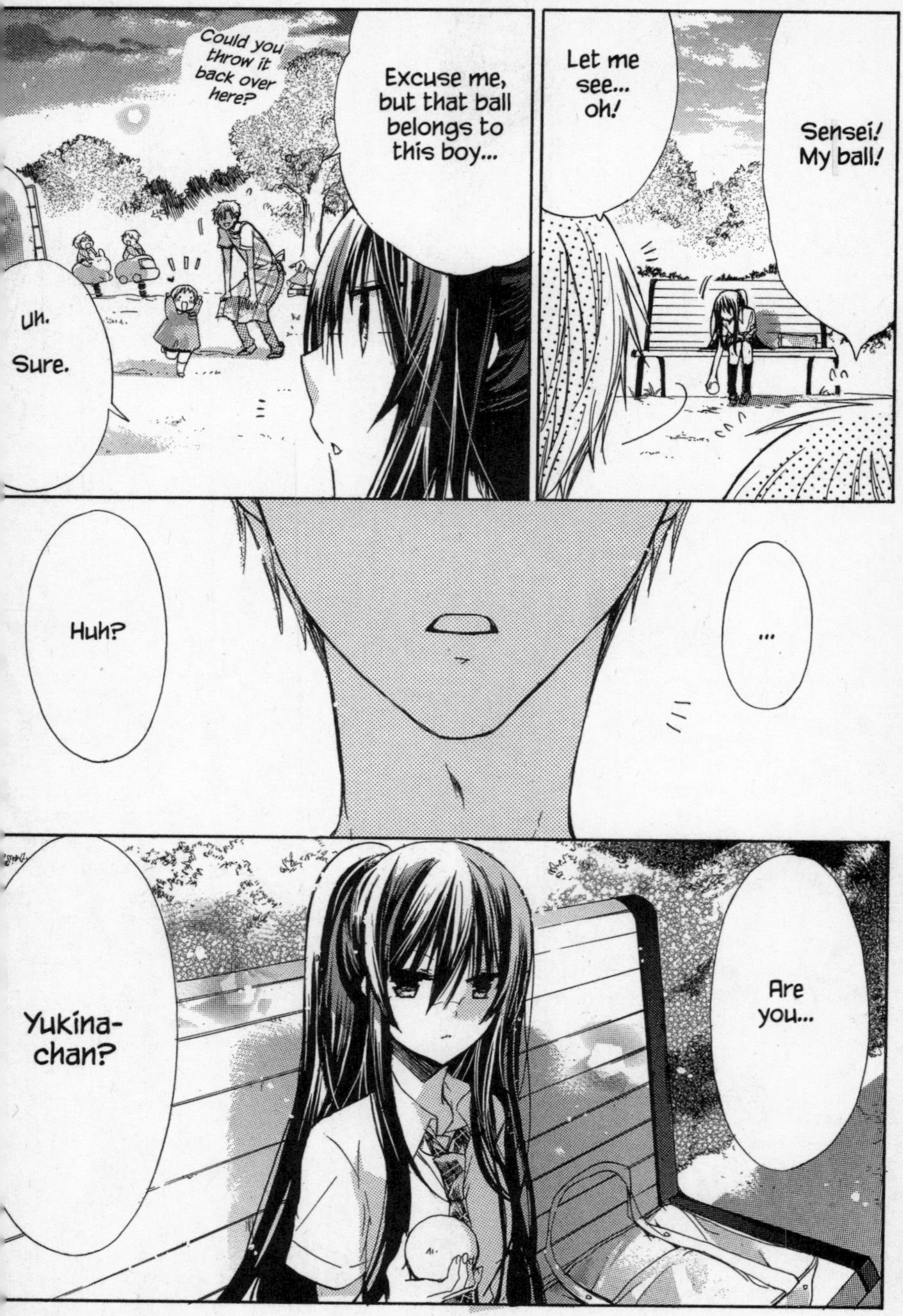

Sensei! My ball!
Let me see... oh!
Excuse me, but that ball belongs to this boy...
Could you throw it back over here?
Uh.
Sure.
...
Huh?
Are you...
Yukina-chan?

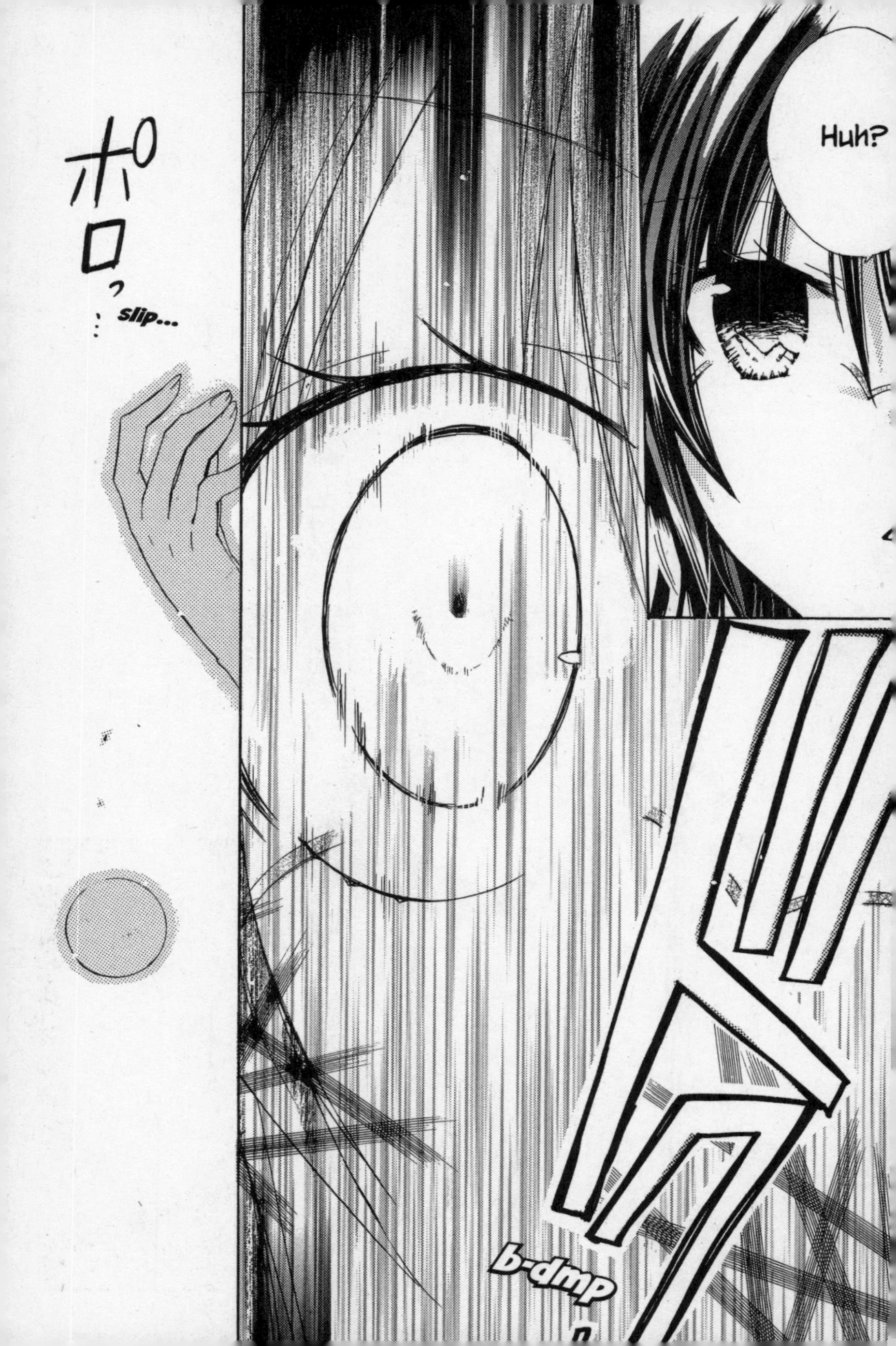
Huh?
b-dmp
ポロっ
slip...

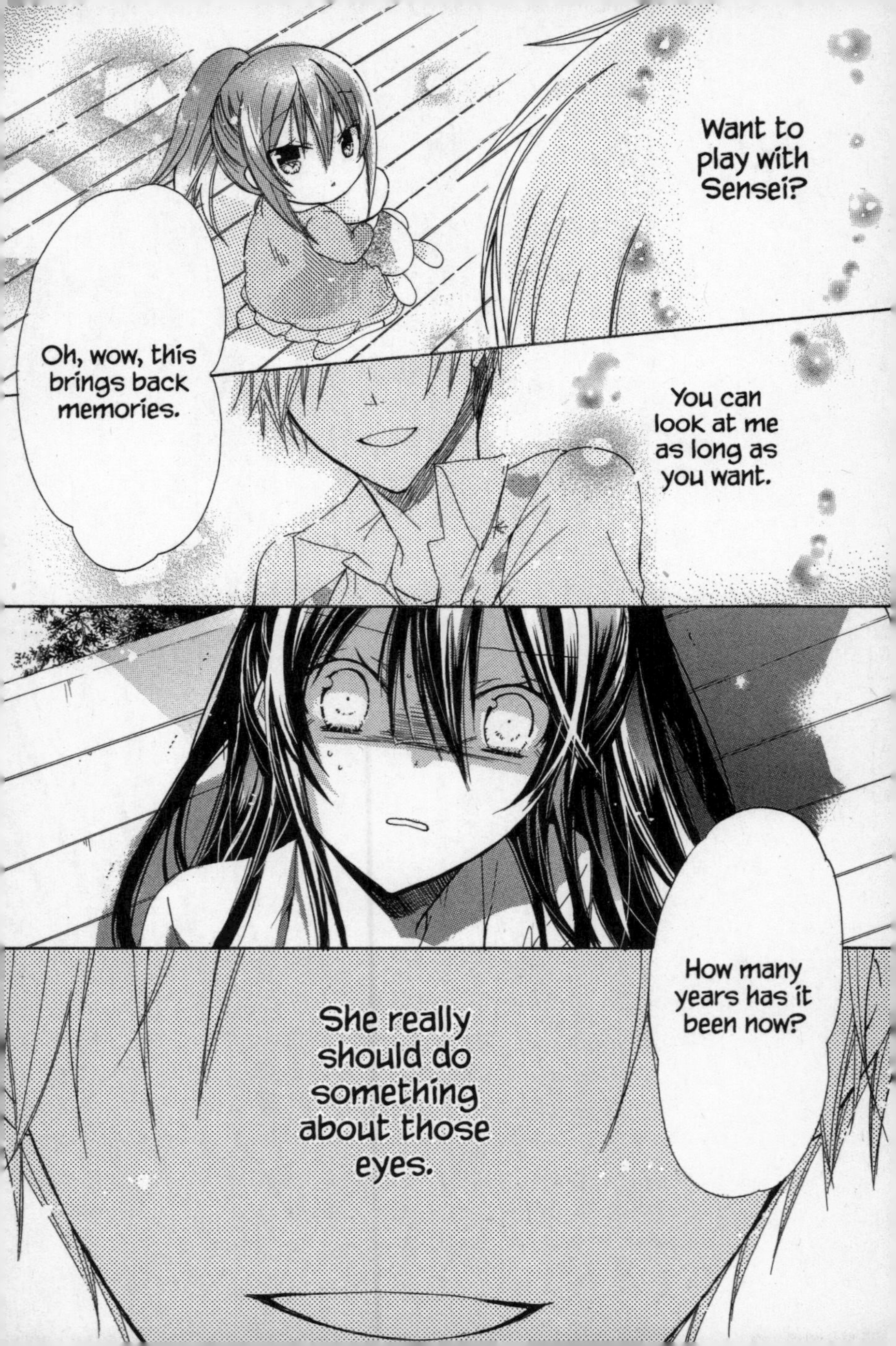
Want to play with Sensei?
You can look at me as long as you want.
Oh, wow, this brings back memories.
How many years has it been now?
She really should do something about those eyes.

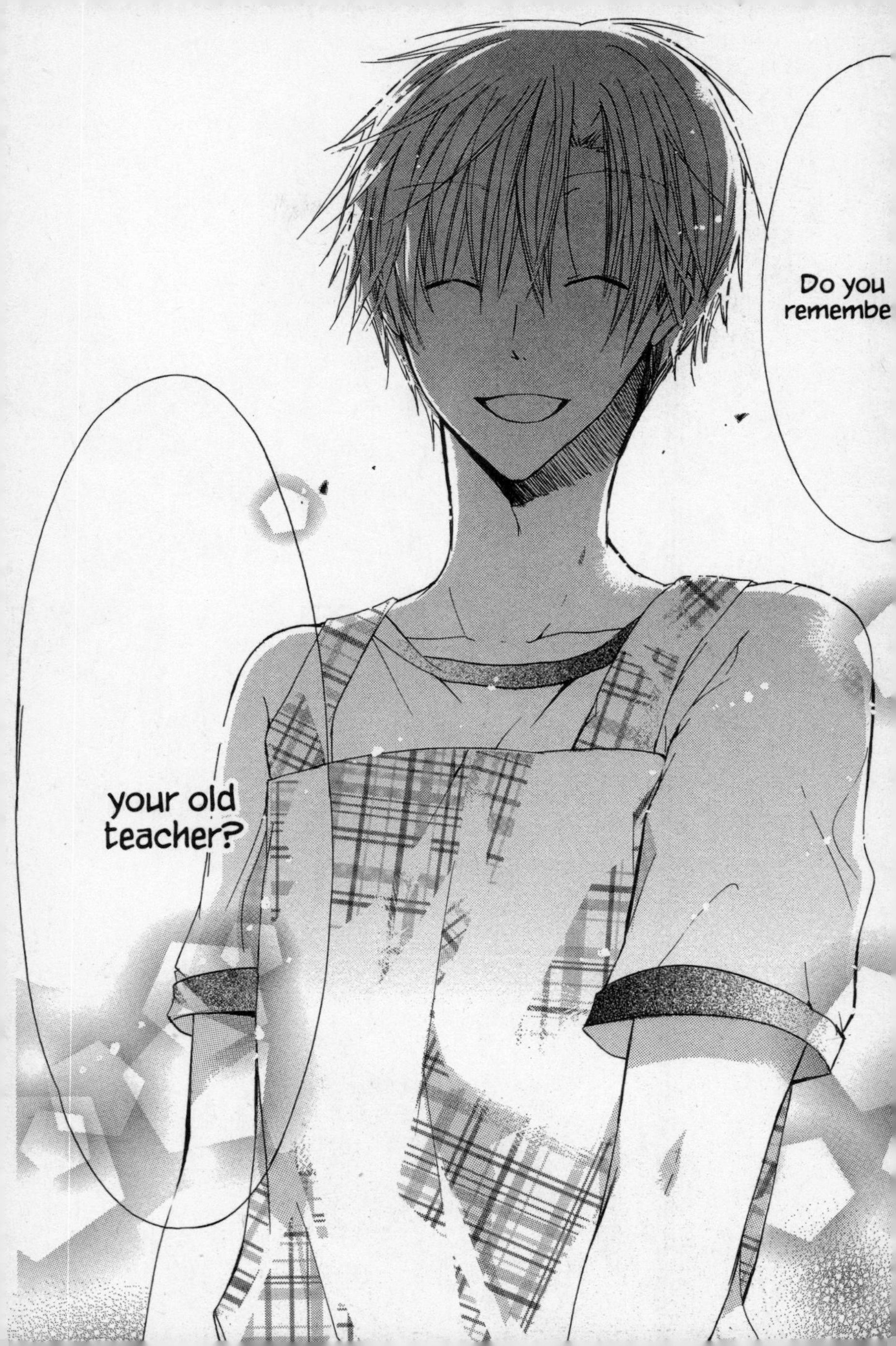
Do you remembe
your old teacher?

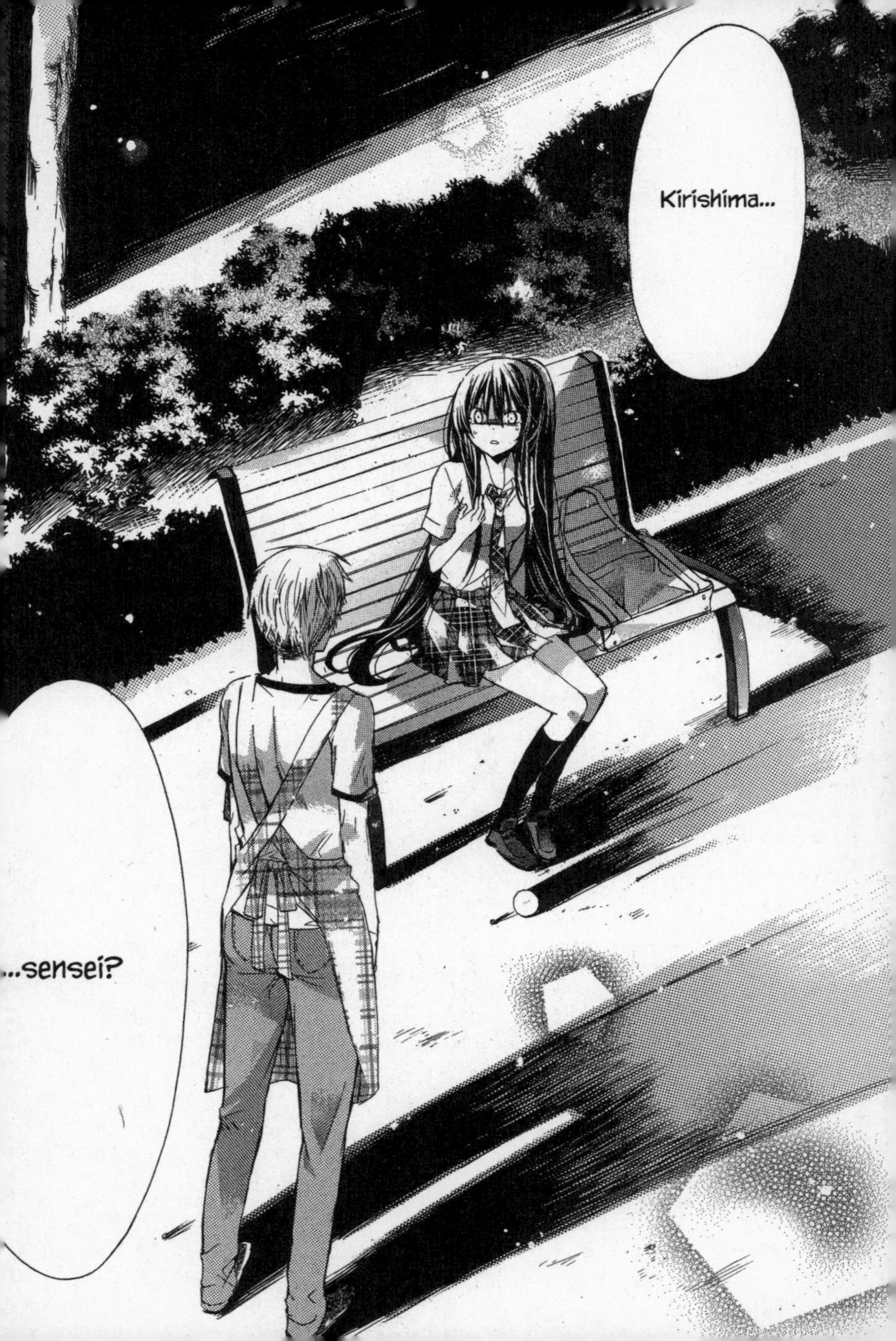
Kirishima...
...sensei?

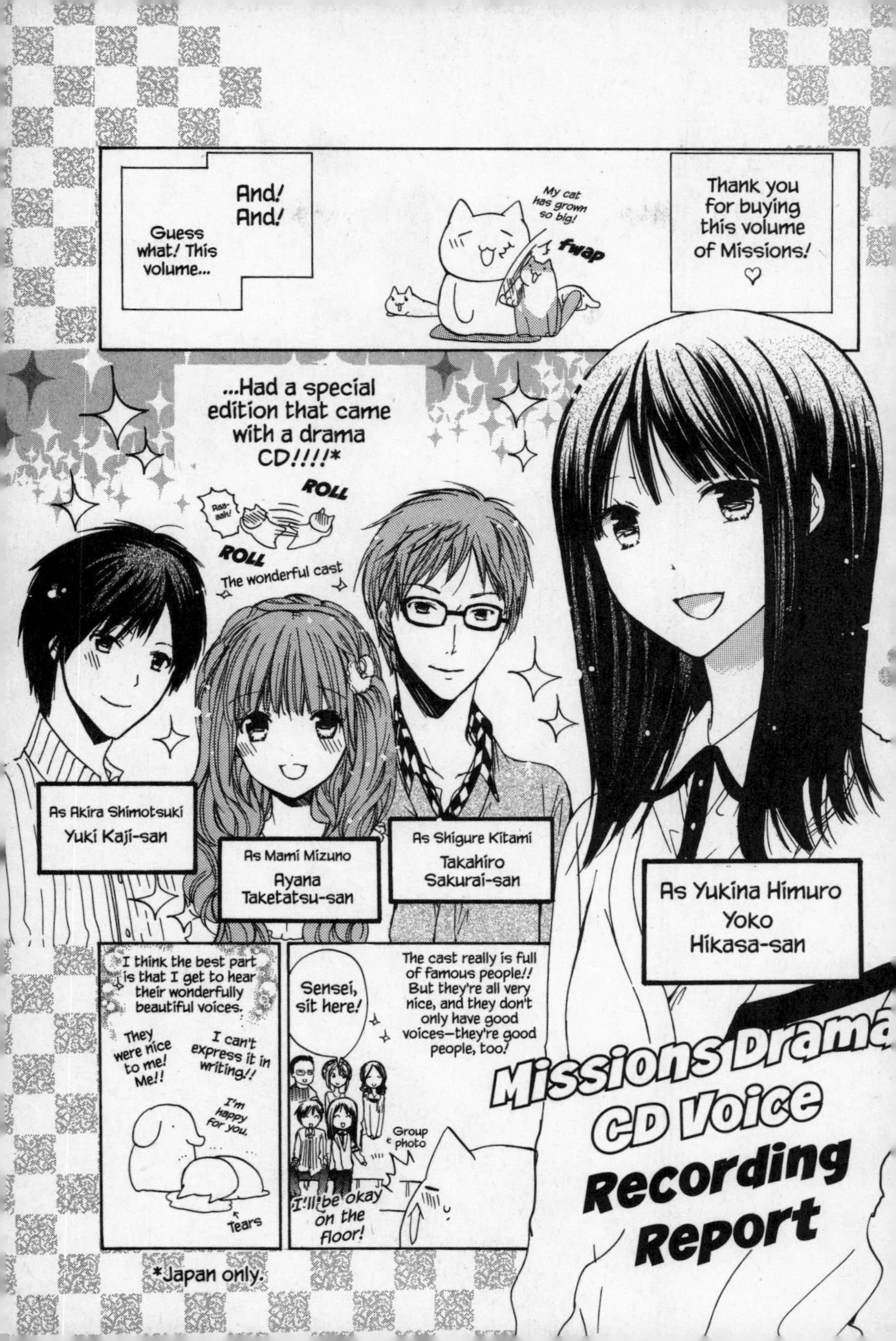
Thank you for buying this volume of Missions! ♡
My cat has grown so big!
fwap
And! And!
Guess what! This volume...
...Had a special edition that came with a drama CD!!!!*
ROLL
Raa-aah!
ROLL
The wonderful cast
Missions Drama CD Voice Recording Report
As Yukina Himuro Yoko Hikasa-san
As Shigure Kitami Takahiro Sakurai-san
As Mami Mizuno Ayana Taketatsu-san
As Akira Shimotsuki Yuki Kaji-san
The cast really is full of famous people!! But they're all very nice, and they don't only have good voices—they're good people, too!
Sensei, sit here!
Group photo
I'll be okay on the floor!
I think the best part is that I get to hear their wonderfully beautiful voices.
I can't express it in writing!!
They were nice to me! Me!!
I'm happy for you.
Tears
*Japan only.

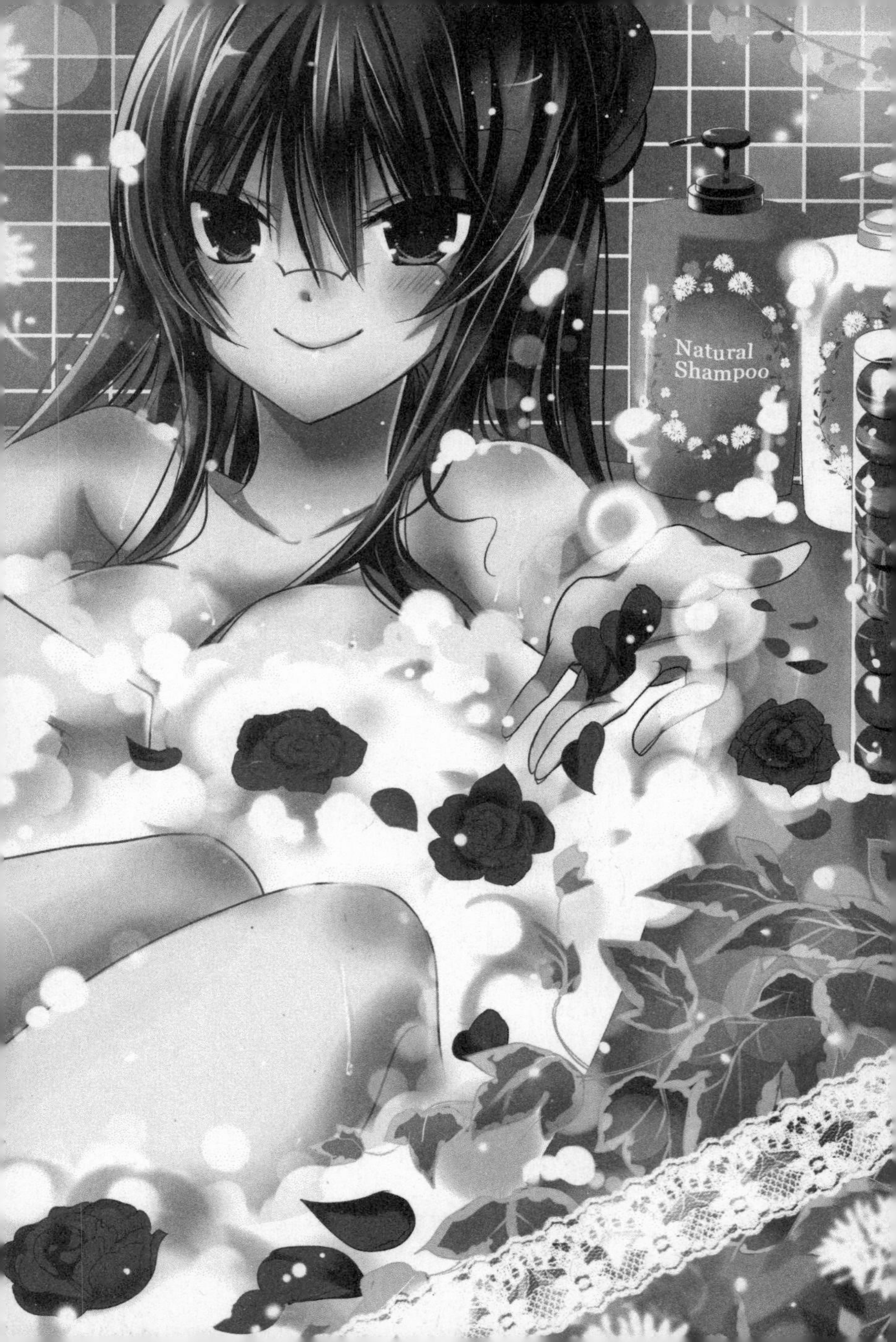
Natural
Shampoo

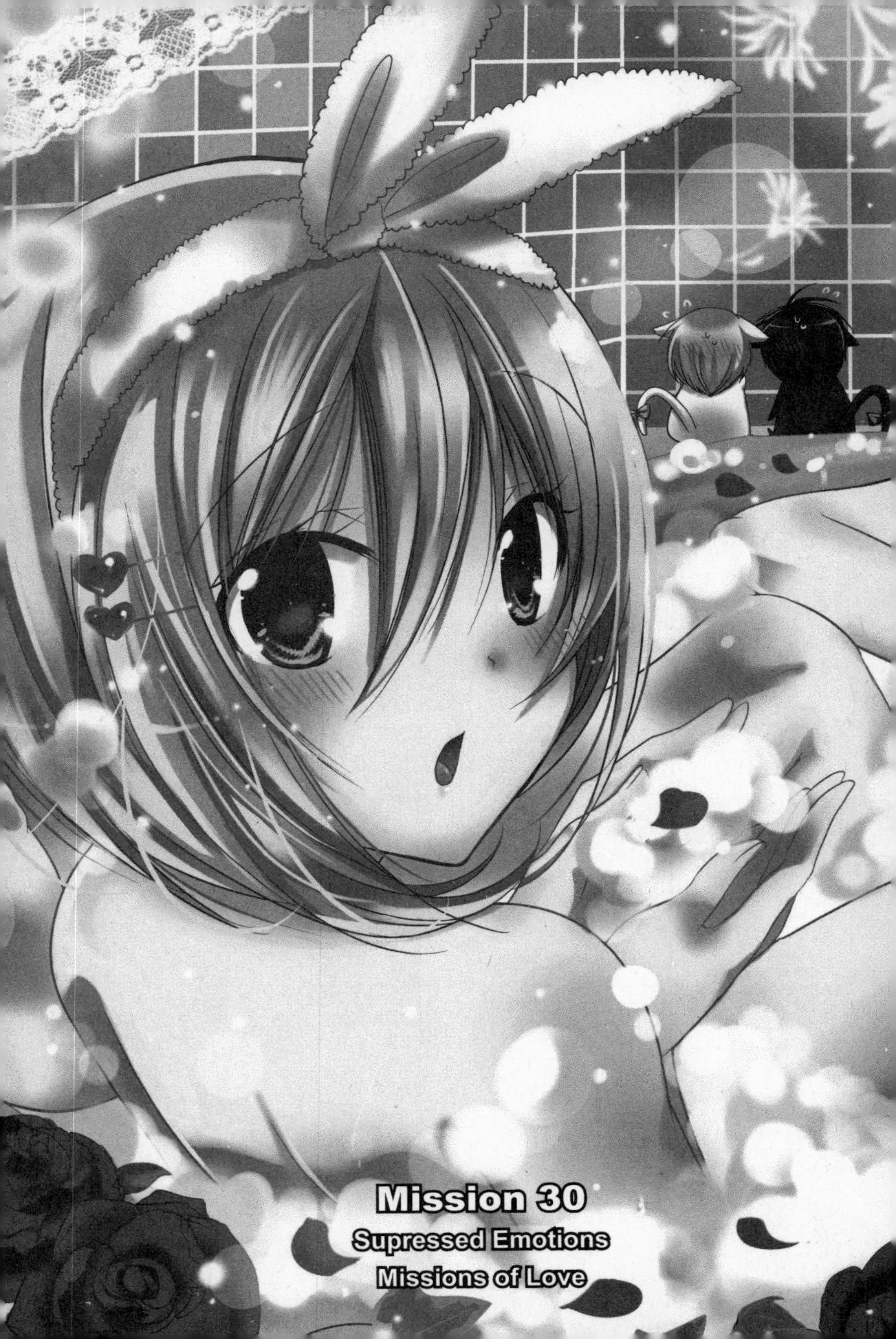
Mission 30
Supressed Emotions
Missions of Love

Digest: Memories from the Recording

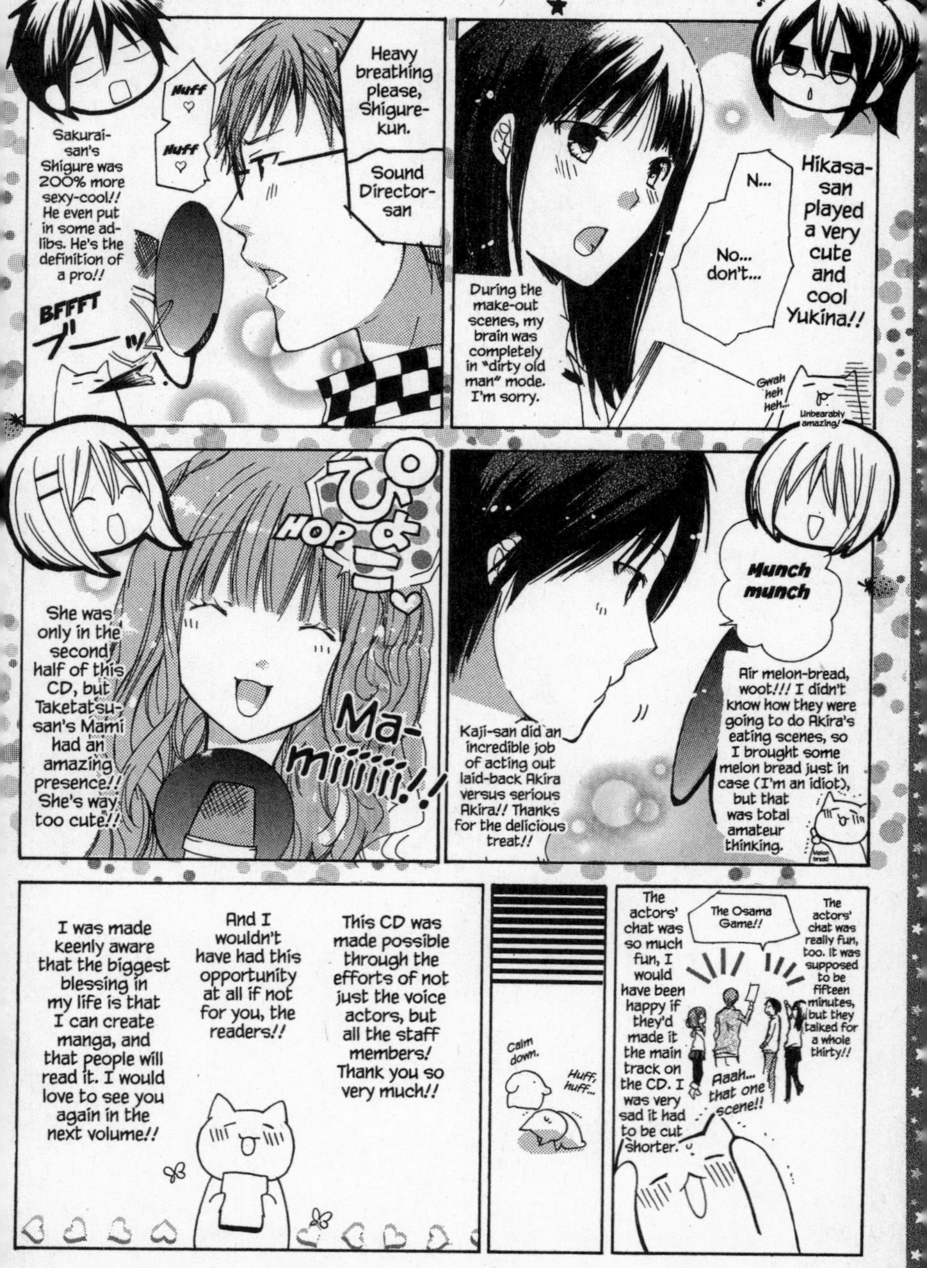
Hikasa-san played a very cute and cool Yukina!!
N...
No... don't...
During the make-out scenes, my brain was completely in "dirty old man" mode. I'm sorry.
Gwah heh heh...
Unbearably amazing!
Heavy breathing please, Shigure-kun.
Sound Director-san
Huff ♡
Huff ♡
Sakurai-san's Shigure was 200% more sexy-cool!! He even put in some ad-libs. He's the definition of a pro!!
BFFFT
Munch munch
Air melon-bread, woot!!! I didn't know how they were going to do Akira's eating scenes, so I brought some melon bread just in case (I'm an idiot), but that was total amateur thinking.
Melon bread
Kaji-san did an incredible job of acting out laid-back Akira versus serious Akira!! Thanks for the delicious treat!!
HOP
Ma-miiiiii!!
She was only in the second half of this CD, but Taketatsu-san's Mami had an amazing presence!! She's way too cute!!
The actors' chat was really fun, too. It was supposed to be fifteen minutes, but they talked for a whole thirty!!
The Osama Game!!
The actors' chat was so much fun, I would have been happy if they'd made it the main track on the CD. I was very sad it had to be cut shorter.
Aaah... that one scene!!
Calm down.
Huff, huff...
I was made keenly aware that the biggest blessing in my life is that I can create manga, and that people will read it. I would love to see you again in the next volume!!
And I wouldn't have had this opportunity at all if not for you, the readers!!
This CD was made possible through the efforts of not just the voice actors, but all the staff members! Thank you so very much!!

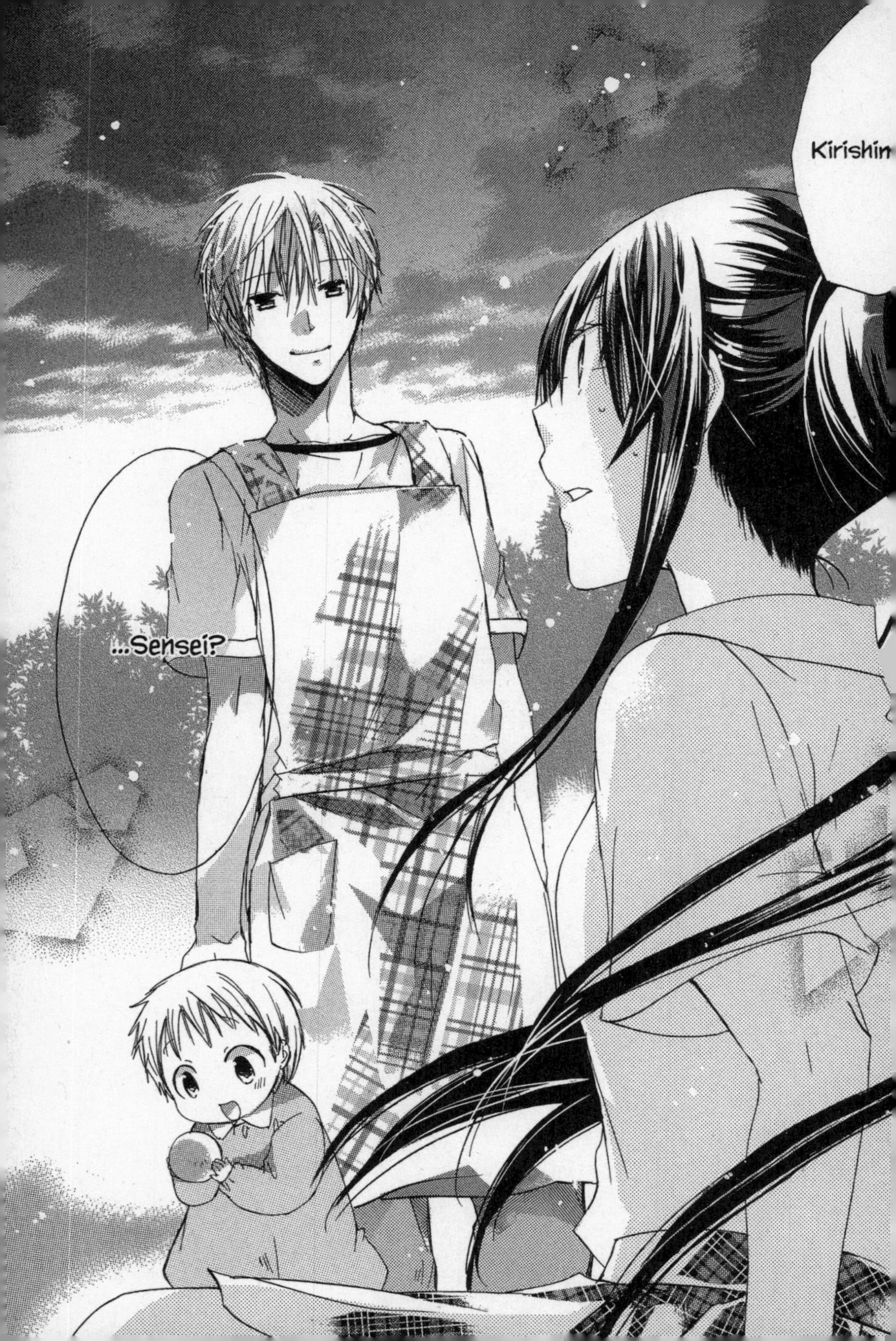
Kirishin
...Sensei?

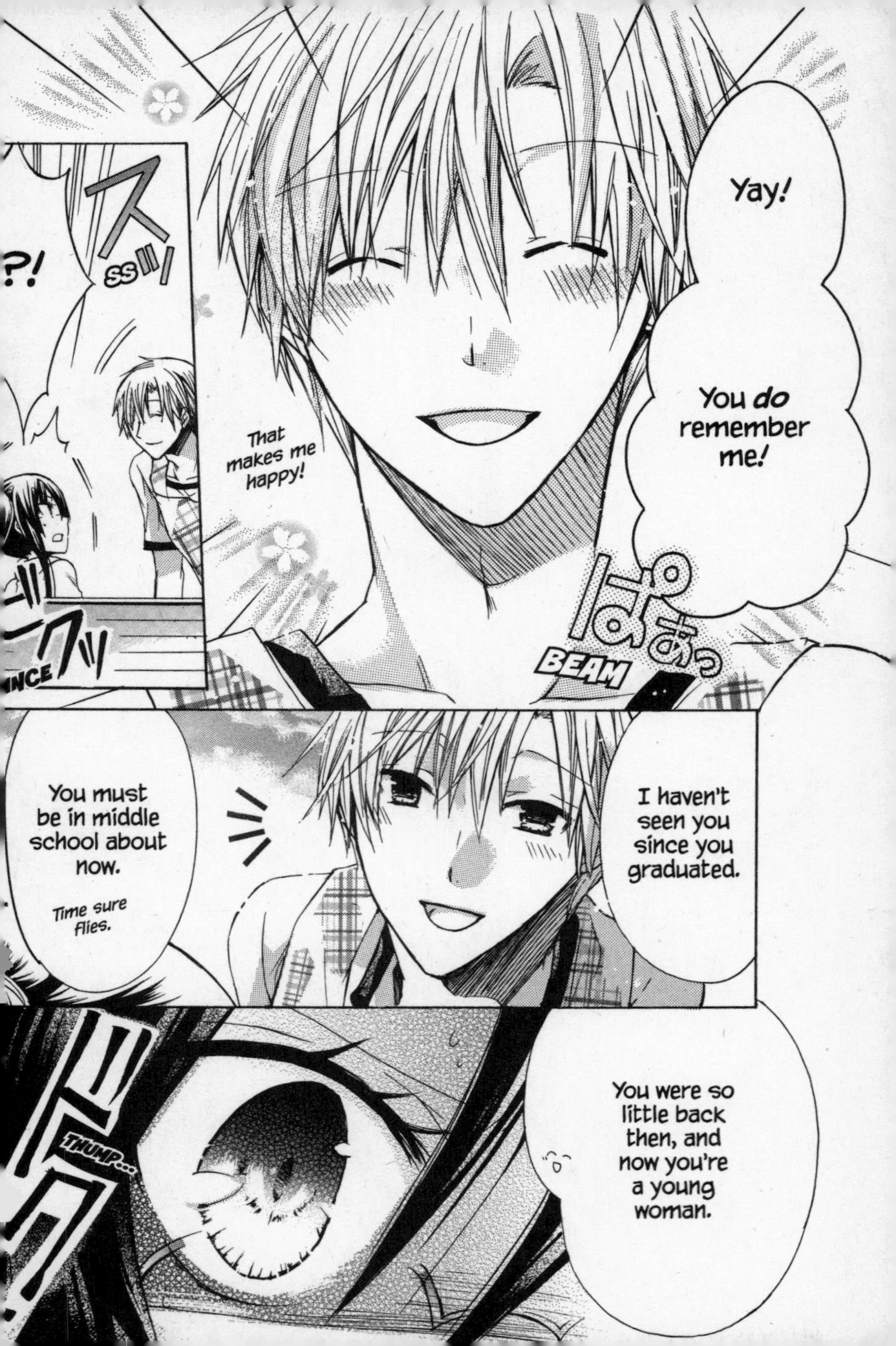
Yay!
You do remember me!
ぱあっ
BEAM
That makes me happy!
SS
?!
INCE
I haven't seen you since you graduated.
You must be in middle school about now.
Time sure flies.
You were so little back then, and now you're a young woman.
THUMP...

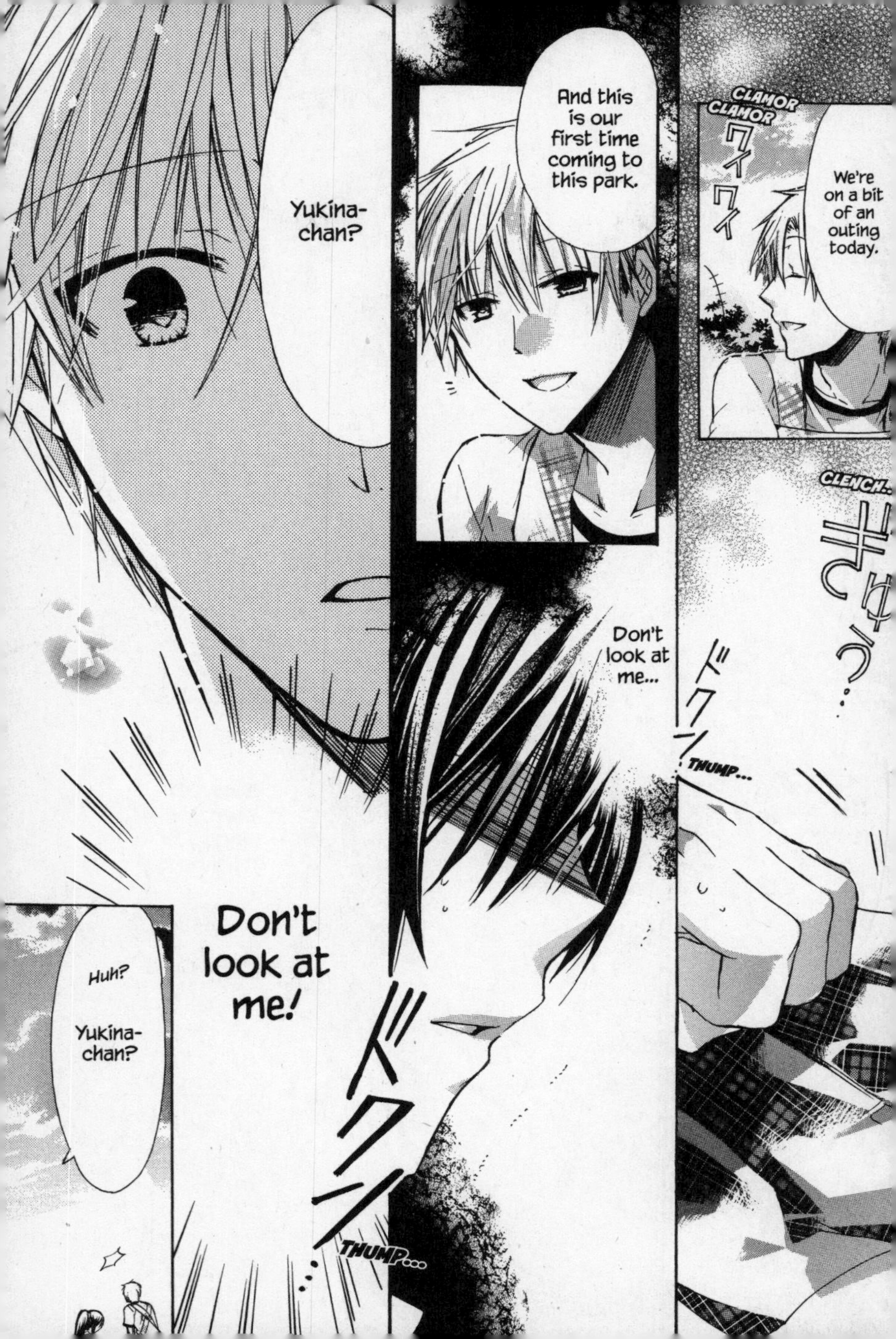
CLAMOR CLAMOR
ワイワイ
We're on a bit of an outing today.
And this is our first time coming to this park.
Yukina-chan?
CLENCH...
THUMP...
Don't look at me...
Don't look at me!
THUMP...
Huh?
Yukina-chan?

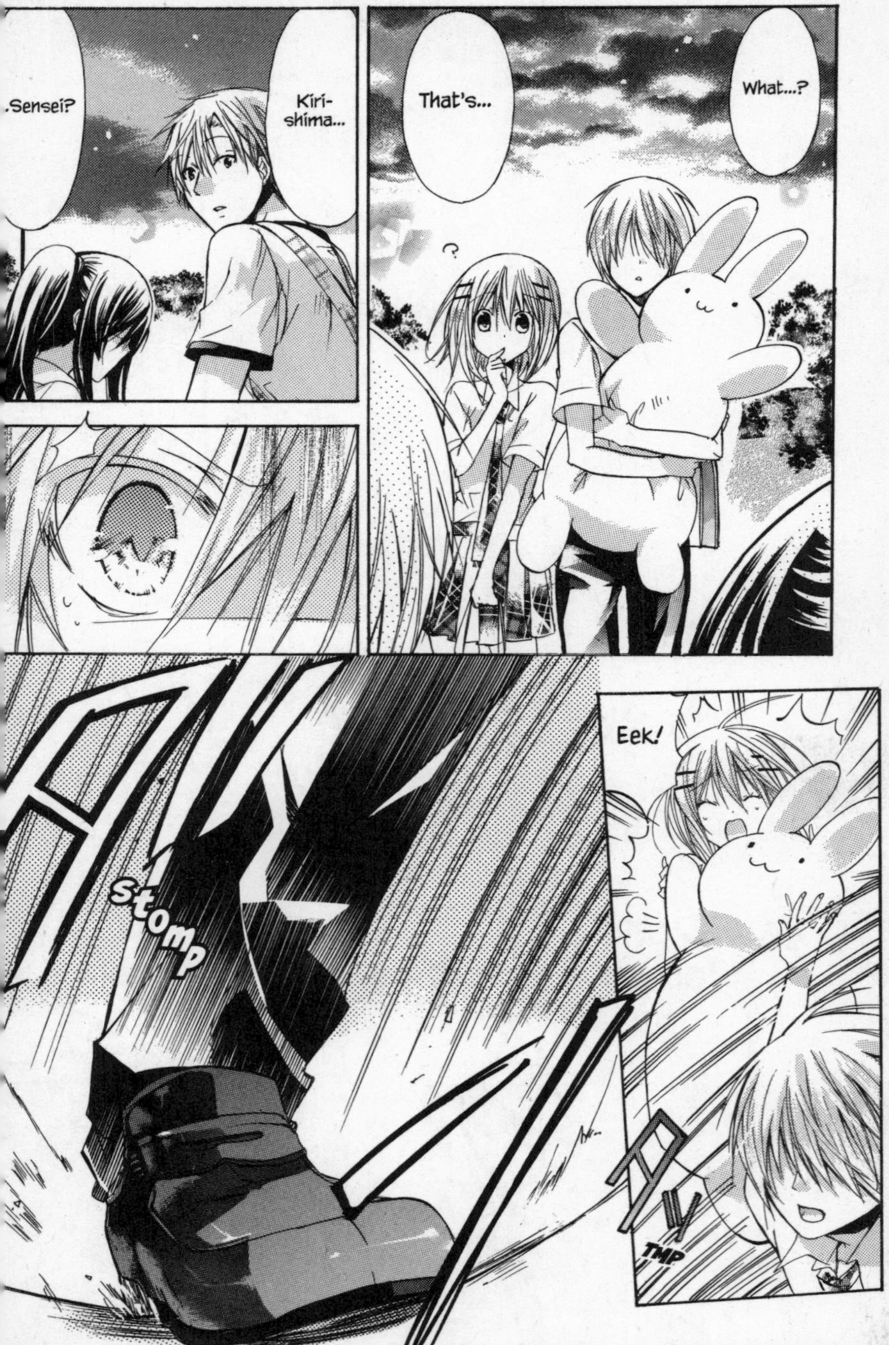
What...?
That's...
Kiri-shima...
.Sensei?
Eek!
TMP
stomp

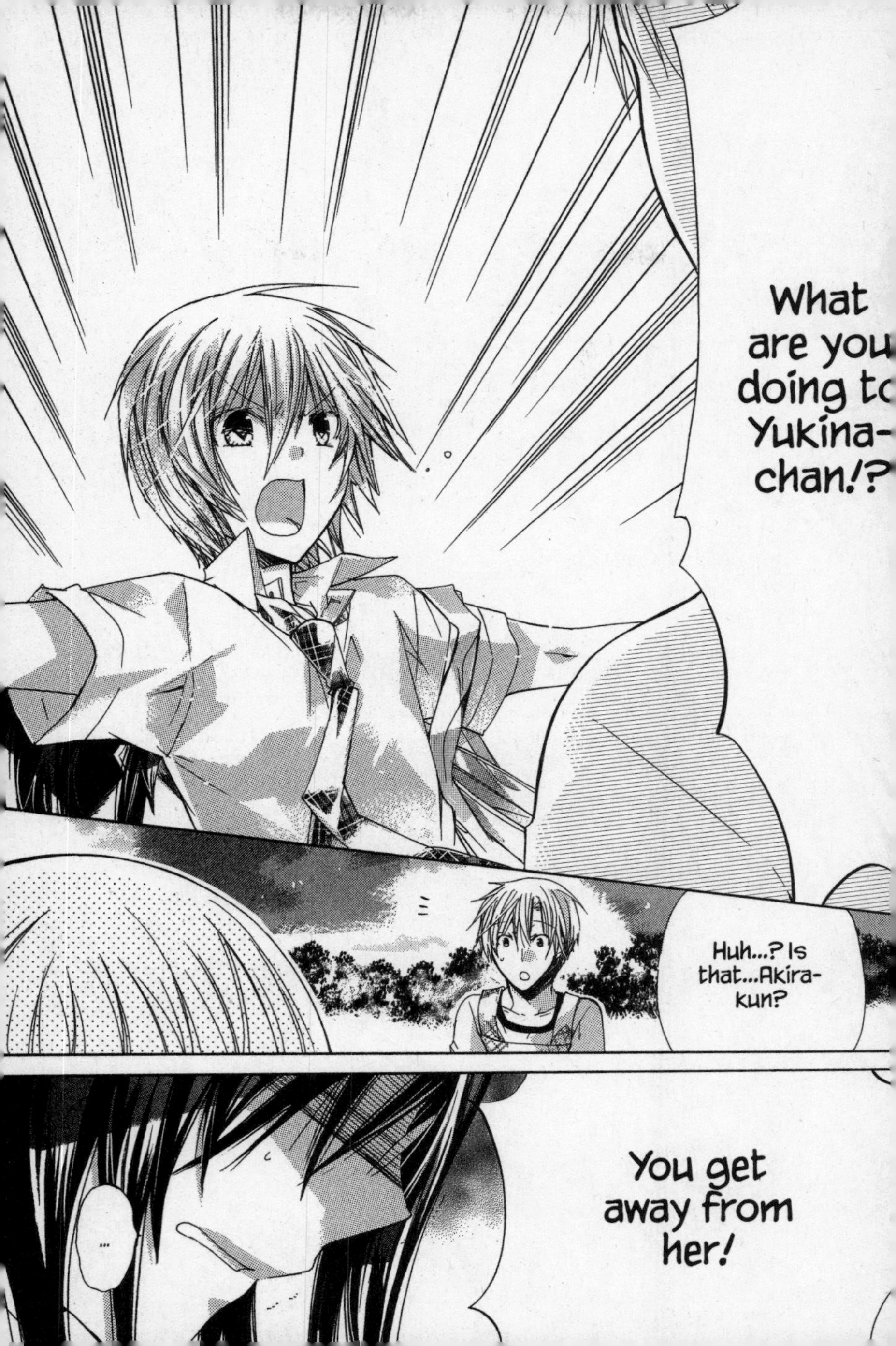
What are you doing to Yukina-chan!?
Huh...? Is that...Akira-kun?
...
You get away from her!

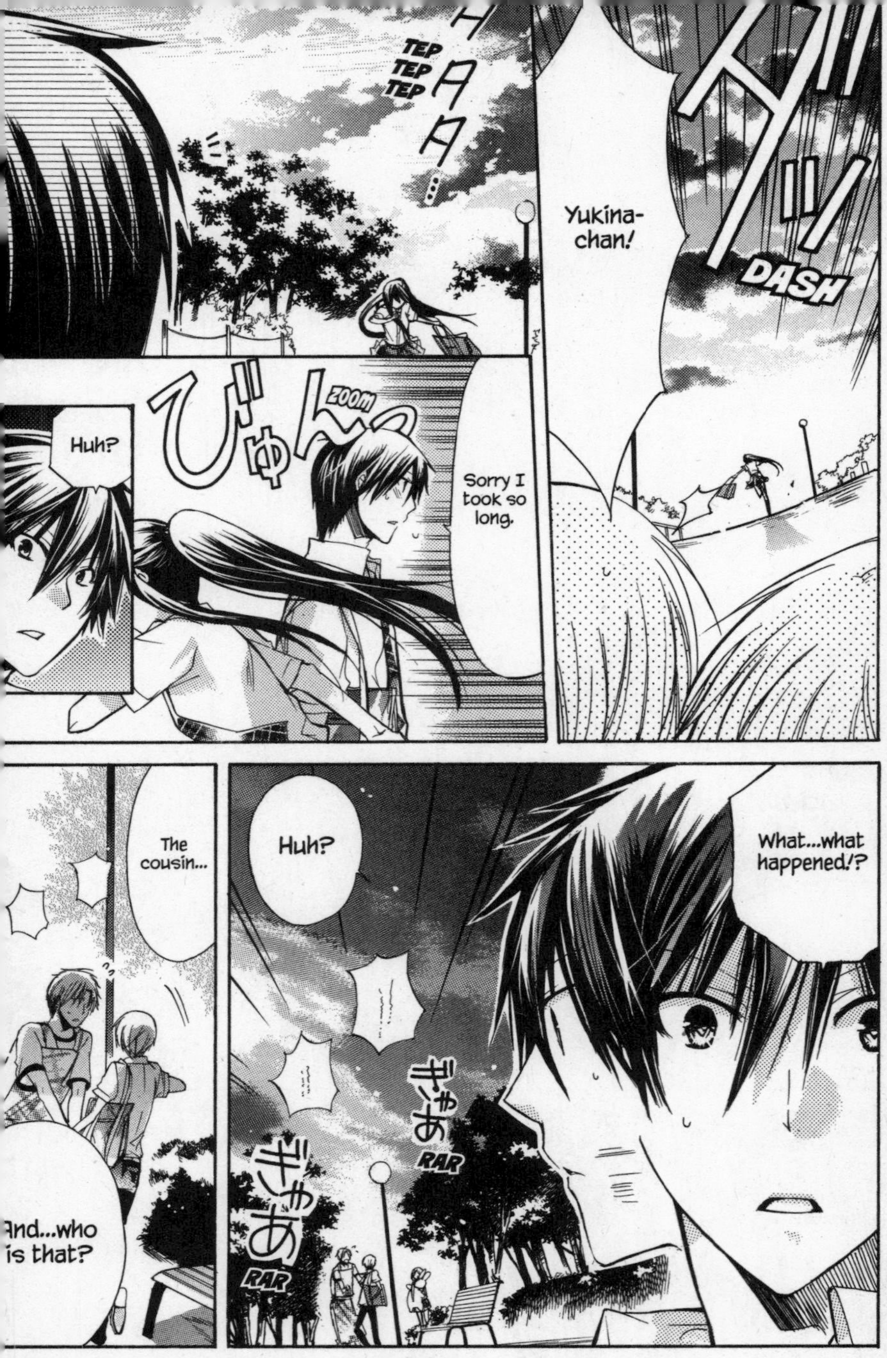

ダッ
DASH
Yukina-chan!
ハァァ…
TEP TEP TEP
びゅんっ
ZOOM
Sorry I took so long.
Huh?
What...what happened!?
Huh?
ぎゃあ
RAR
ぎゃあ
RAR
The cousin...
And...who is that?

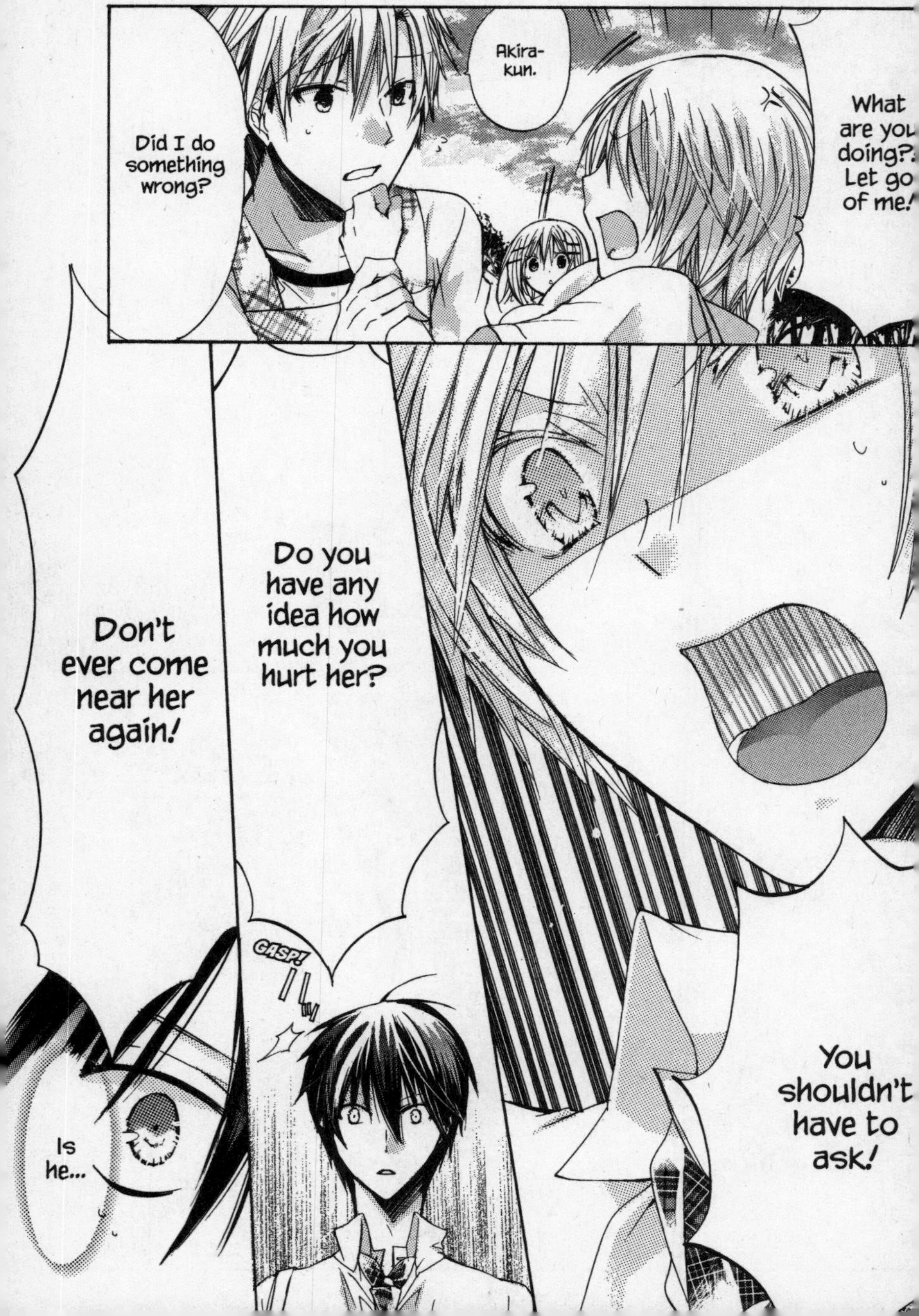
What are you doing?! Let go of me!
Akira-kun.
Did I do something wrong?
You shouldn't have to ask!
Do you have any idea how much you hurt her?
Don't ever come near her again!
GASP!
Is he...

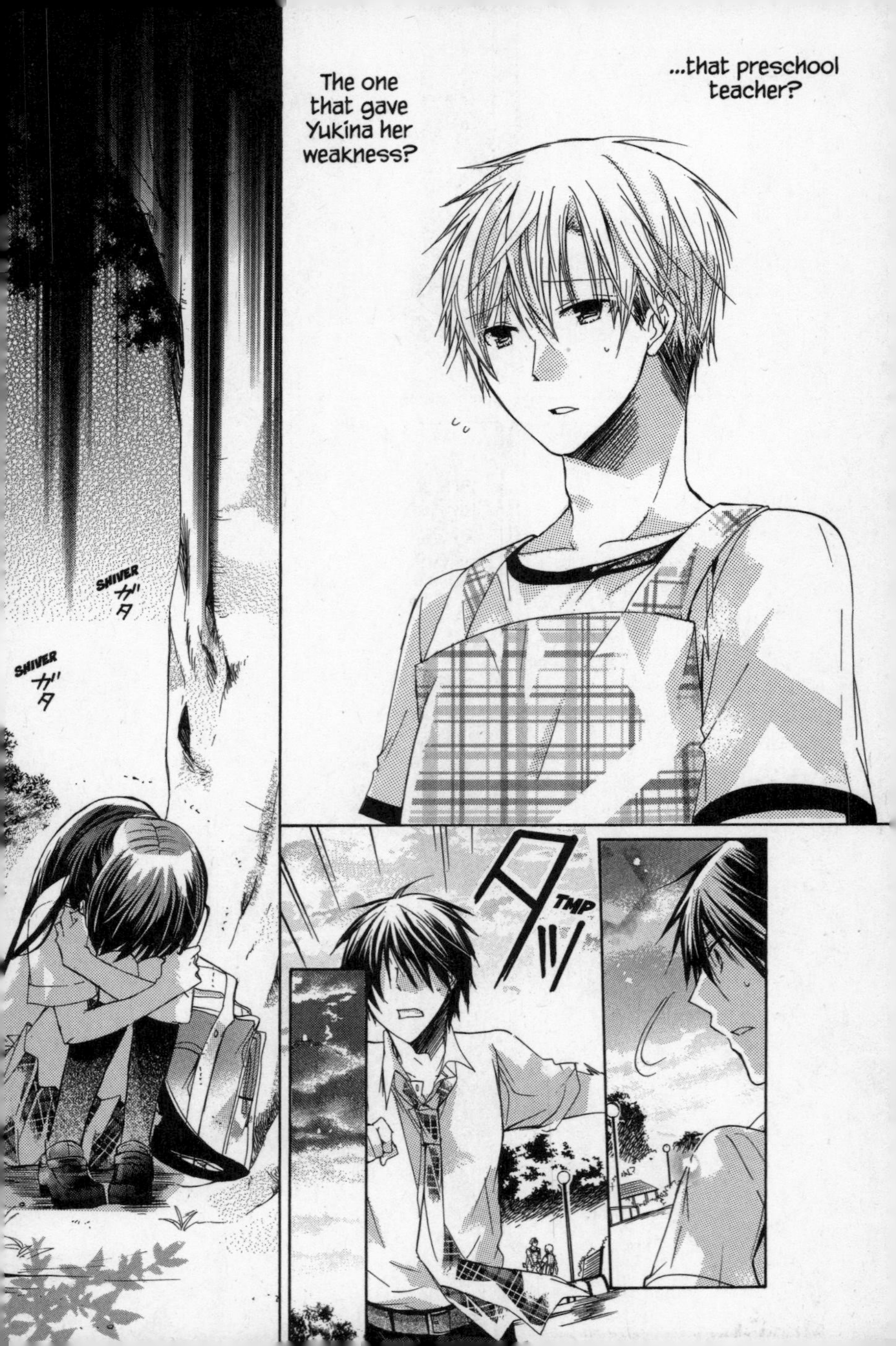
...that preschool teacher?
The one that gave Yukina her weakness?
TMP
タッ
SHIVER
ガタ
SHIVER
ガタ

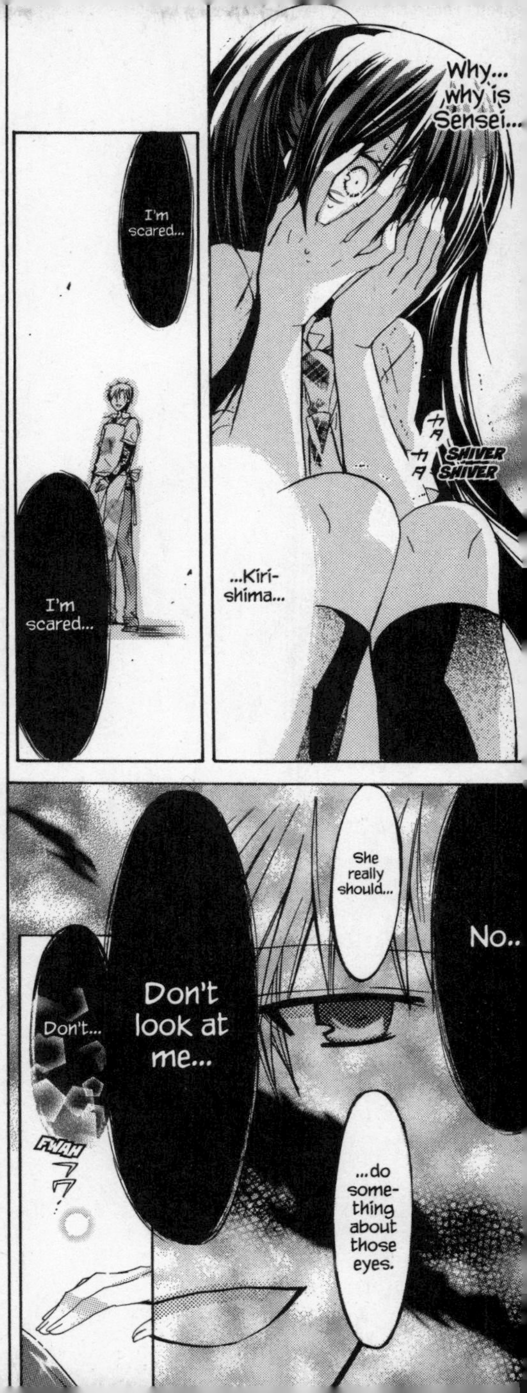
Why... why is Sensei...
SHIVER SHIVER
...Kiri-shima...
I'm scared...
I'm scared...
No...
She really should...
...do some-thing about those eyes.
Don't look at me...
Don't...
FWAH

The Secret to Staying Solid 2

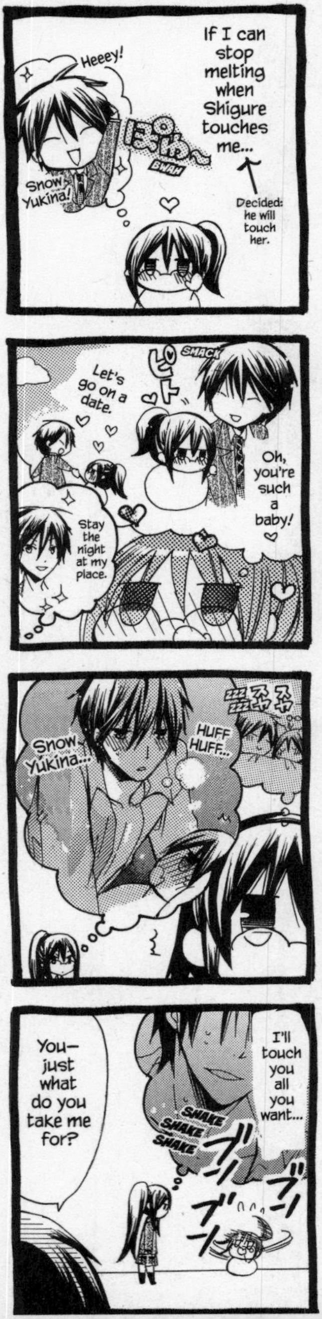
If I can stop melting when Shigure touches me...
Heeey!
BWAH
Snow Yukina!
Decided: he will touch her.
SMACK
Let's go on a date.
Oh, you're such a baby!
Stay the night at my place.
HUFF HUFF...
Snow Yukina...
I'll touch you all you want...
You— just what do you take me for?
SHAKE SHAKE SHAKE

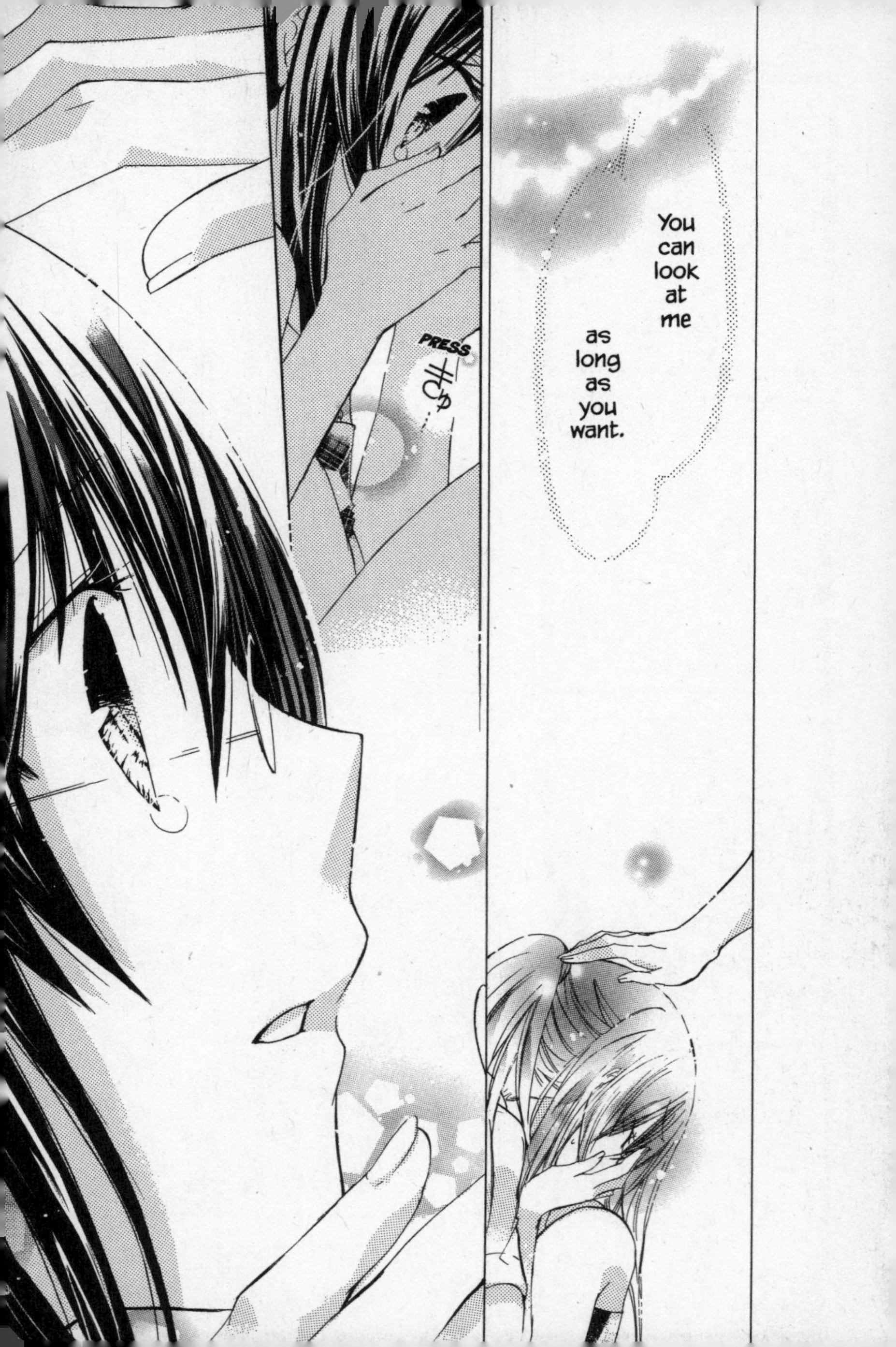
You can look at me as long as you want.
PRESS

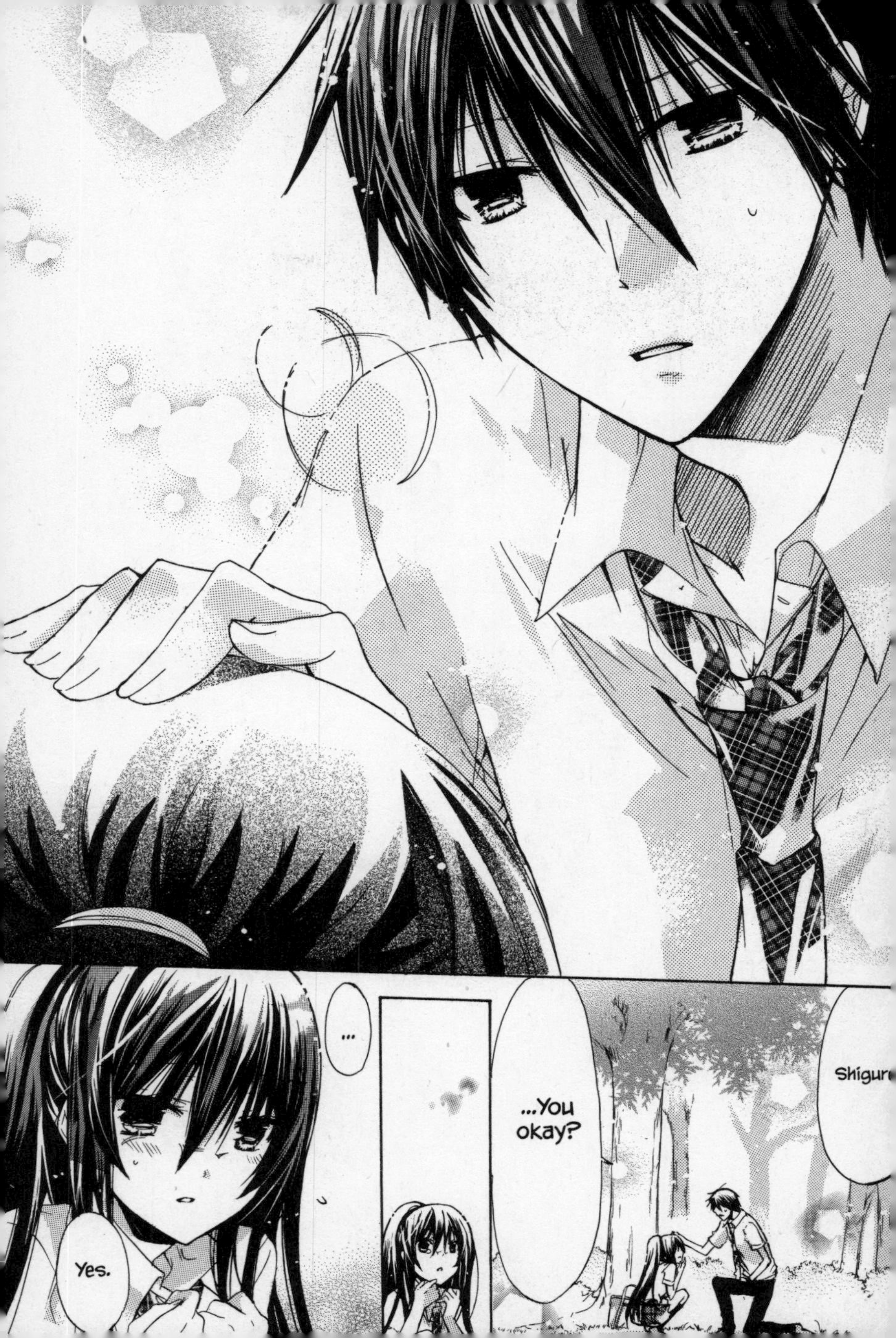
Shigur
...You okay?
...
Yes.

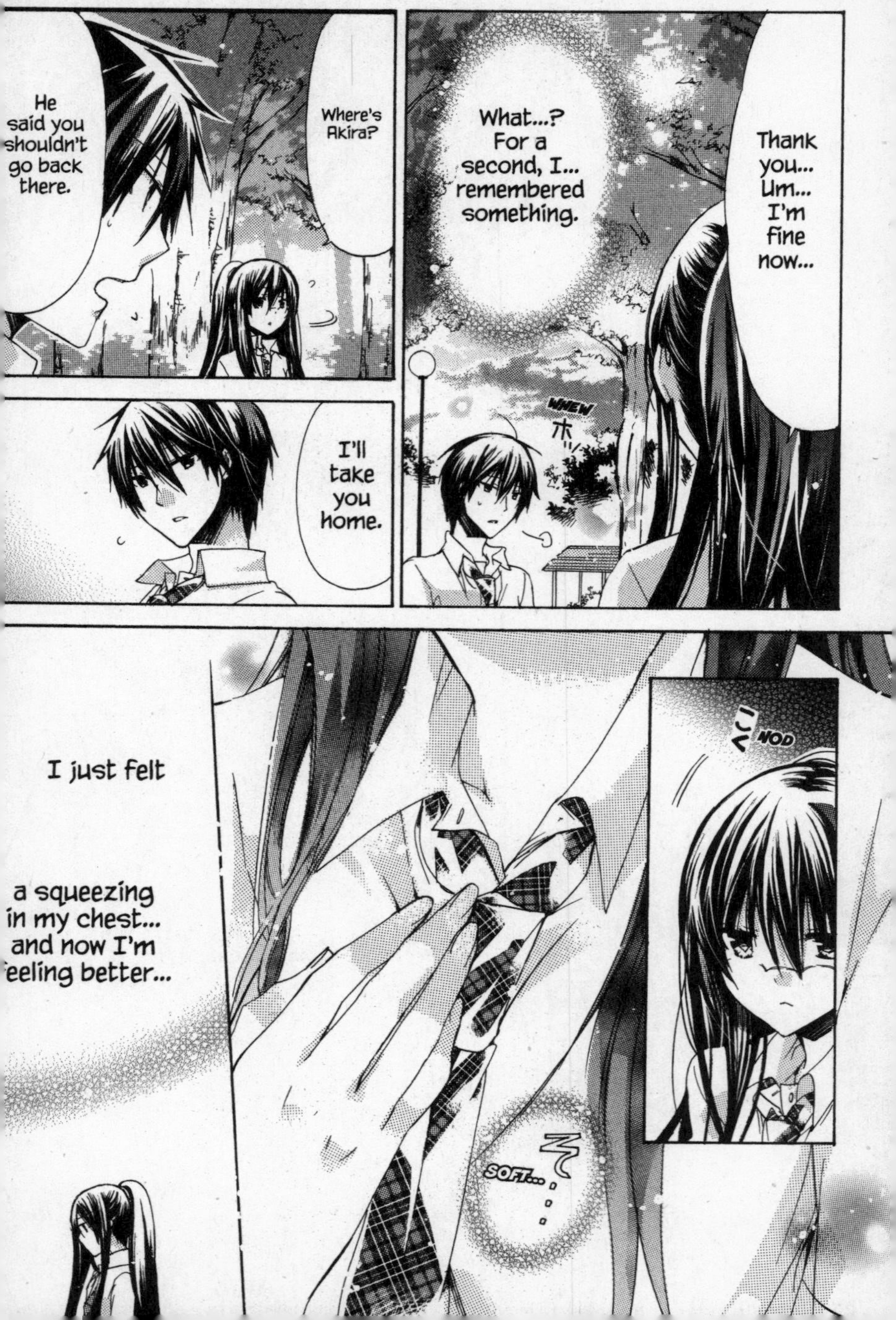
Thank you... Um... I'm fine now...
What...? For a second, I... remembered something.
WHEW
Where's Akira?
He said you shouldn't go back there.
I'll take you home.
NOD
SOFT...
I just felt
a squeezing in my chest... and now I'm feeling better...

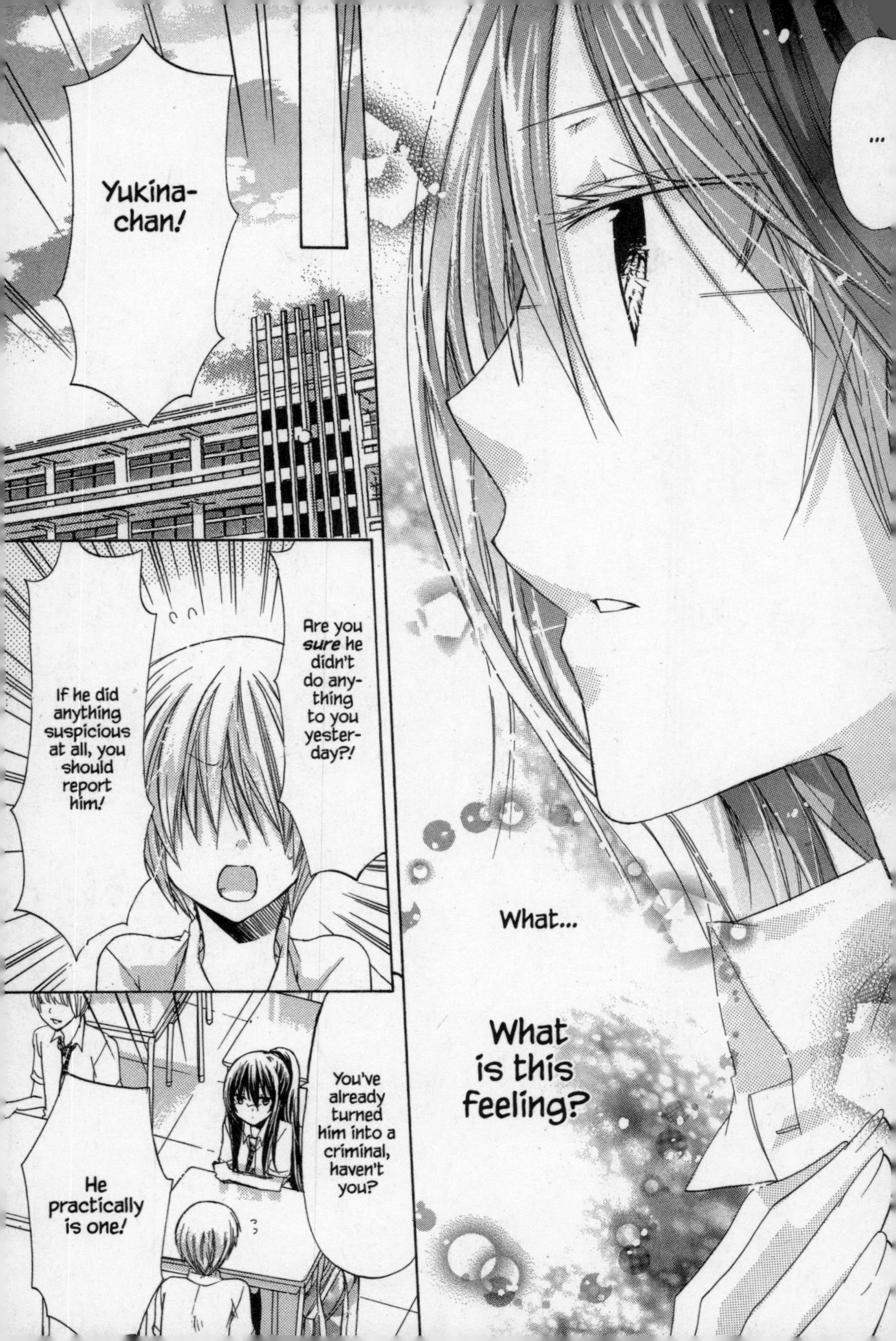
...
Yukina-chan!
Are you *sure* he didn't do anything to you yesterday?!
If he did anything suspicious at all, you should report him!
What...
What is this feeling?
You've already turned him into a criminal, haven't you?
He practically is one!

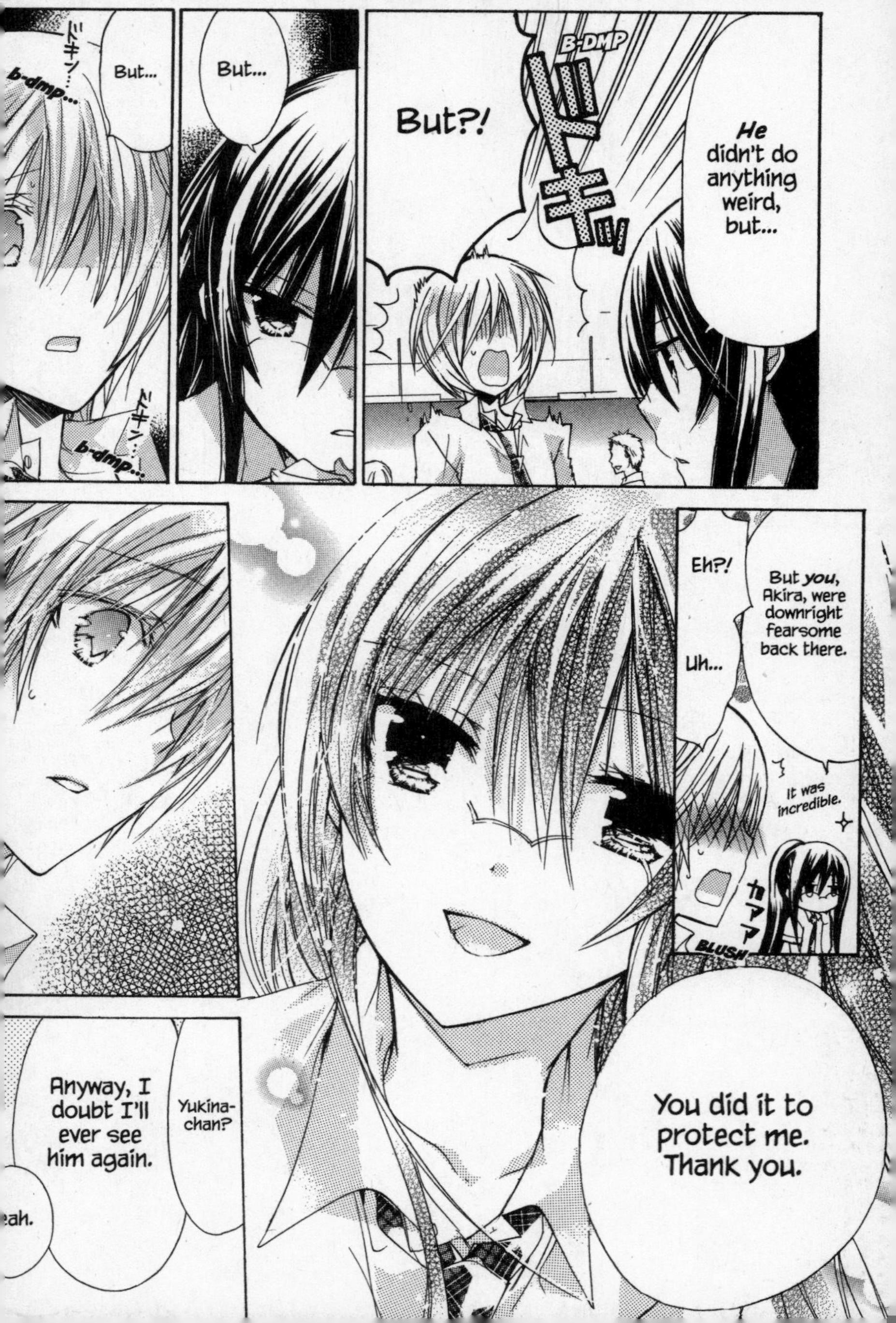

He didn't do anything weird, but...
B-DMP
ドキッ
But?!
But...
But...
ドキン…
b-dmp...
ドキン…
b-dmp...
But you, Akira, were downright fearsome back there.
Eh?!
Uh...
It was incredible.
カァァ
BLUSH
You did it to protect me. Thank you.
Yukina-chan?
Anyway, I doubt I'll ever see him again.
eah.

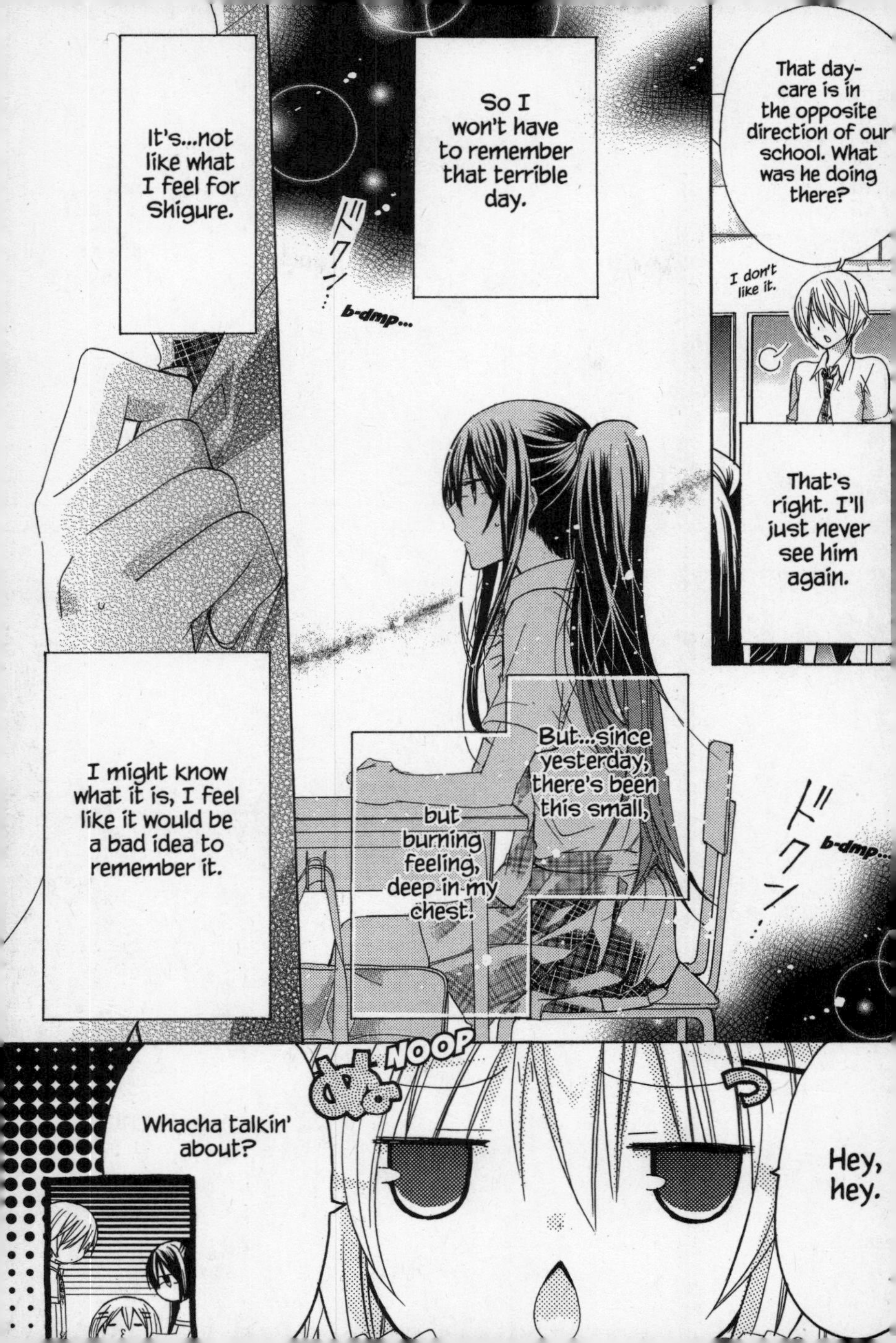
That day-care is in the opposite direction of our school. What was he doing there?
I don't like it.
That's right. I'll just never see him again.
So I won't have to remember that terrible day.
ドクン…
b-dmp...
But...since yesterday, there's been this small,
but burning feeling, deep in my chest.
ドクン…
b-dmp...
It's...not like what I feel for Shigure.
I might know what it is, I feel like it would be a bad idea to remember it.
Hey, hey.
ぬっ
NOOP
Whacha talkin' about?

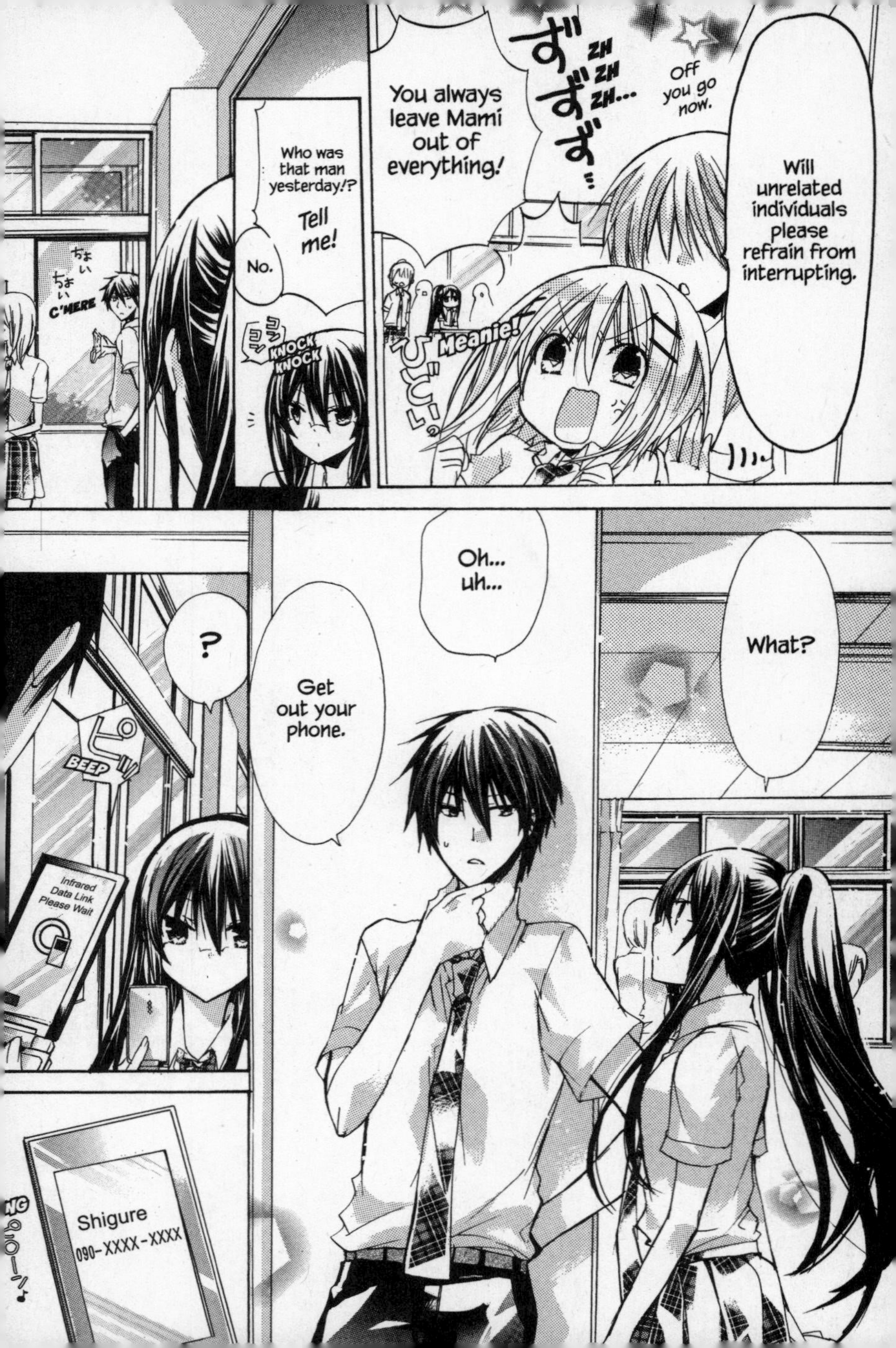
Will unrelated individuals please refrain from interrupting.
Off you go now.
ずずず
ZH ZH ZH...
You always leave Mami out of everything!
ひどい
Meanie!
Who was that man yesterday!?
Tell me!
No.
コンコン
KNOCK KNOCK
ちょいちょい
C'MERE
What?
Oh... uh...
Get out your phone.
?
ピッ
BEEP
Infrared Data Link Please Wait
Shigure
090-XXXX-XXXX

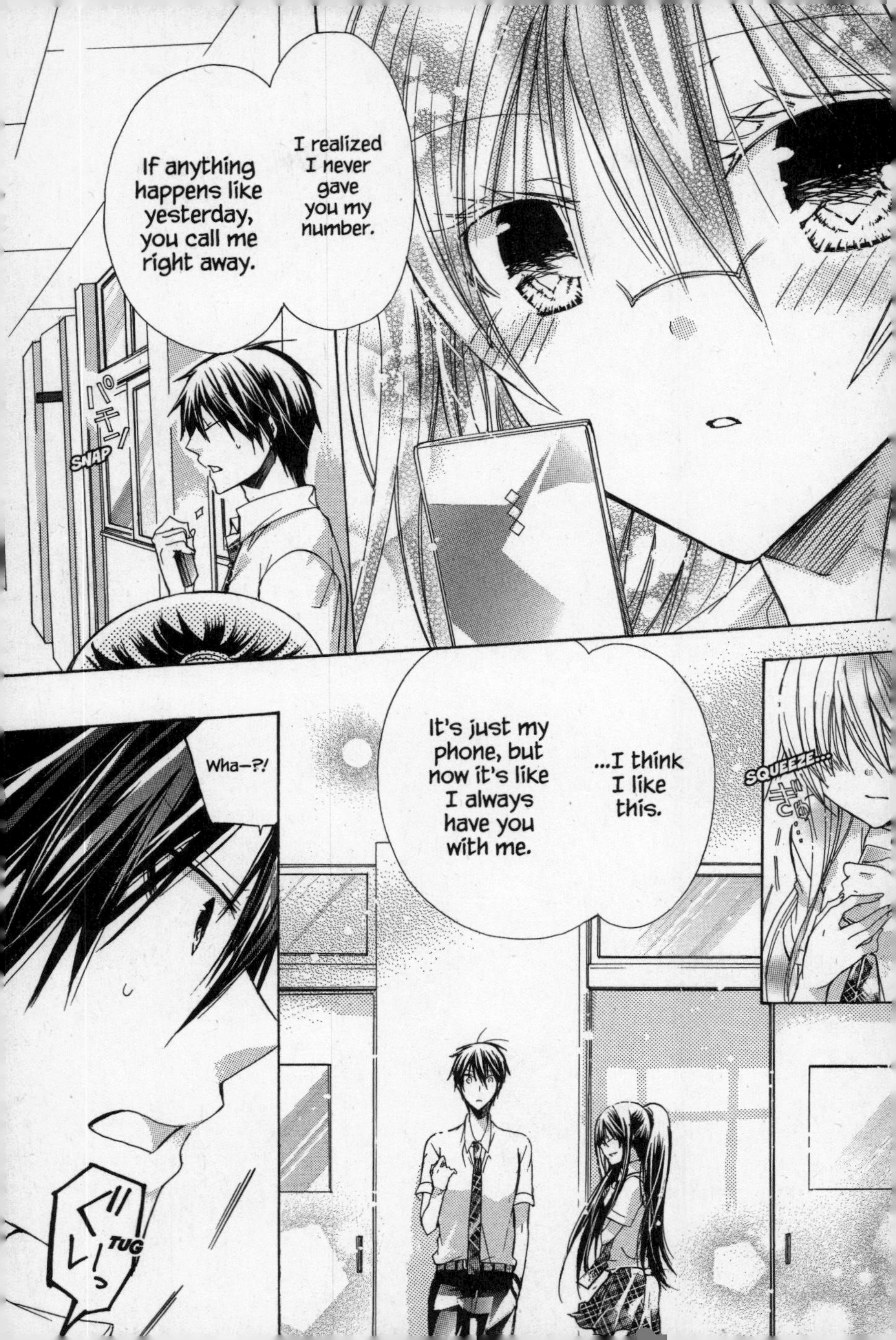
I realized I never gave you my number.
If anything happens like yesterday, you call me right away.
SNAP
SQUEEZE...
...I think I like this.
It's just my phone, but now it's like I always have you with me.
Wha-?!
TUG

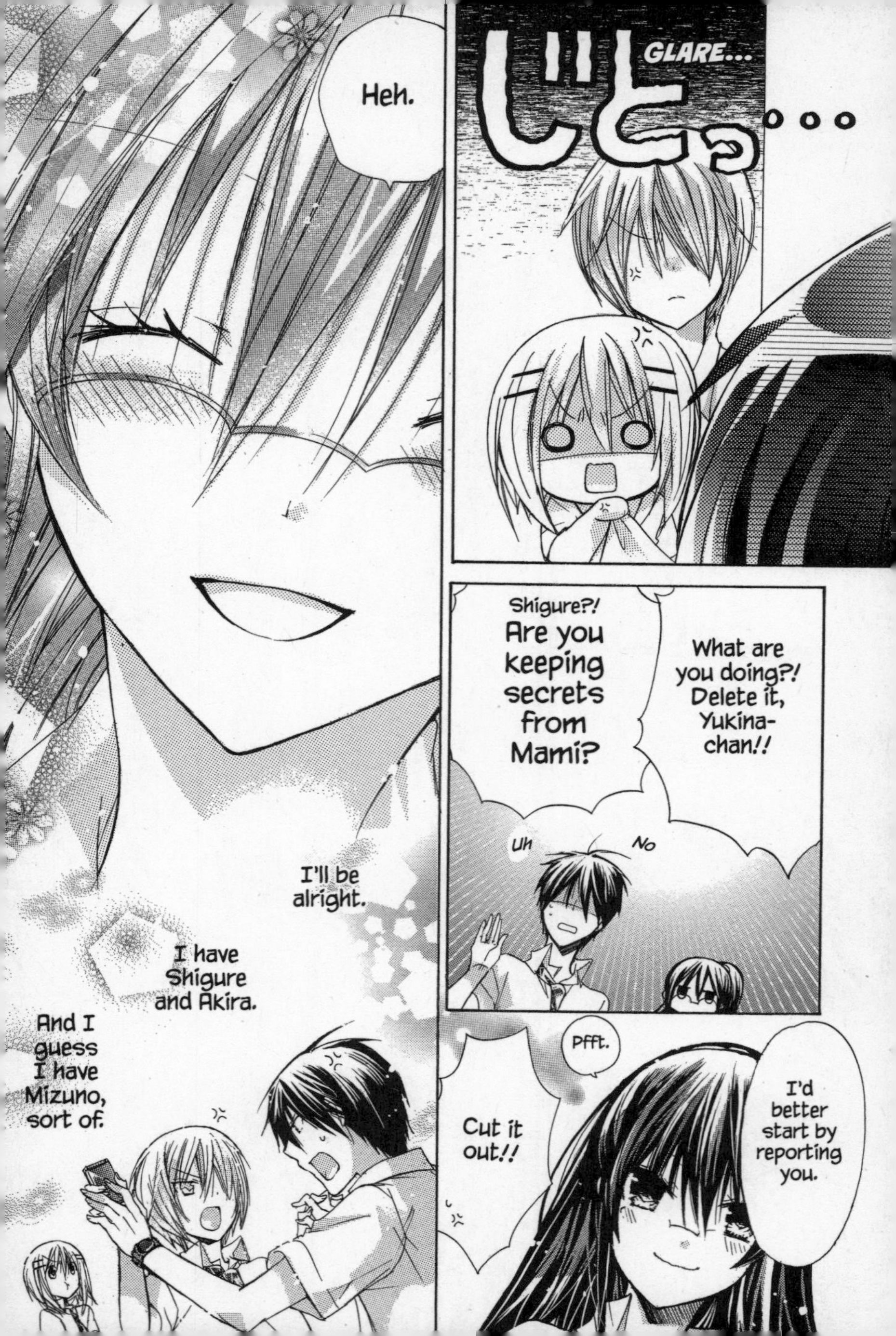
GLARE...
じーっ…
What are you doing?! Delete it, Yukina-chan!!
Shigure?! Are you keeping secrets from Mami?
No
Uh
I'd better start by reporting you.
Pfft.
Cut it out!!
Heh.
I'll be alright.
I have Shigure and Akira.
And I guess I have Mizuno, sort of.

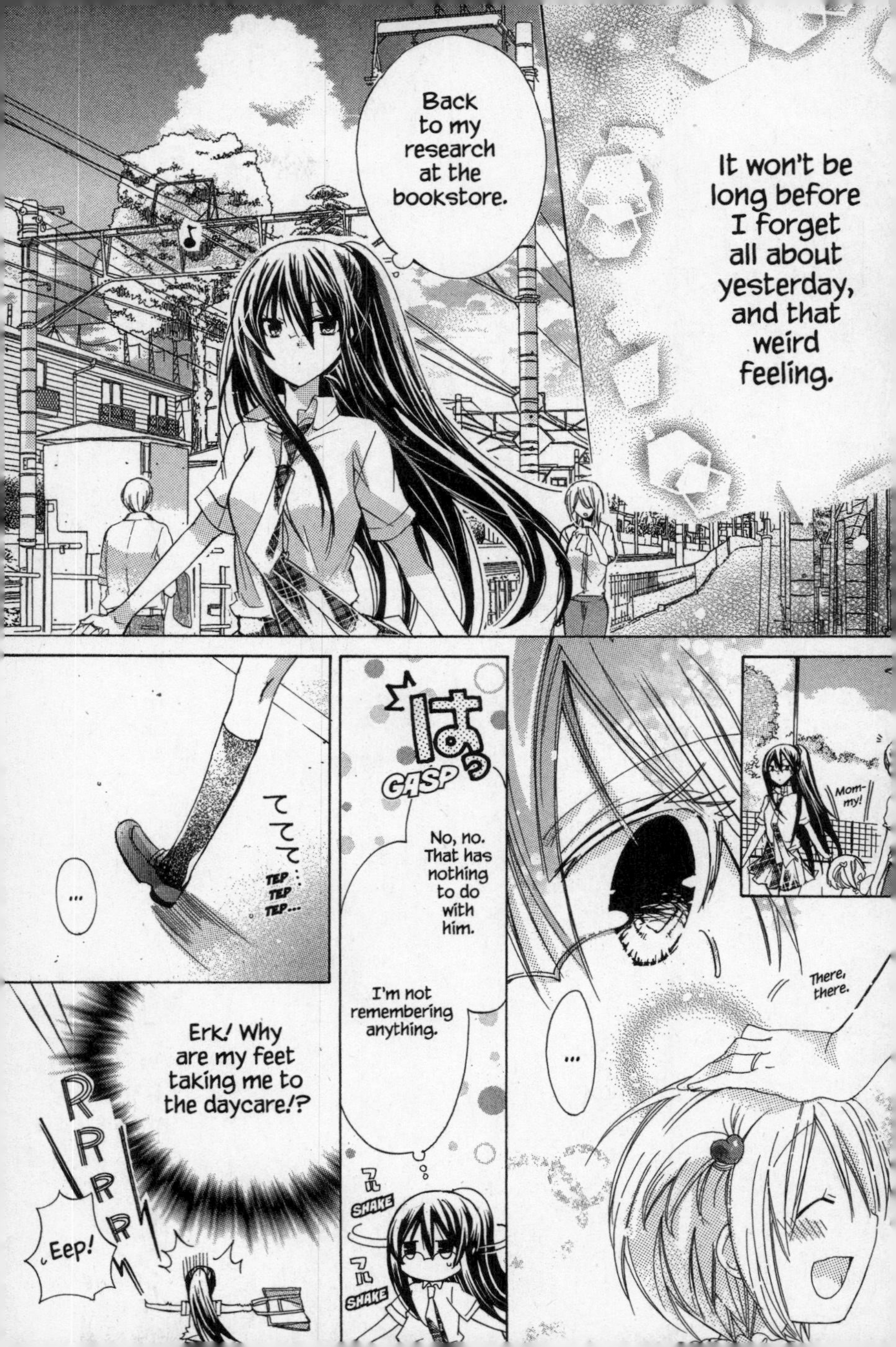

It won't be long before I forget all about yesterday, and that weird feeling.
Back to my research at the bookstore.
Mom-my!
There, there.
...
はっ
GASP
No, no. That has nothing to do with him.
I'm not remembering anything.
フル
SHAKE
フル
SHAKE
てててて
TEP TEP TEP...
...
Erk! Why are my feet taking me to the daycare!?
RRRRM
Eep!

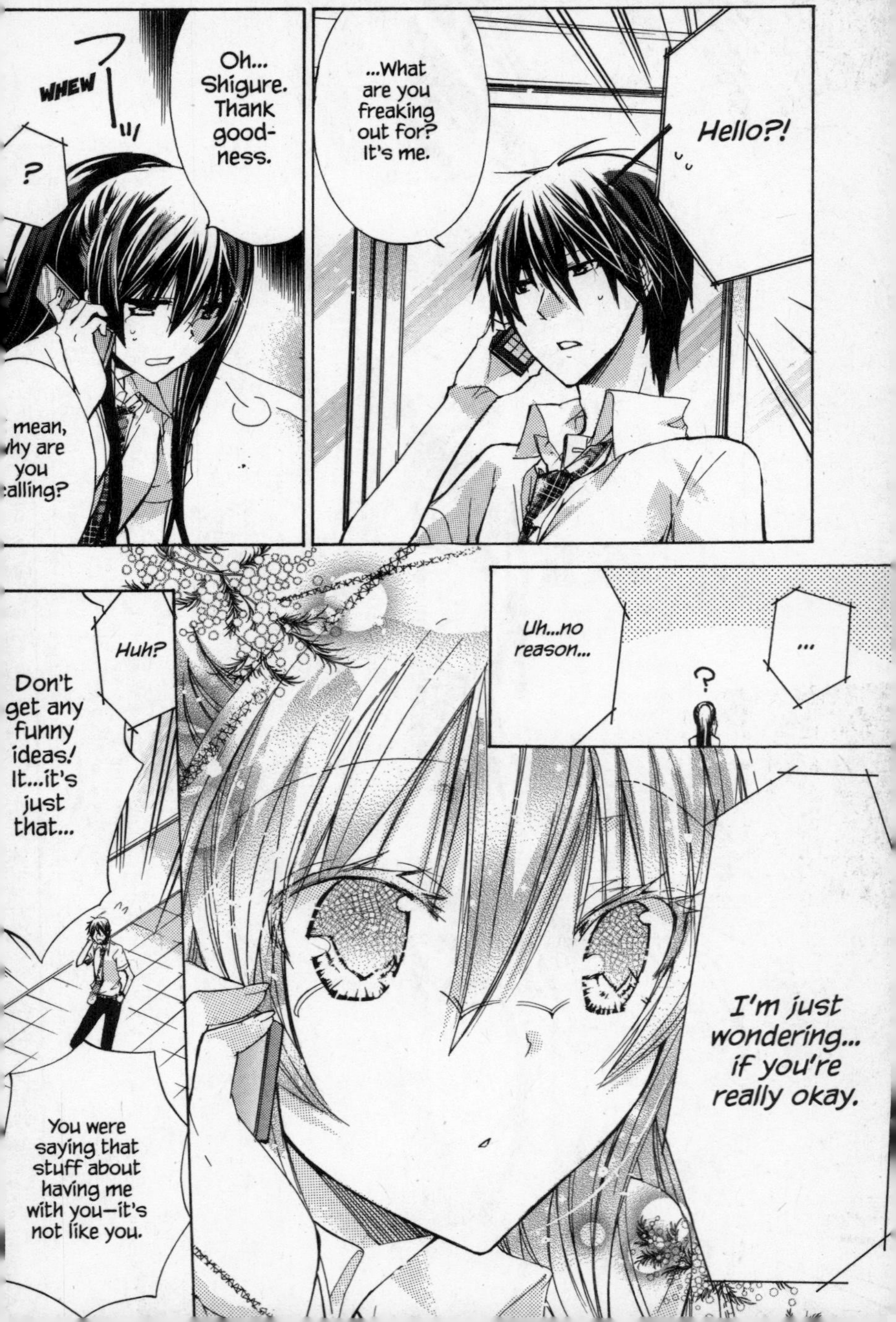
Hello?!
...What are you freaking out for? It's me.
Oh... Shigure. Thank goodness.
WHEW
?
mean, hy are you alling?
...
?
Uh...no reason...
I'm just wondering... if you're really okay.
You were saying that stuff about having me with you—it's not like you.
Huh?
Don't get any funny ideas! It...it's just that...

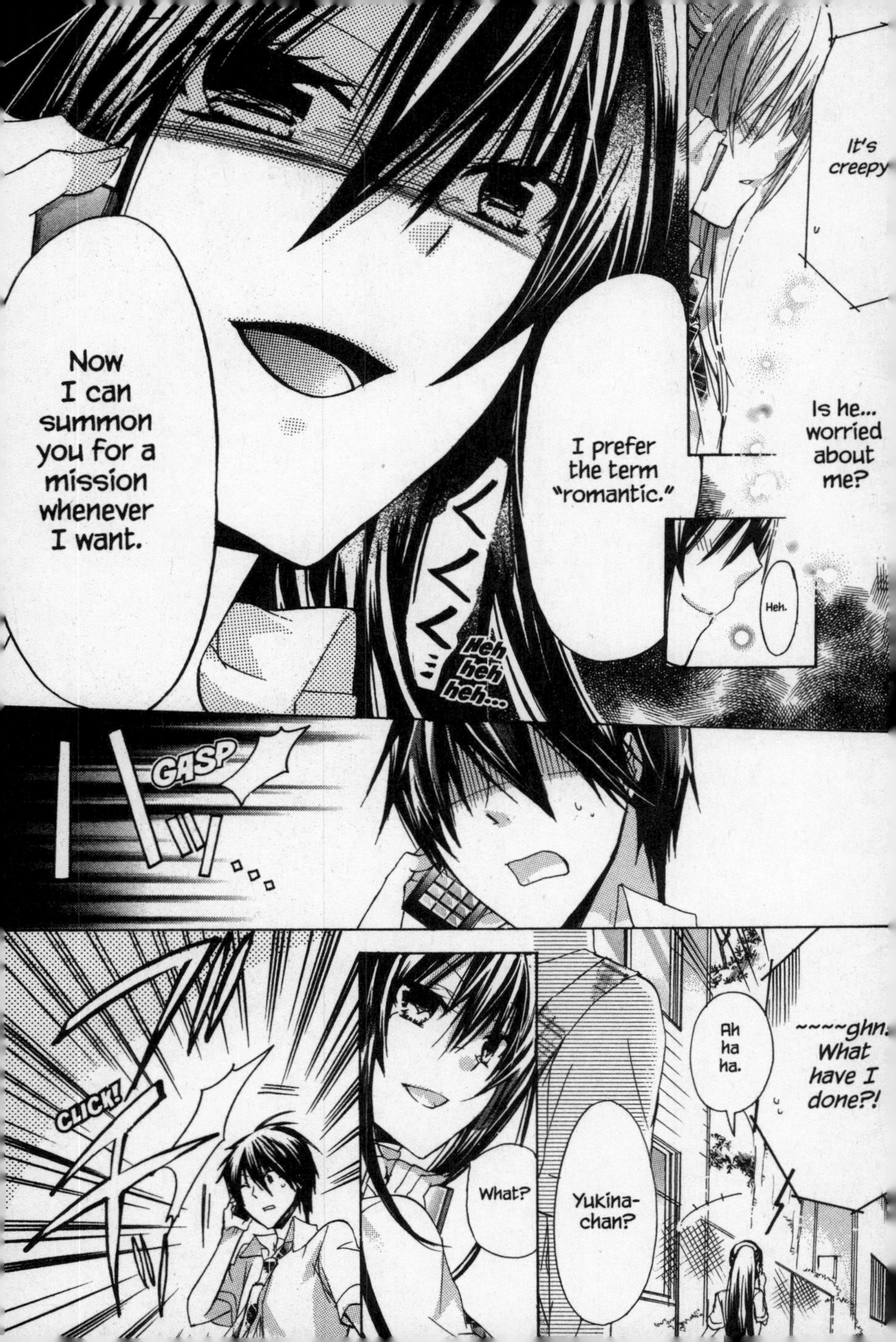
It's creepy
Is he... worried about me?
Heh.
I prefer the term "romantic."
Now I can summon you for a mission whenever I want.
Heh heh heh...
GASP
~~~~ghn. What have I done?!
Ah ha ha.
Yukina-chan?
What?
CLICK!
~~~~

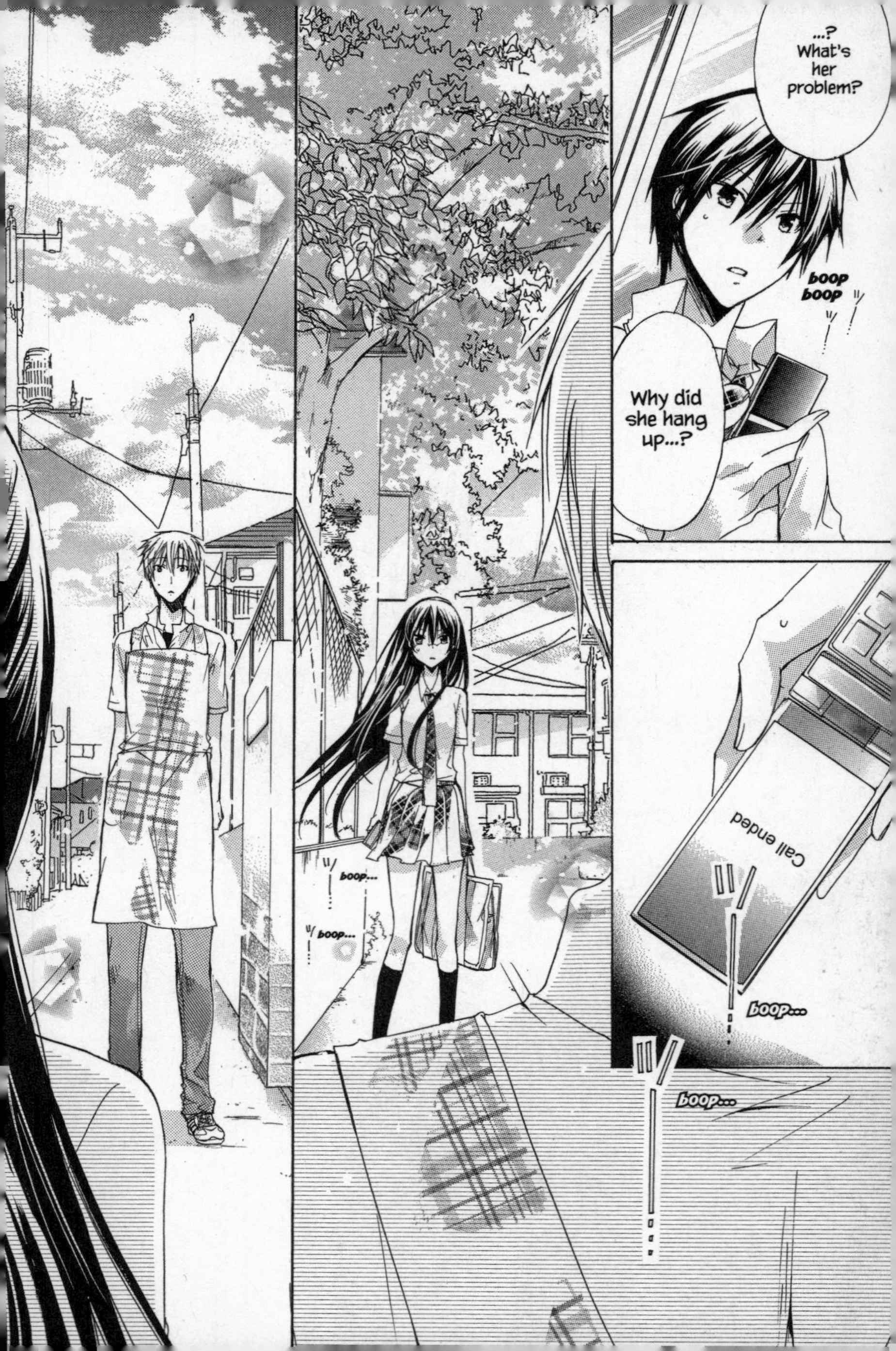
...? What's her problem?
boop boop
Why did she hang up...?
Call ended
boop...
boop...
boop...
boop...

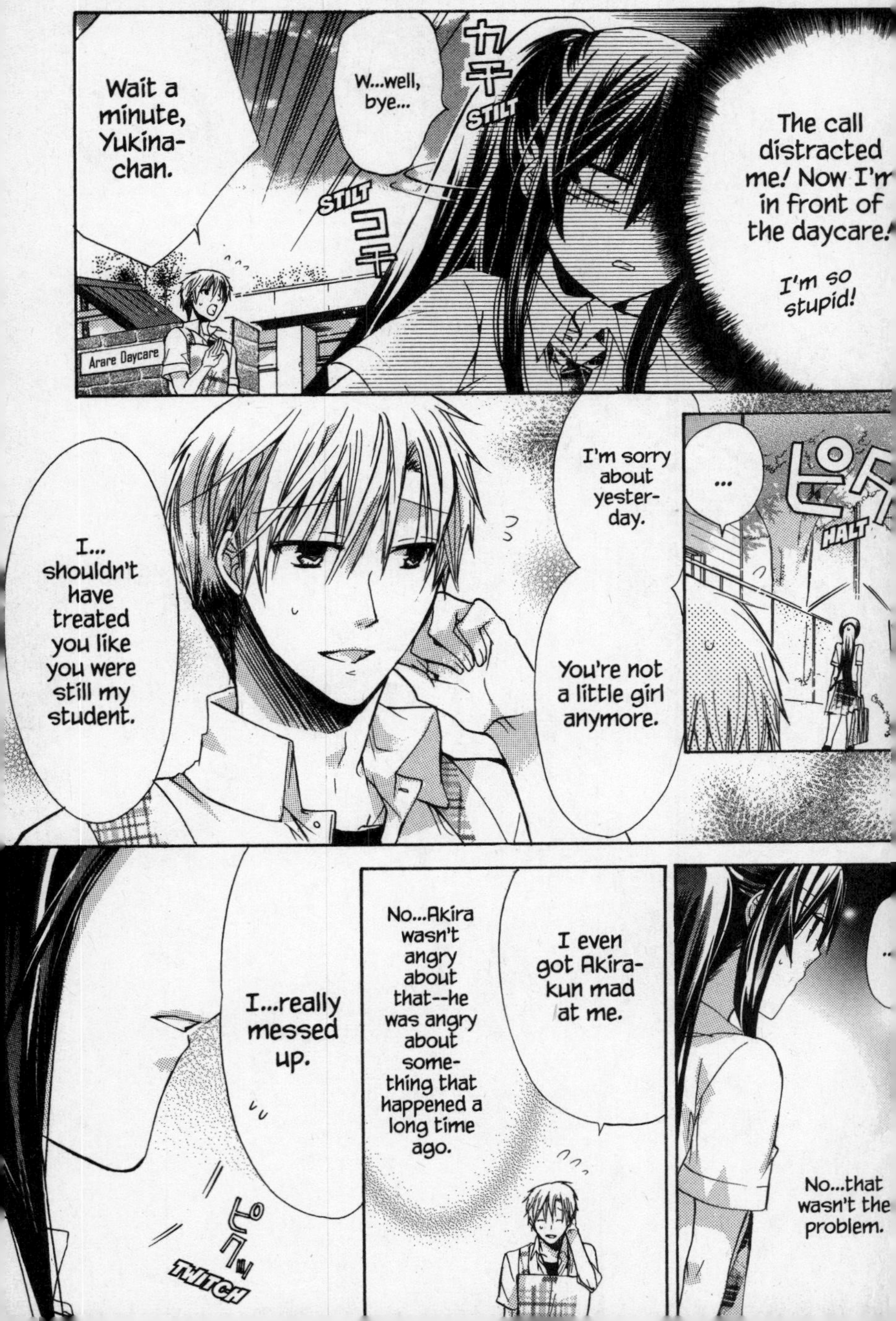
The call distracted me! Now I'm in front of the daycare!
I'm so stupid!
カチ
STILT
W...well, bye...
Wait a minute, Yukina-chan.
STILT
コチ
Arare Daycare
...
HALT
I'm sorry about yesterday.
You're not a little girl anymore.
I... shouldn't have treated you like you were still my student.
...
No...that wasn't the problem.
I even got Akira-kun mad at me.
No...Akira wasn't angry about that--he was angry about something that happened a long time ago.
I...really messed up.
TWITCH

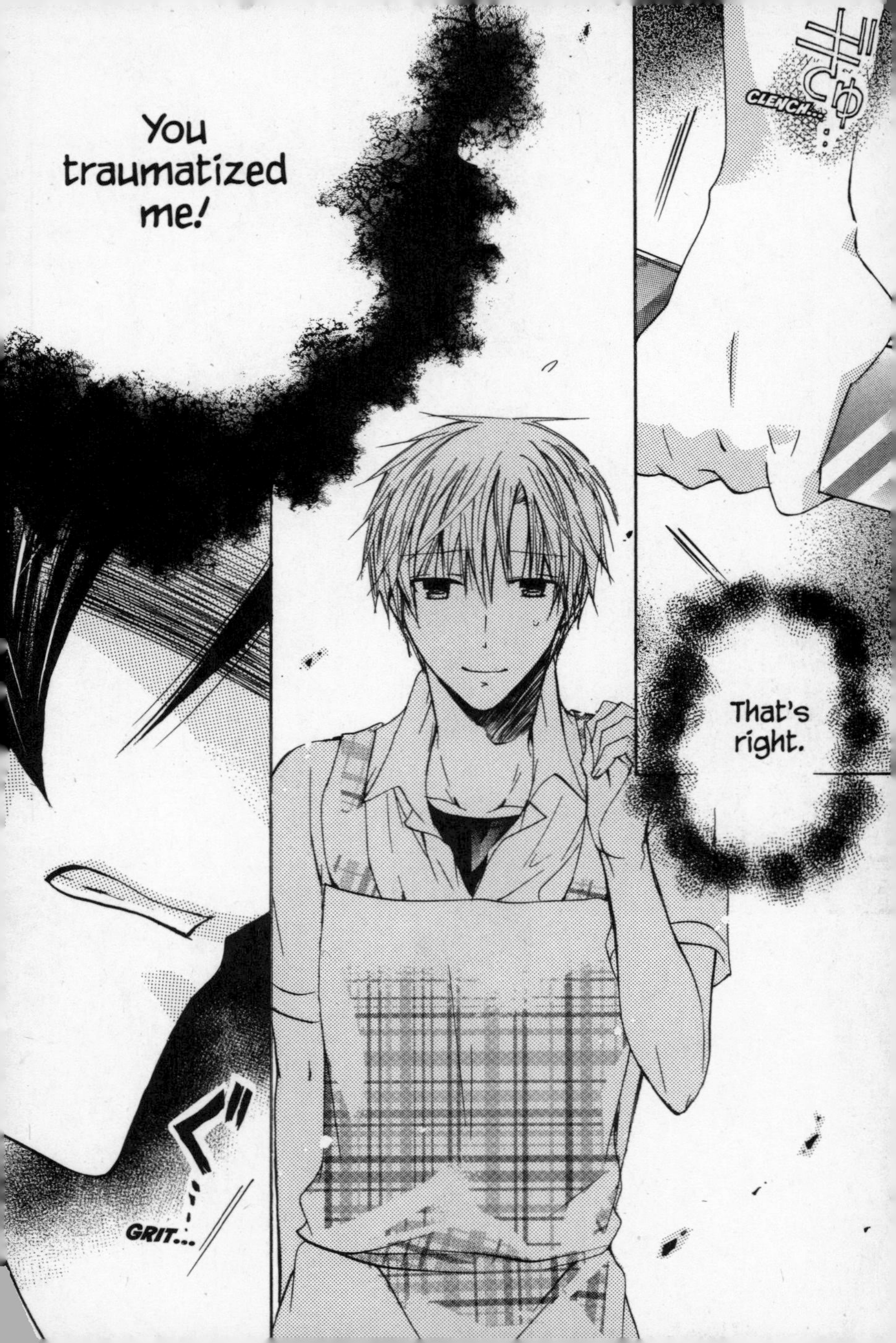
CLENCH...
That's right.
You traumatized me!
GRIT...

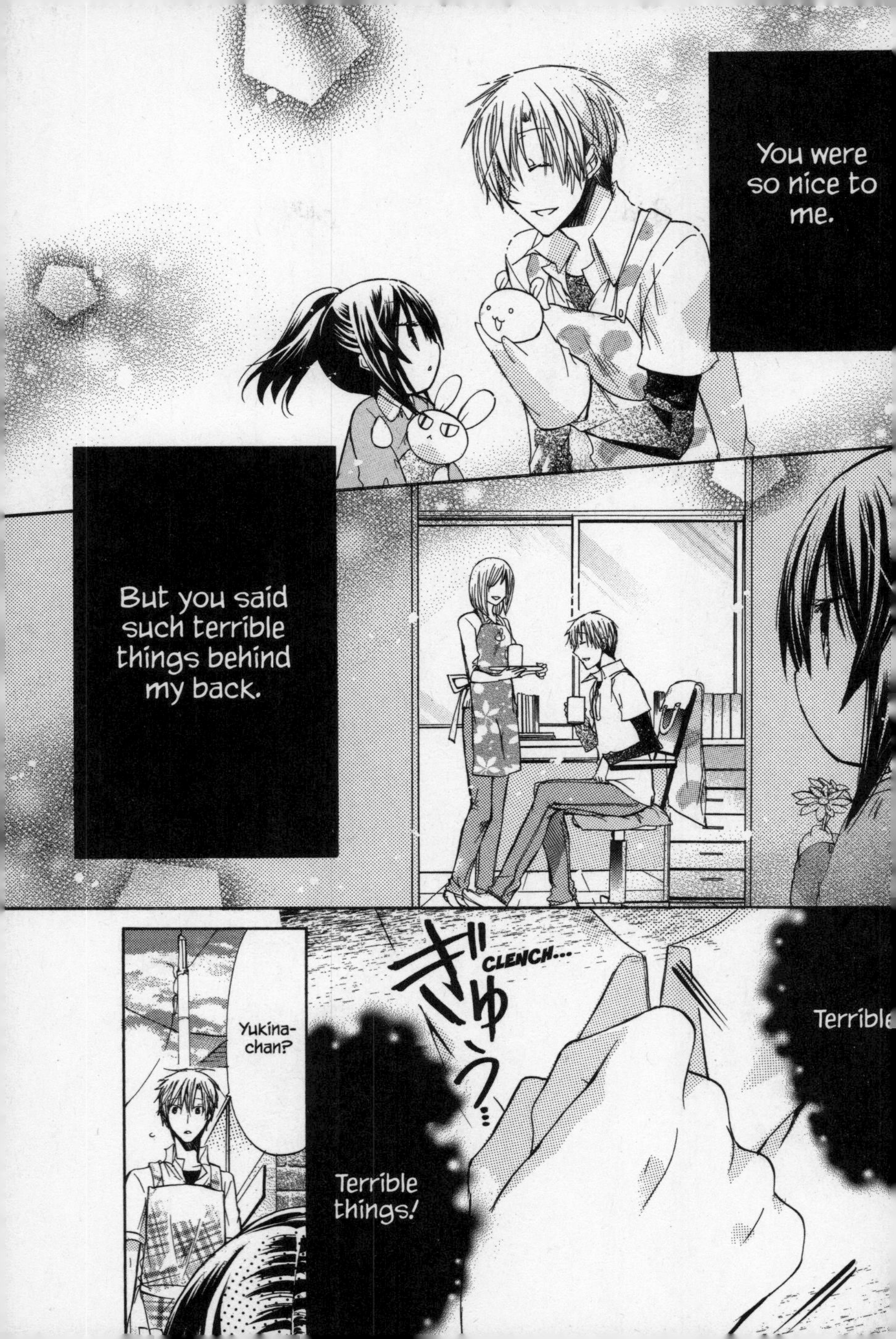
You were so nice to me.
But you said such terrible things behind my back.
Terrible
ぎゅう…
CLENCH...
Terrible things!
Yukina-chan?

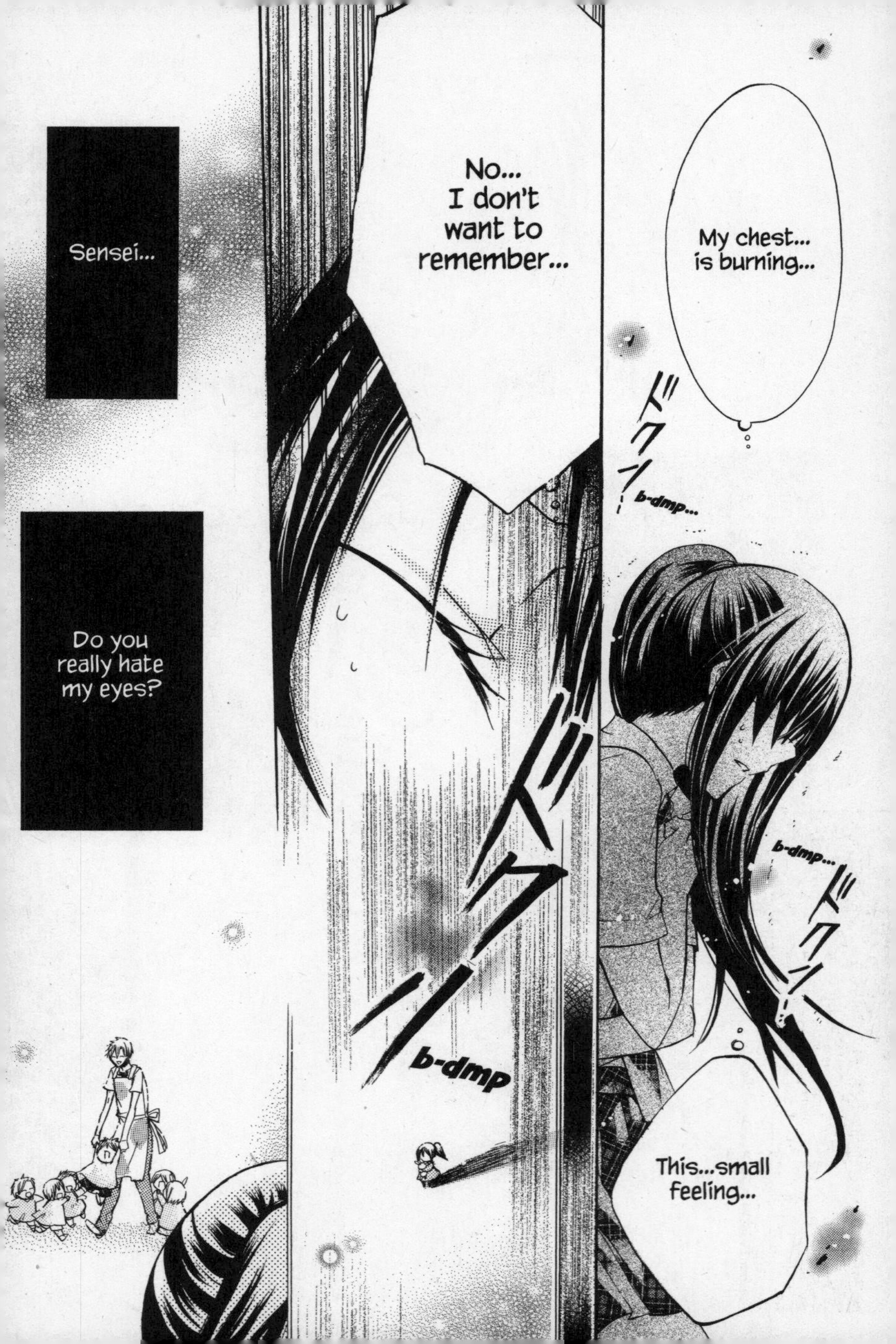
My chest... is burning...
ドクン
b-dmp...
b-dmp...
ドクン
This...small feeling...
No... I don't want to remember...
ドクン
b-dmp
Sensei...
Do you really hate my eyes?

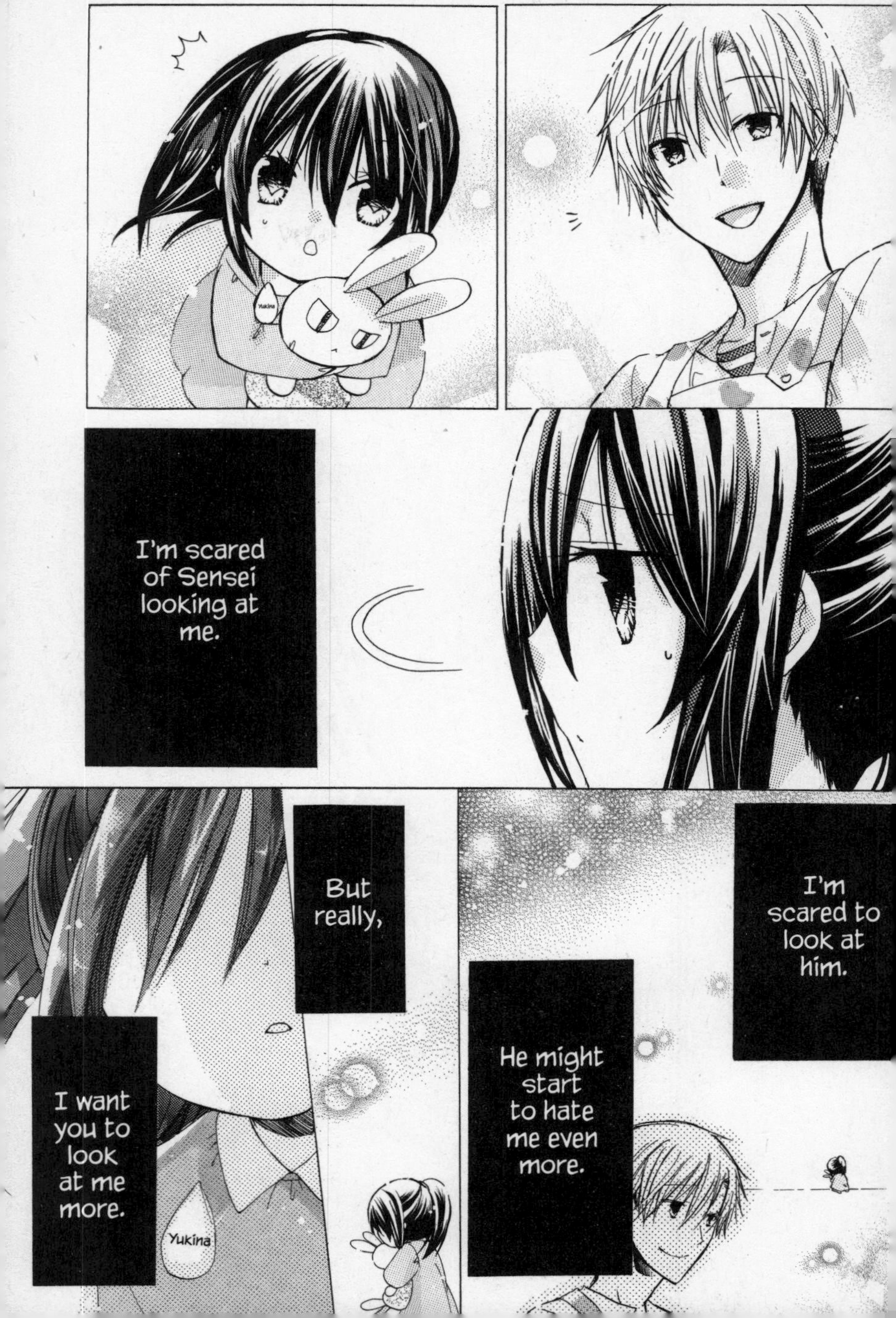
I'm scared of Sensei looking at me.
I'm scared to look at him.
He might start to hate me even more.
But really,
I want you to look at me more.
Yukina

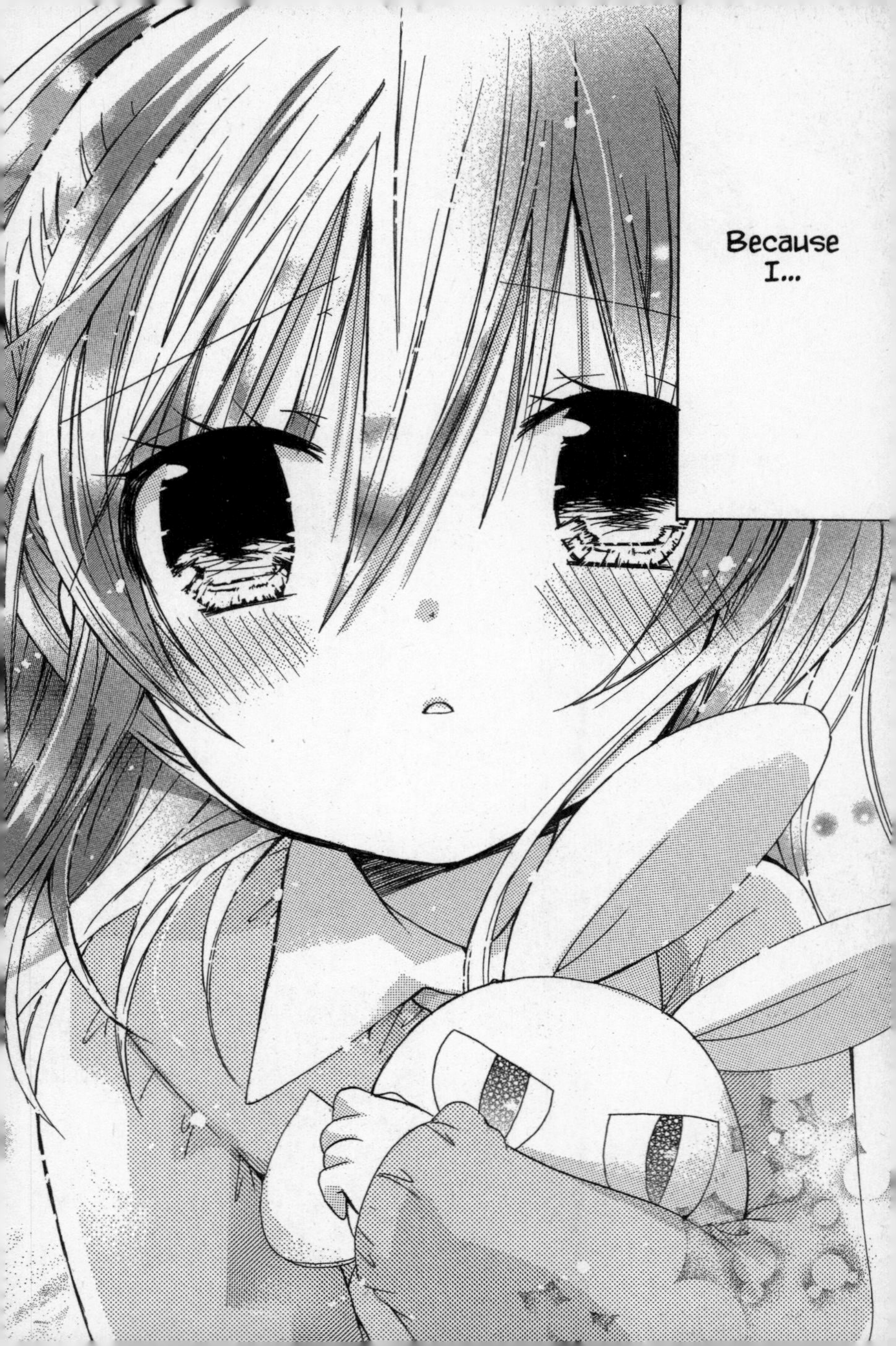
Because I...

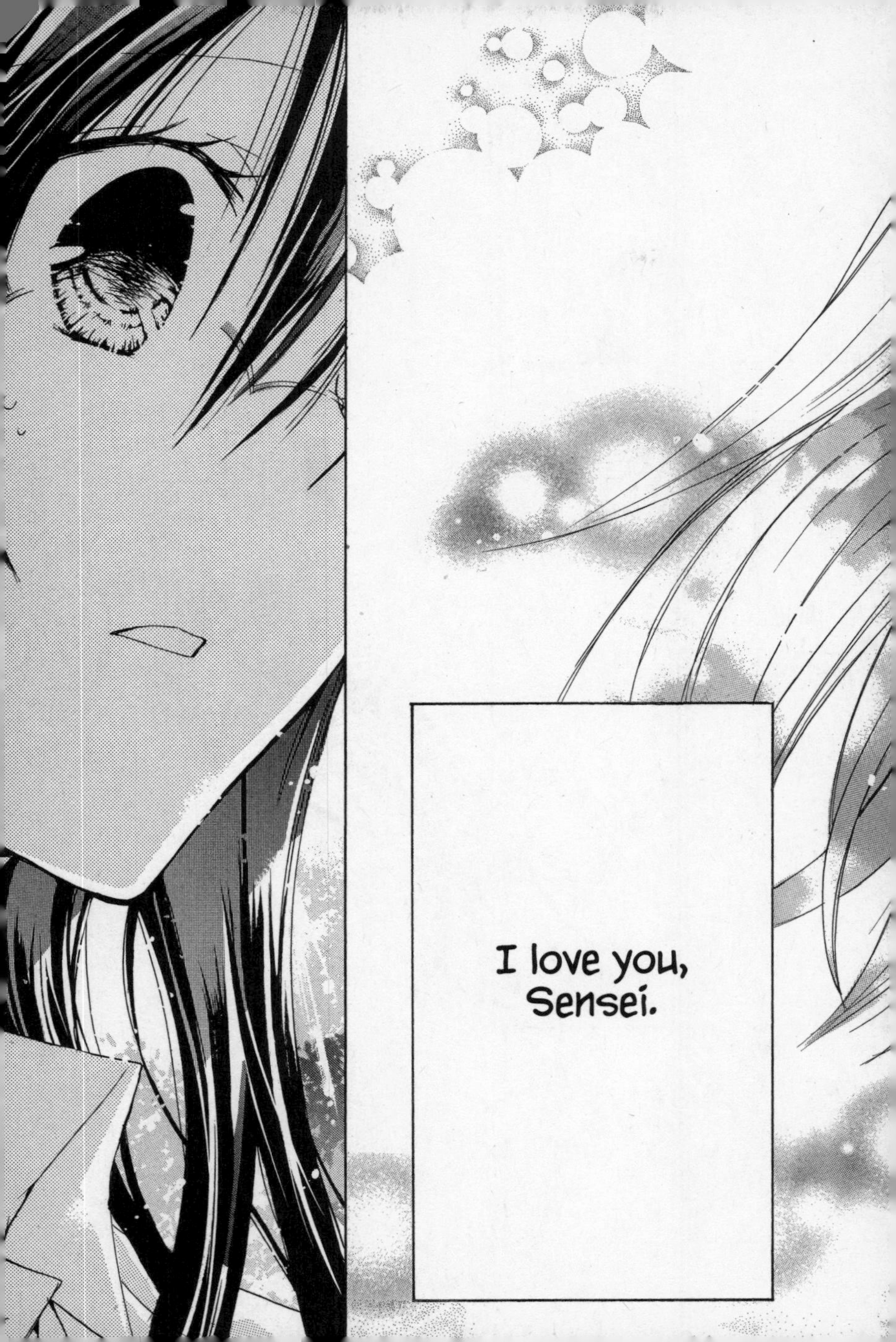
I love you, Sensei.

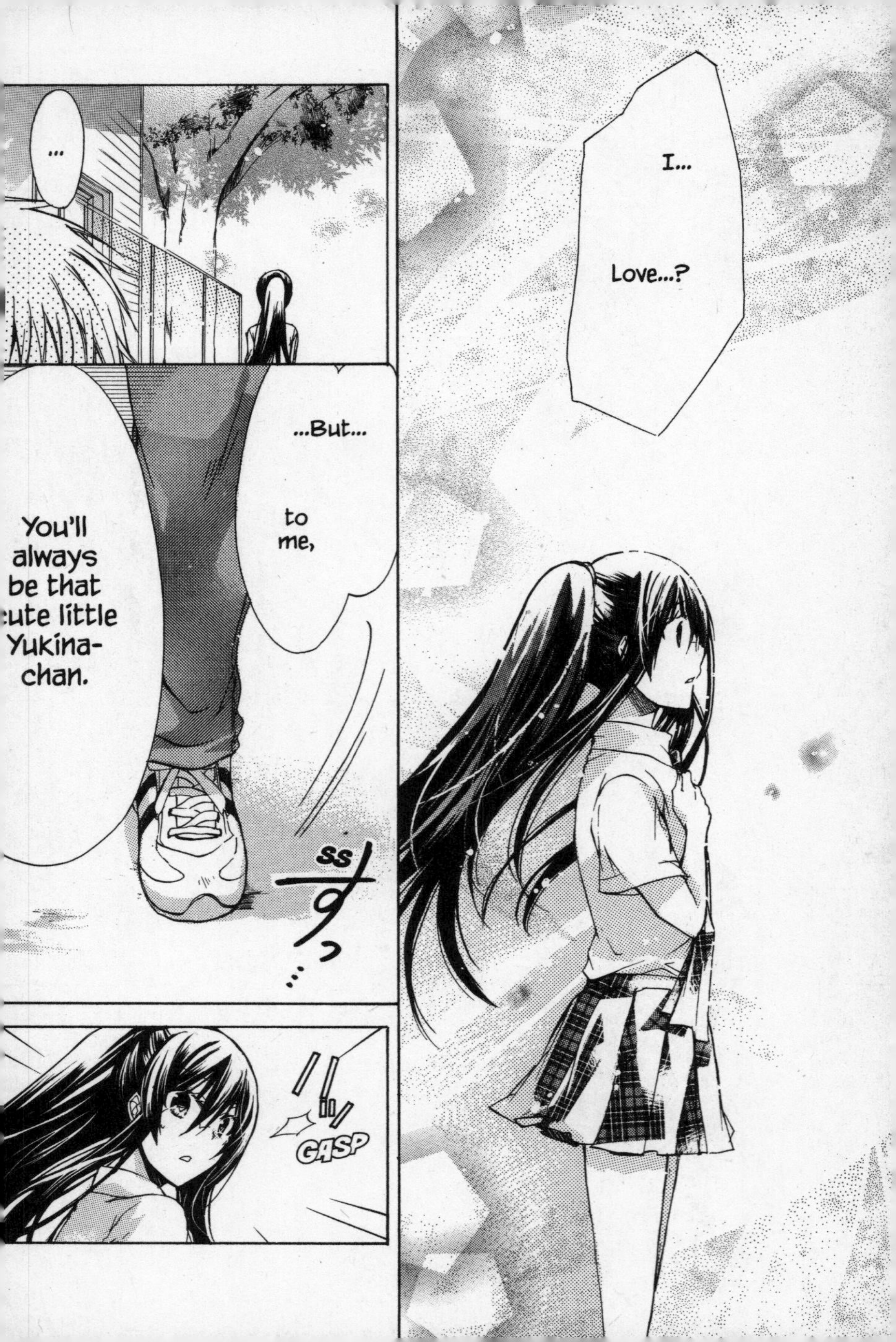
I...
Love...?
...
...But...
to me,
You'll always be that cute little Yukina-chan.
SS
GASP

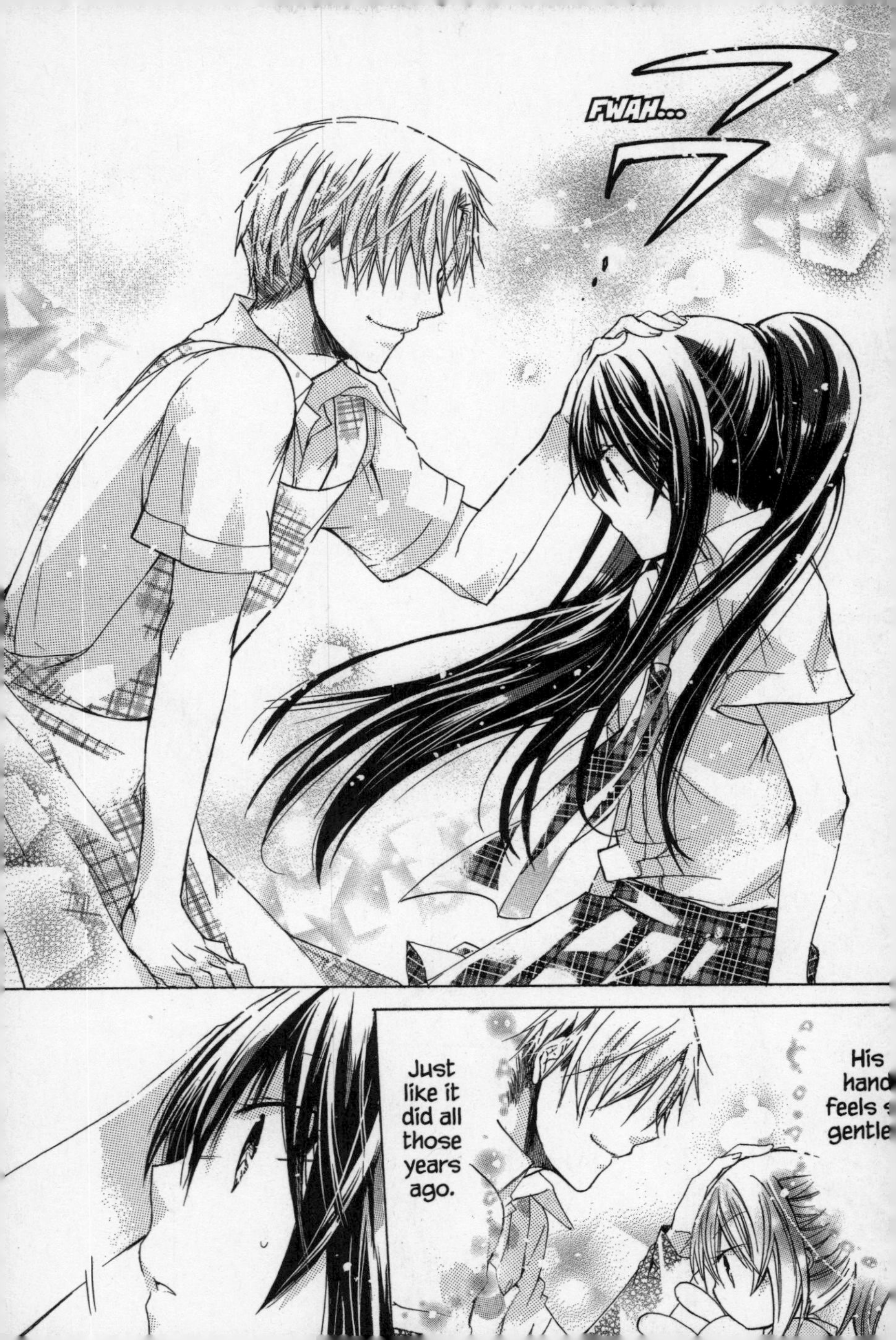
FWAH...
His hand feels s gentle
Just like it did all those years ago.

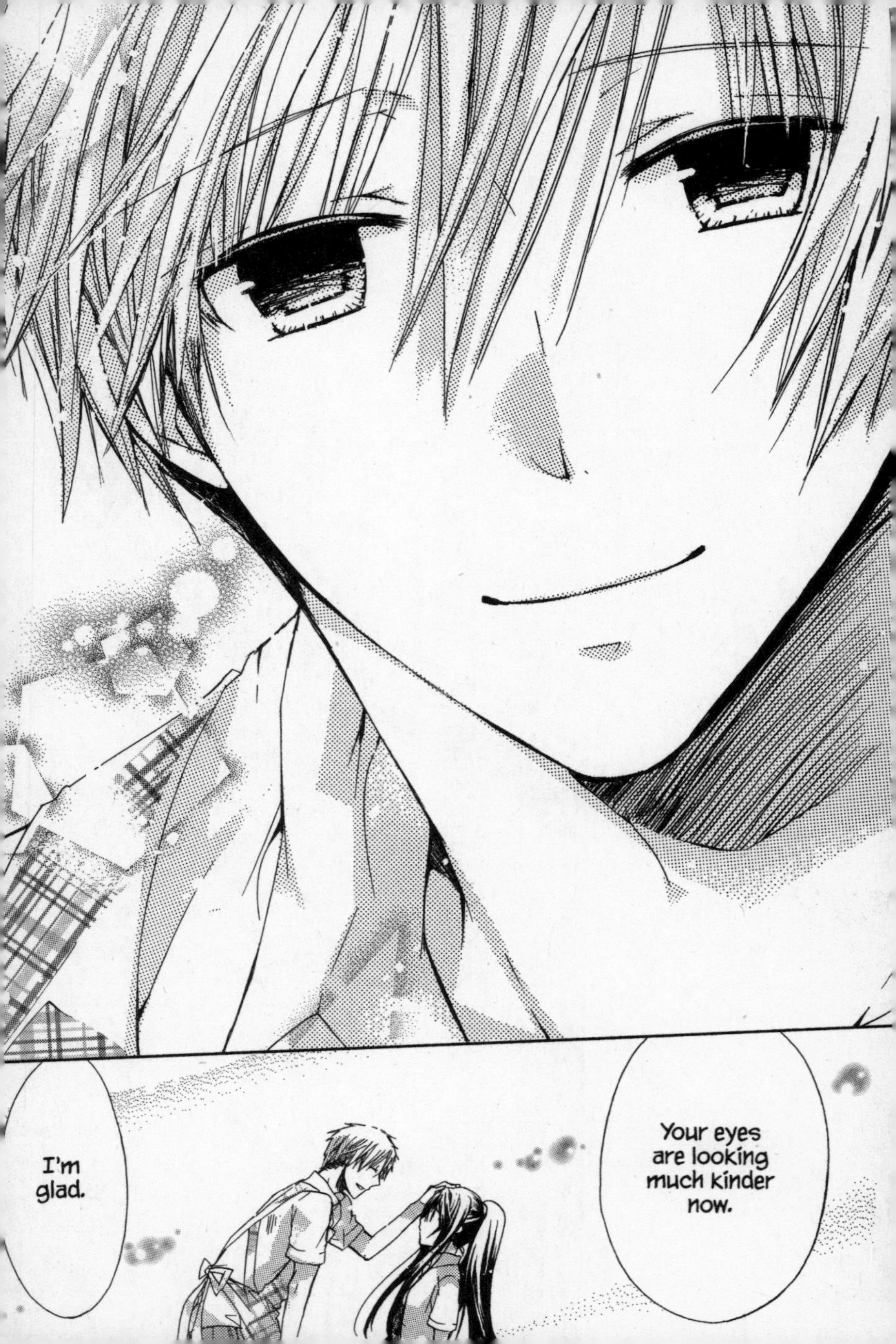
Your eyes are looking much kinder now.
I'm glad.

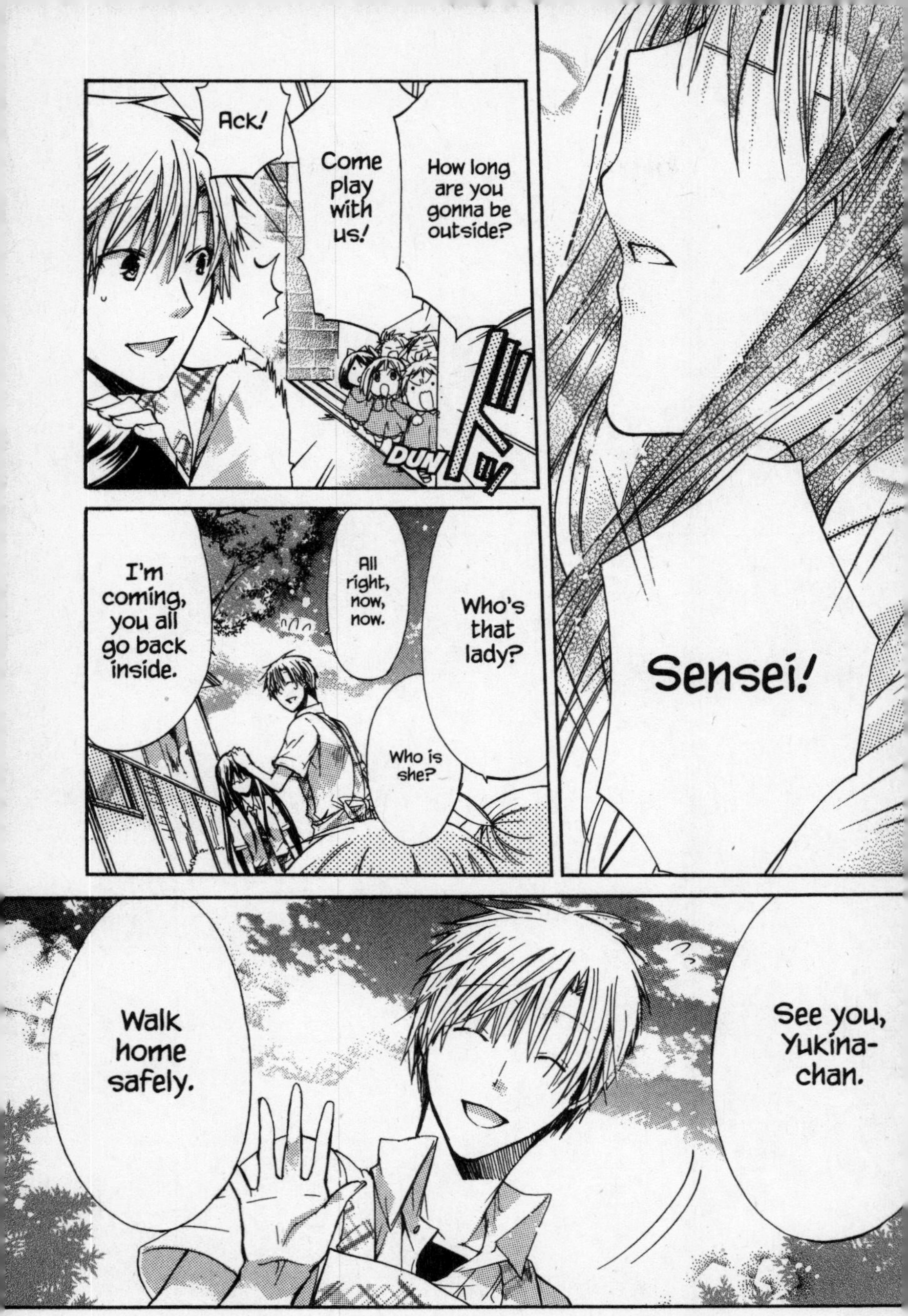
Sensei!
How long are you gonna be outside?
Come play with us!
Ack!
DUN
Who's that lady?
All right, now, now.
Who is she?
I'm coming, you all go back inside.
See you, Yukina-chan.
Walk home safely.

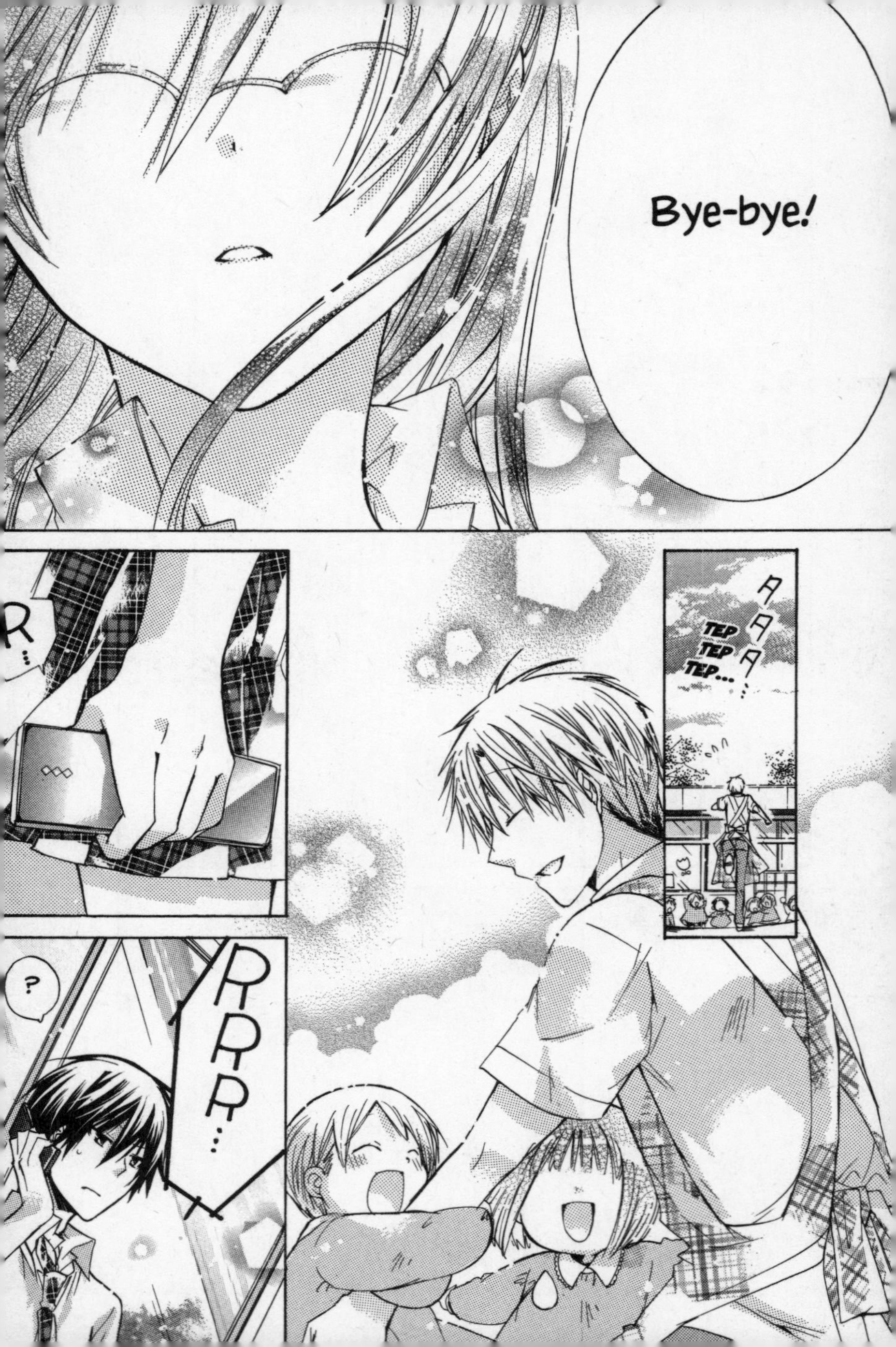
Bye-bye!
AAA...
TEP TEP TEP...
R...
?
RRR...

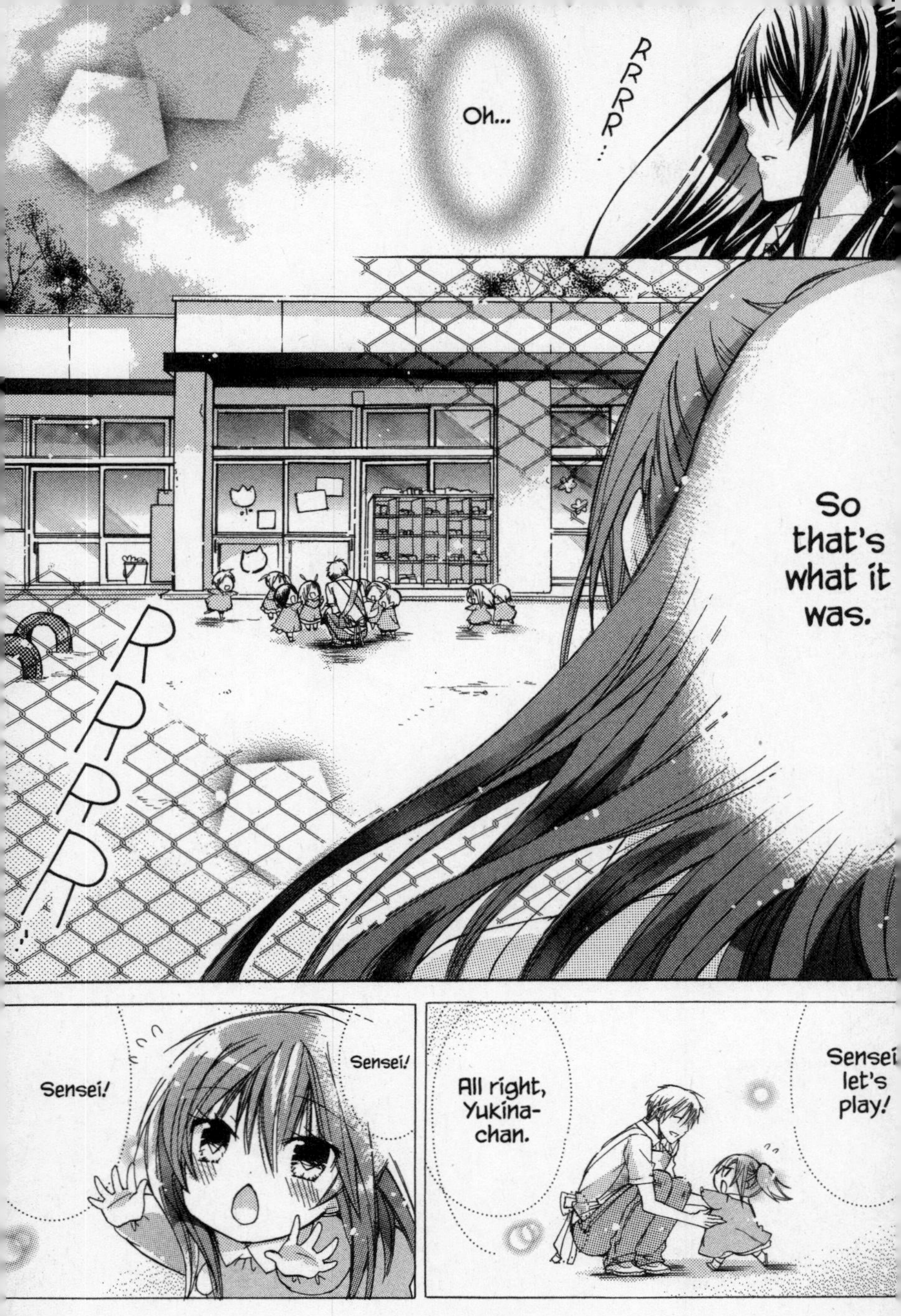
RRRR...
Oh...
So that's what it was.
RRRRR...
Sensei let's play!
All right, Yukina-chan.
Sensei!
Sensei!

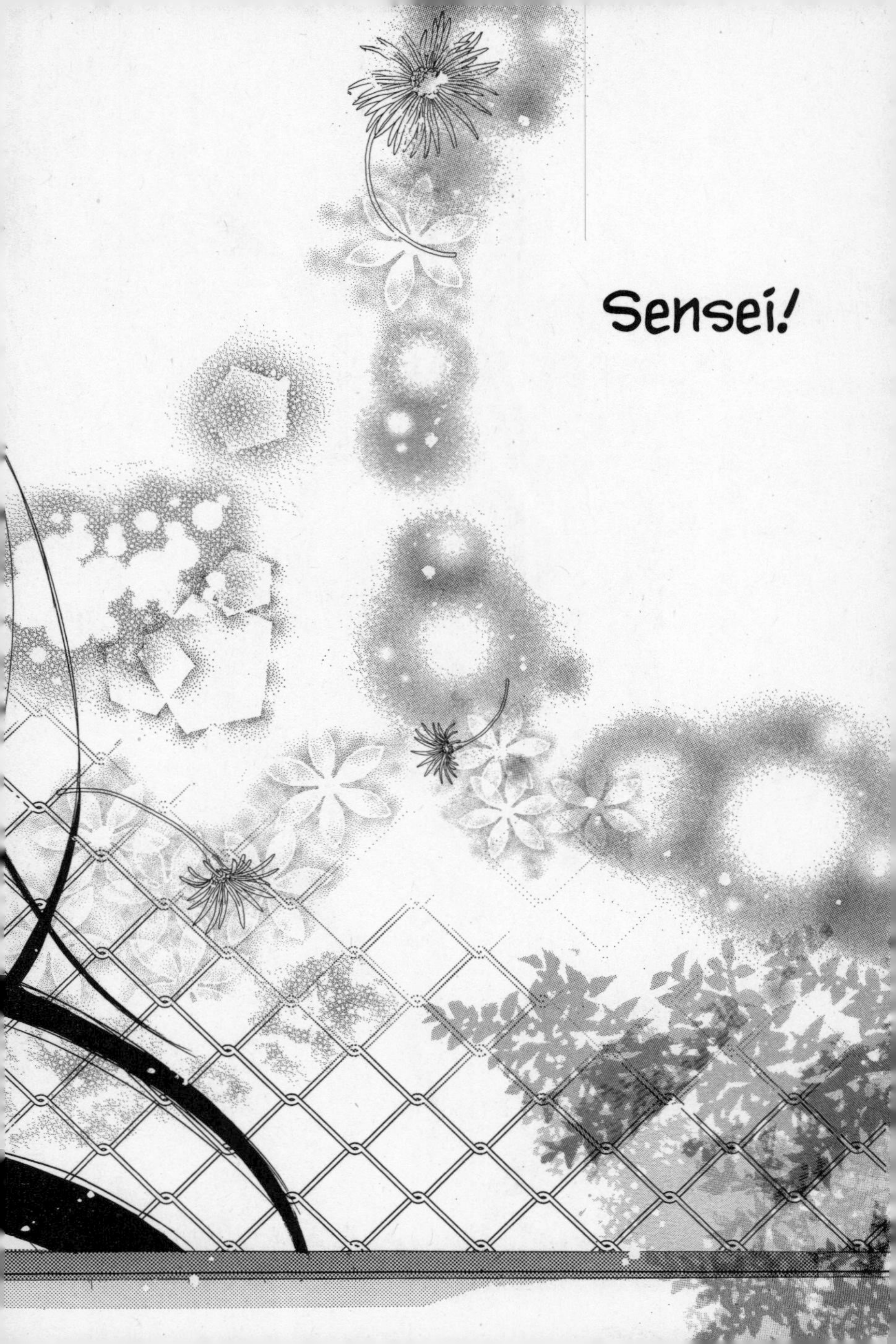
Sensei!

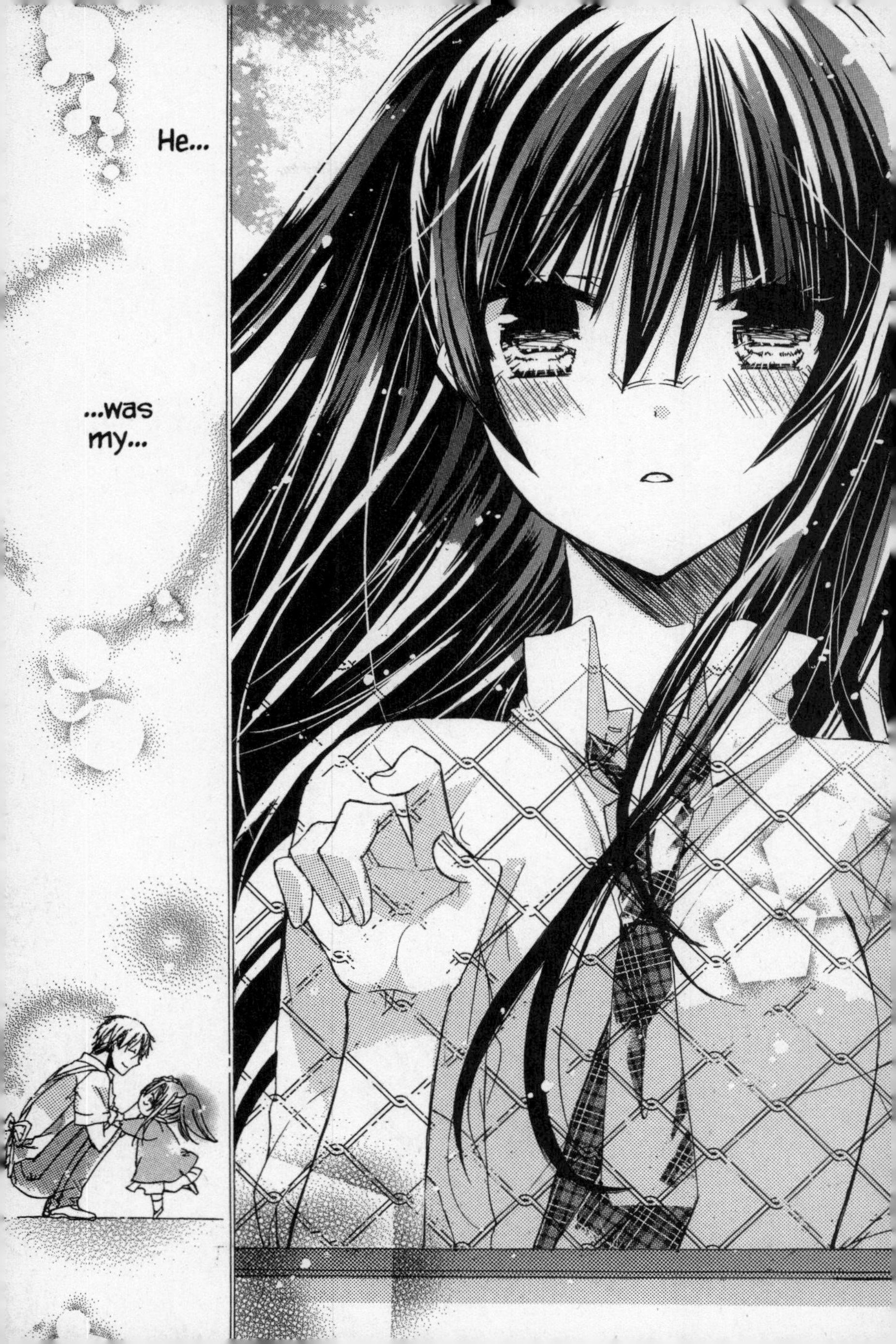
He...
...was my...

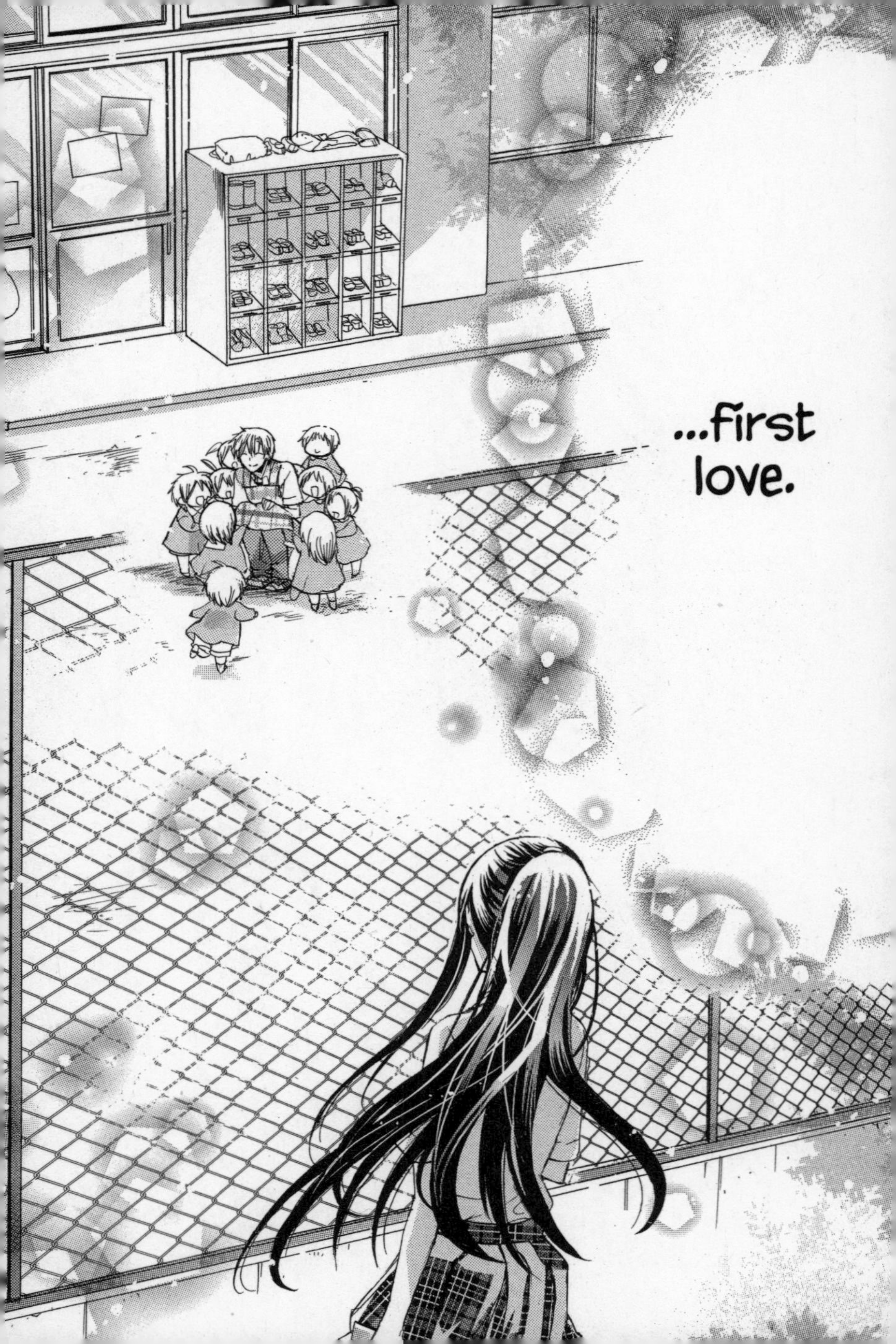
...first love.

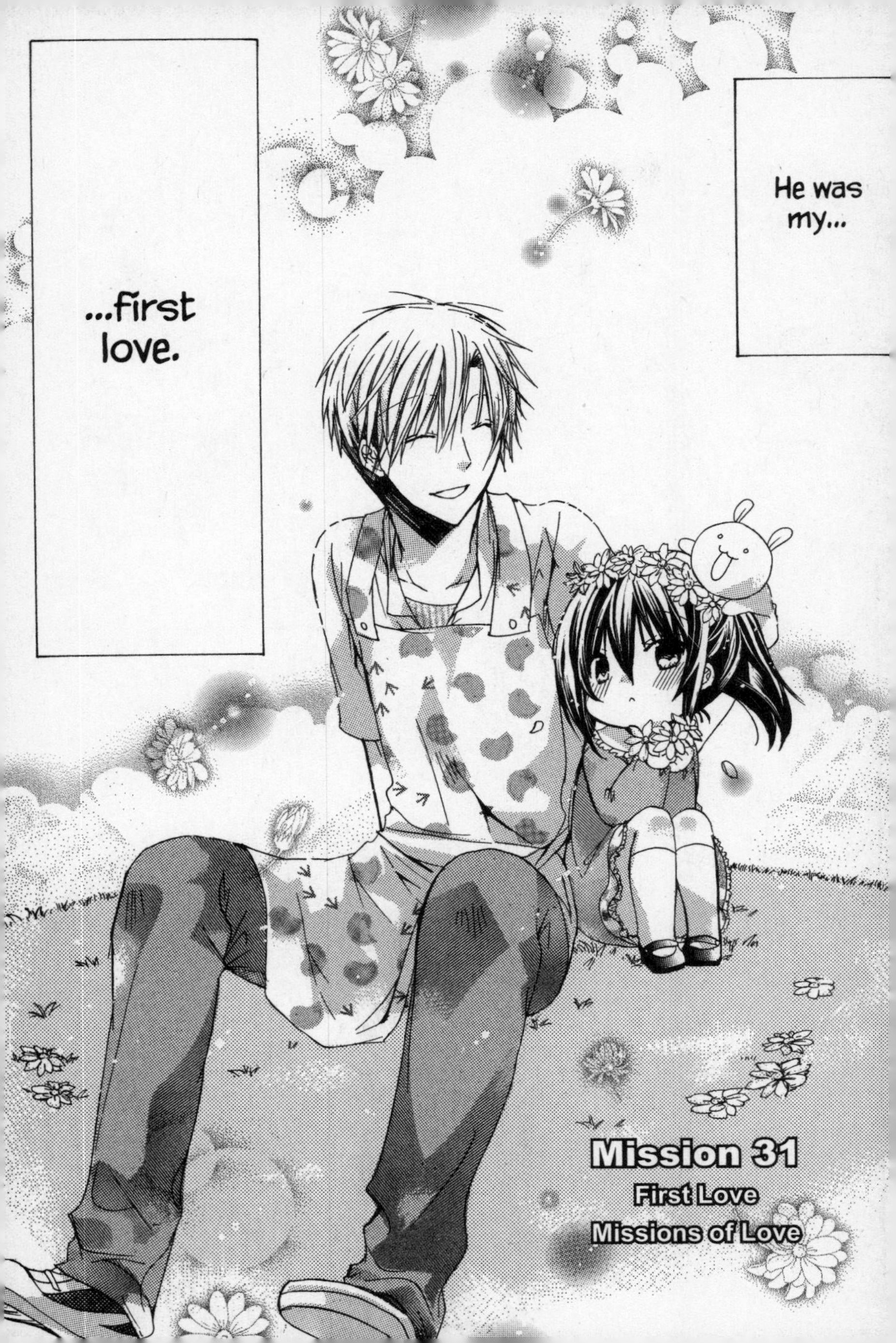
He was my...
...first love.
Mission 31
First Love
Missions of Love

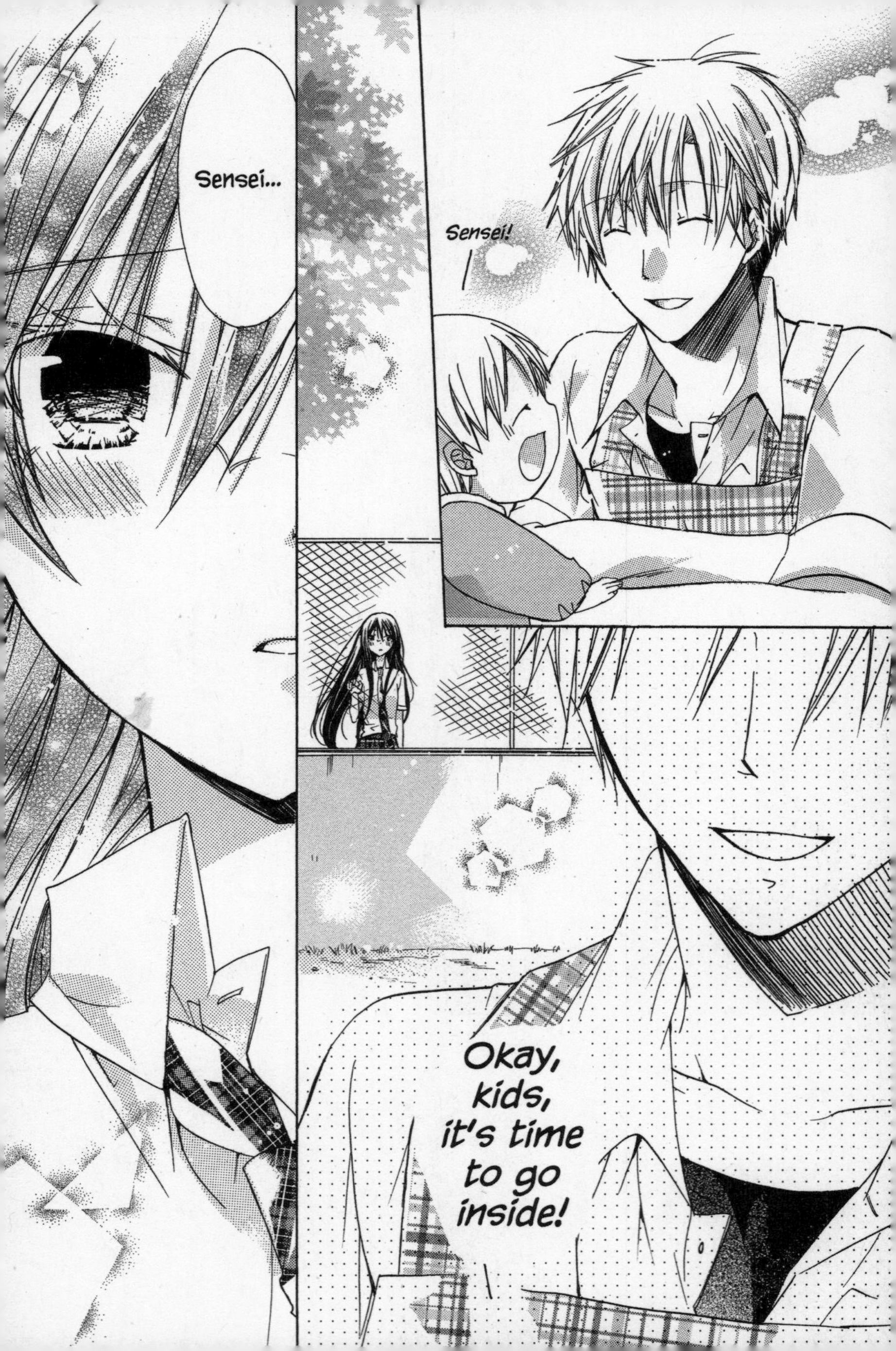
Sensei!
Okay, kids, it's time to go inside!
Sensei...

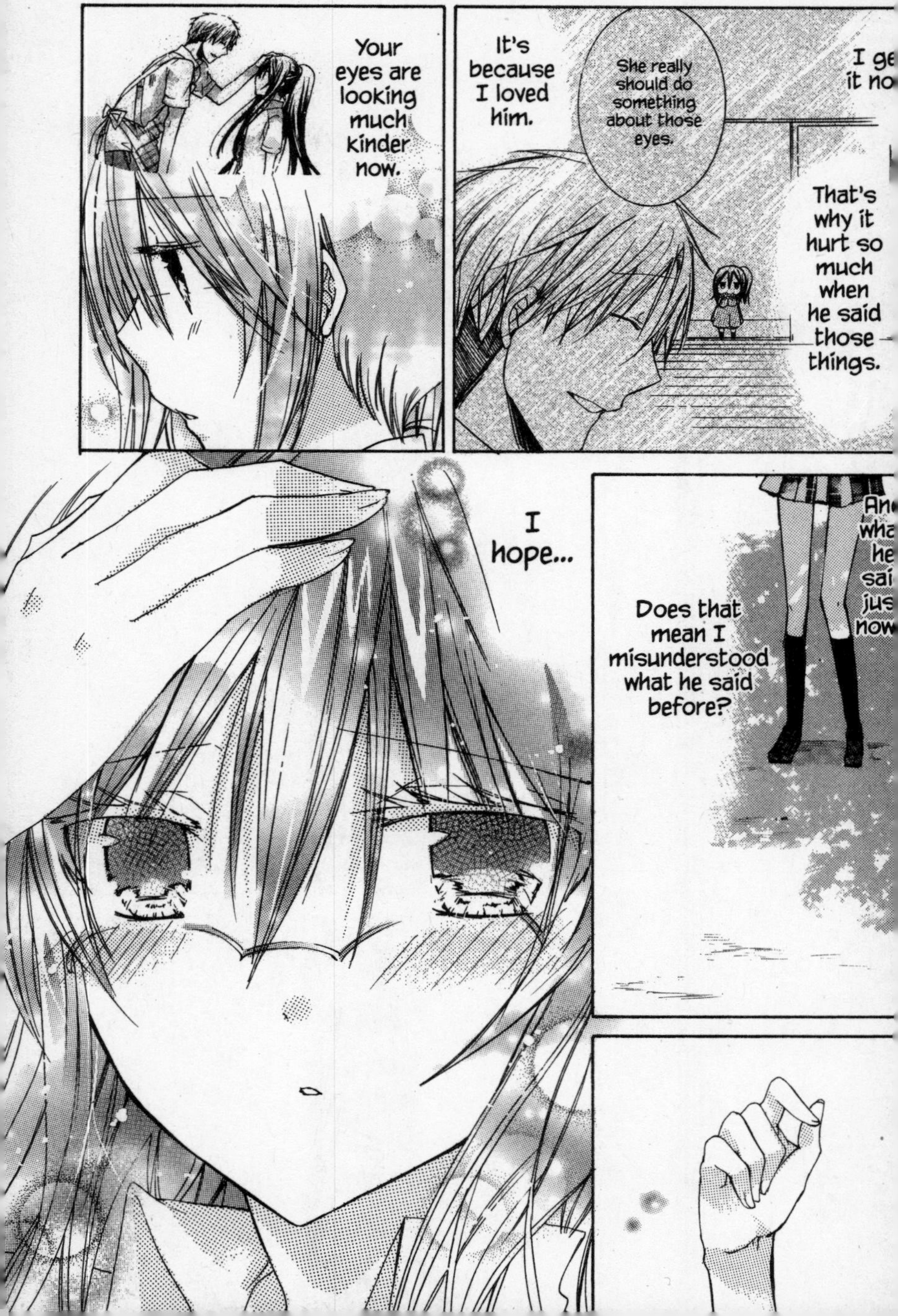
I ge it no
That's why it hurt so much when he said those things.
She really should do something about those eyes.
It's because I loved him.
Your eyes are looking much kinder now.
An wha he sai jus now
Does that mean I misunderstood what he said before?
I hope...

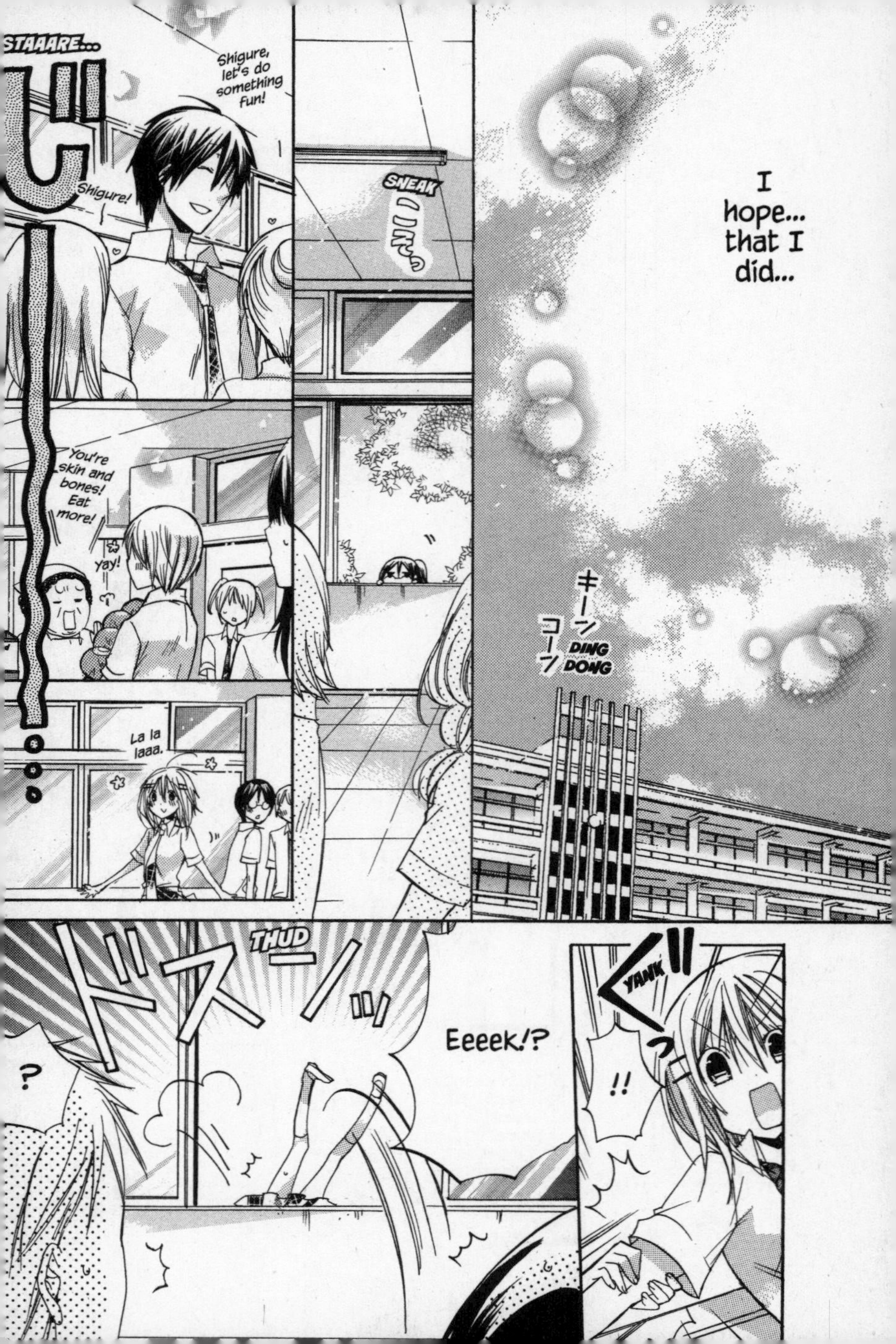

I hope... that I did...
キーン
コーン
DING DONG
SNEAK
STAAARE...
Shigure, let's do something fun!
Shigure!
You're skin and bones! Eat more!
yay!
La la laaa.
YANK
!!
THUD
Eeeek!?
?

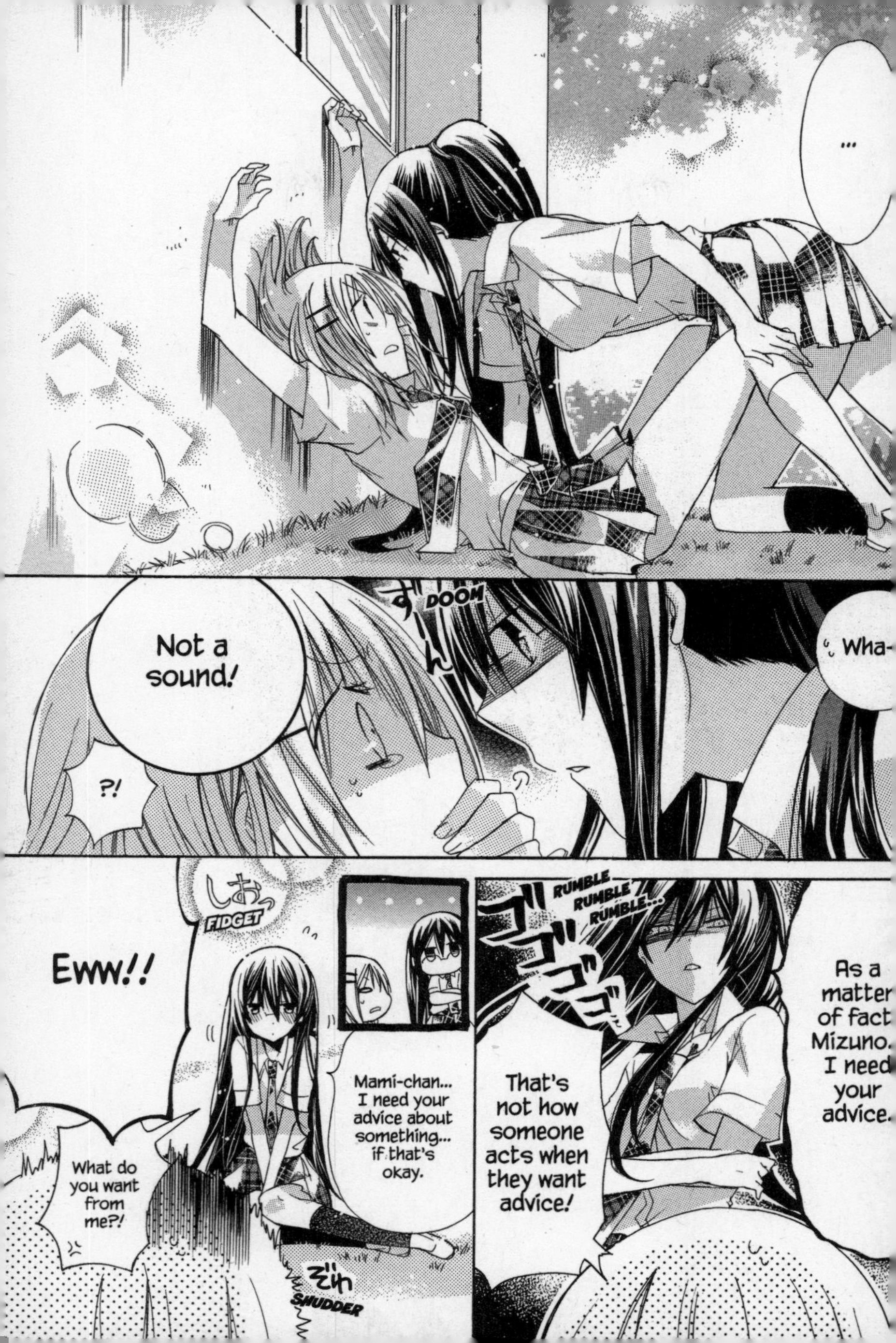
...
Wha-
ずーん
DOOM
Not a sound!
?!
As a matter of fact Mizuno. I need your advice.
RUMBLE RUMBLE RUMBLE...
That's not how someone acts when they want advice!
Mami-chan... I need your advice about something... if that's okay.
しおっ
FIDGET
Eww!!
What do you want from me?!
ぞわ
SHUDDER

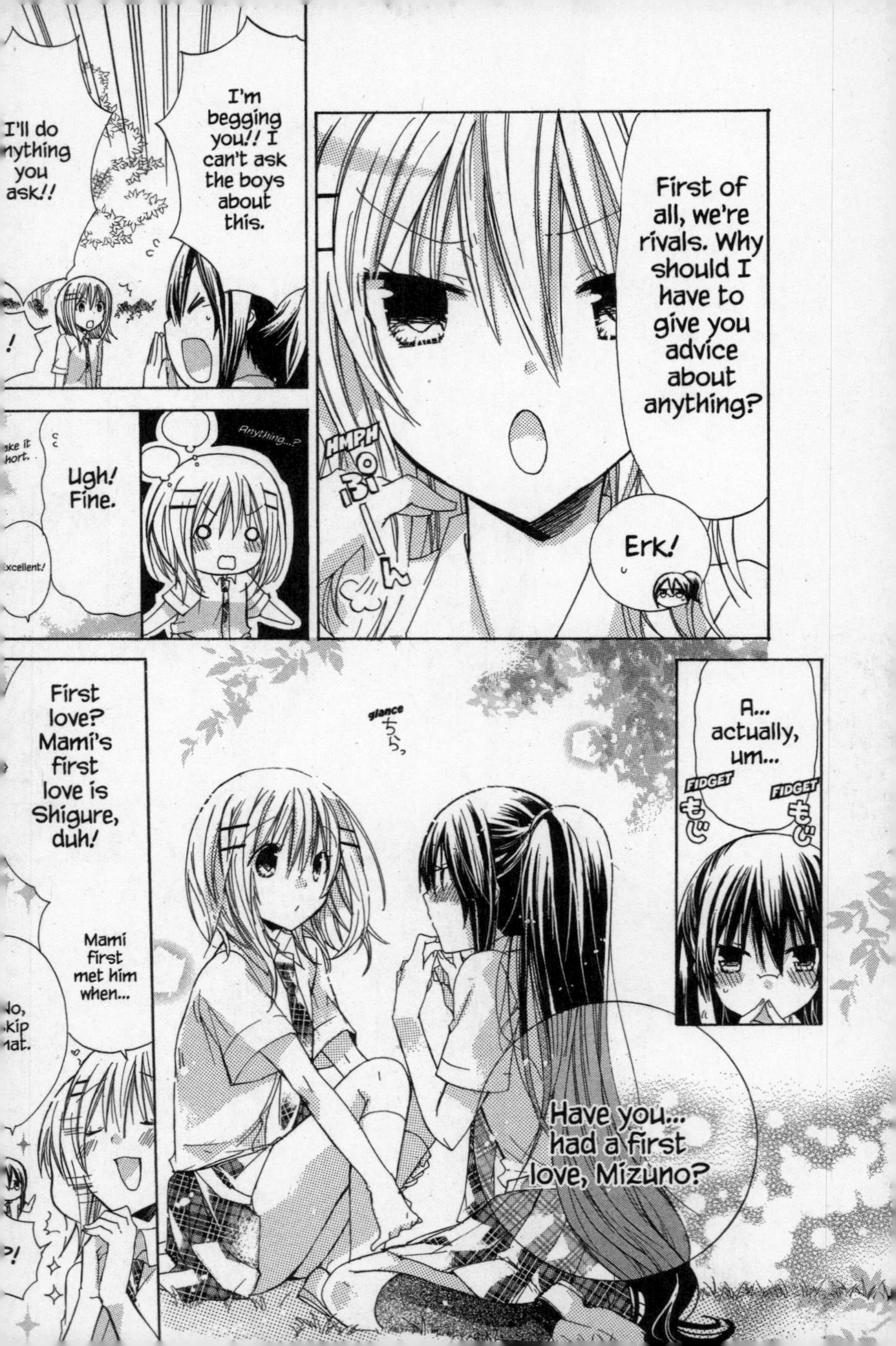
First of all, we're rivals. Why should I have to give you advice about anything?
HMPH
Erk!
I'm begging you!! I can't ask the boys about this.
I'll do nything you ask!!
Anything...?
Ugh! Fine.
Excellent!
A... actually, um...
FIDGET
FIDGET
glance
Have you... had a first love, Mizuno?
First love? Mami's first love is Shigure, duh!
Mami first met him when...

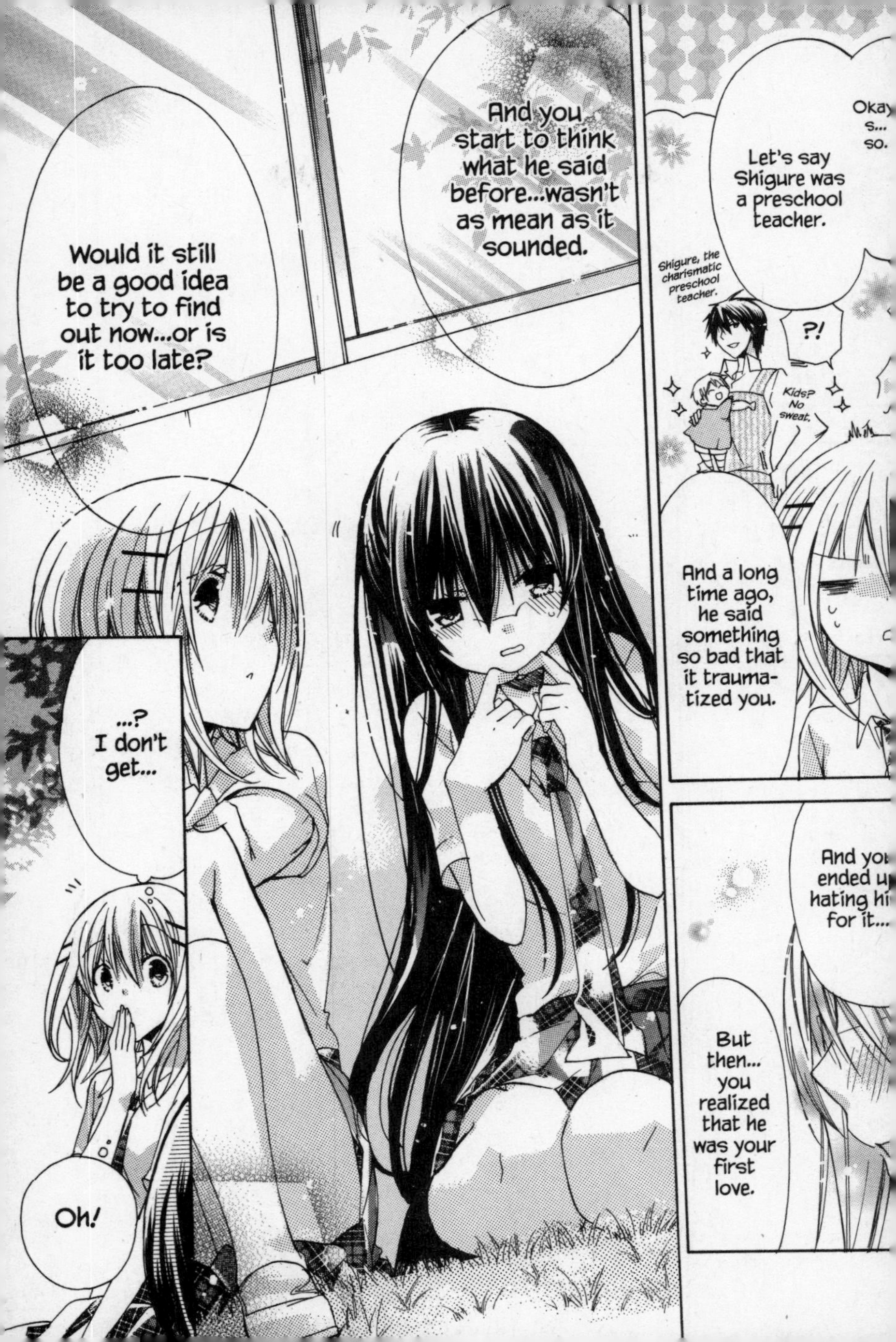
Okay s... so.
Let's say Shigure was a preschool teacher.
Shigure, the charismatic preschool teacher.
?!
Kids? No sweat.
And a long time ago, he said something so bad that it traumatized you.
And you ended up hating hi for it...
But then... you realized that he was your first love.
And you start to think what he said before...wasn't as mean as it sounded.
Would it still be a good idea to try to find out now...or is it too late?
...? I don't get...
Oh!

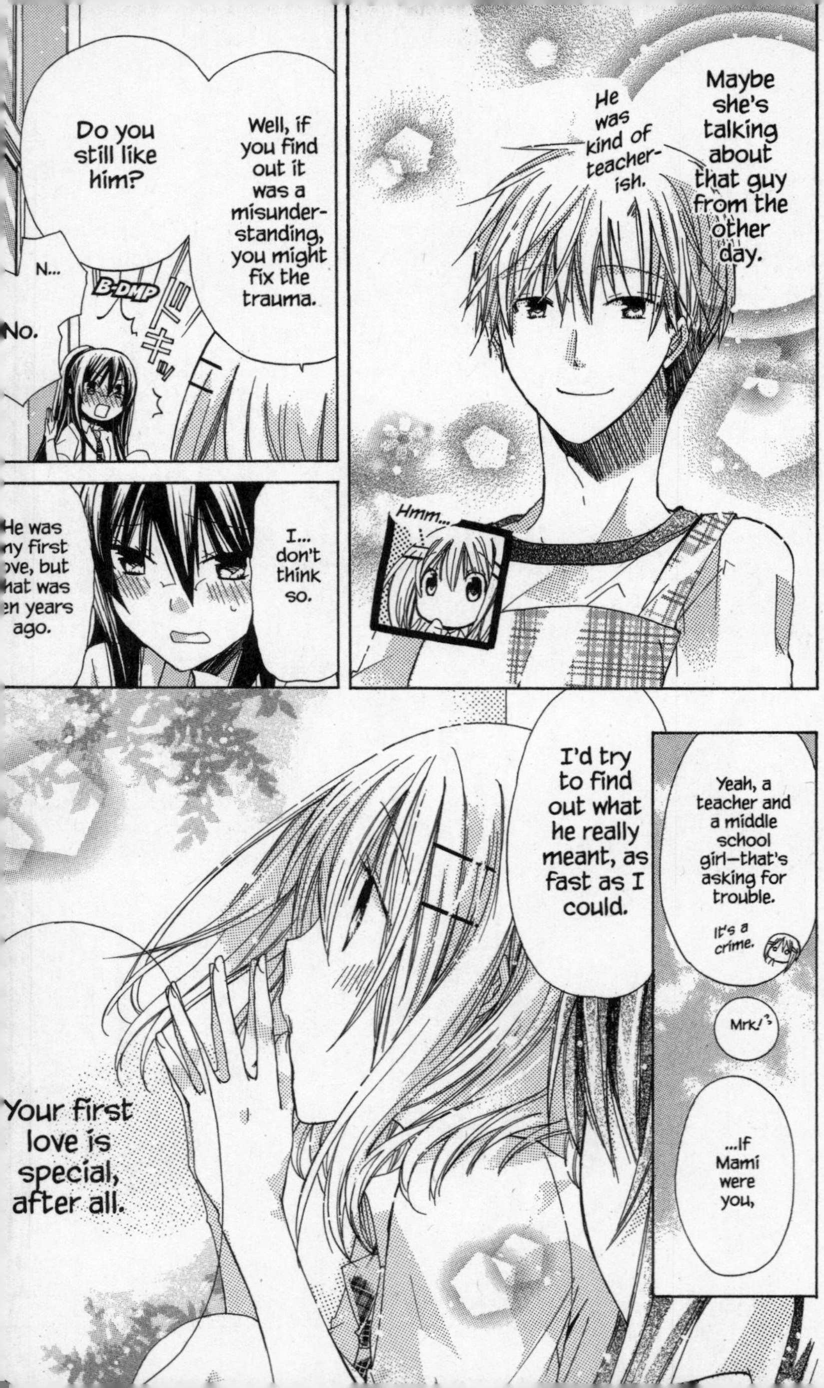
Maybe she's talking about that guy from the other day.
He was kind of teacher-ish.
Hmm...
Well, if you find out it was a misunderstanding, you might fix the trauma.
Do you still like him?
B-DMP
N...
No.
I... don't think so.
He was ny first ove, but hat was en years ago.
Yeah, a teacher and a middle school girl—that's asking for trouble.
It's a crime.
Mrk!
...If Mami were you,
I'd try to find out what he really meant, as fast as I could.
Your first love is special, after all.

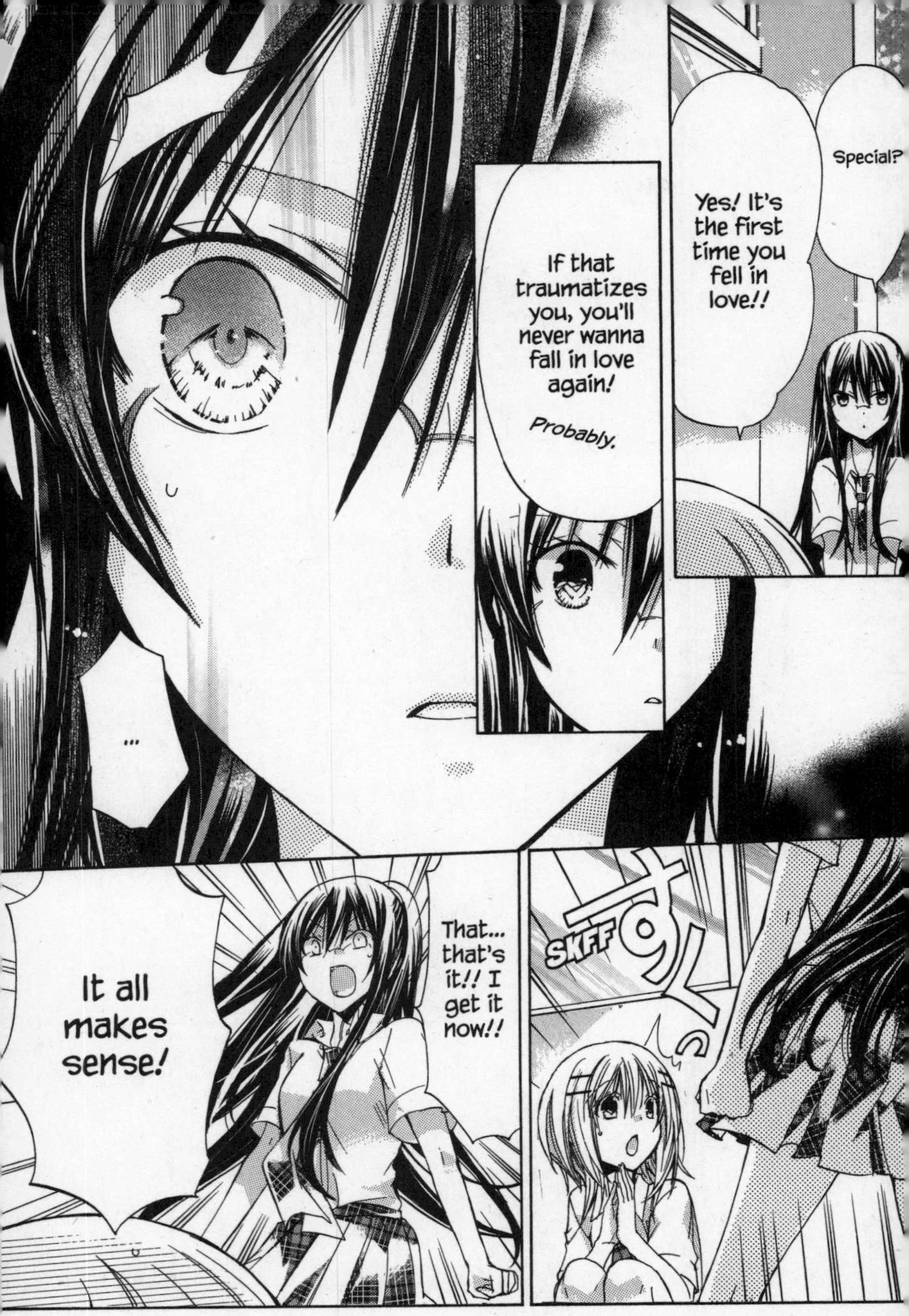
Special?
Yes! It's the first time you fell in love!!
If that traumatizes you, you'll never wanna fall in love again!
Probably.
...
SKFF
That... that's it!! I get it now!!
It all makes sense!

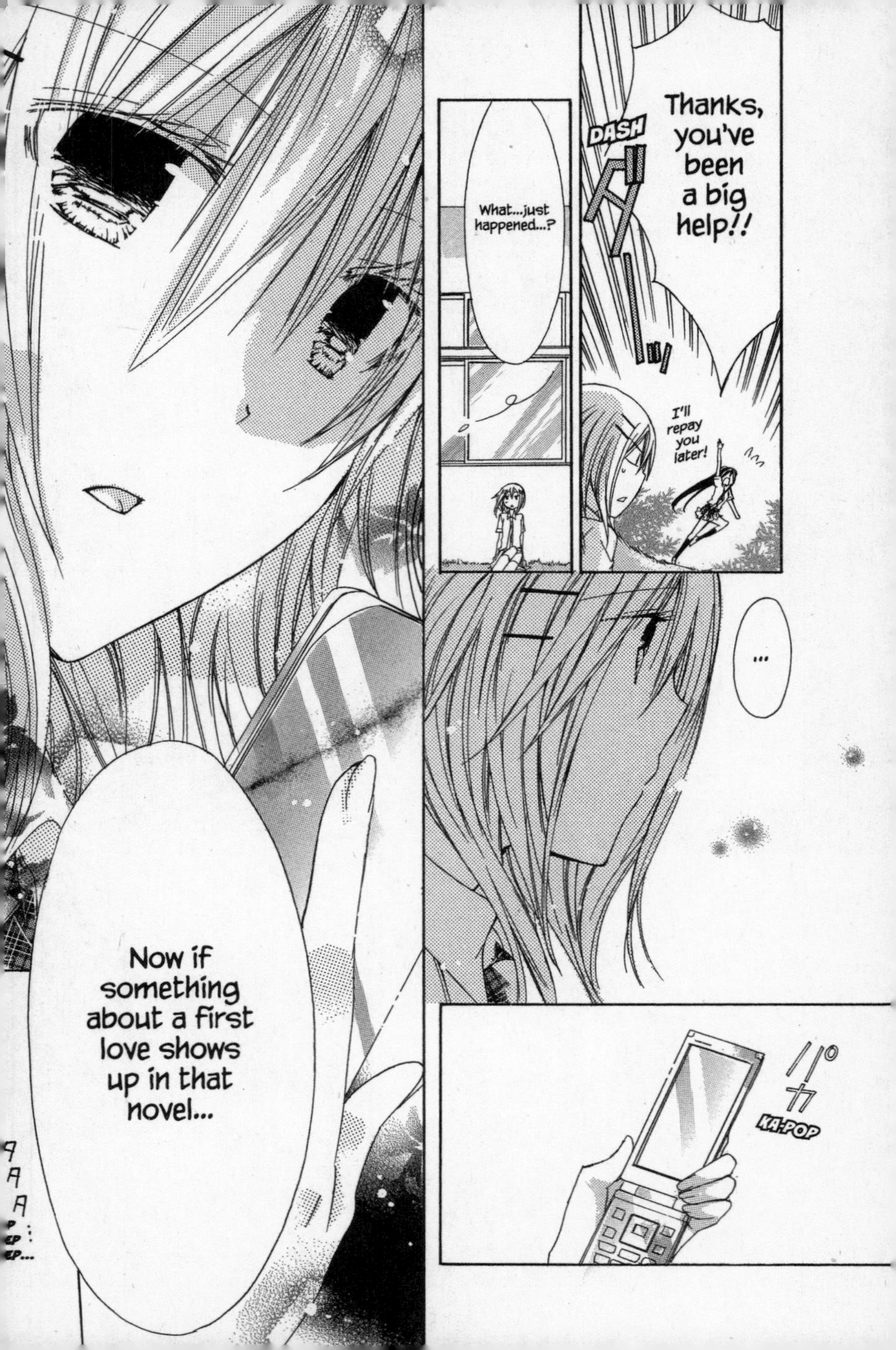
Thanks, you've been a big help!!
DASH
I'll repay you later!
What...just happened...?
...
KA-POP
Now if something about a first love shows up in that novel...

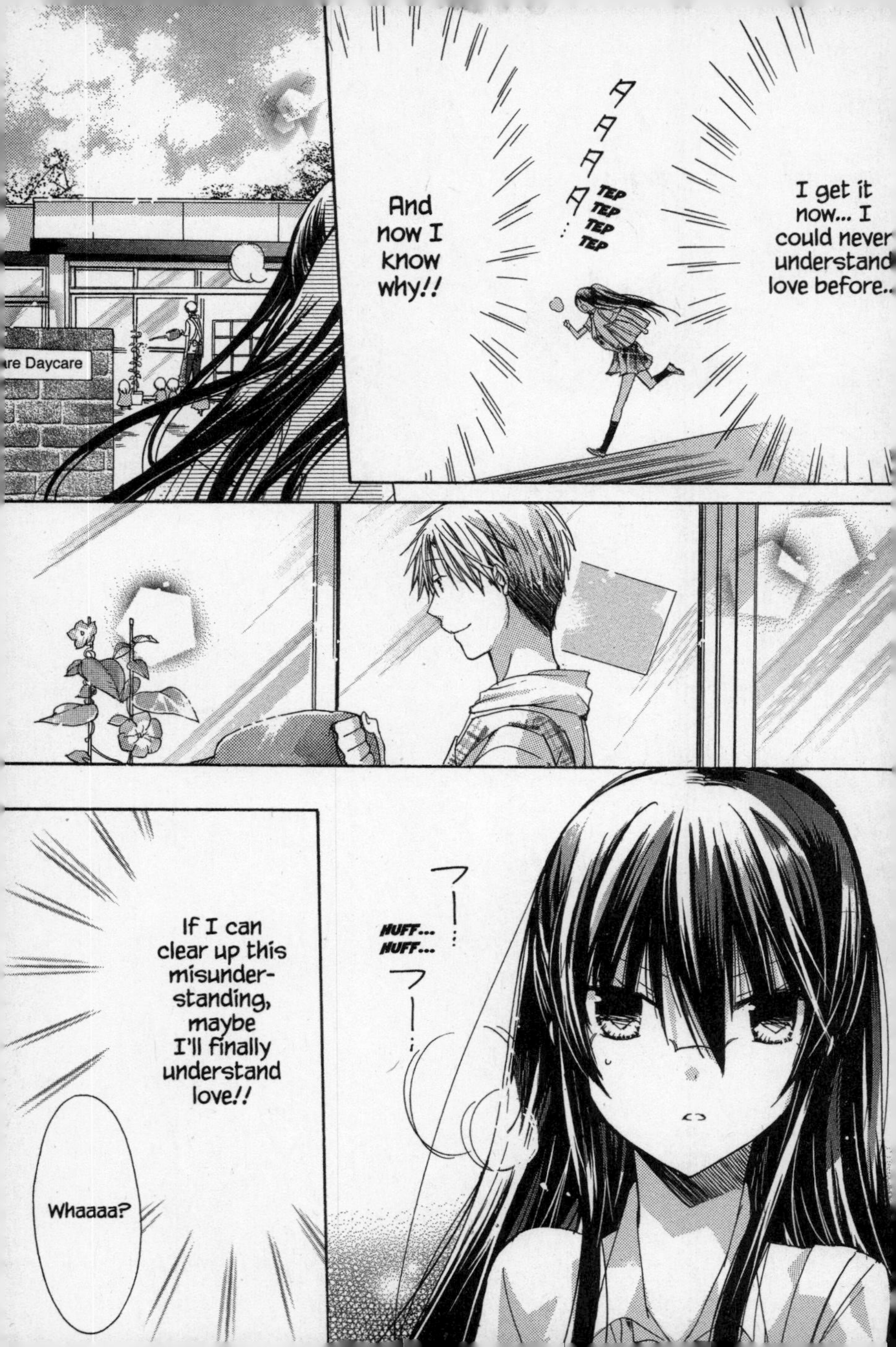
I get it now... I could never understand love before..
タタタタ…
TEP TEP TEP TEP
And now I know why!!
are Daycare
フー…
HUFF... HUFF...
フー…
If I can clear up this misunderstanding, maybe I'll finally understand love!!
Whaaaa?

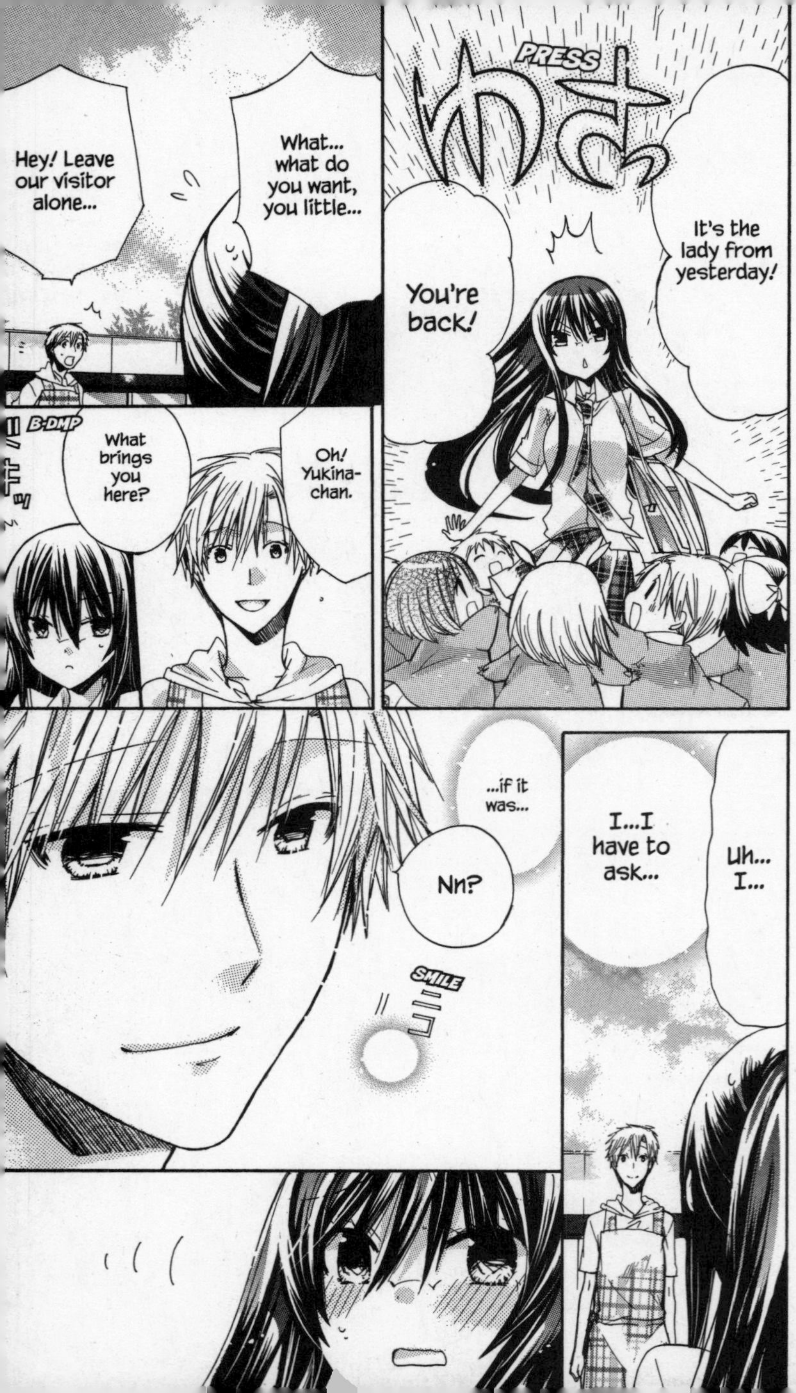
PRESS
It's the lady from yesterday!
You're back!
What... what do you want, you little...
Hey! Leave our visitor alone...
Oh! Yukina-chan.
What brings you here?
B-DMP
Uh... I...
I...I have to ask...
...if it was...
Nn?
SMILE

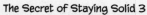

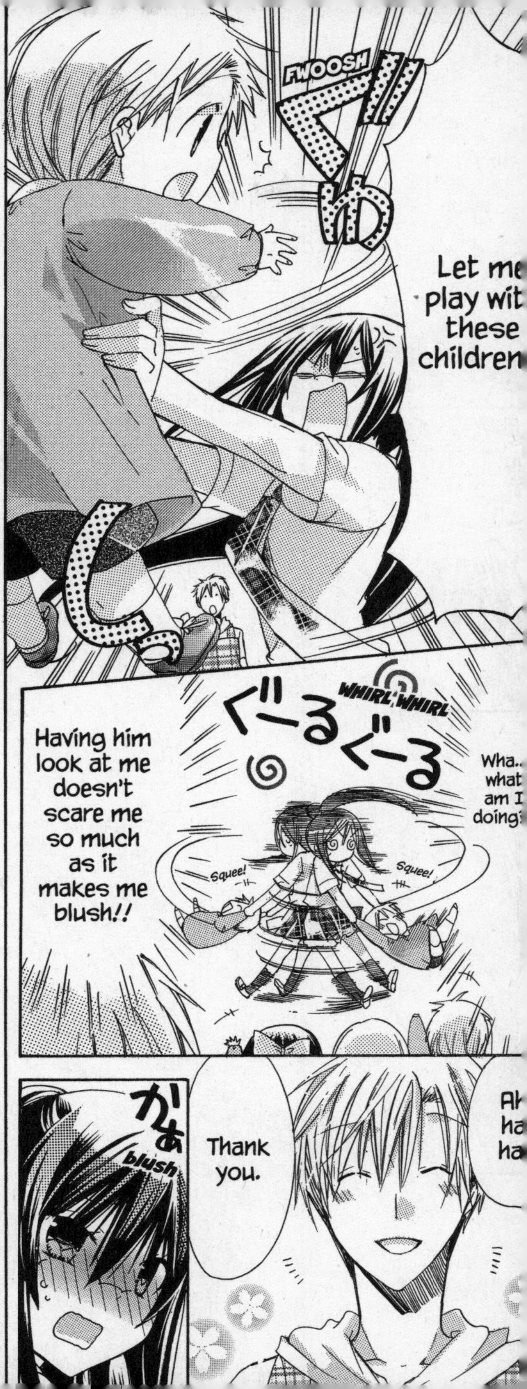
FWOOSH
Let me play wit these children
WHIRL WHIRL
ぐーるぐーる
Wha... what am I doing
Having him look at me doesn't scare me so much as it makes me blush!!
Squee!
Squee!
Ah ha ha
Thank you.
かぁ
blush

The Secret of Staying Solid 3

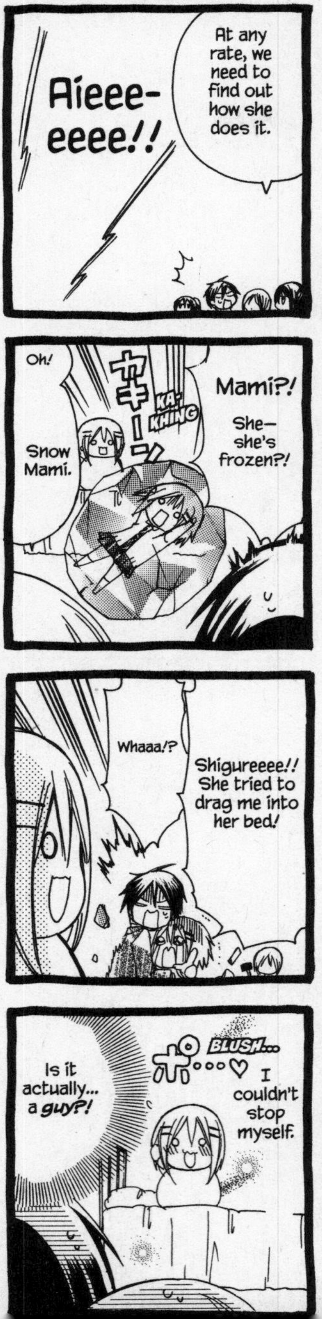
At any rate, we need to find out how she does it.
Aieee-eeee!!
Mami?!
She—she's frozen?!
カキーン
KA-KHING
Oh!
Snow Mami.
Shigureeee!! She tried to drag me into her bed!
Whaaa!?
I couldn't stop myself.
BLUSH...
ポ...♡
Is it actually... a guy?!

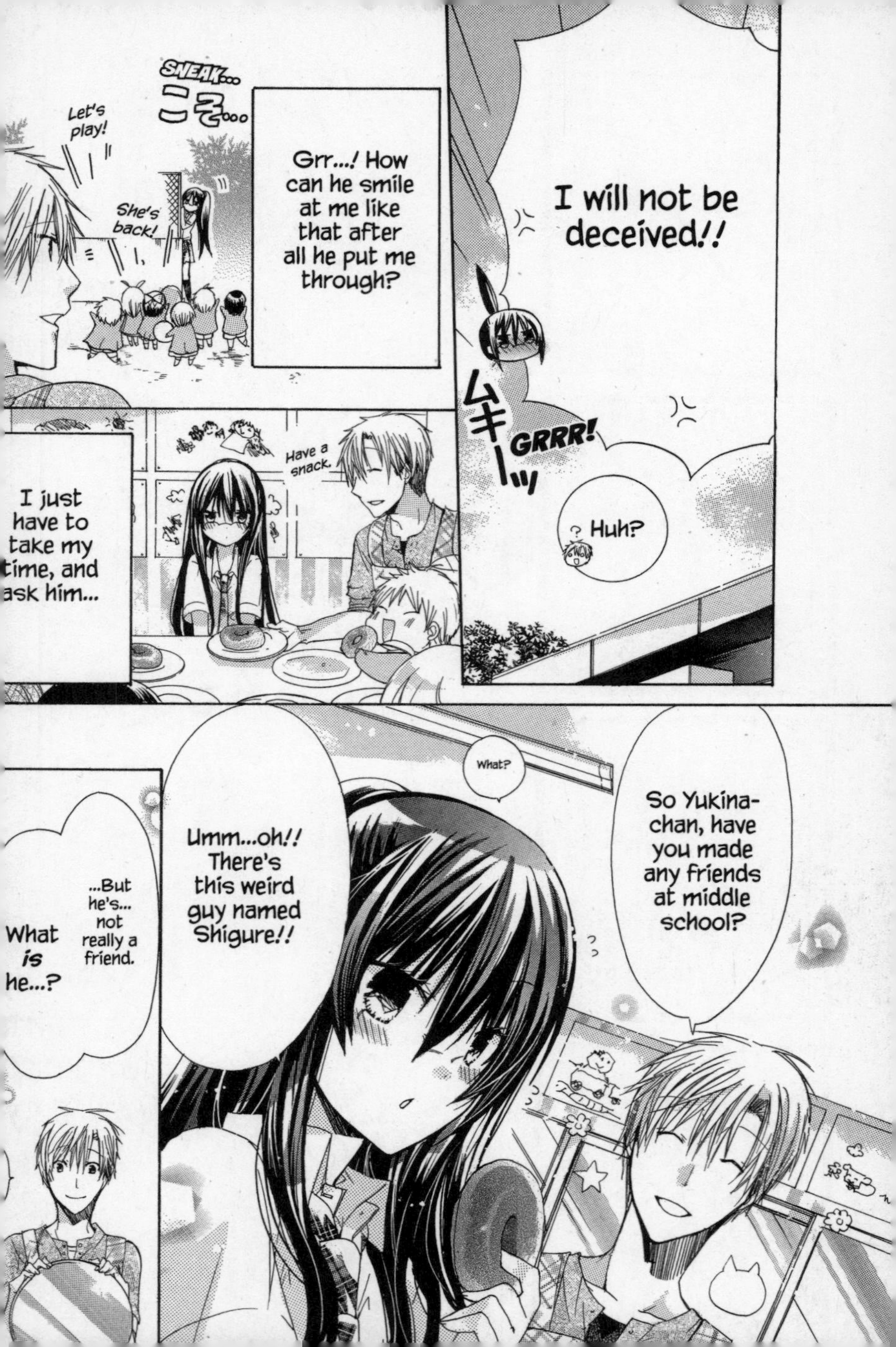
I will not be deceived!!
ムキーッ
GRRR!
Huh?
Grr...! How can he smile at me like that after all he put me through?
SNEAK...
こそ...
Let's play!
She's back!
Have a snack.
I just have to take my time, and ask him...
So Yukina-chan, have you made any friends at middle school?
What?
Umm...oh!! There's this weird guy named Shigure!!
...But he's... not really a friend.
What *is* he...?

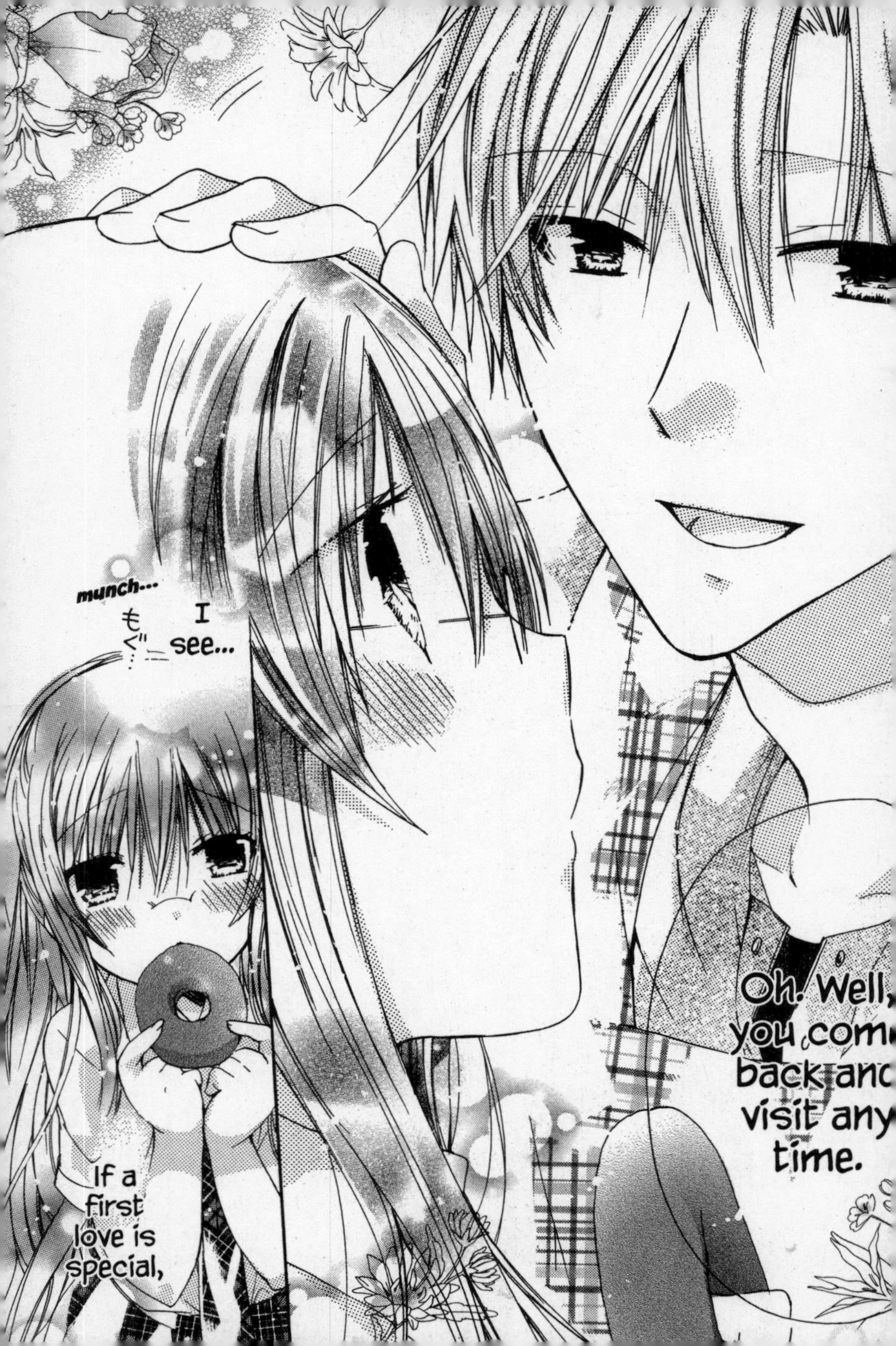
Oh. Well, you com back anc visit any time.
I see...
munch...
もぐ…
If a first love is special,

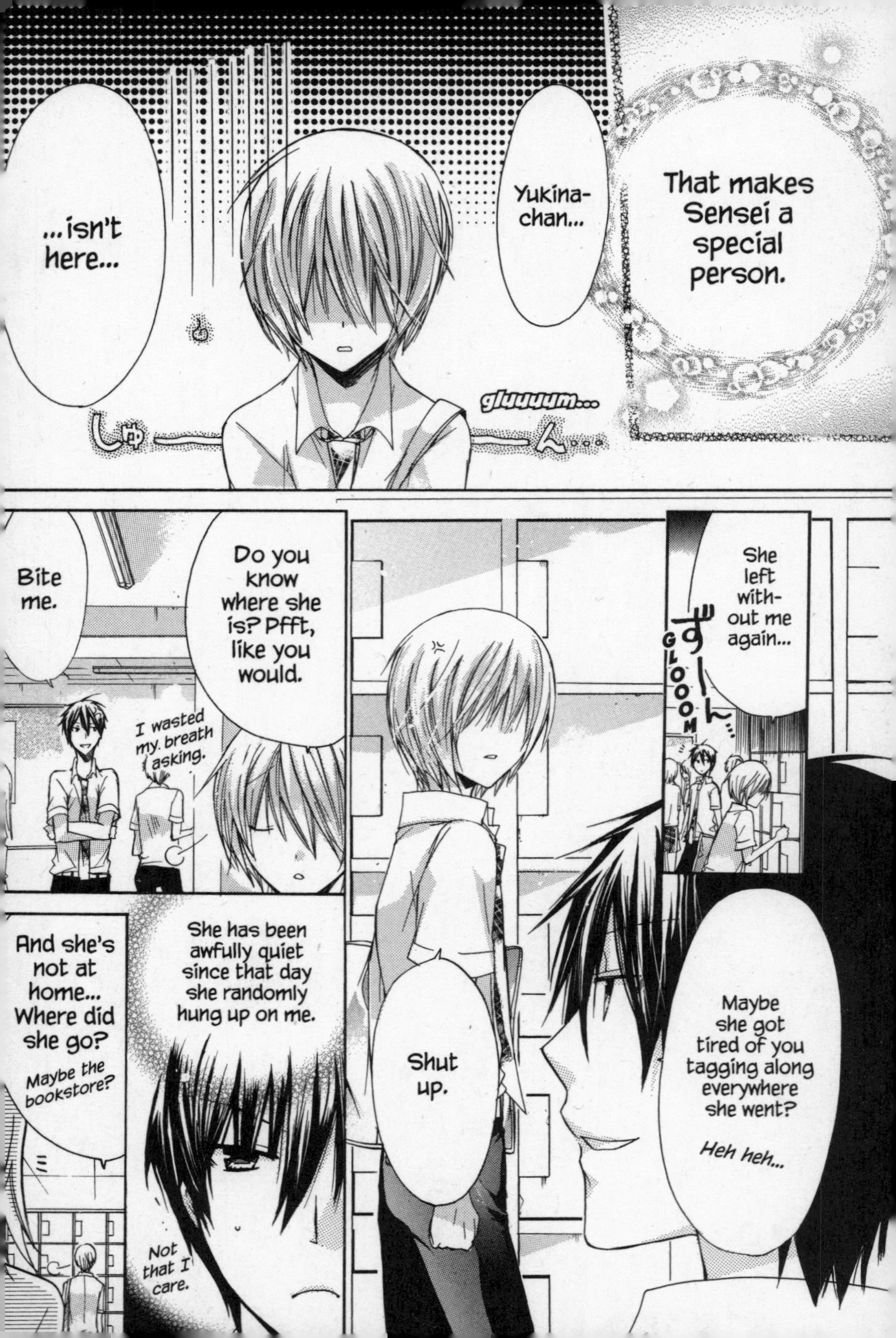
That makes Sensei a special person.
Yukina-chan...
...isn't here...
gluuuum...
しゅーーーーん...
She left without me again...
GLOOOOM
ずーん...
Do you know where she is? Pfft, like you would.
Bite me.
I wasted my breath asking.
Maybe she got tired of you tagging along everywhere she went?
Heh heh...
Shut up.
She has been awfully quiet since that day she randomly hung up on me.
And she's not at home... Where did she go?
Maybe the bookstore?
Not that I care.

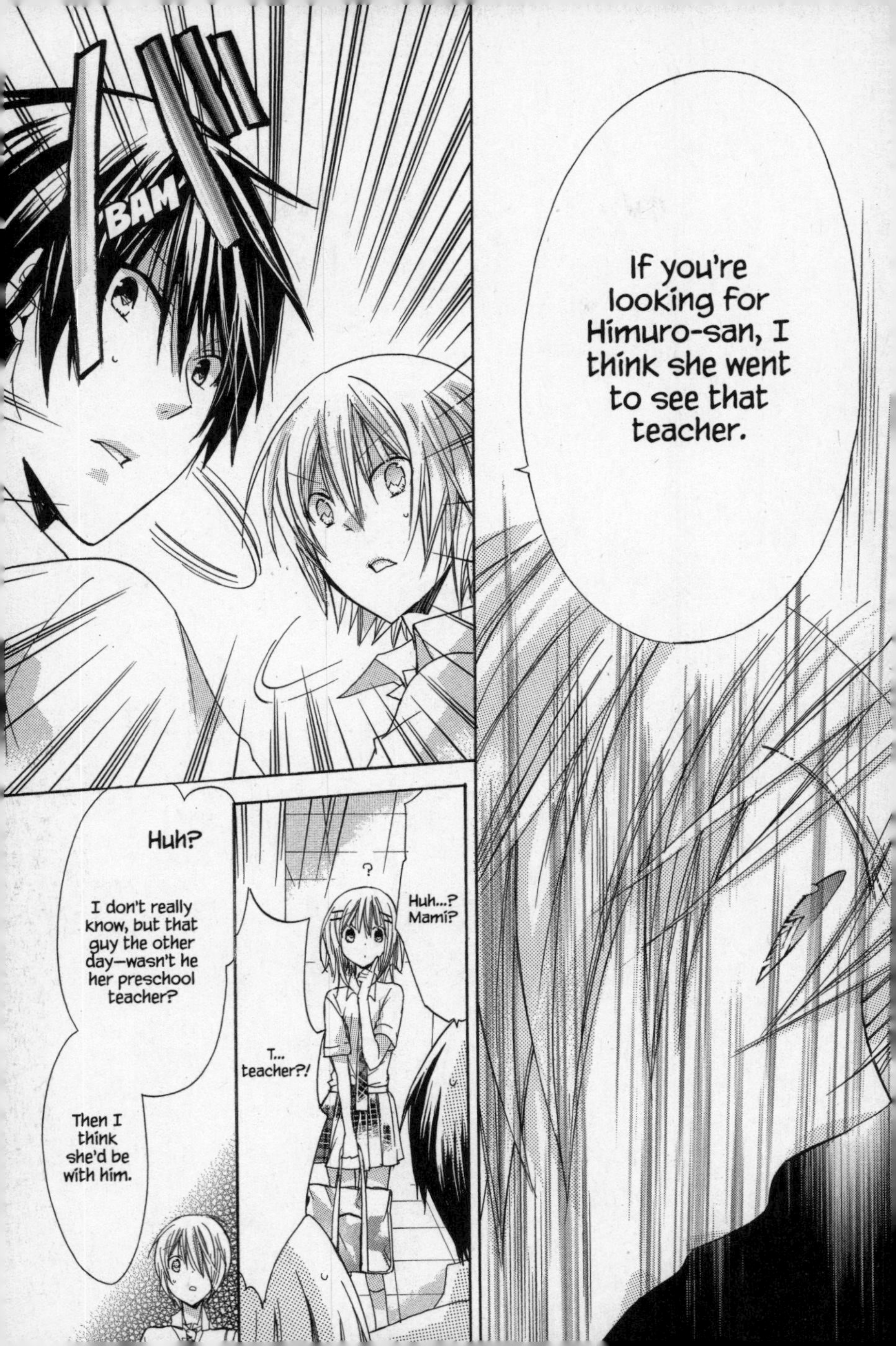
If you're looking for Himuro-san, I think she went to see that teacher.
BAM
?
Huh...? Mami?
T... teacher?!
Huh?
I don't really know, but that guy the other day—wasn't he her preschool teacher?
Then I think she'd be with him.

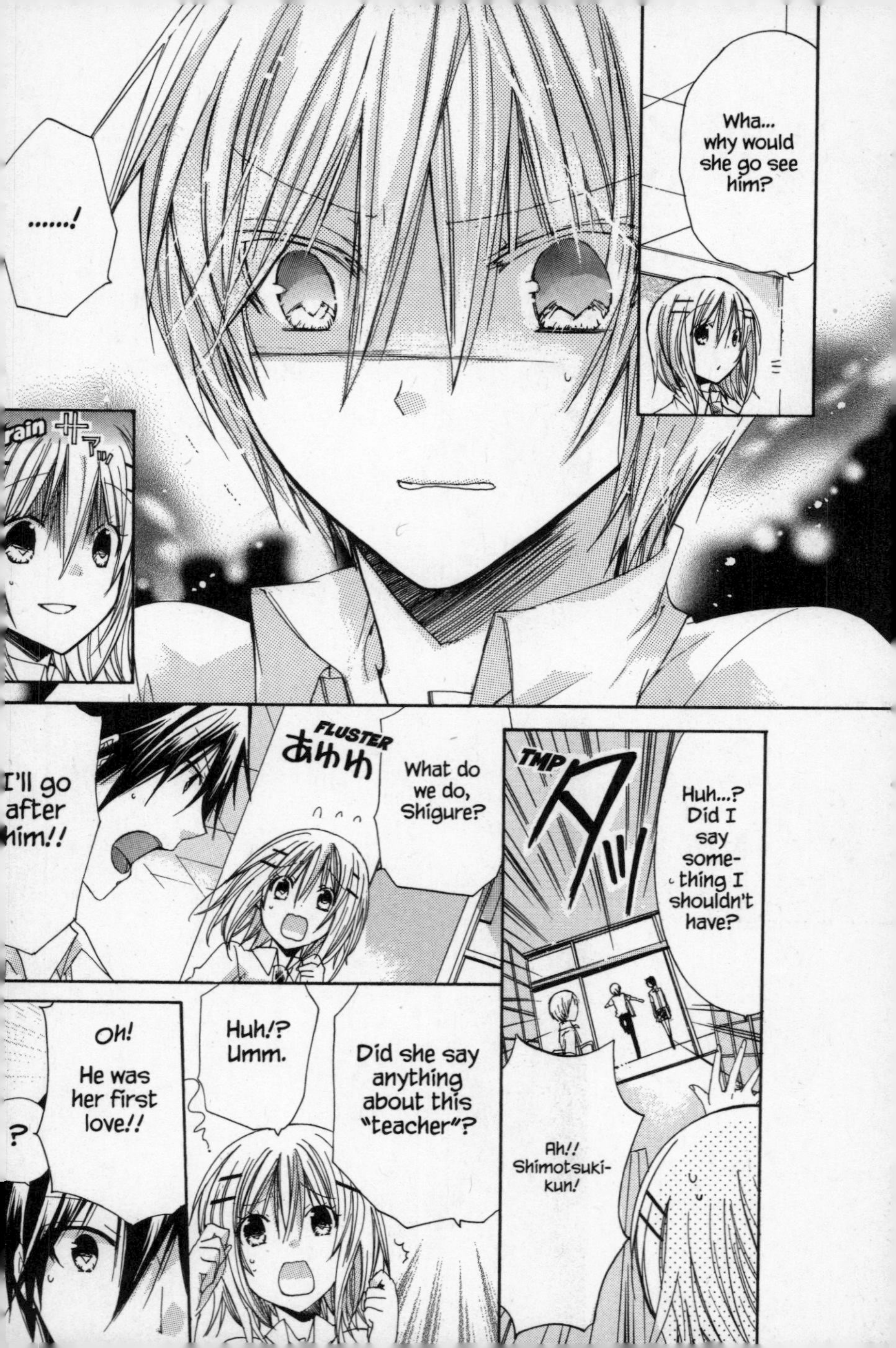

Wha... why would she go see him?
......!
TMP
Huh...? Did I say something I shouldn't have?
FLUSTER
What do we do, Shigure?
I'll go after him!!
Ah!! Shimotsuki-kun!
Did she say anything about this "teacher"?
Huh!? Umm.
Oh! He was her first love!!
?

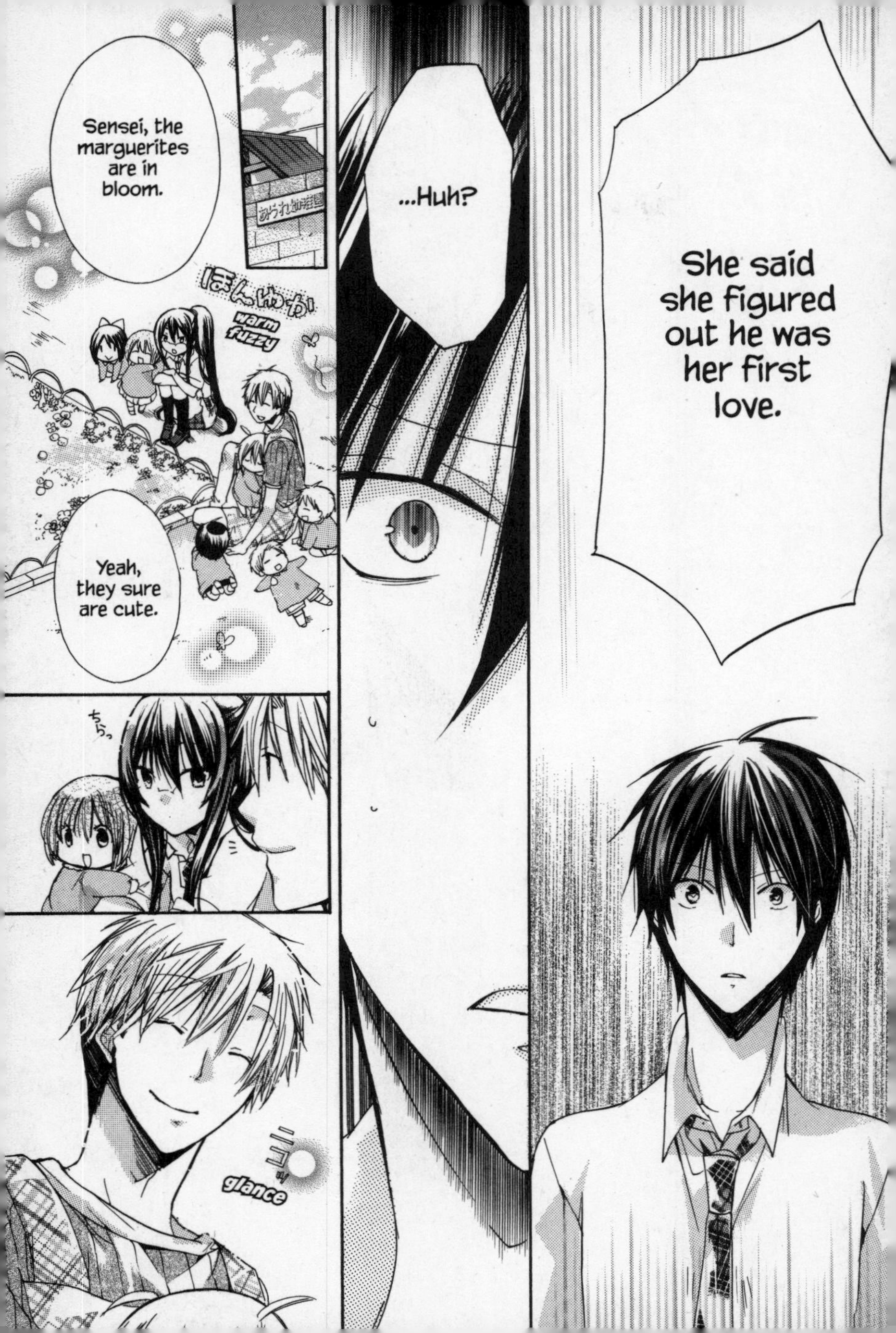
She said she figured out he was her first love.
...Huh?
Sensei, the marguerites are in bloom.
ほんわか
warm fuzzy
Yeah, they sure are cute.
ちらっ
ニコッ
glance

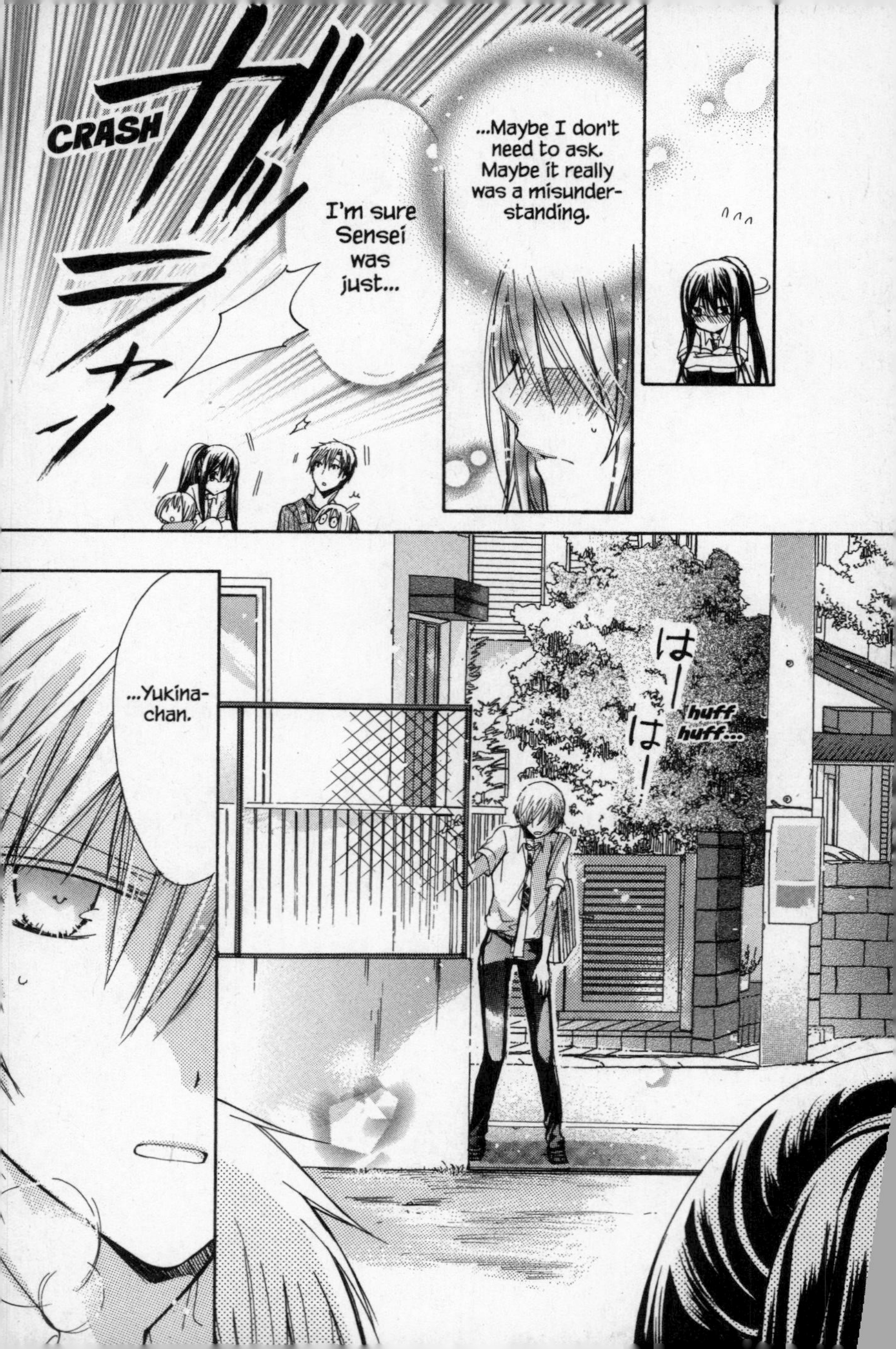
...Maybe I don't need to ask. Maybe it really was a misunderstanding.
I'm sure Sensei was just...
ガシャン
CRASH
はーはー
huff huff...
...Yukina-chan.

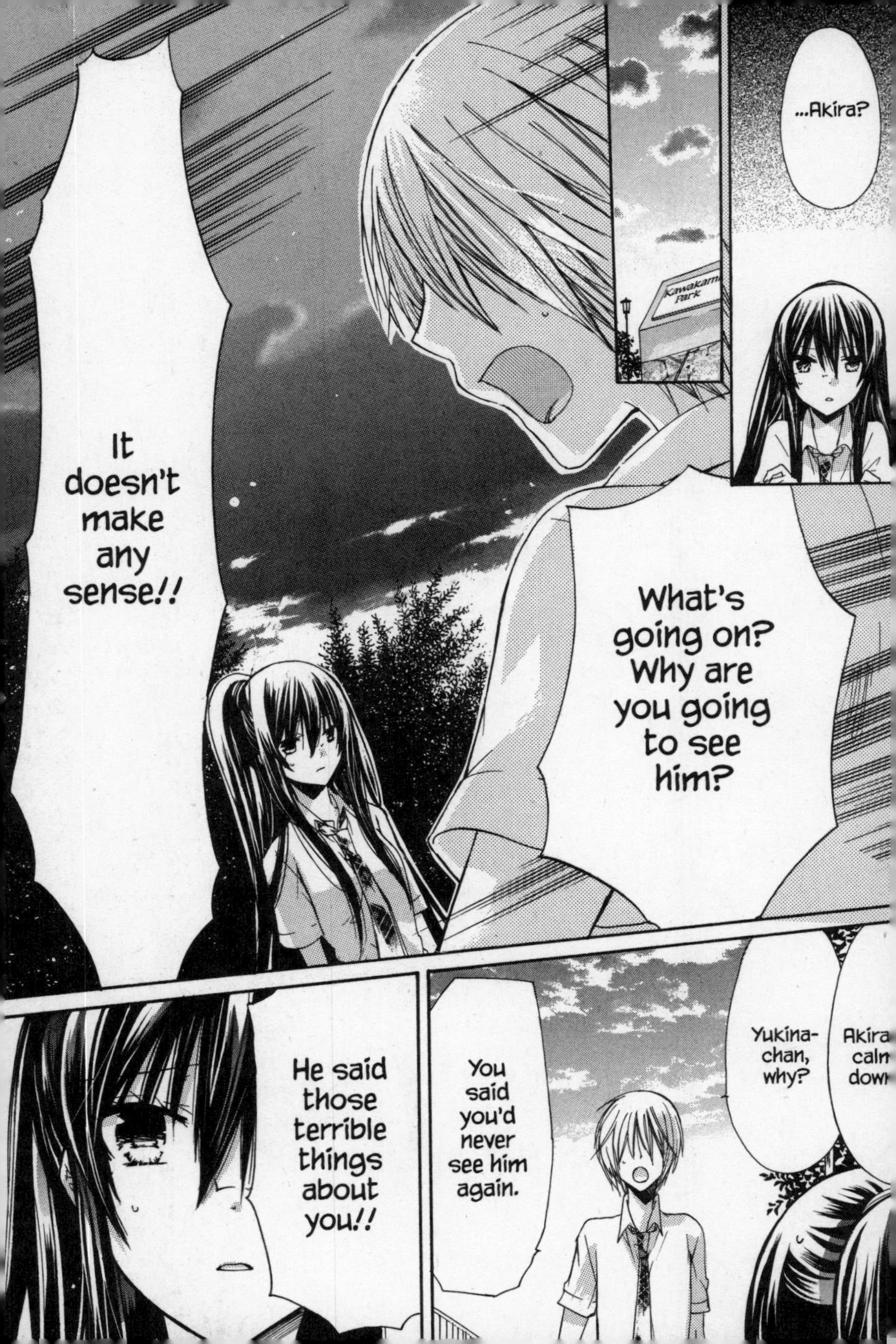
...Akira?
Kawakami Park
What's going on? Why are you going to see him?
It doesn't make any sense!!
Akira calm down
Yukina-chan, why?
You said you'd never see him again.
He said those terrible things about you!!

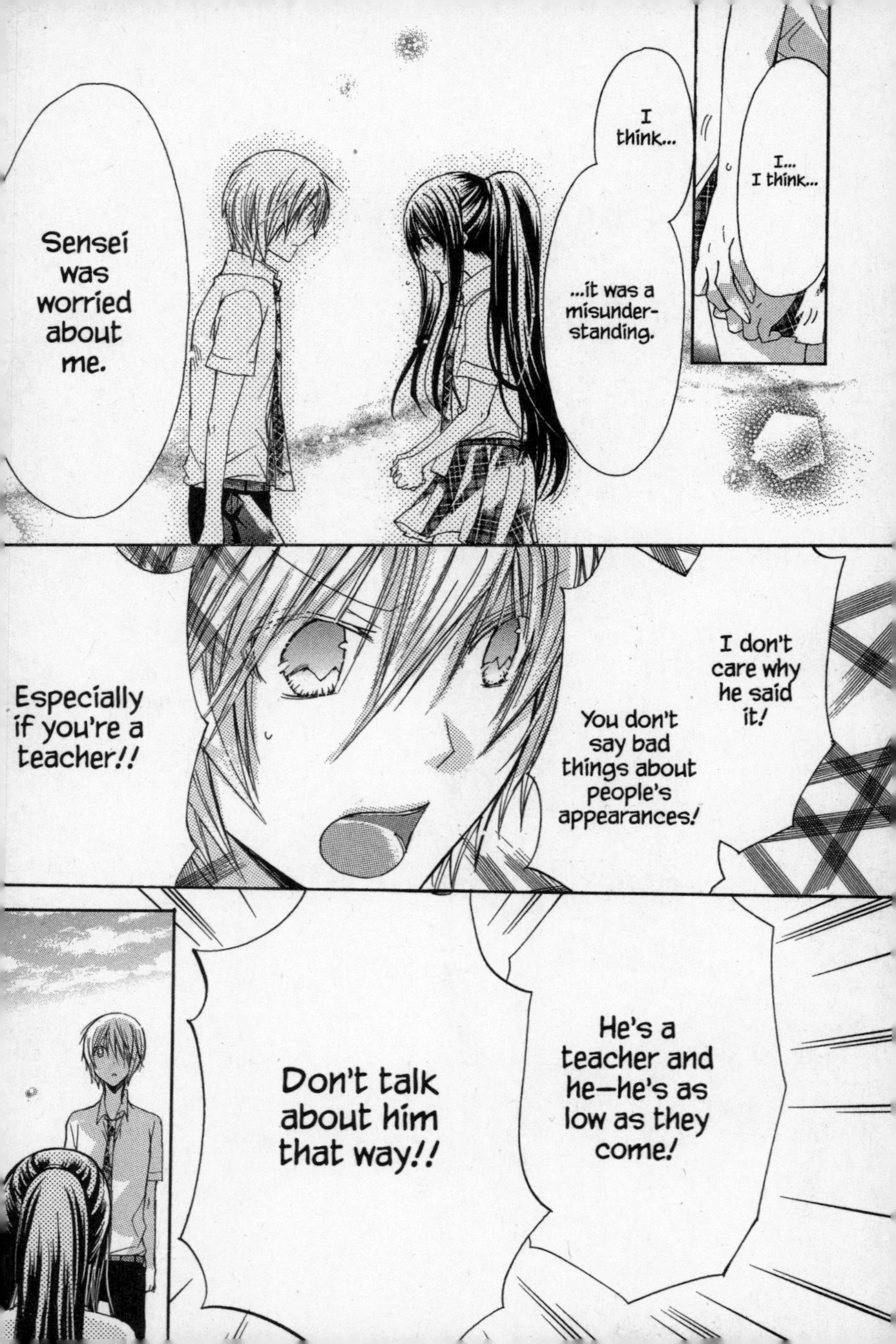
I...
I think...
I think...
...it was a misunder-standing.
Sensei was worried about me.
I don't care why he said it!
You don't say bad things about people's appearances!
Especially if you're a teacher!!
He's a teacher and he—he's as low as they come!
Don't talk about him that way!!

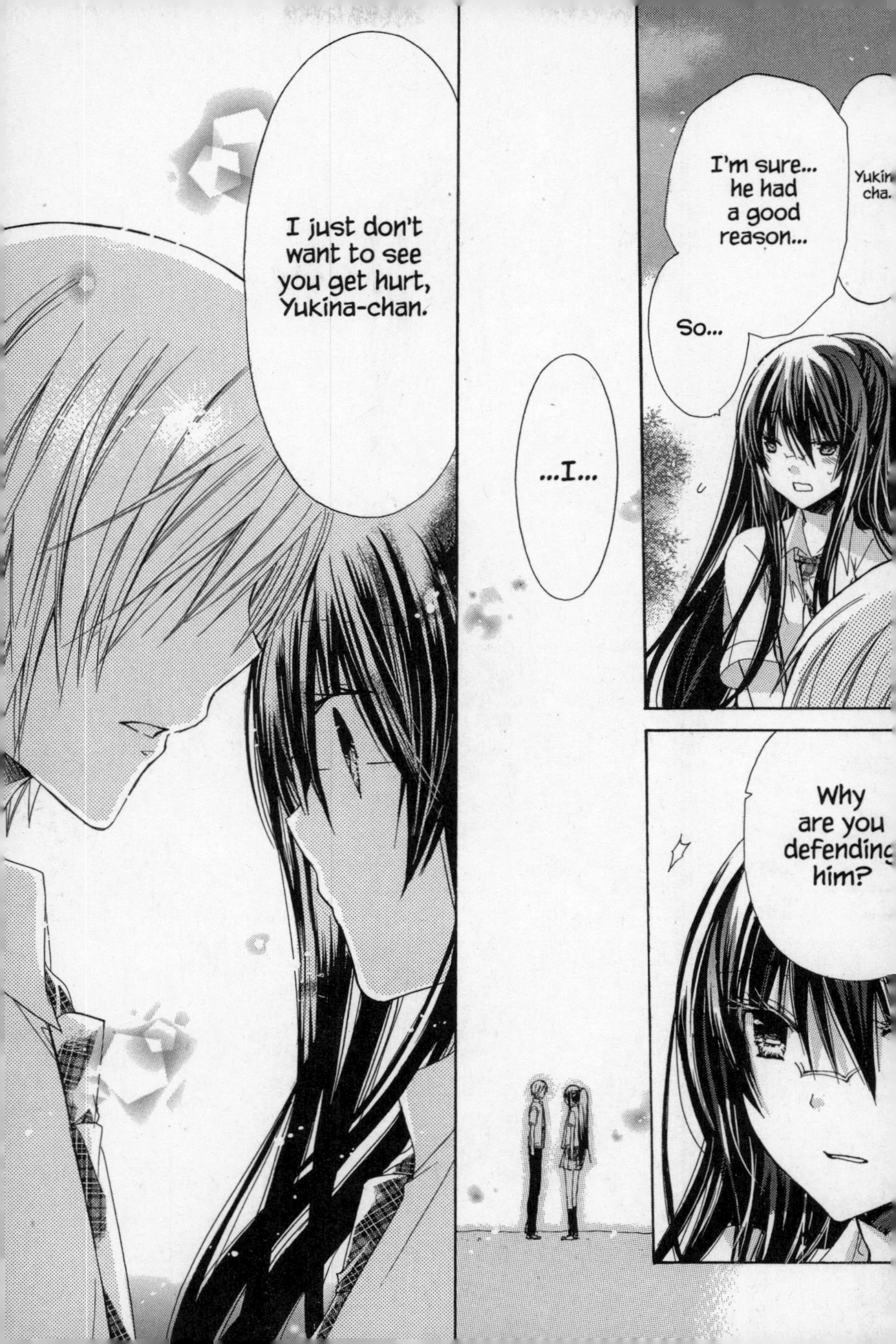
Yukin cha.
I'm sure... he had a good reason...
So...
Why are you defending him?
...I...
I just don't want to see you get hurt, Yukina-chan.

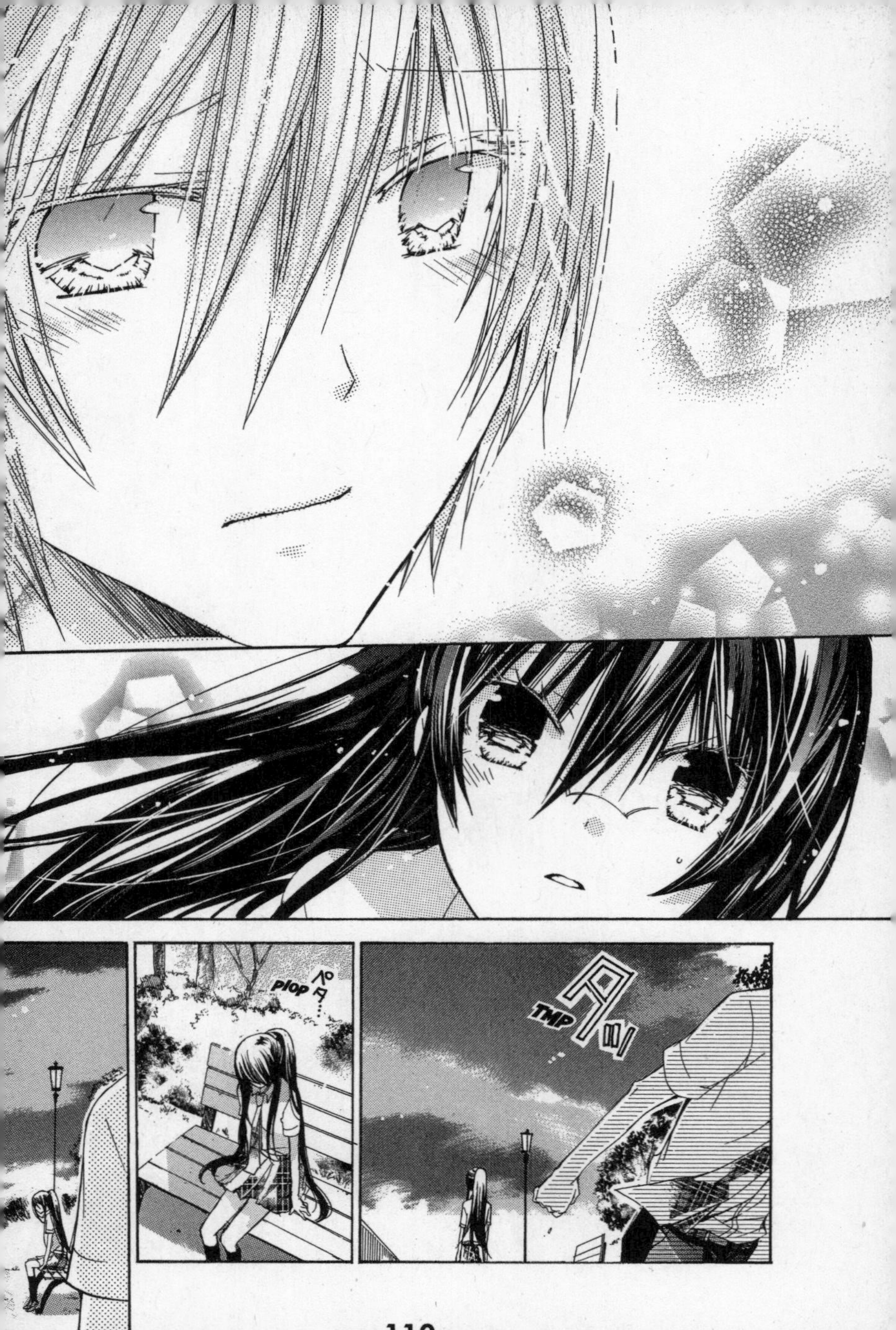
TMP
PLOP

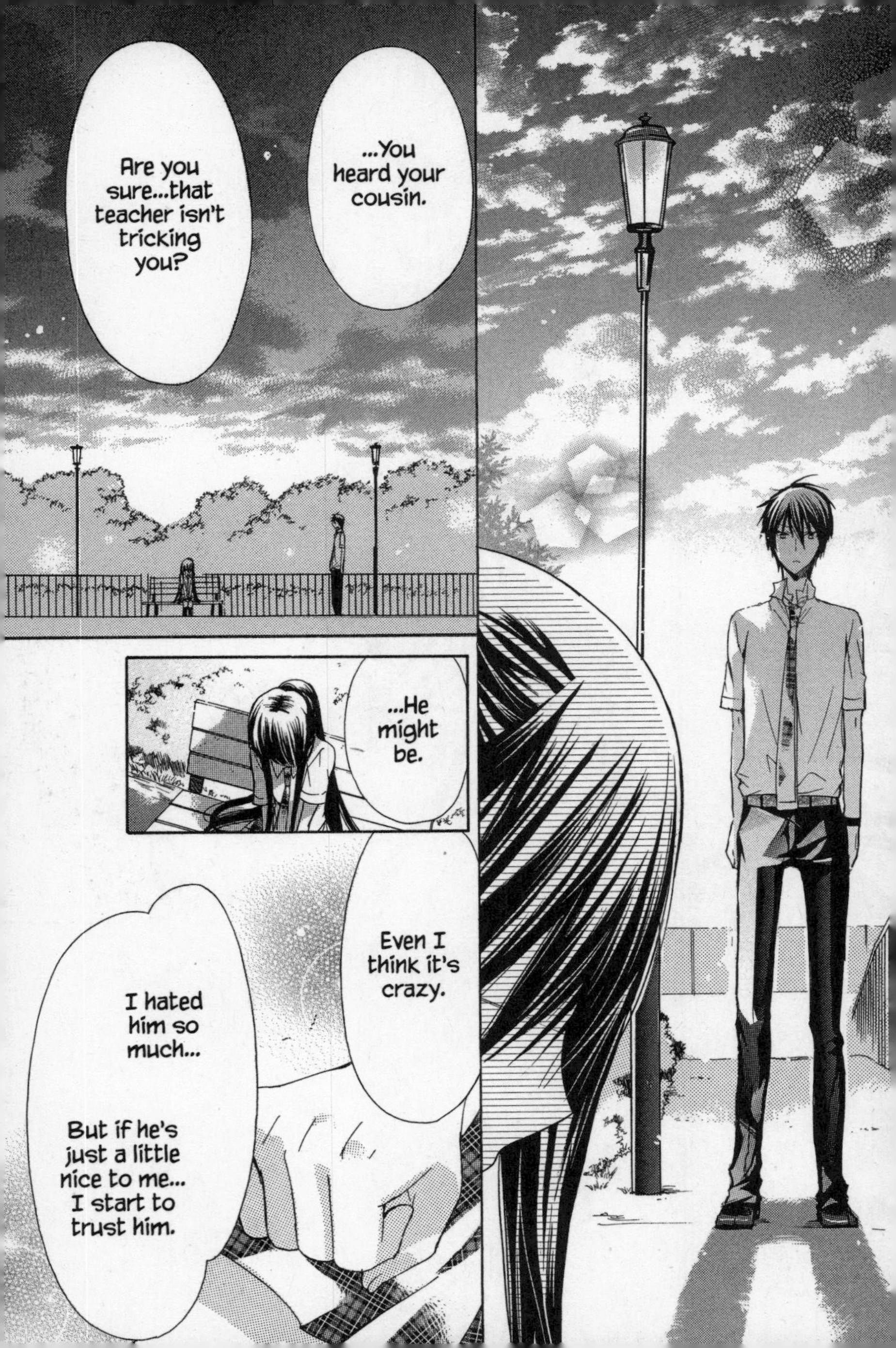
...You heard your cousin.
Are you sure...that teacher isn't tricking you?
...He might be.
Even I think it's crazy.
I hated him so much...
But if he's just a little nice to me... I start to trust him.

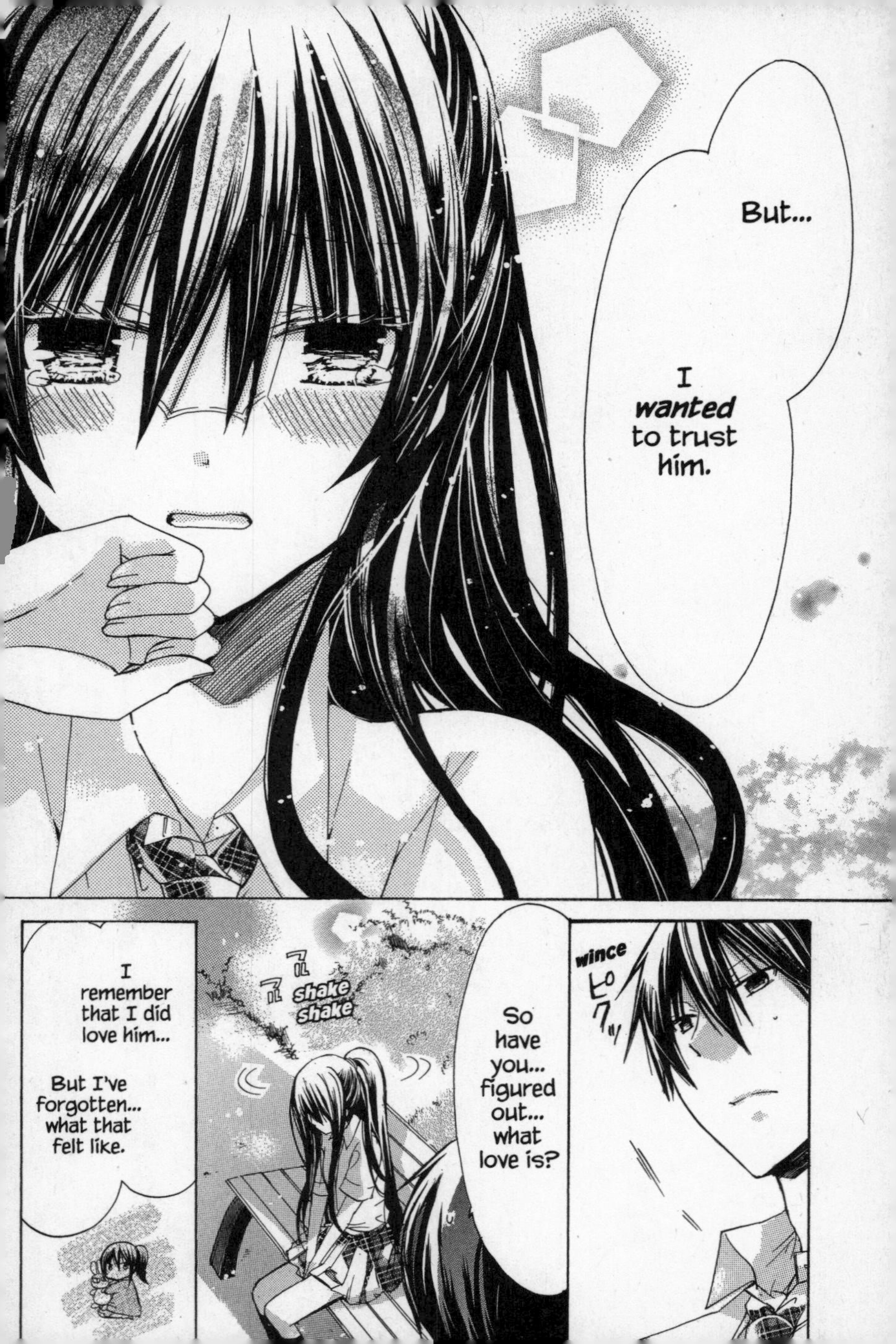
But...
I *wanted* to trust him.
wince
So have you... figured out... what love is?
shake shake
I remember that I did love him...
But I've forgotten... what that felt like.

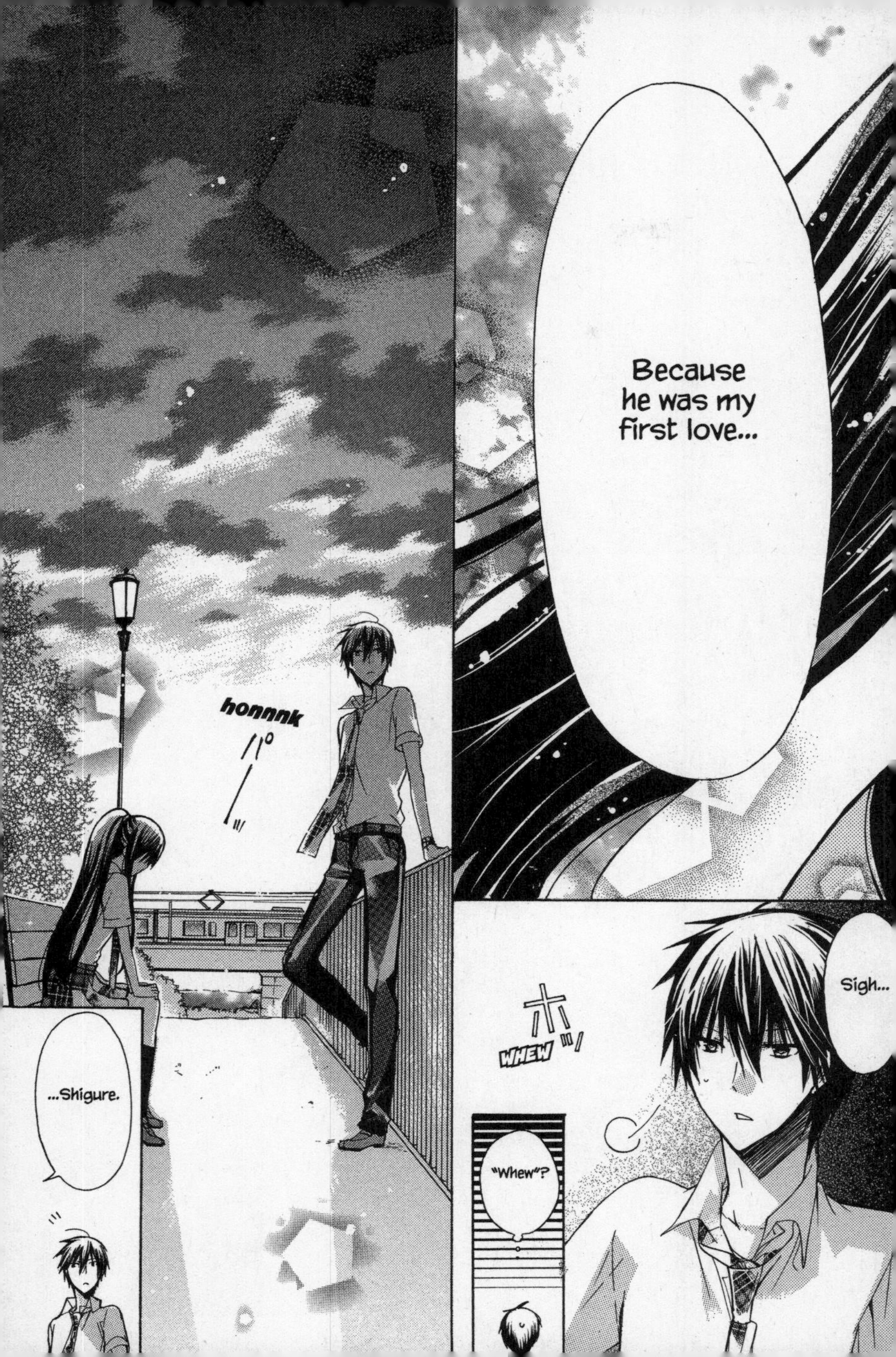

Because he was my first love...
Sigh...
WHEW
"Whew"?
honnnk
...Shigure.

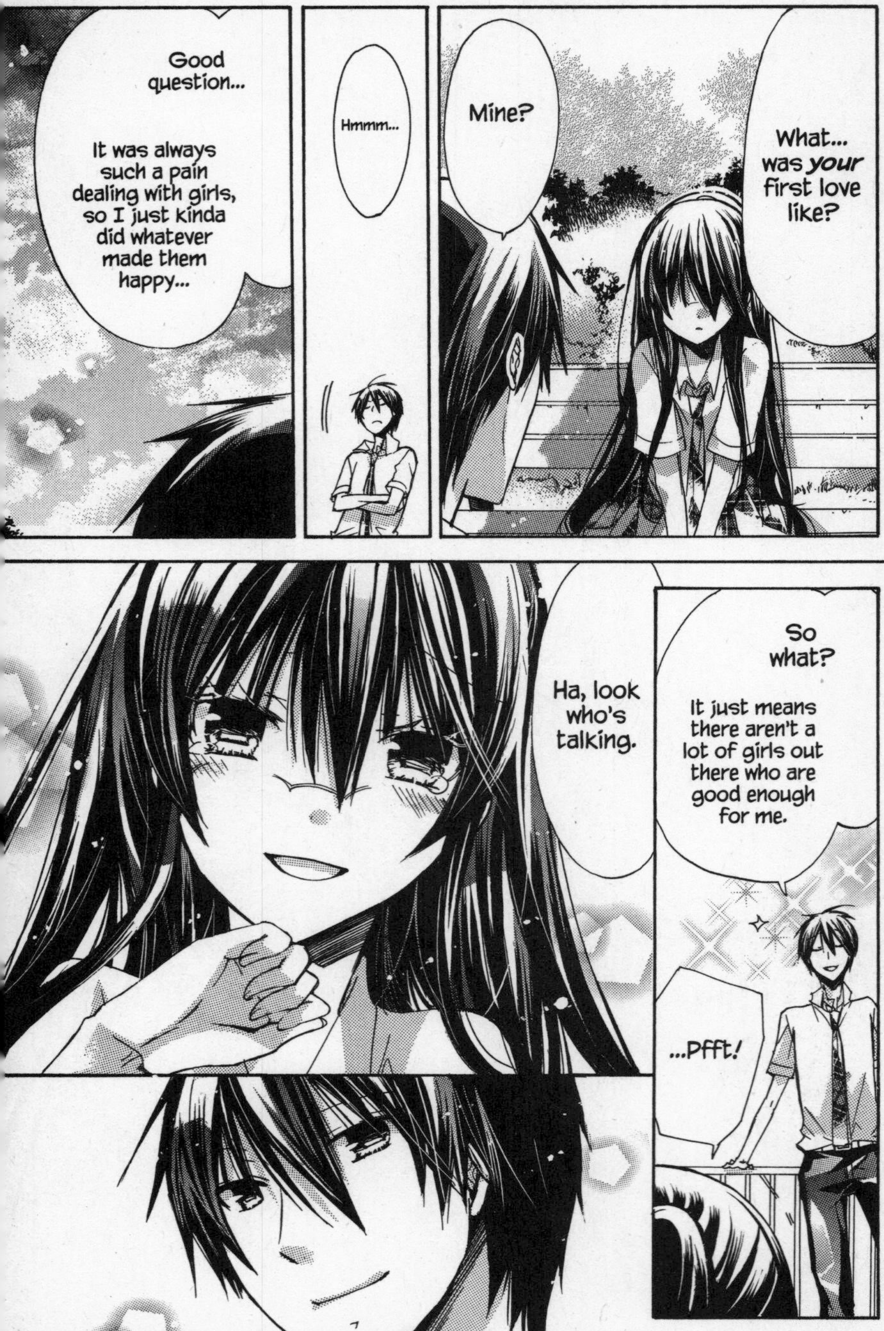
What... was *your* first love like?
Mine?
Hmmm...
Good question...
It was always such a pain dealing with girls, so I just kinda did whatever made them happy...
So what?
It just means there aren't a lot of girls out there who are good enough for me.
...Pfft!
Ha, look who's talking.

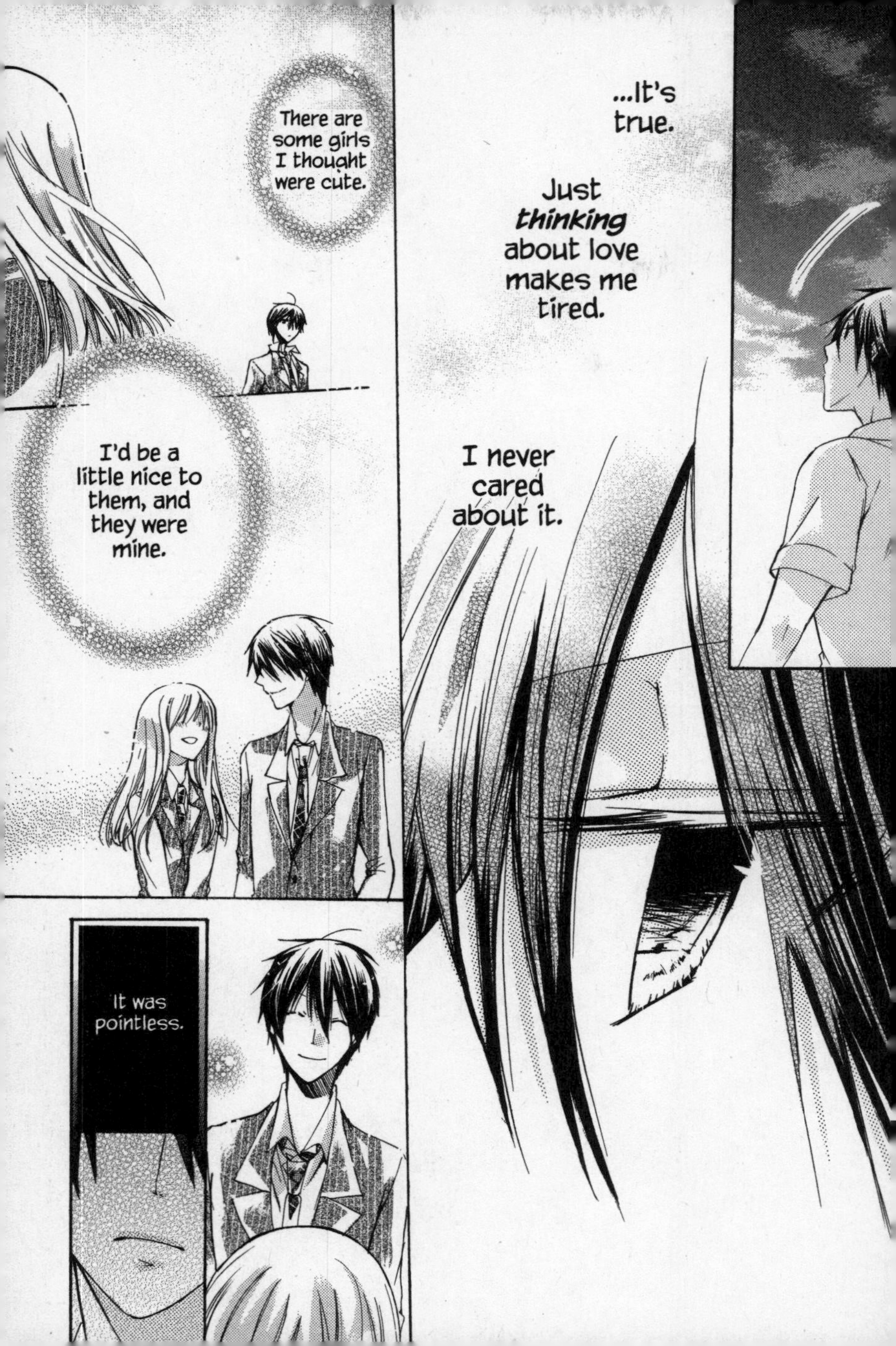
...It's true.
Just *thinking* about love makes me tired.
I never cared about it.
There are some girls I thought were cute.
I'd be a little nice to them, and they were mine.
It was pointless.

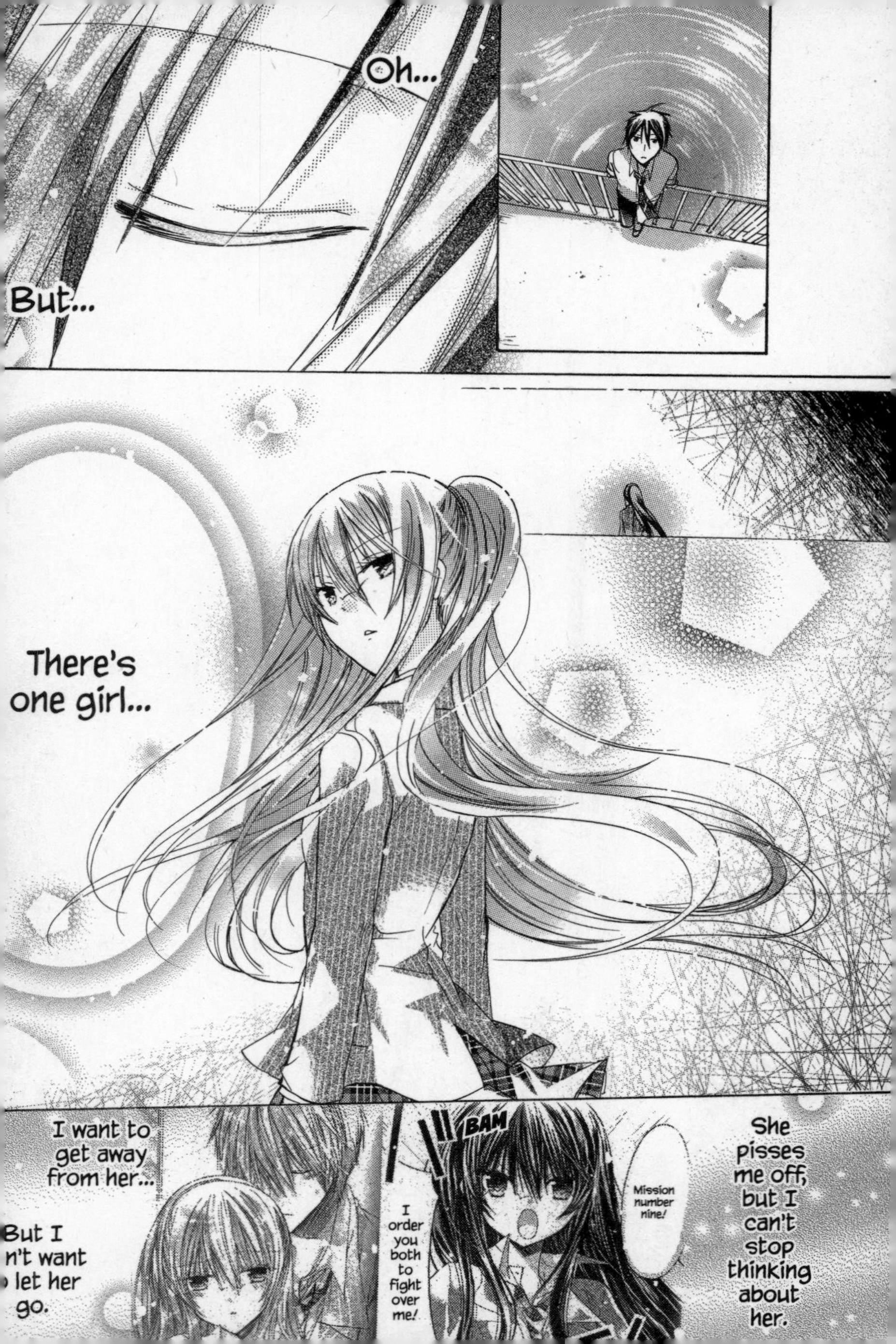

Oh...
But...
There's one girl...
She pisses me off, but I can't stop thinking about her.
BAM
Mission number nine!
I order you both to fight over me!
I want to get away from her...
But I n't want let her go.

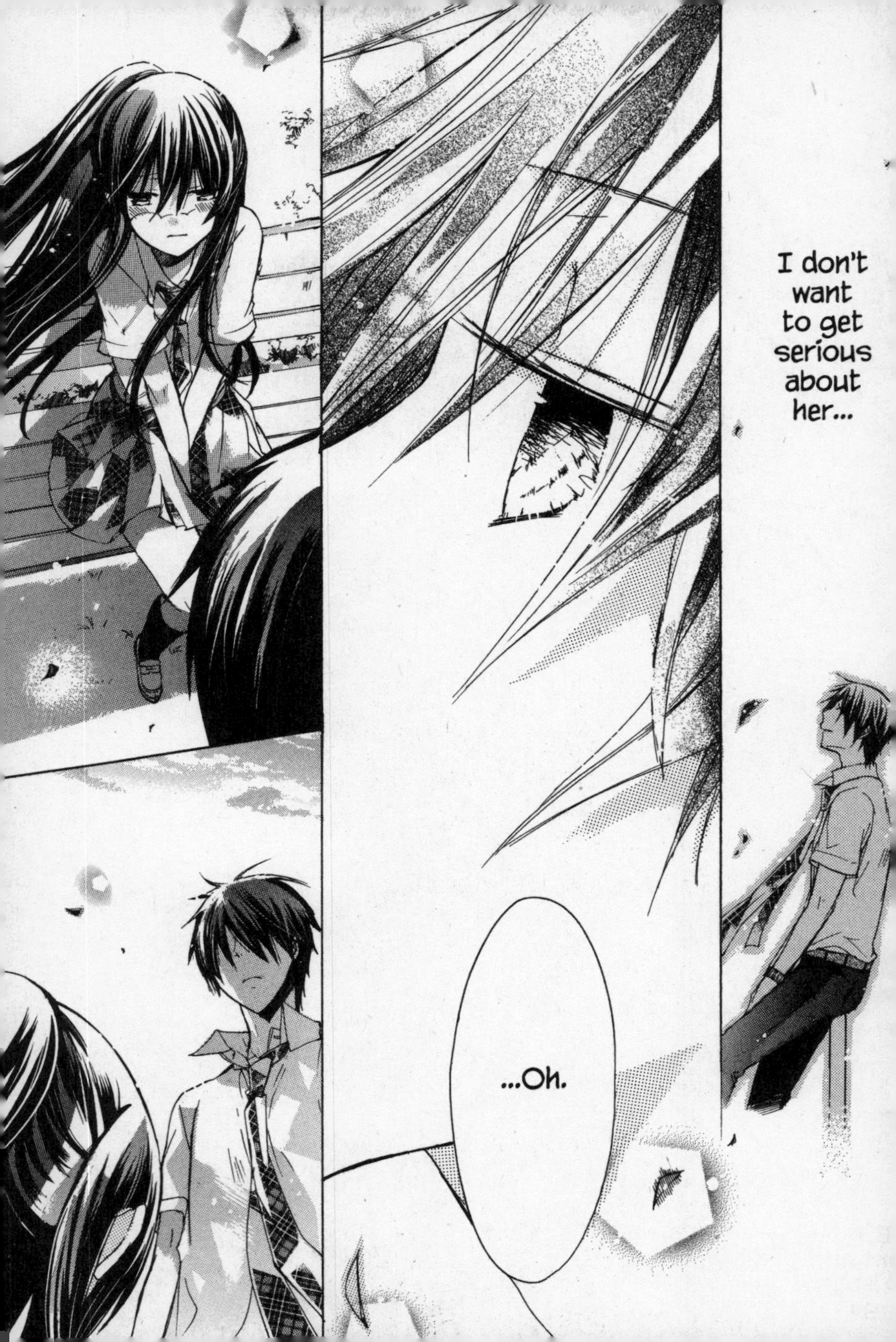
I don't want to get serious about her...
...Oh.

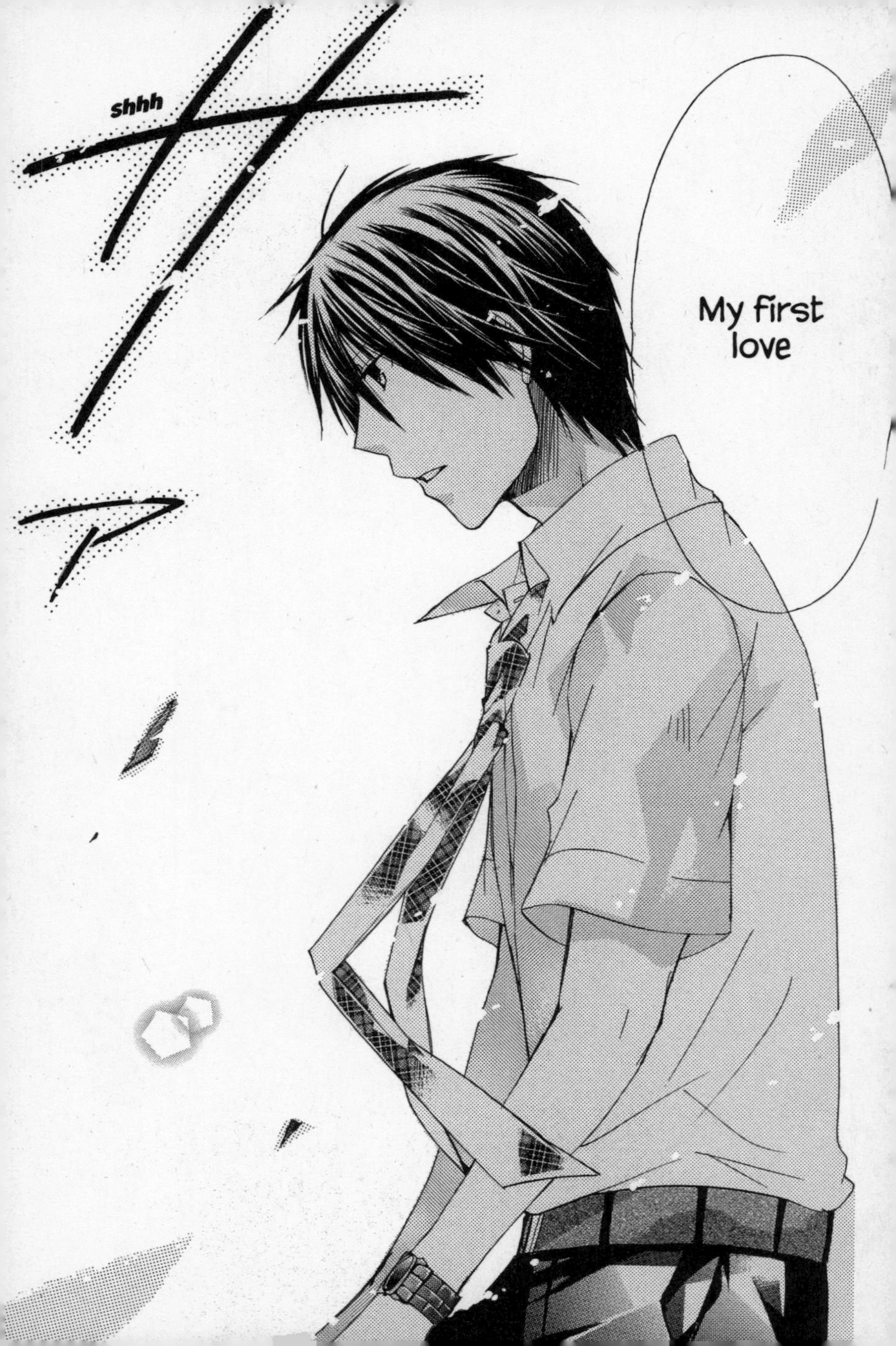
My first love
shhh

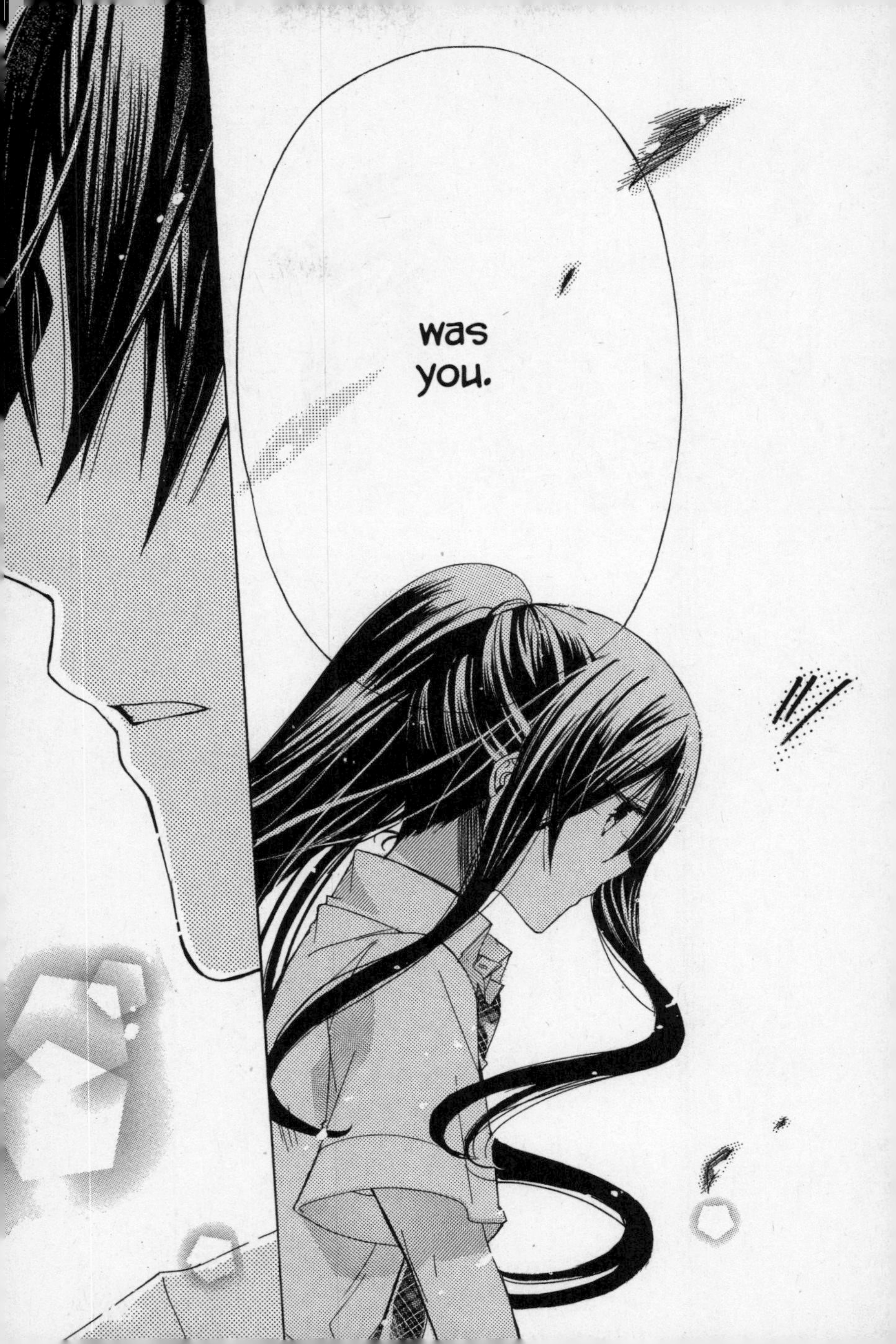
was you.

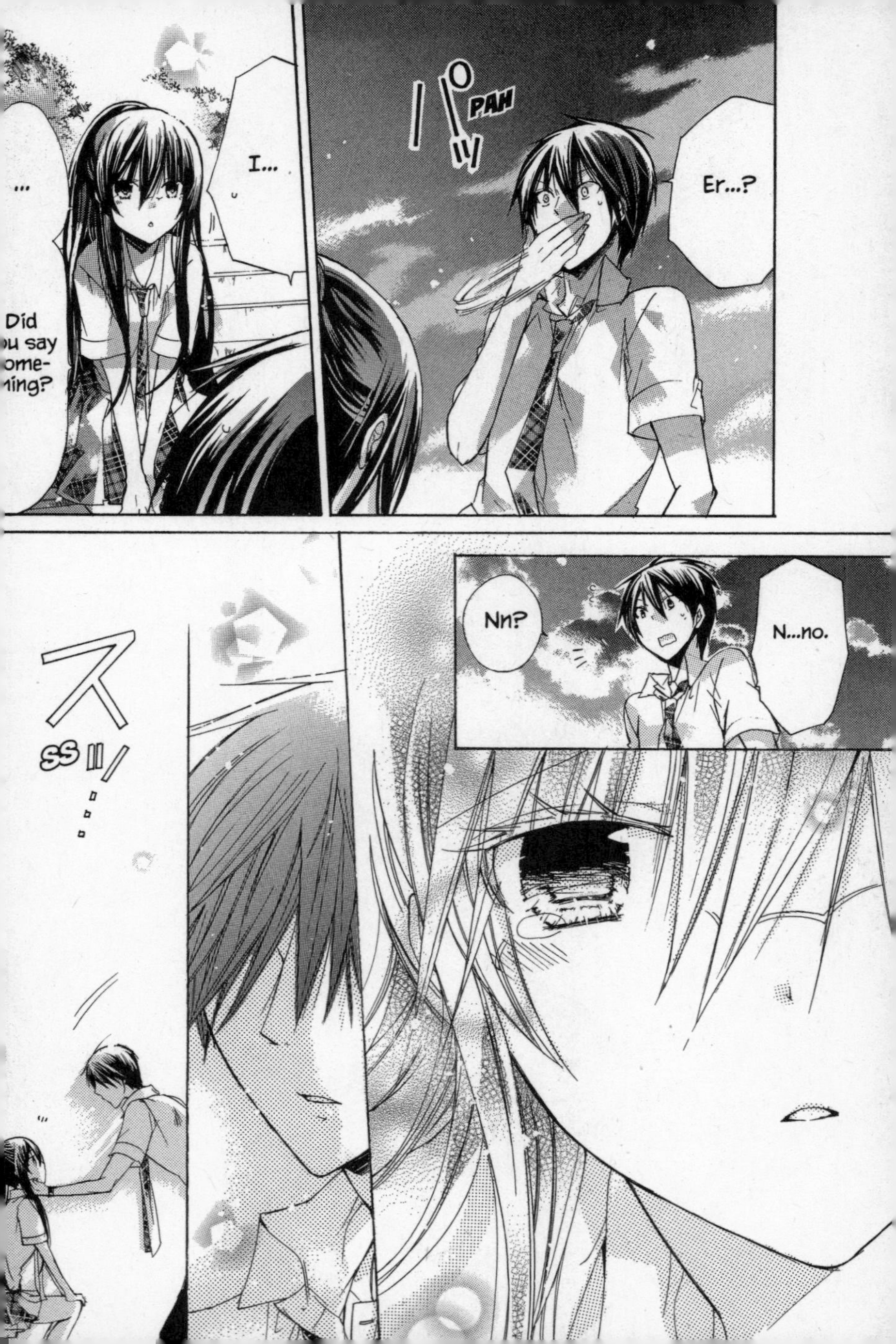
パッ
PAH
Er...?
I...
...
Did
ou say
ome-
ning?
N...no.
Nn?
ス
SS

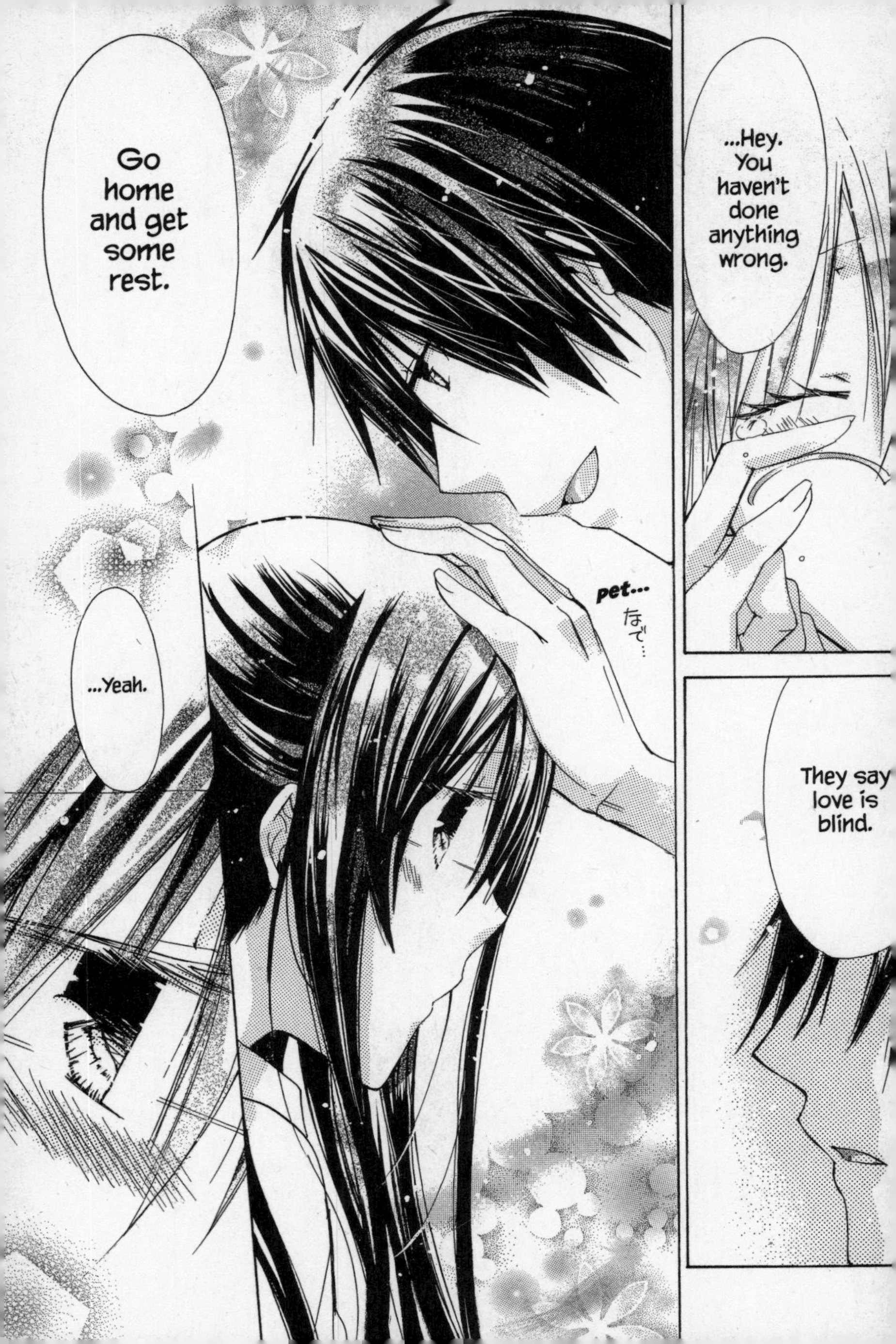
...Hey. You haven't done anything wrong.
They say love is blind.
Go home and get some rest.
pet...
なで…
...Yeah.

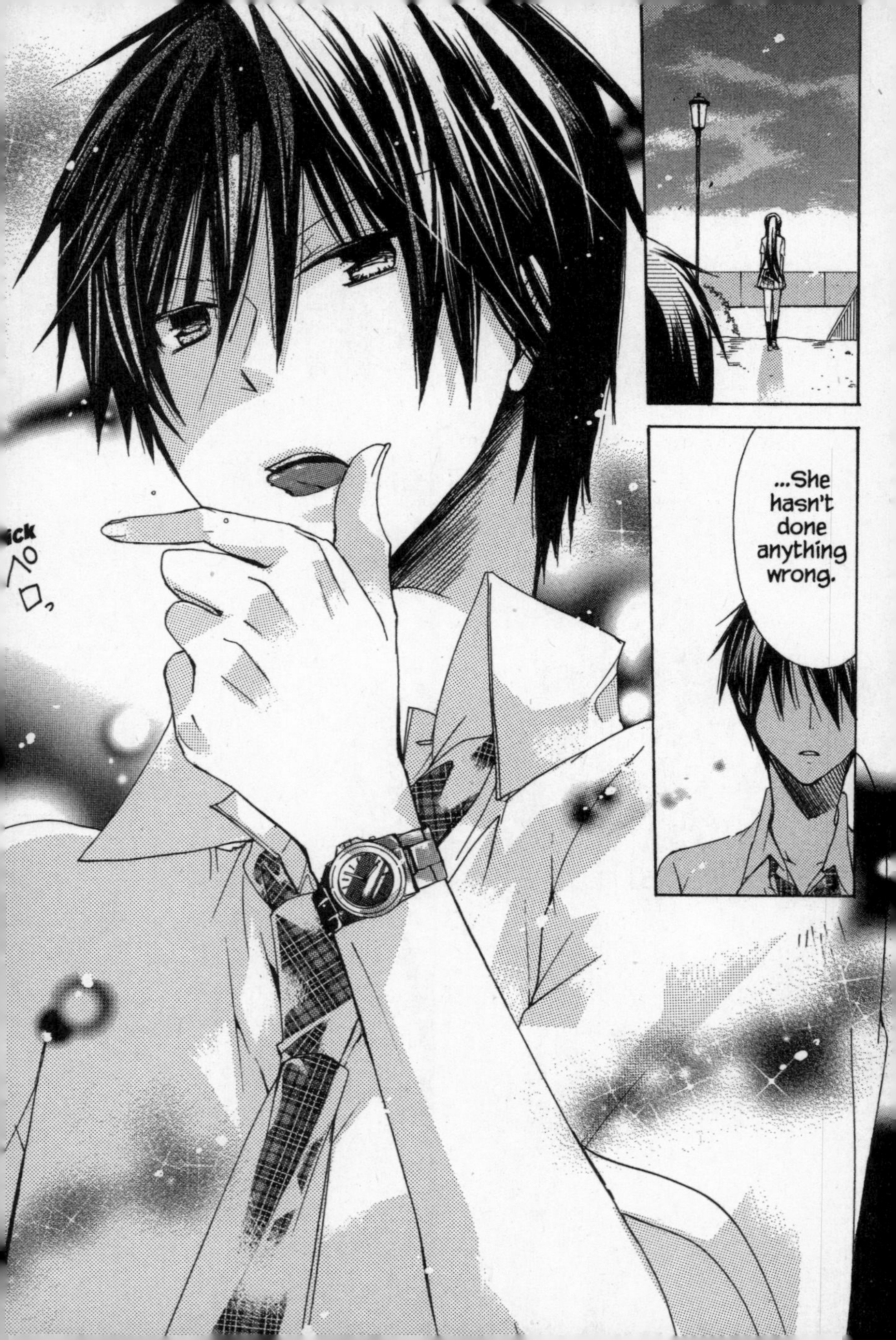
...She hasn't done anything wrong.
ick

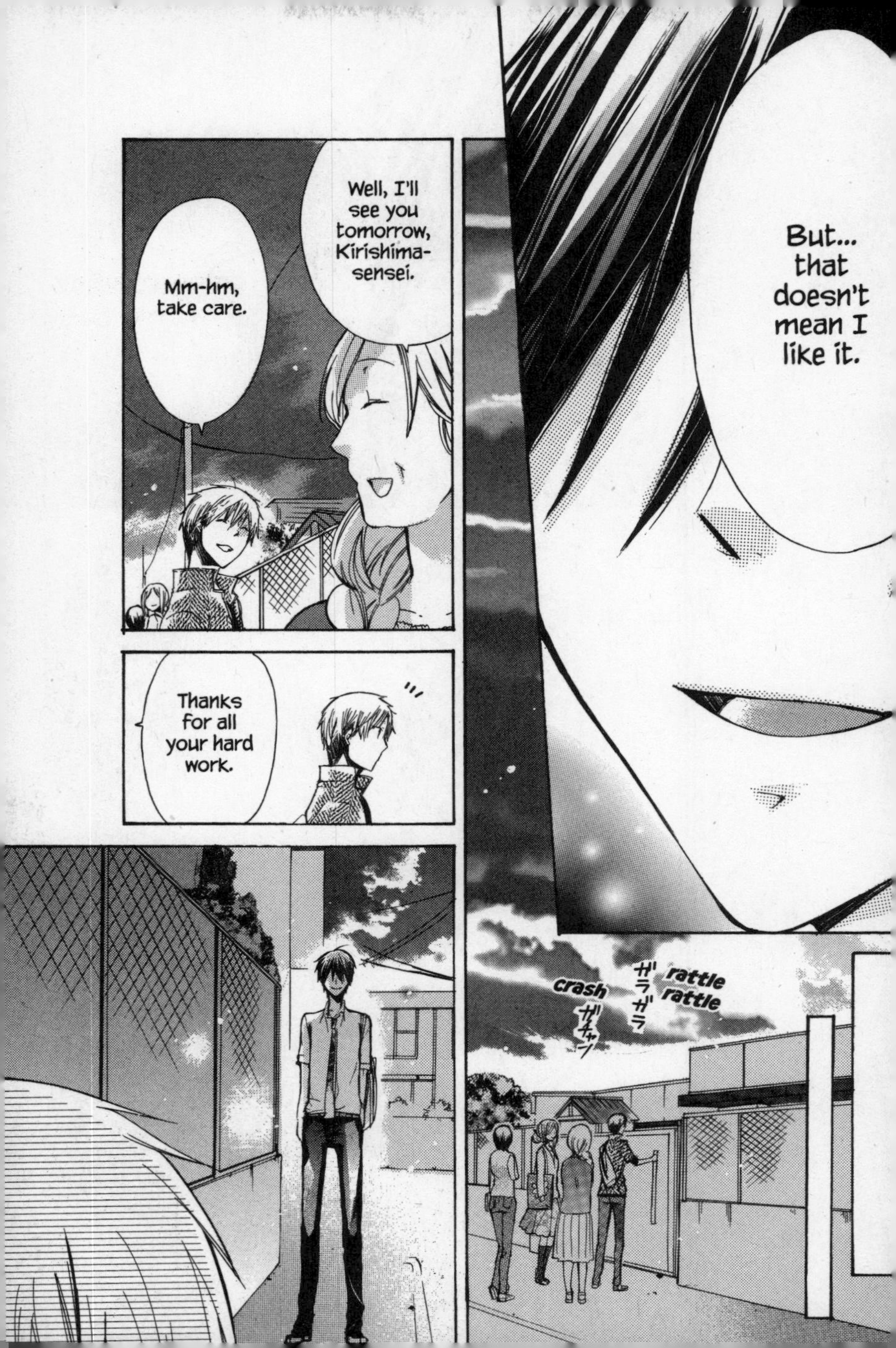
But... that doesn't mean I like it.
Well, I'll see you tomorrow, Kirishima-sensei.
Mm-hm, take care.
Thanks for all your hard work.
ガラガラ
rattle rattle
ガチャン
crash

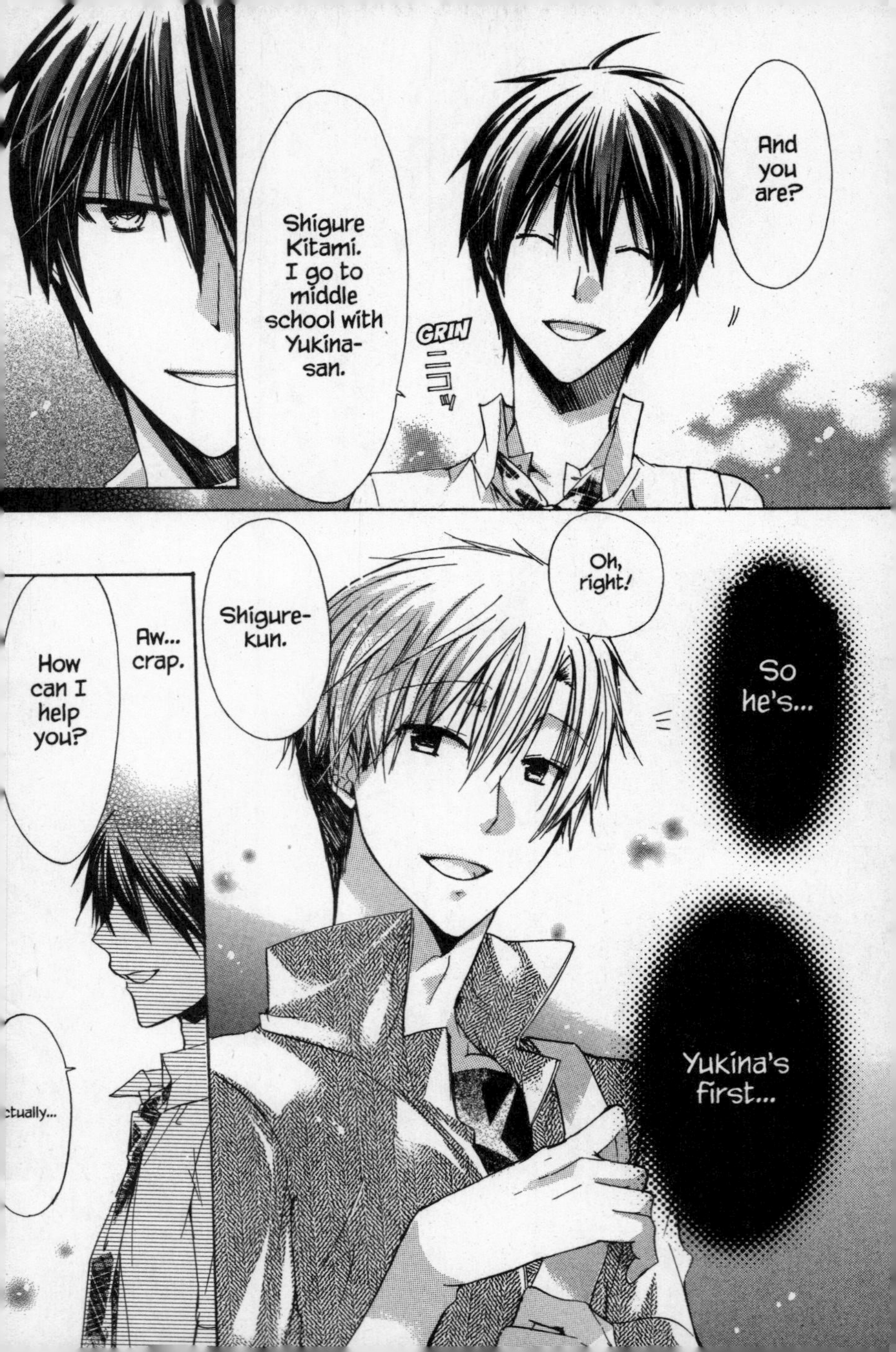
And you are?
GRIN
ニコッ
Shigure Kitami. I go to middle school with Yukina-san.
So he's...
Yukina's first...
Oh, right!
Shigure-kun.
Aw... crap.
How can I help you?
ctually...

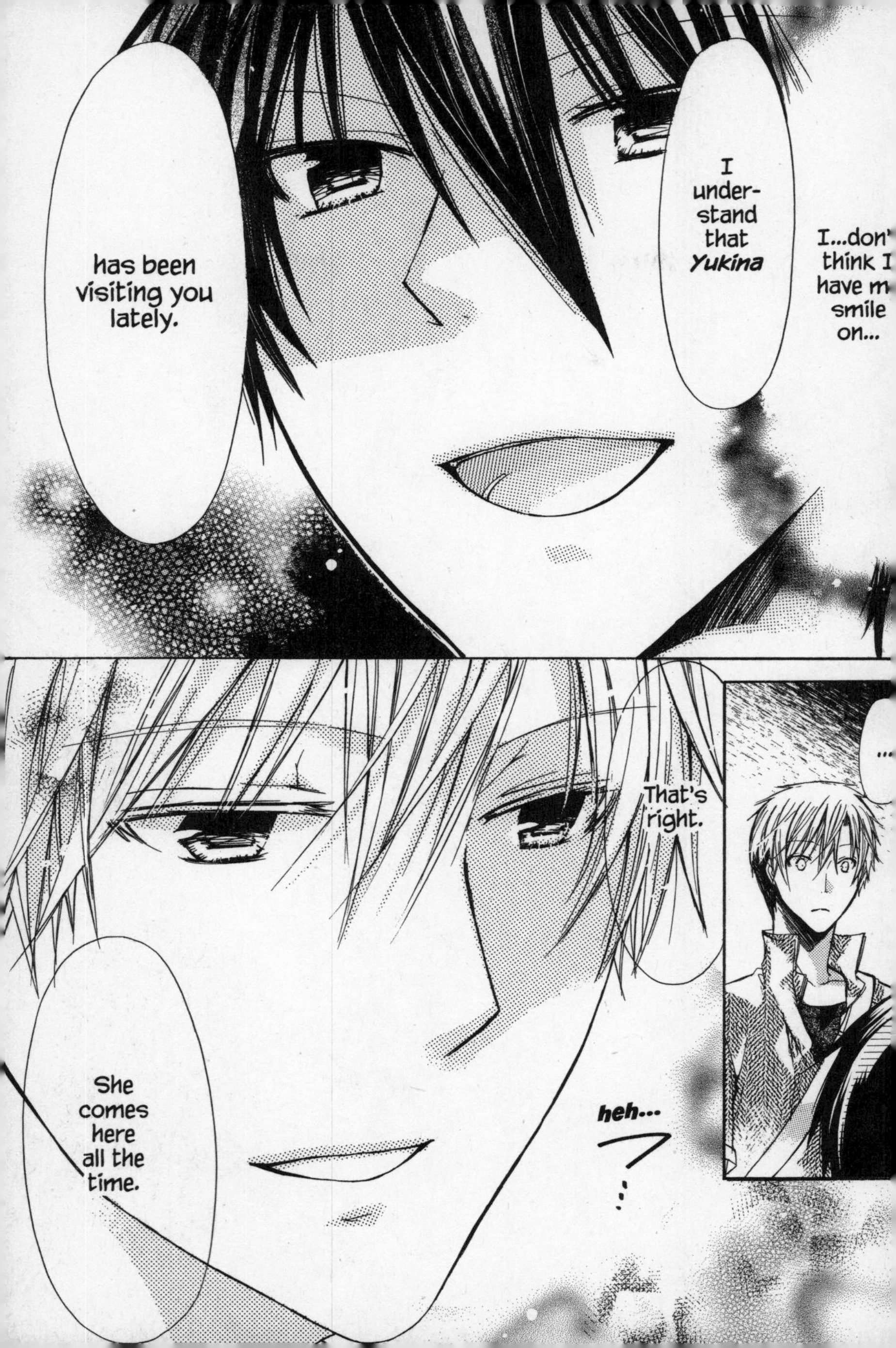
I...don' think I have m smile on...
I understand that *Yukina*
has been visiting you lately.
...
That's right.
heh...
She comes here all the time.

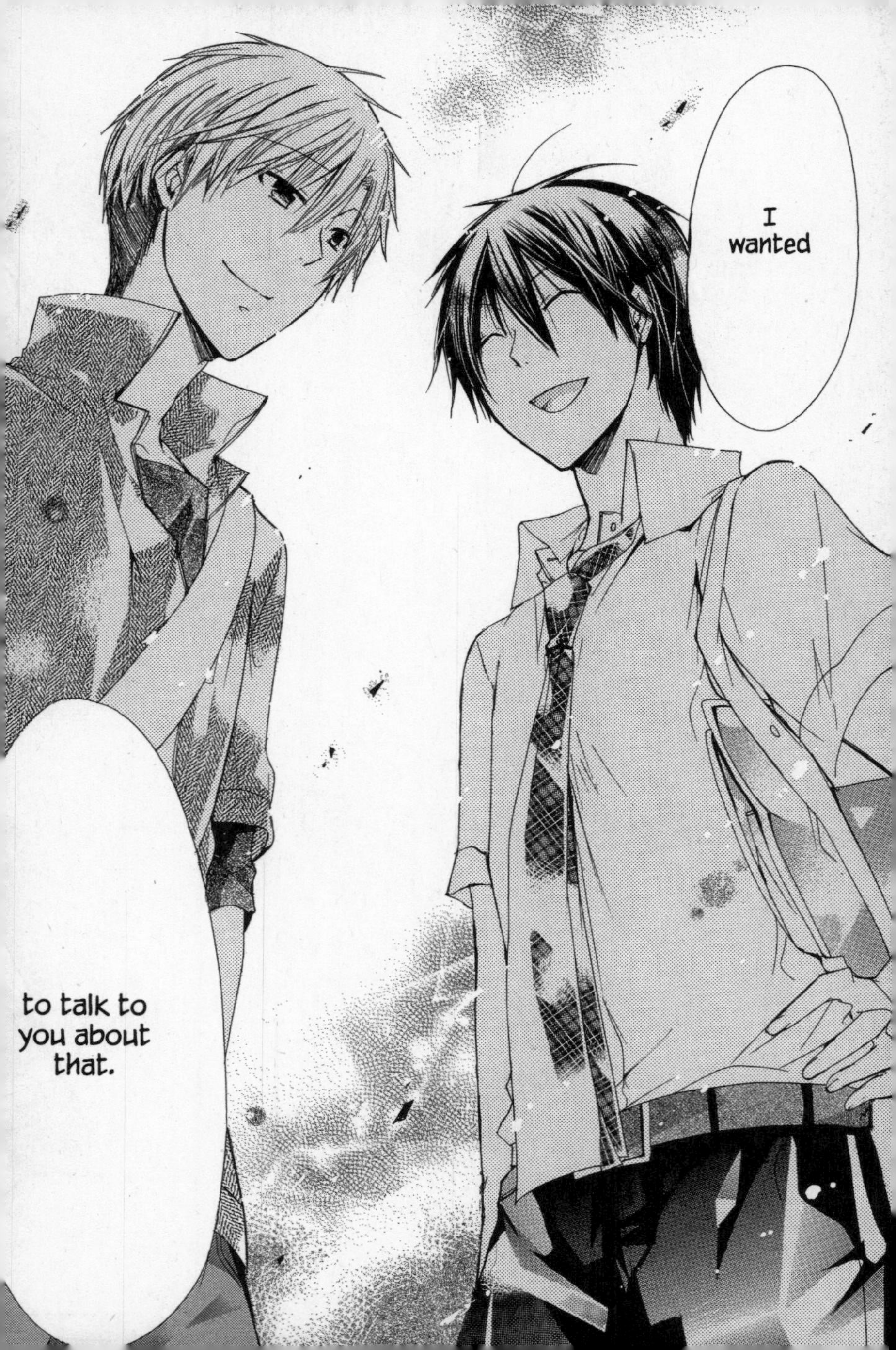
I wanted
to talk to you about that.

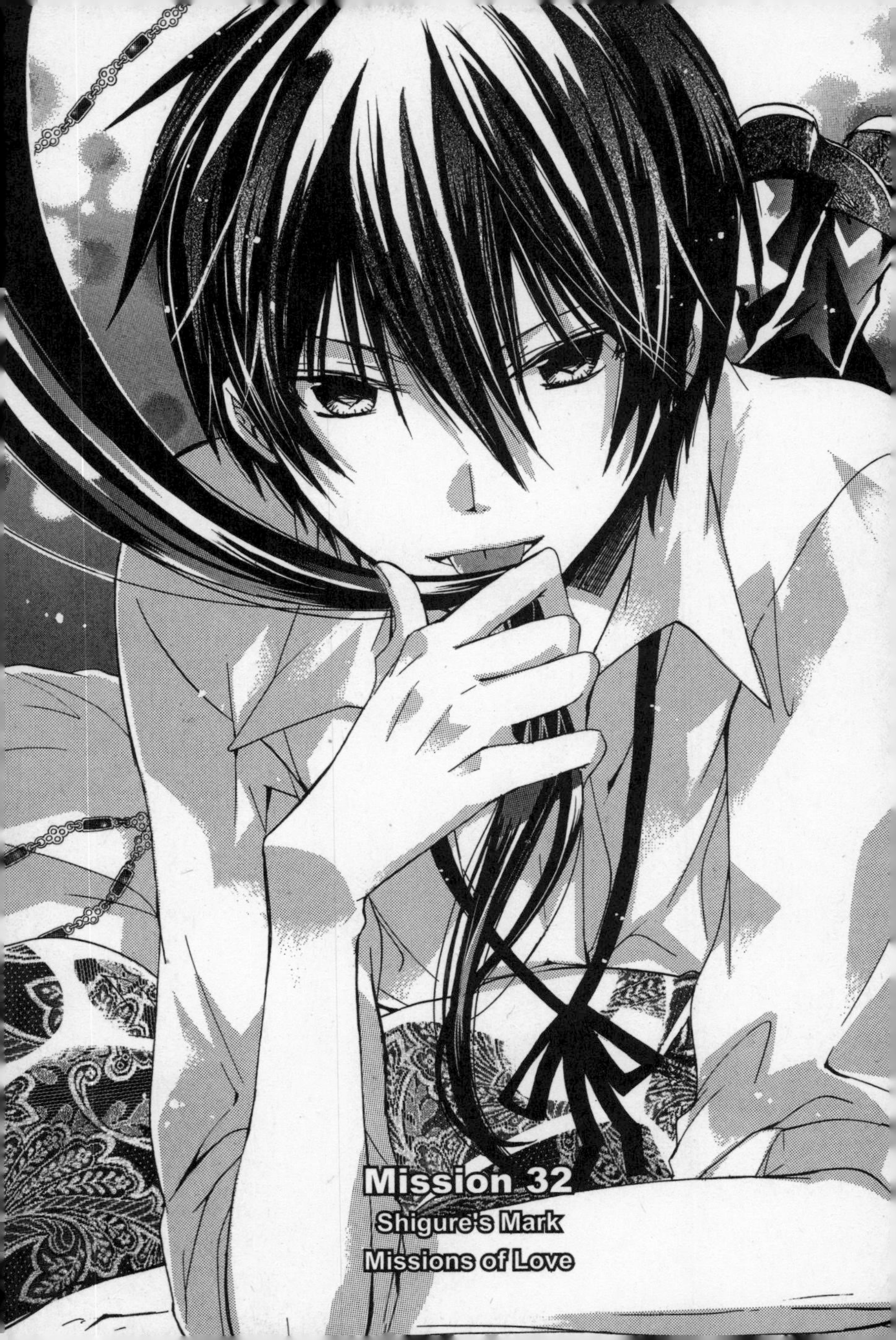
Mission 32
Shigure's Mark
Missions of Love

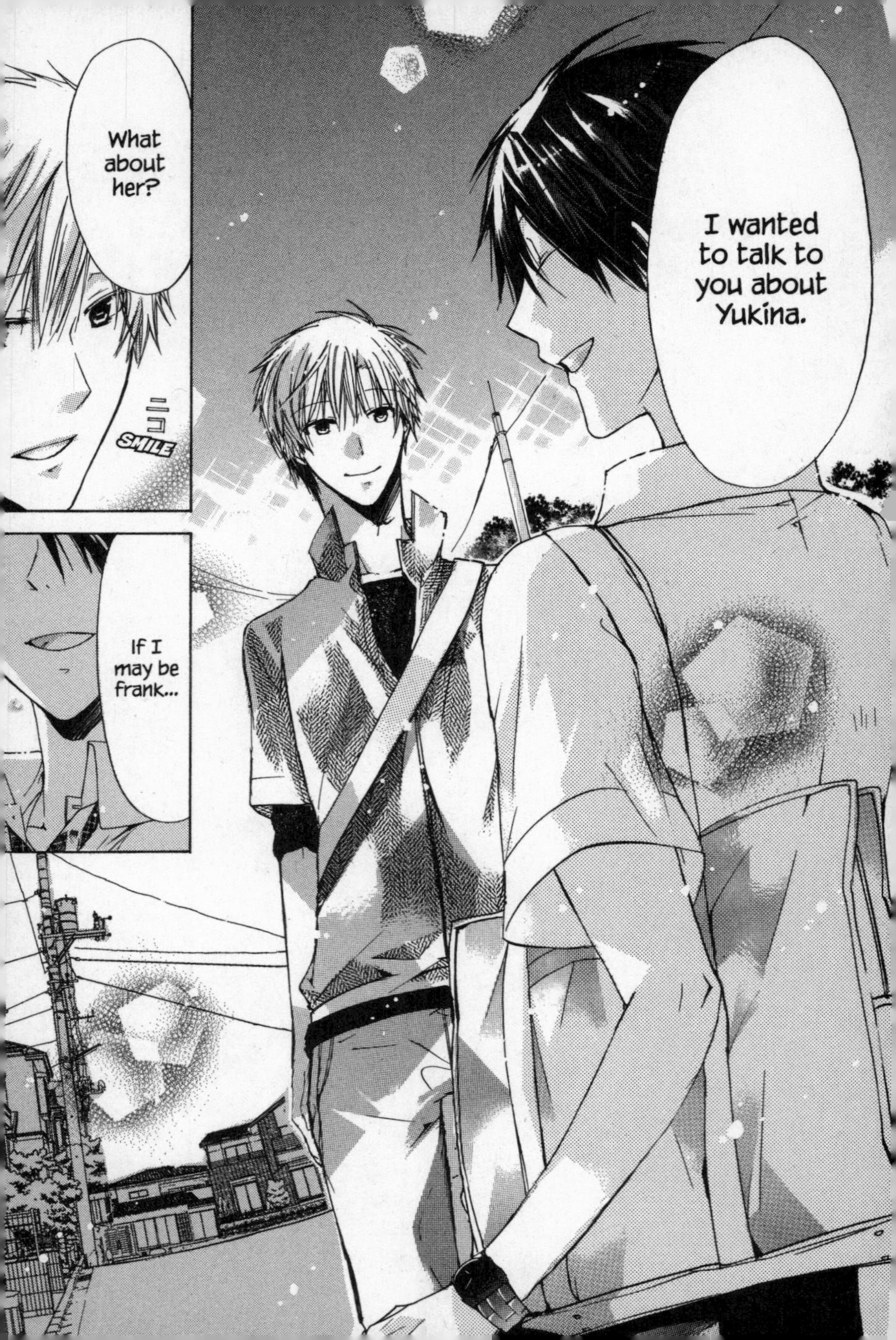
I wanted to talk to you about Yukina.
What about her?
ニコ
SMILE
If I may be frank...

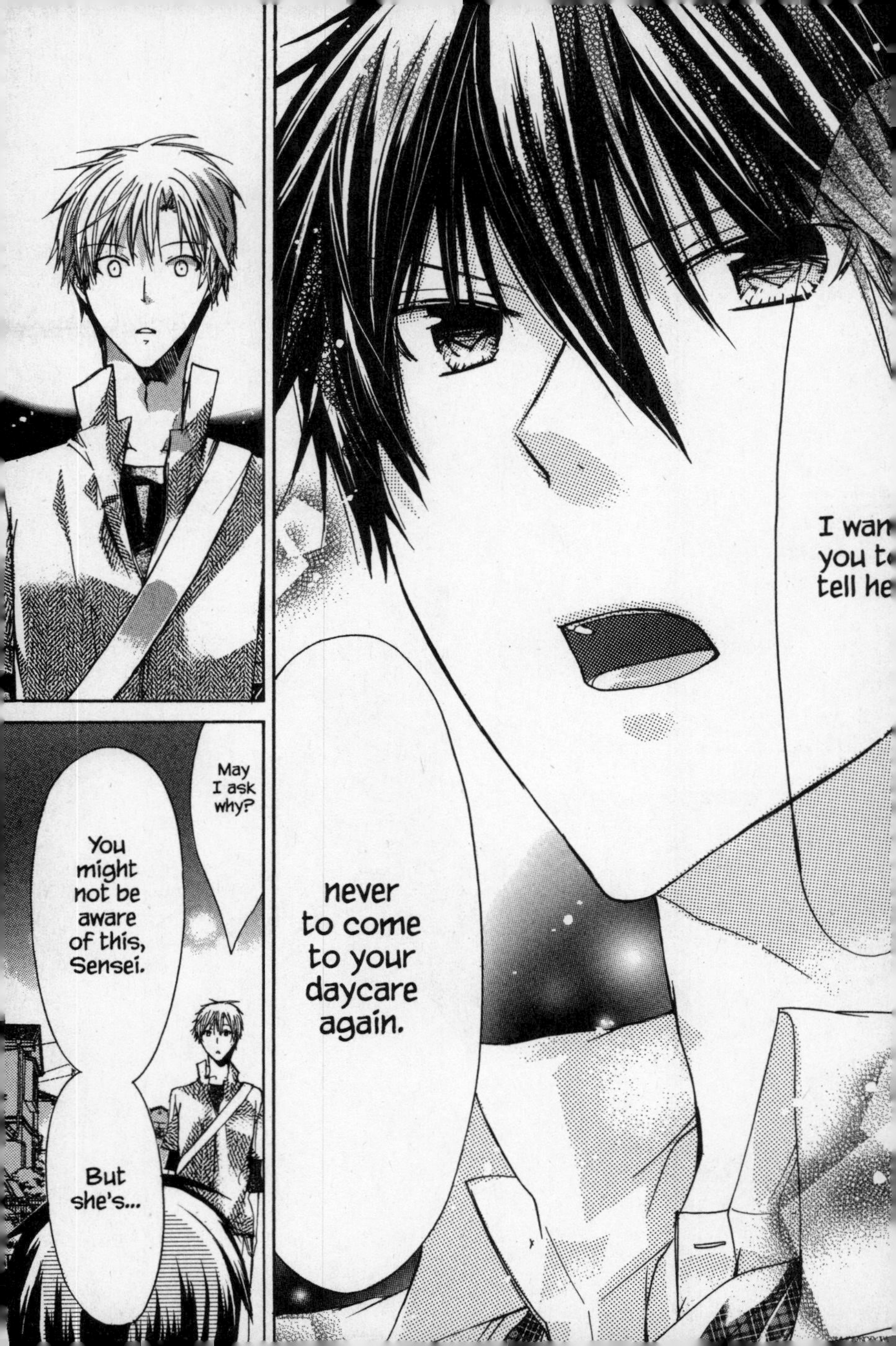
I wan you t tell he
never to come to your daycare again.
May I ask why?
You might not be aware of this, Sensei.
But she's...

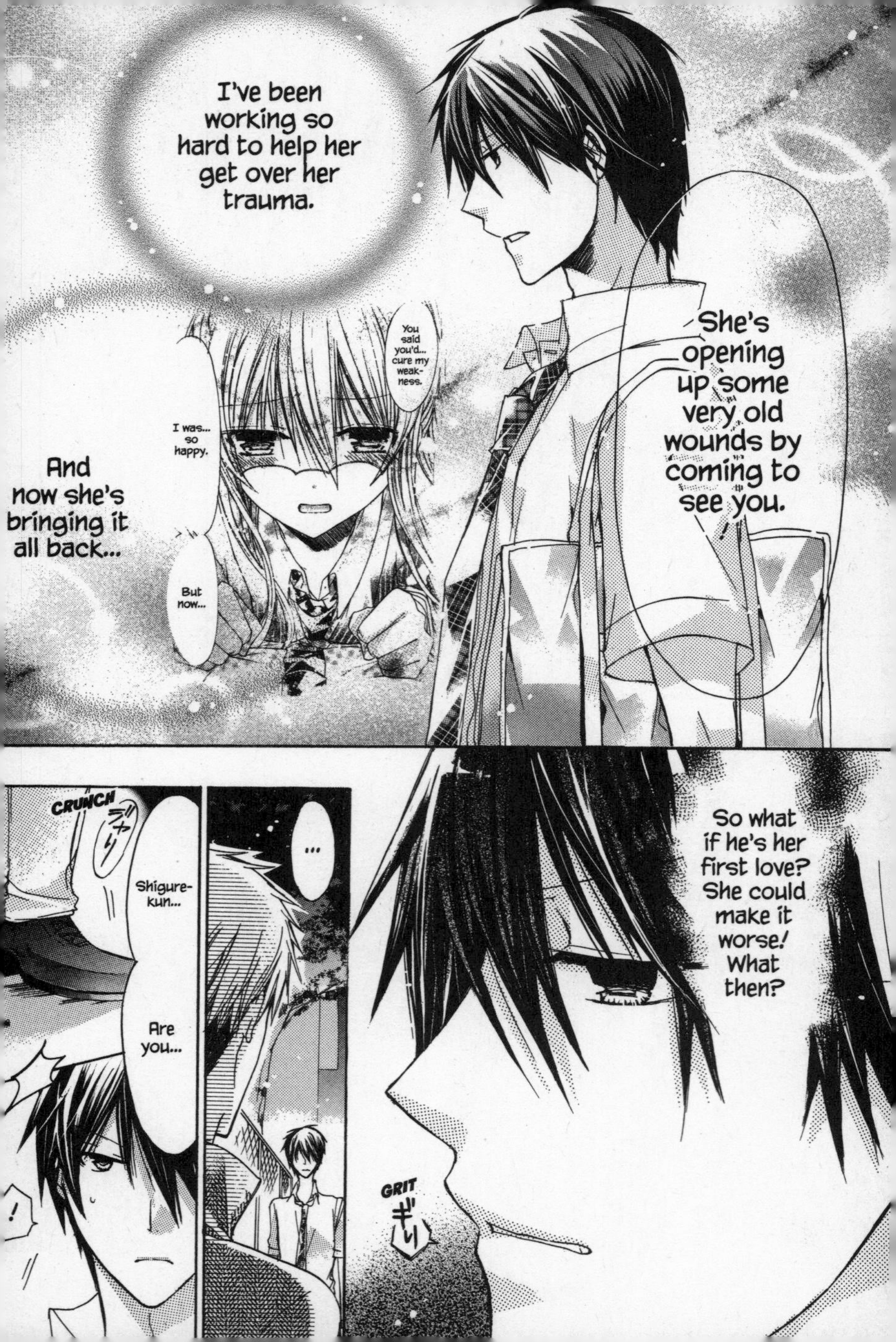
She's opening up some very old wounds by coming to see you.
I've been working so hard to help her get over her trauma.
You said you'd... cure my weak-ness.
I was... so happy.
And now she's bringing it all back...
But now...
So what if he's her first love? She could make it worse! What then?
GRIT
ギリ
...
CRUNCH
ジャリ
Shigure-kun...
Are you...
!

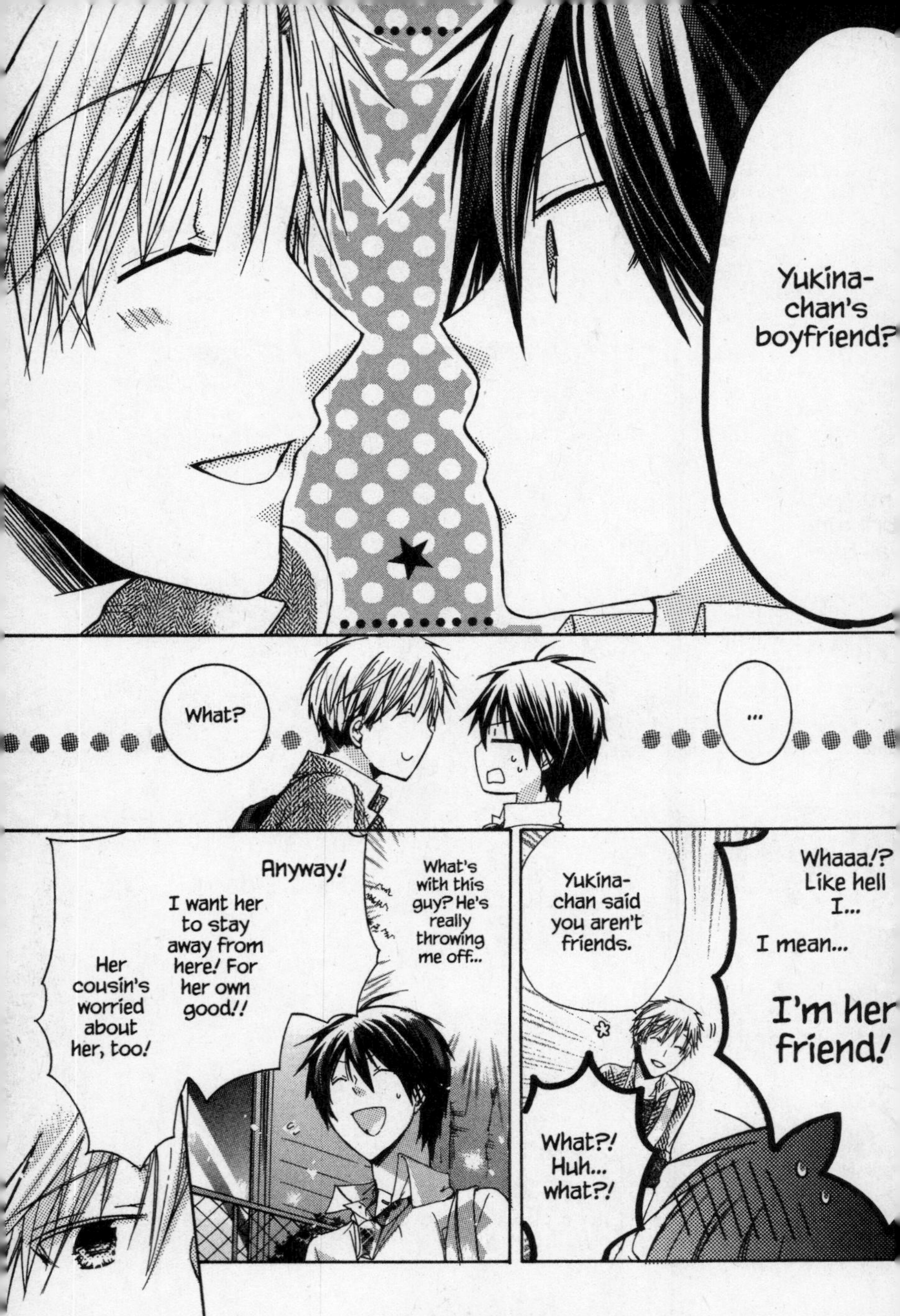
Yukina-chan's boyfriend?
...
What?
Whaaa!? Like hell I...
I mean...
I'm her friend!
Yukina-chan said you aren't friends.
What?! Huh... what?!
What's with this guy? He's really throwing me off...
Anyway!
I want her to stay away from here! For her own good!!
Her cousin's worried about her, too!

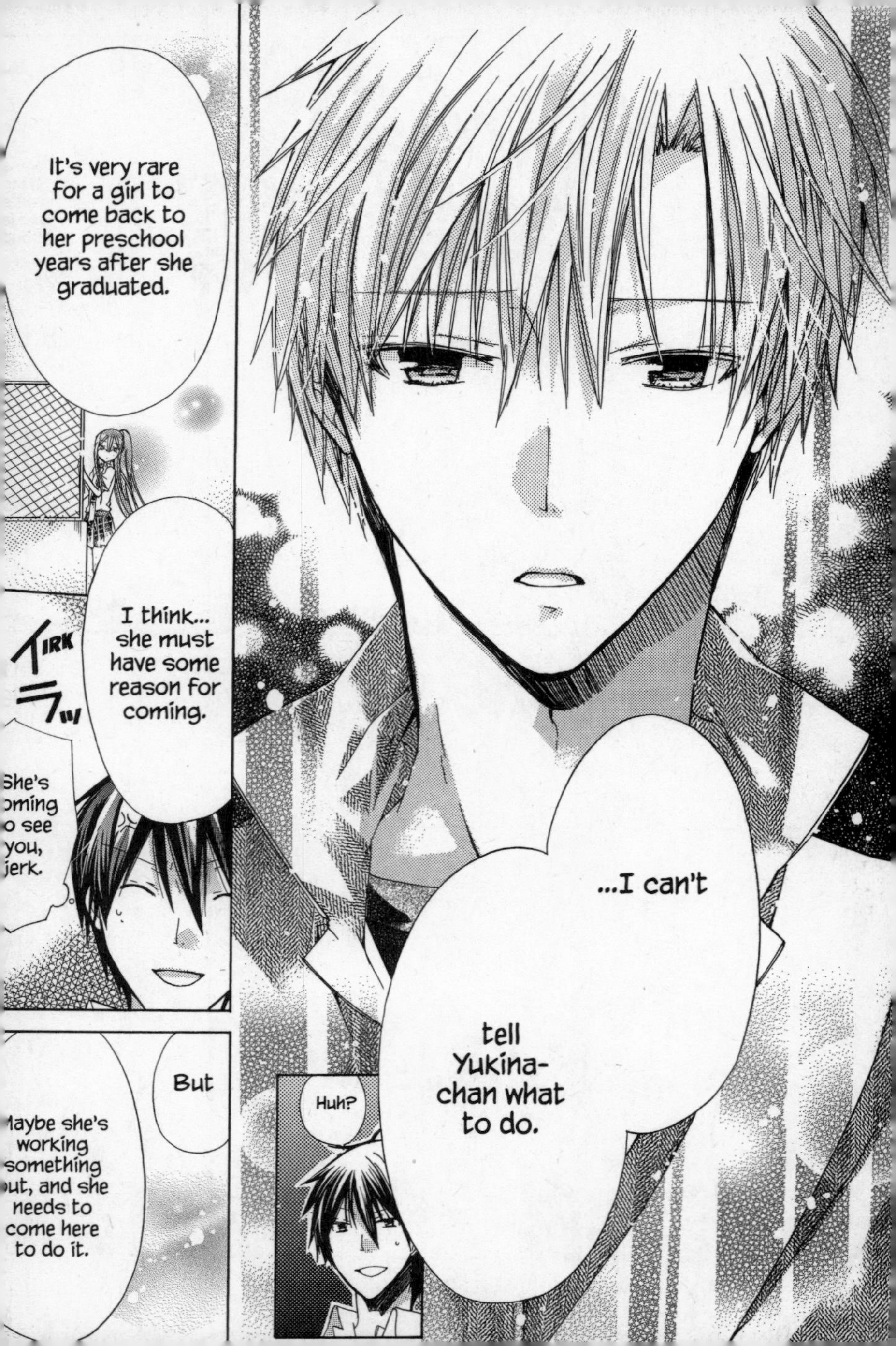

...I can't
tell Yukina-chan what to do.
Huh?
It's very rare for a girl to come back to her preschool years after she graduated.
I think... she must have some reason for coming.
TIRK
She's oming o see you, jerk.
But
laybe she's working something ut, and she needs to come here to do it.

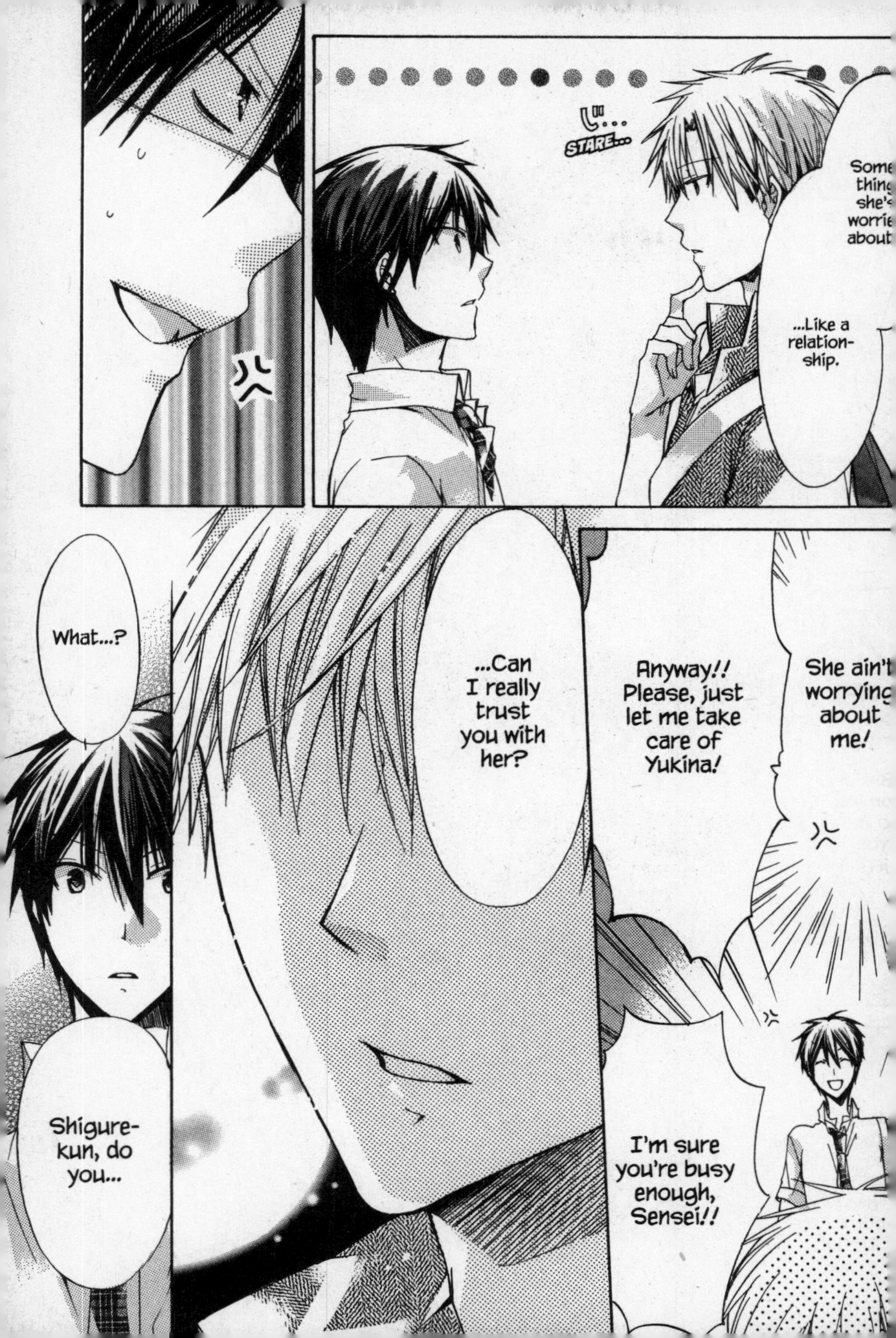
じ...
STARE...
Some thing she's worrie about
...Like a relationship.
She ain't worrying about me!
Anyway!! Please, just let me take care of Yukina!
I'm sure you're busy enough, Sensei!!
...Can I really trust you with her?
What...?
Shigure-kun, do you...

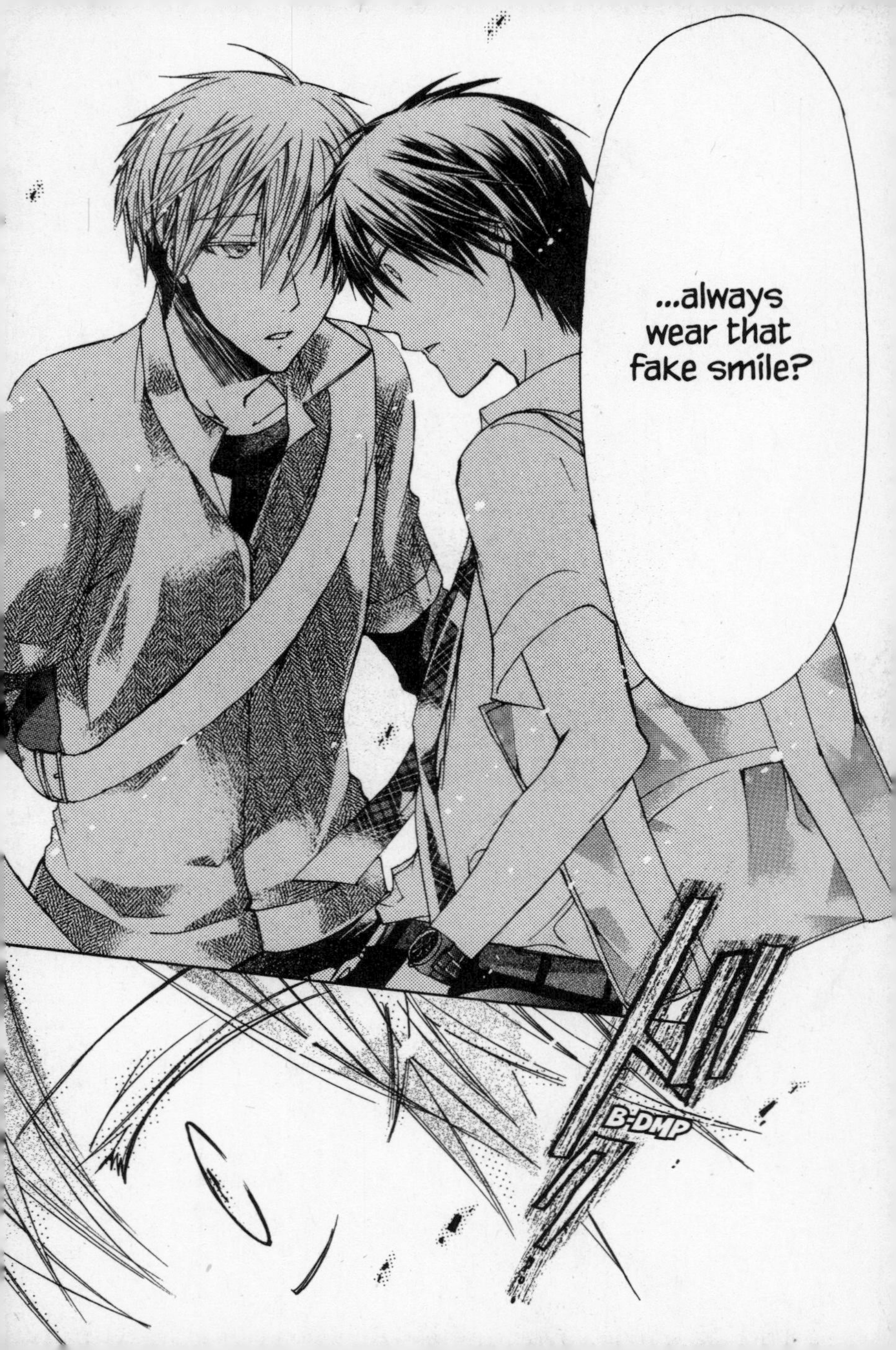
...always wear that fake smile?
B-DMP

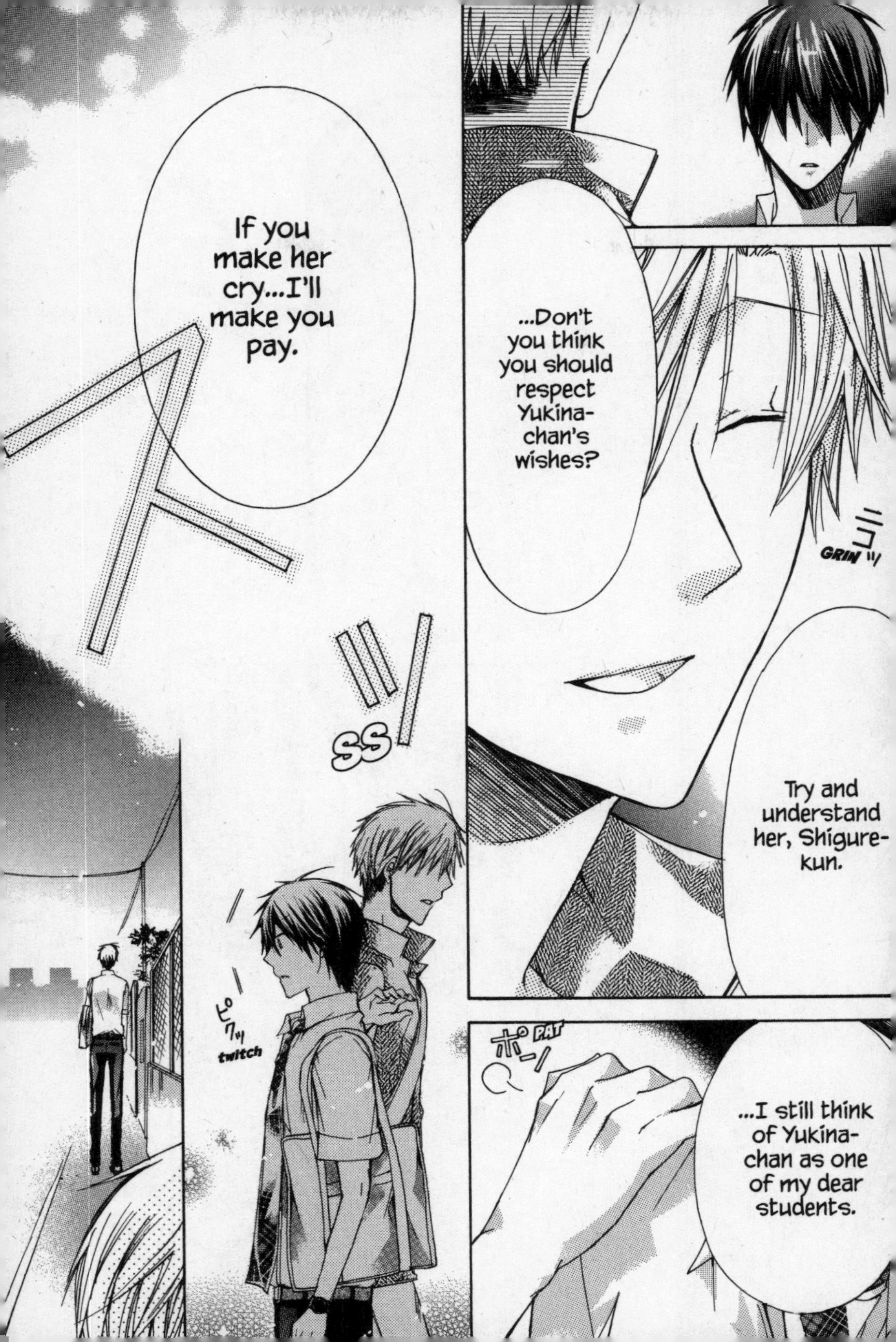
...Don't you think you should respect Yukina-chan's wishes?
GRIN
Try and understand her, Shigure-kun.
PAT
...I still think of Yukina-chan as one of my dear students.
If you make her cry...I'll make you pay.
SS
twitch

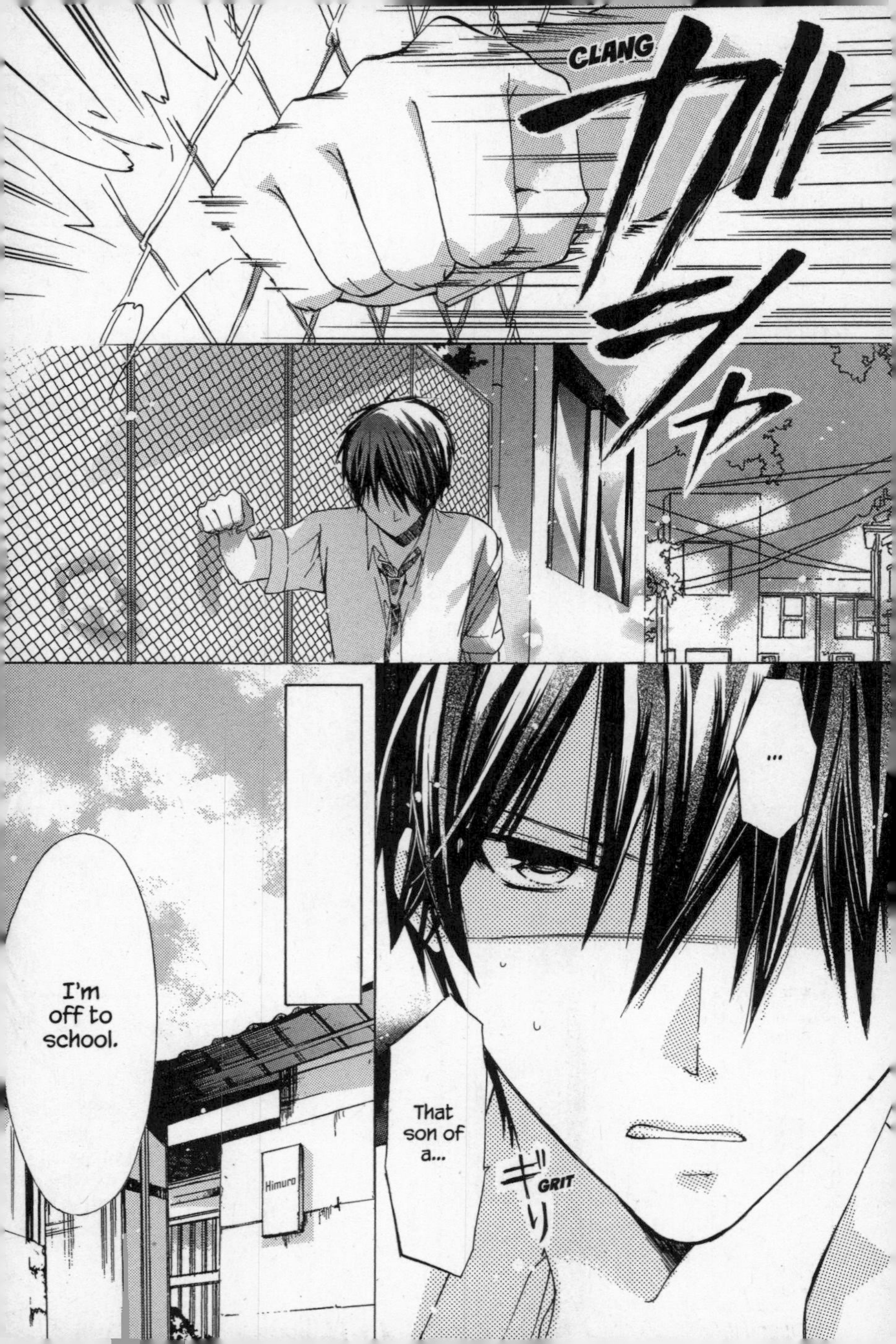
CLANG
...
That son of a...
GRIT
I'm off to school.
Himuro

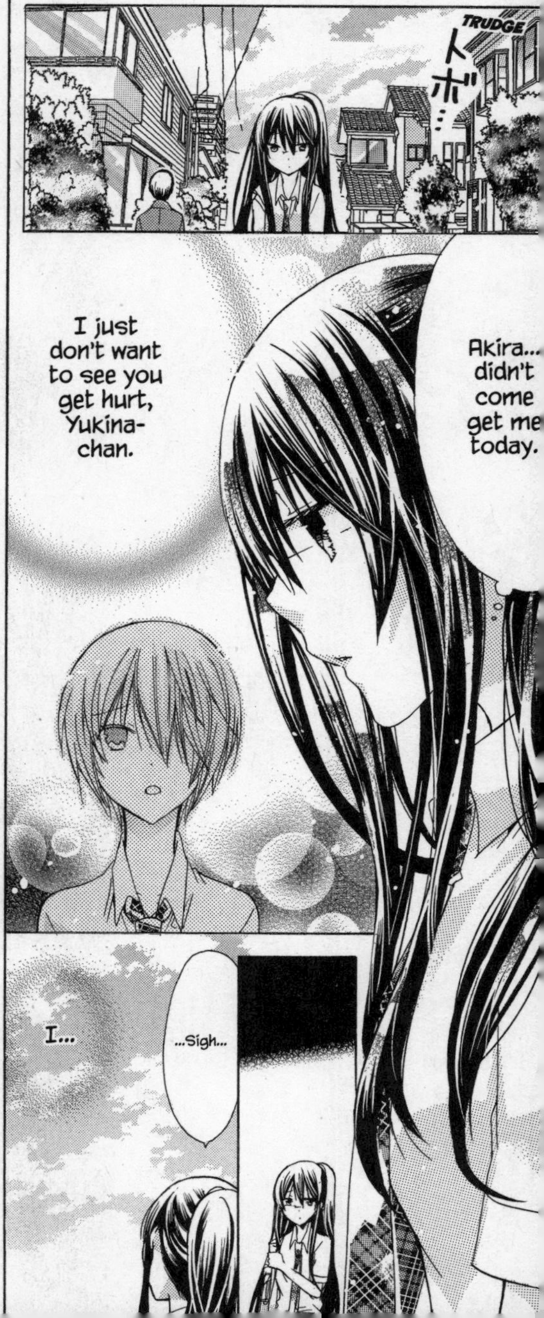
TRUDGE
トボ…
Akira... didn't come get me today.
I just don't want to see you get hurt, Yukina-chan.
...Sigh...
I...

The Secret of Staying Solid 4

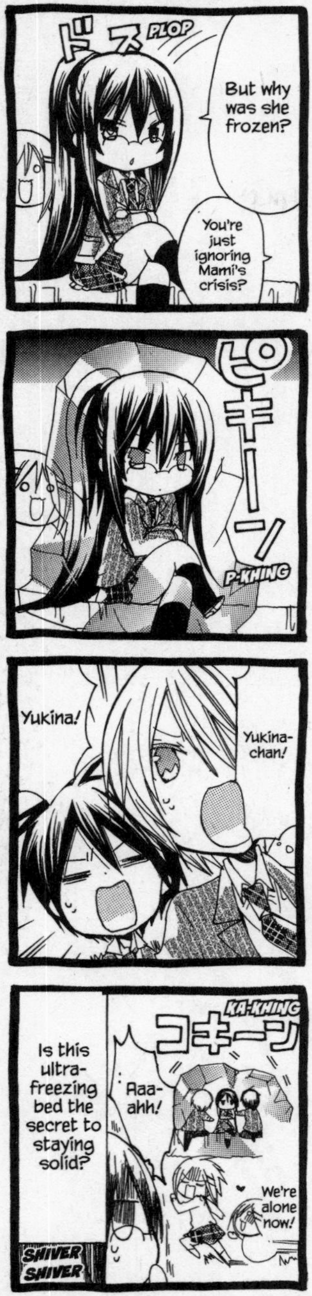
ドス
PLOP
But why was she frozen?
You're just ignoring Mami's crisis?
ピキーン
P-KHING
Yukina-chan!
Yukina!
KA-KHING
コキーン
Is this ultra-freezing bed the secret to staying solid?
Aaa-ahh!
We're alone now!
SHIVER SHIVER

In the midst of this chaos... To be continued!!

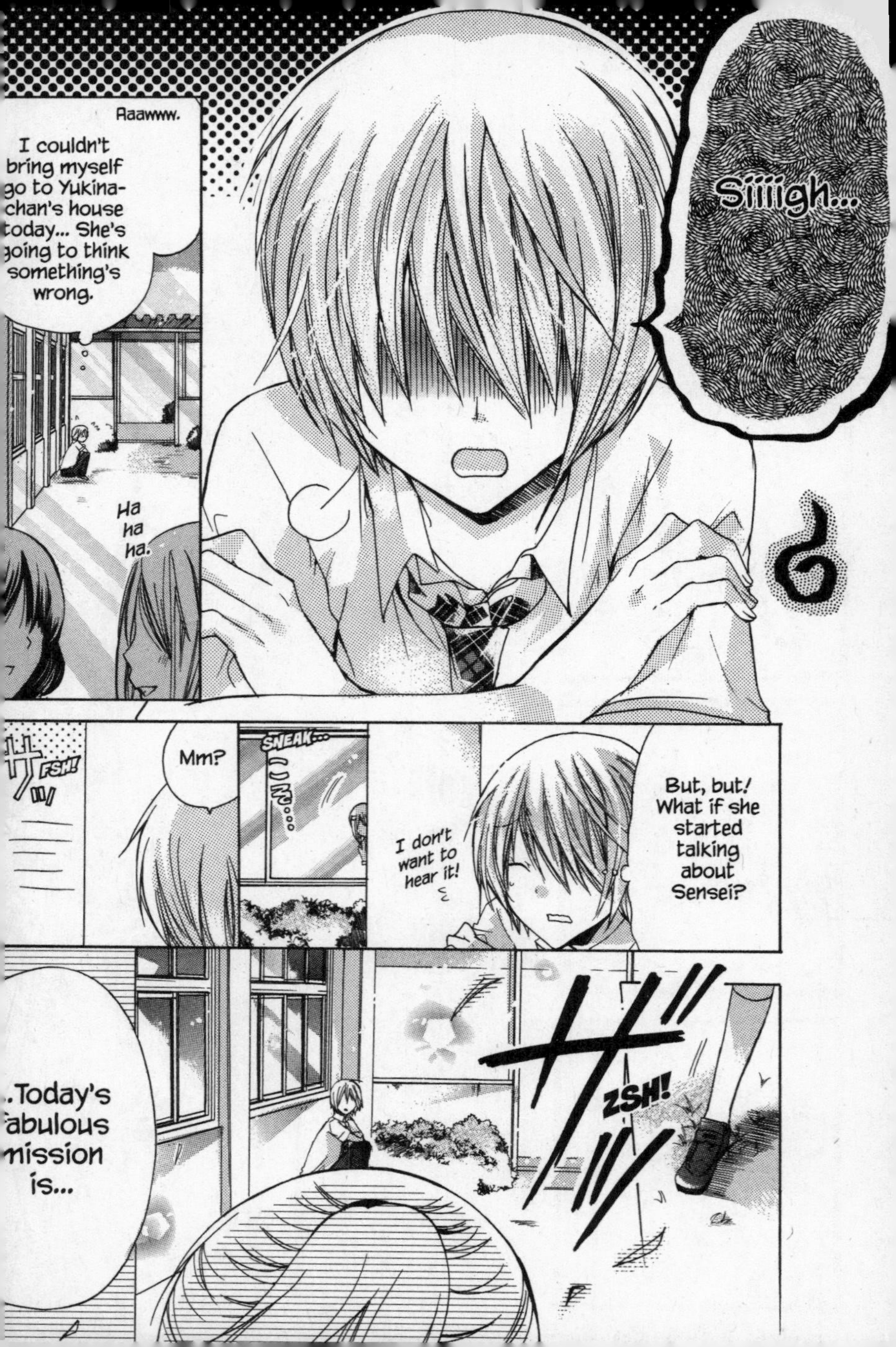
Siiiigh...
Raawww.
I couldn't bring myself go to Yukina-chan's house today... She's going to think something's wrong.
Ha ha ha.
But, but! What if she started talking about Sensei?
I don't want to hear it!
SNEAK...
Mm?
FSH!
ZSH!
..Today's fabulous mission is...

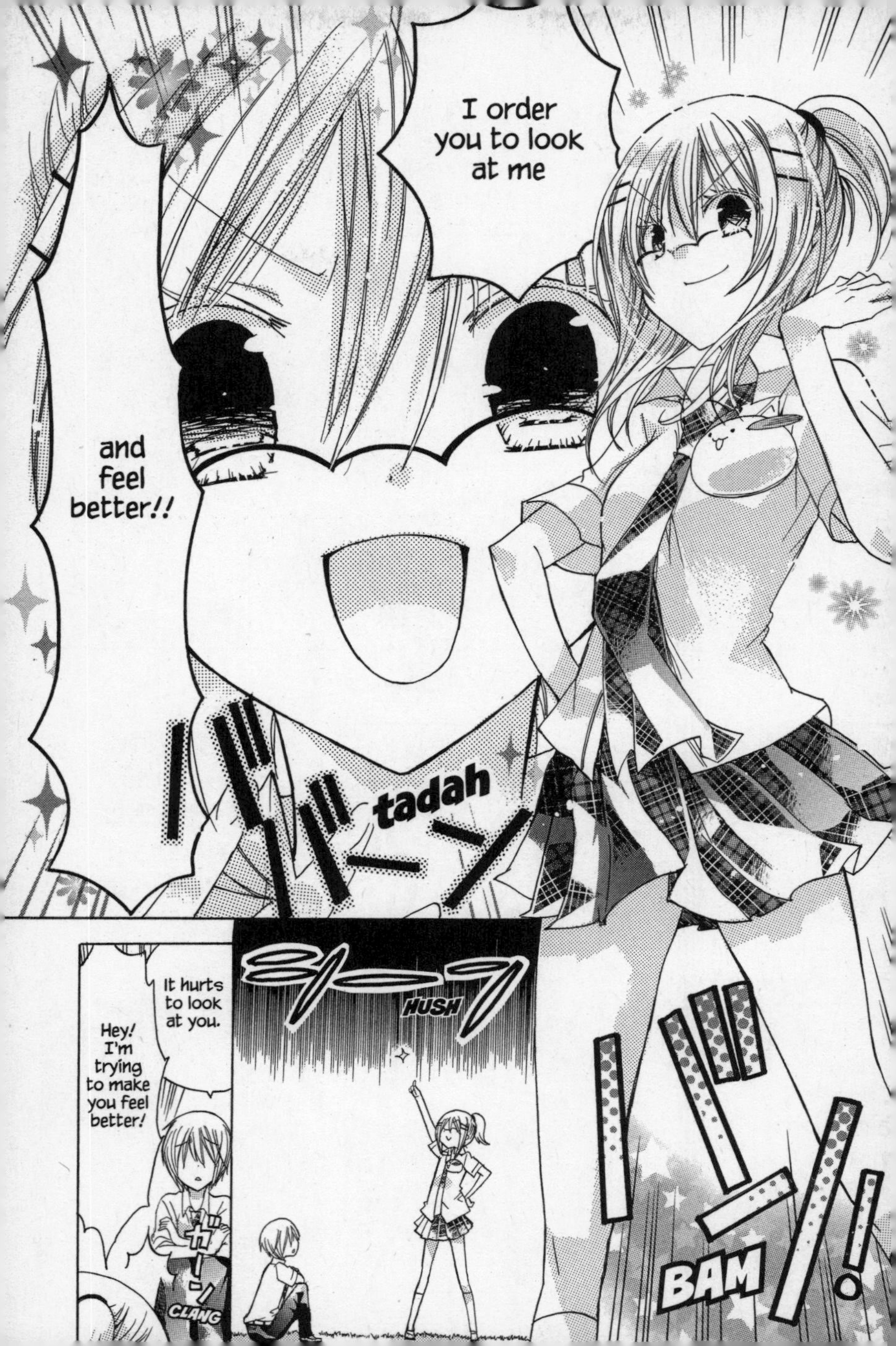
I order you to look at me
and feel better!!
tadah
BAM
HUSH
It hurts to look at you.
Hey! I'm trying to make you feel better!
CLANG

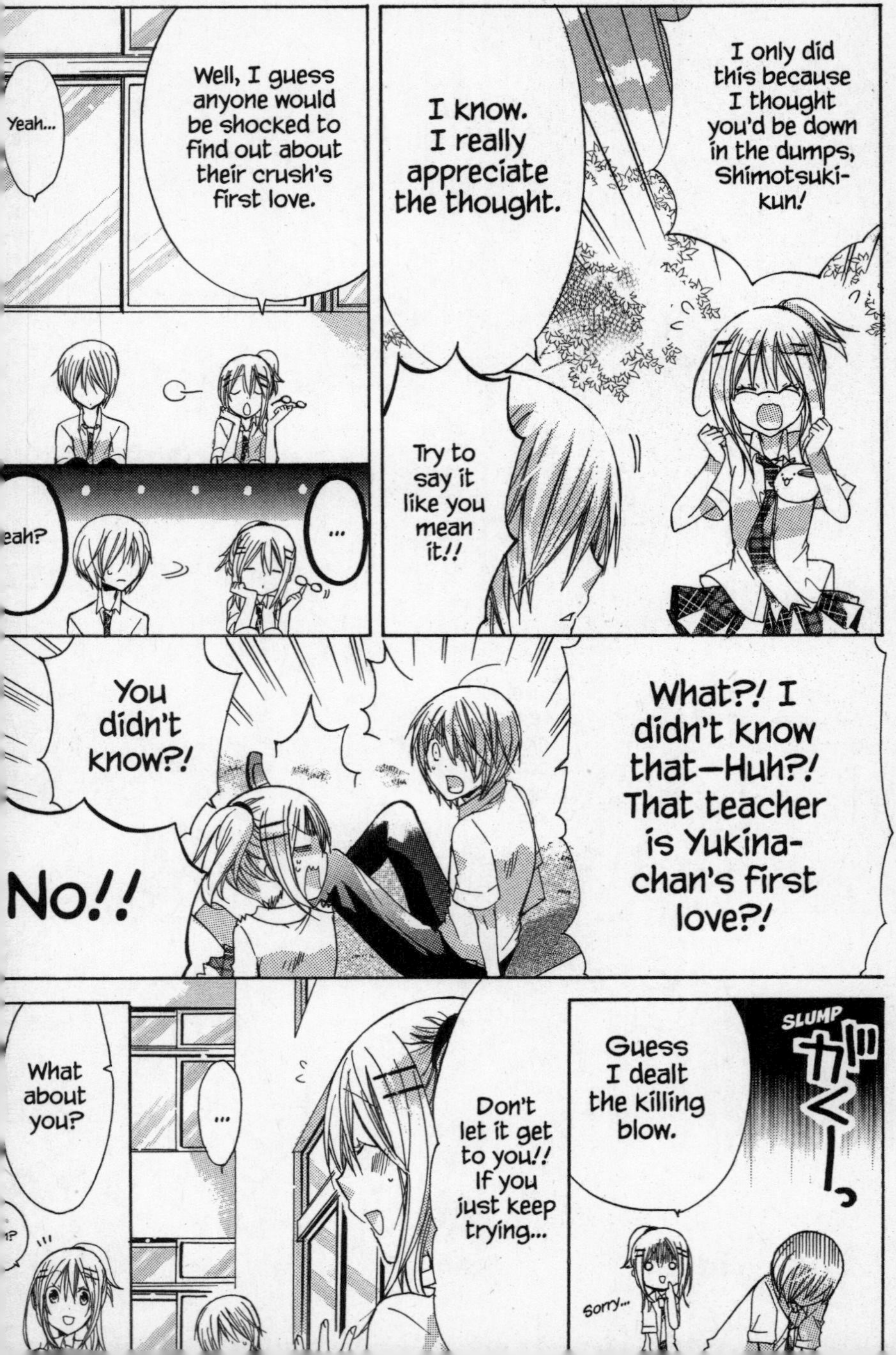
I only did this because I thought you'd be down in the dumps, Shimotsuki-kun!
I know. I really appreciate the thought.
Try to say it like you mean it!!
Well, I guess anyone would be shocked to find out about their crush's first love.
Yeah...
...
eah?
What?! I didn't know that—Huh?! That teacher is Yukina-chan's first love?!
You didn't know?!
No!!
SLUMP
がくーっ
Guess I dealt the killing blow.
Sorry...
Don't let it get to you!! If you just keep trying...
...
What about you?

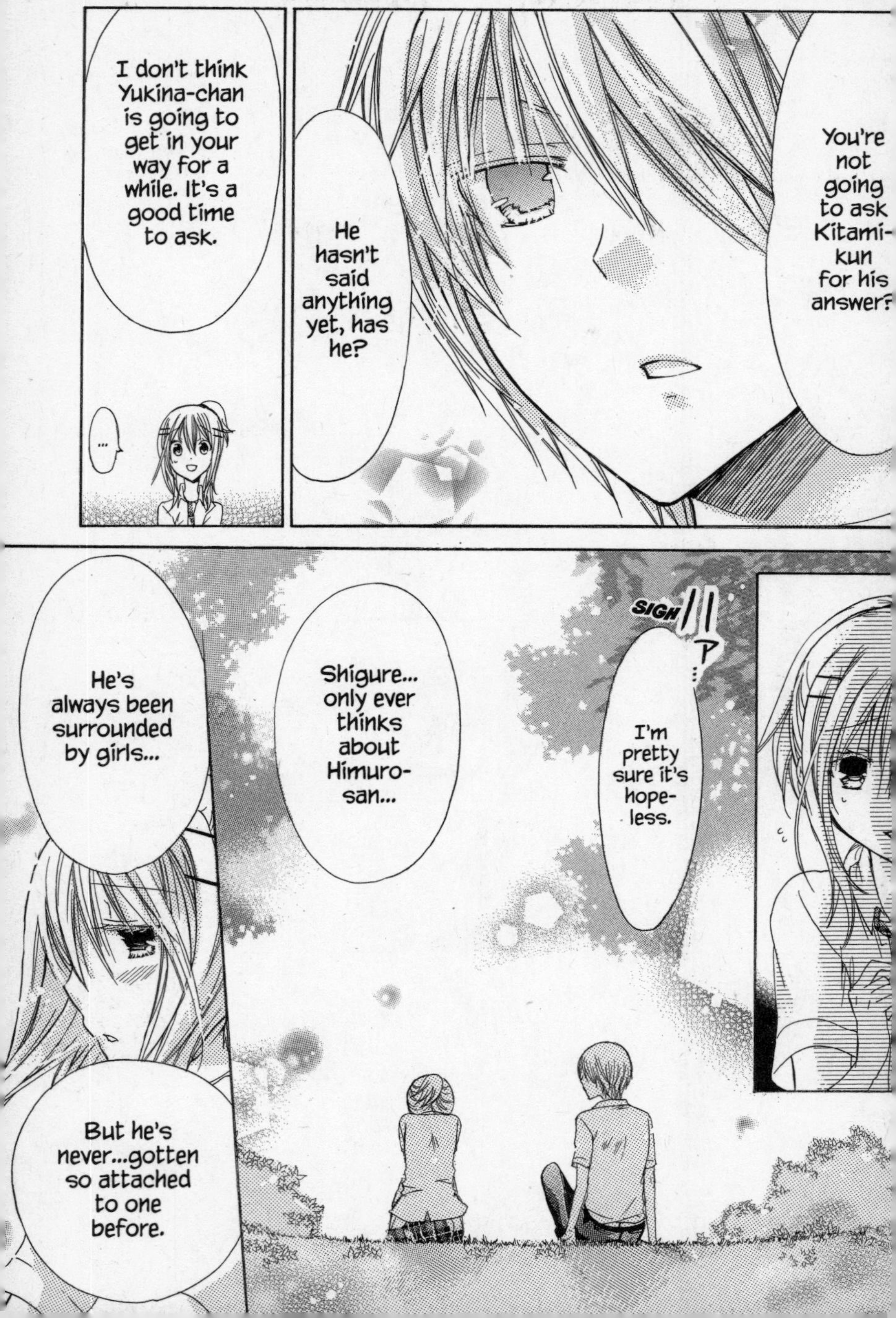
You're not going to ask Kitami-kun for his answer?
He hasn't said anything yet, has he?
I don't think Yukina-chan is going to get in your way for a while. It's a good time to ask.
...
SIGH
I'm pretty sure it's hope-less.
Shigure... only ever thinks about Himuro-san...
He's always been surrounded by girls...
But he's never...gotten so attached to one before.

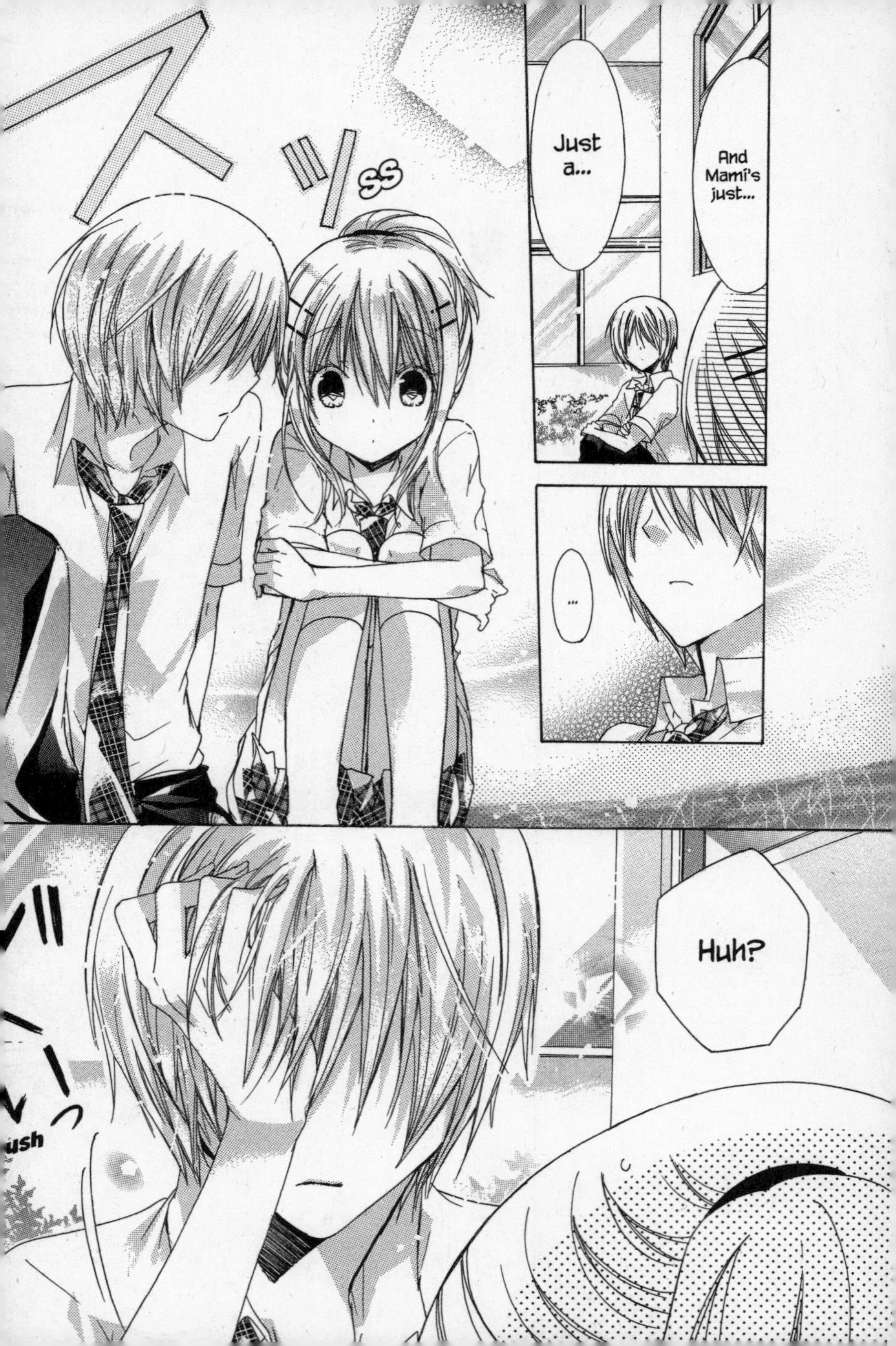
And Mami's just...
Just a...
...
SS
Huh?
ush

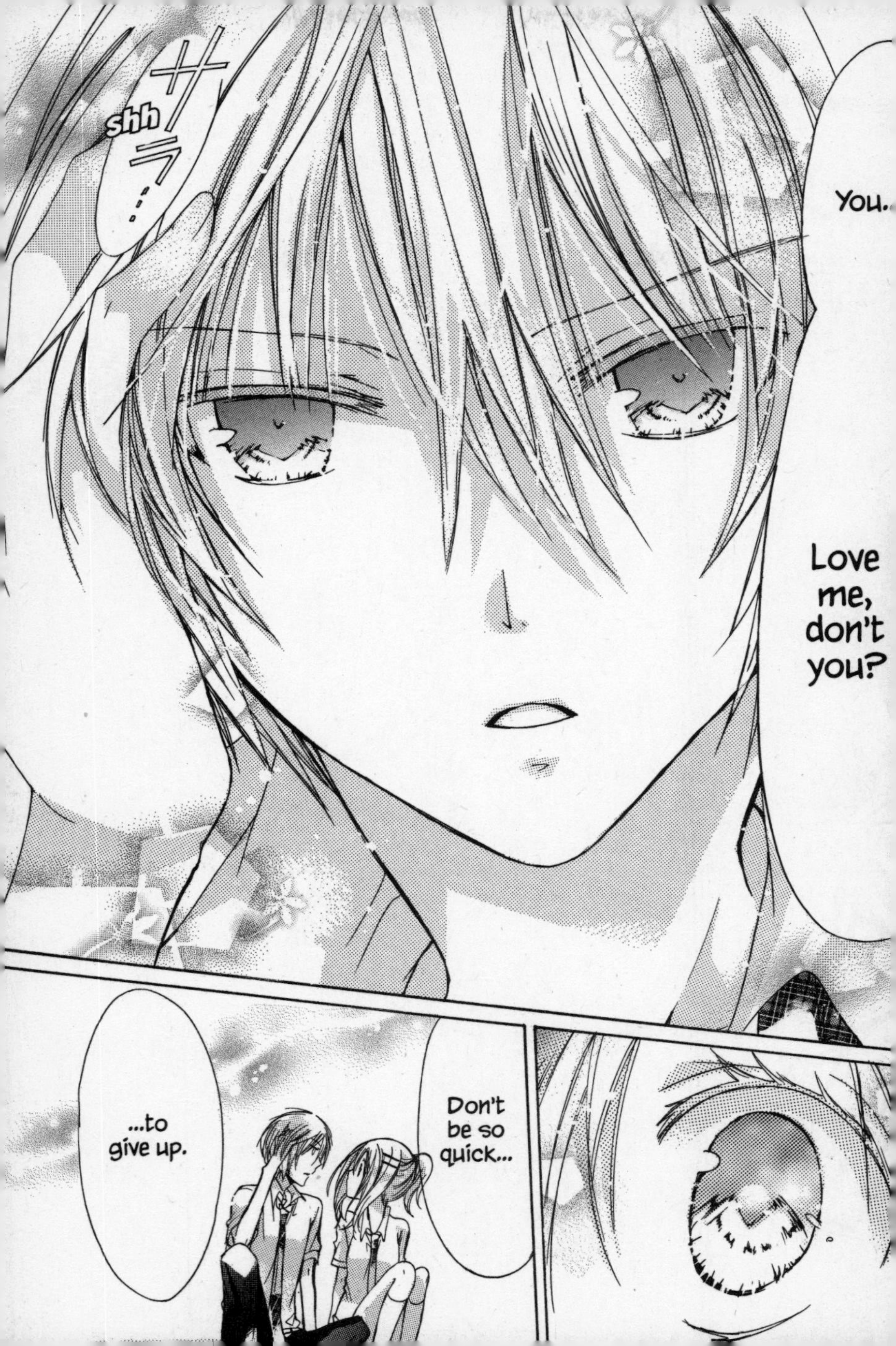

You.
Love me, don't you?
shh
サラ...
Don't be so quick...
...to give up.

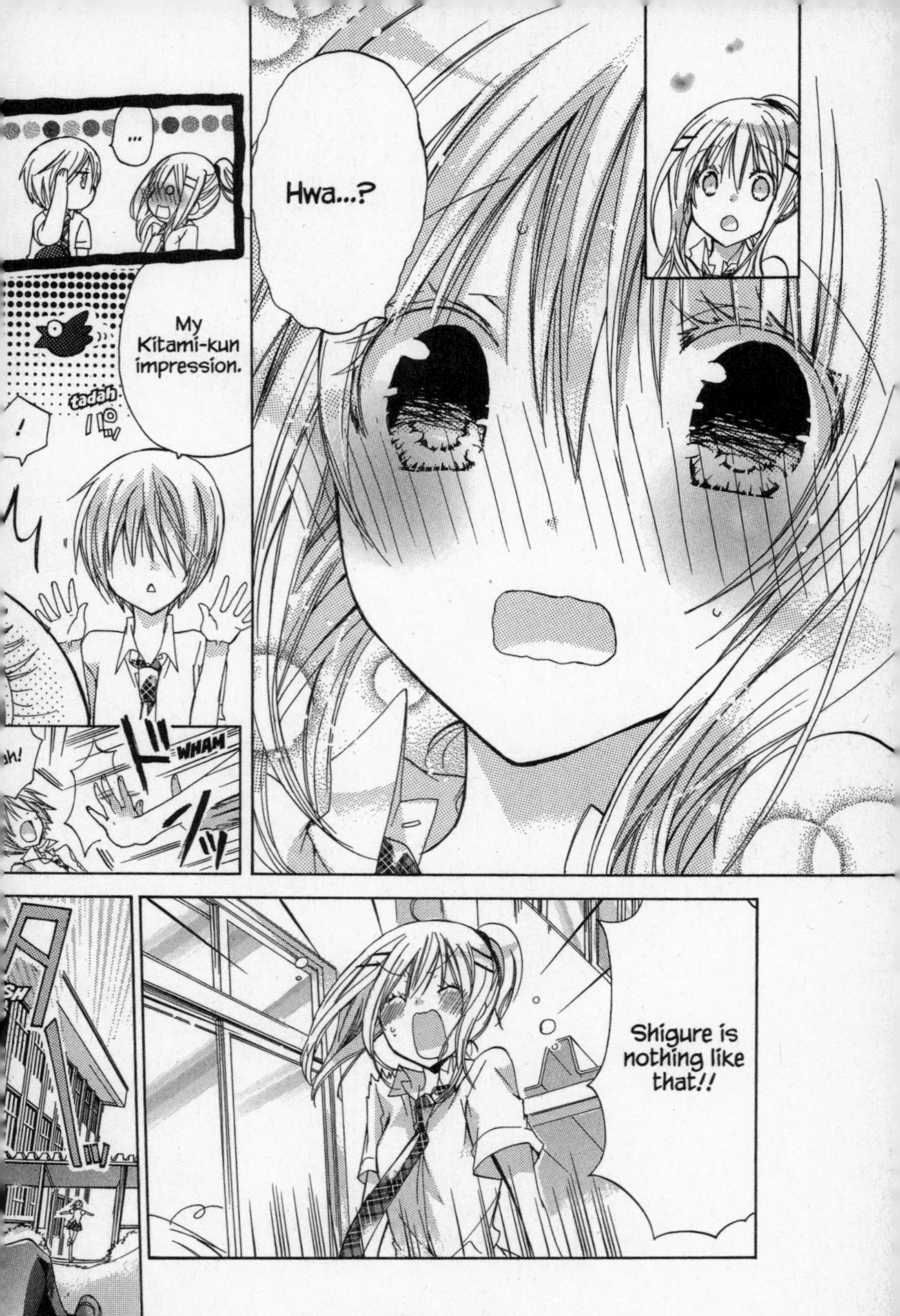
Hwa...?
...
My Kitami-kun impression.
tadah
!
WHAM
Shigure is nothing like that!!

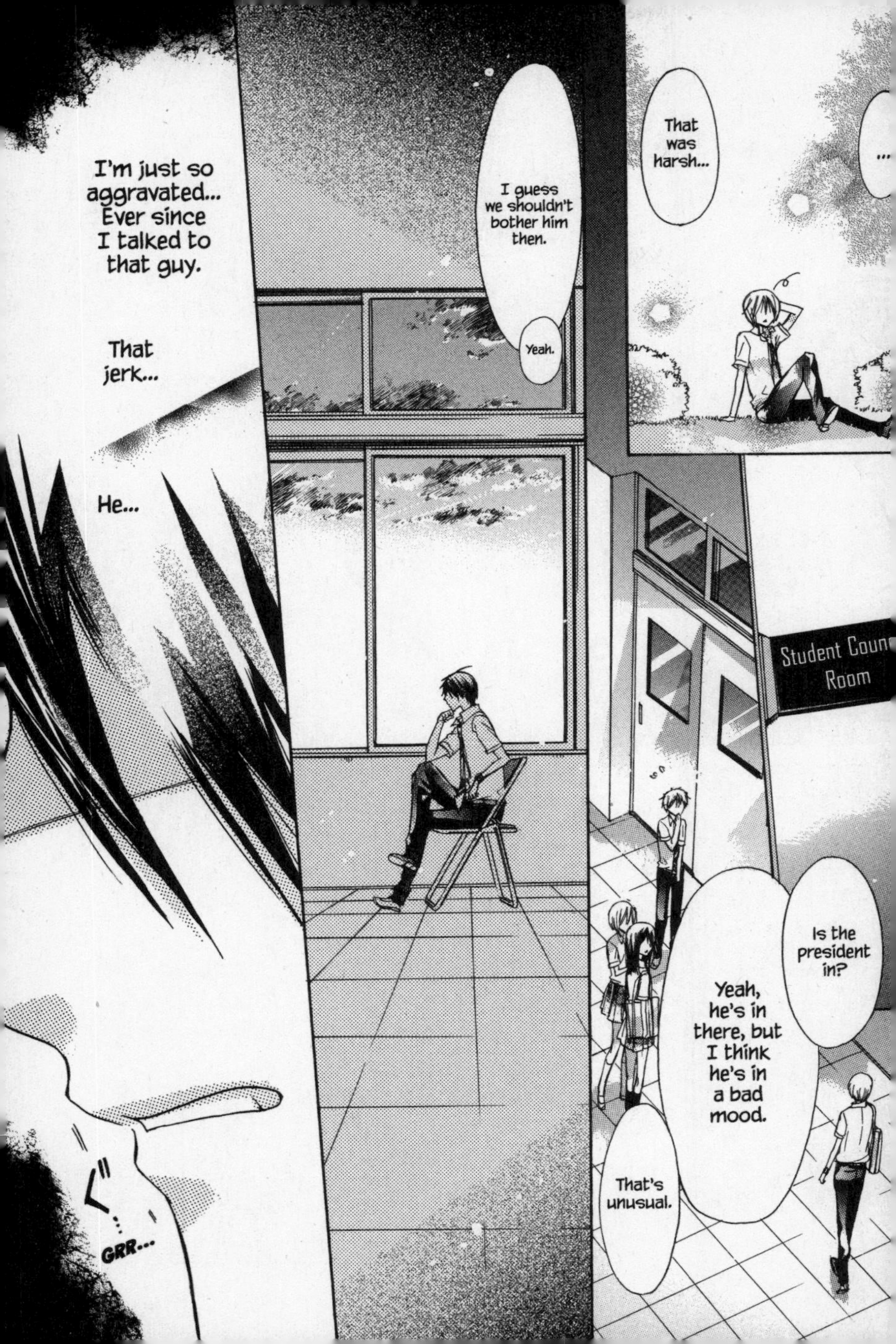
...
That was harsh...
Student Coun
Room
Is the president in?
Yeah, he's in there, but I think he's in a bad mood.
That's unusual.
I guess we shouldn't bother him then.
Yeah.
I'm just so aggravated... Ever since I talked to that guy.
That jerk...
He...
GRR...

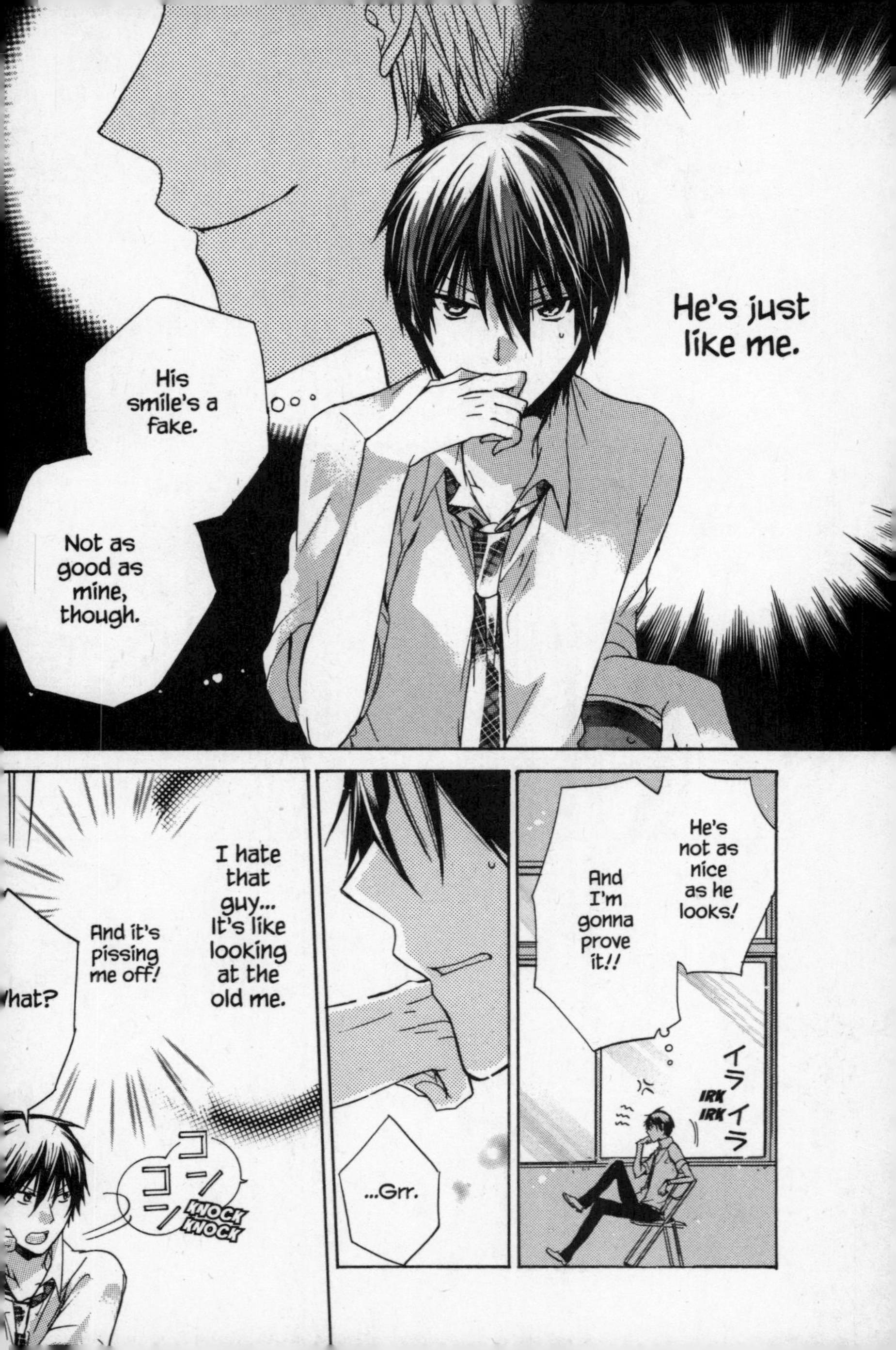
He's just like me.
His smile's a fake.
Not as good as mine, though.
He's not as nice as he looks!
And I'm gonna prove it!!
イライラ
IRK IRK
...Grr.
I hate that guy... It's like looking at the old me.
And it's pissing me off!
hat?
KNOCK KNOCK

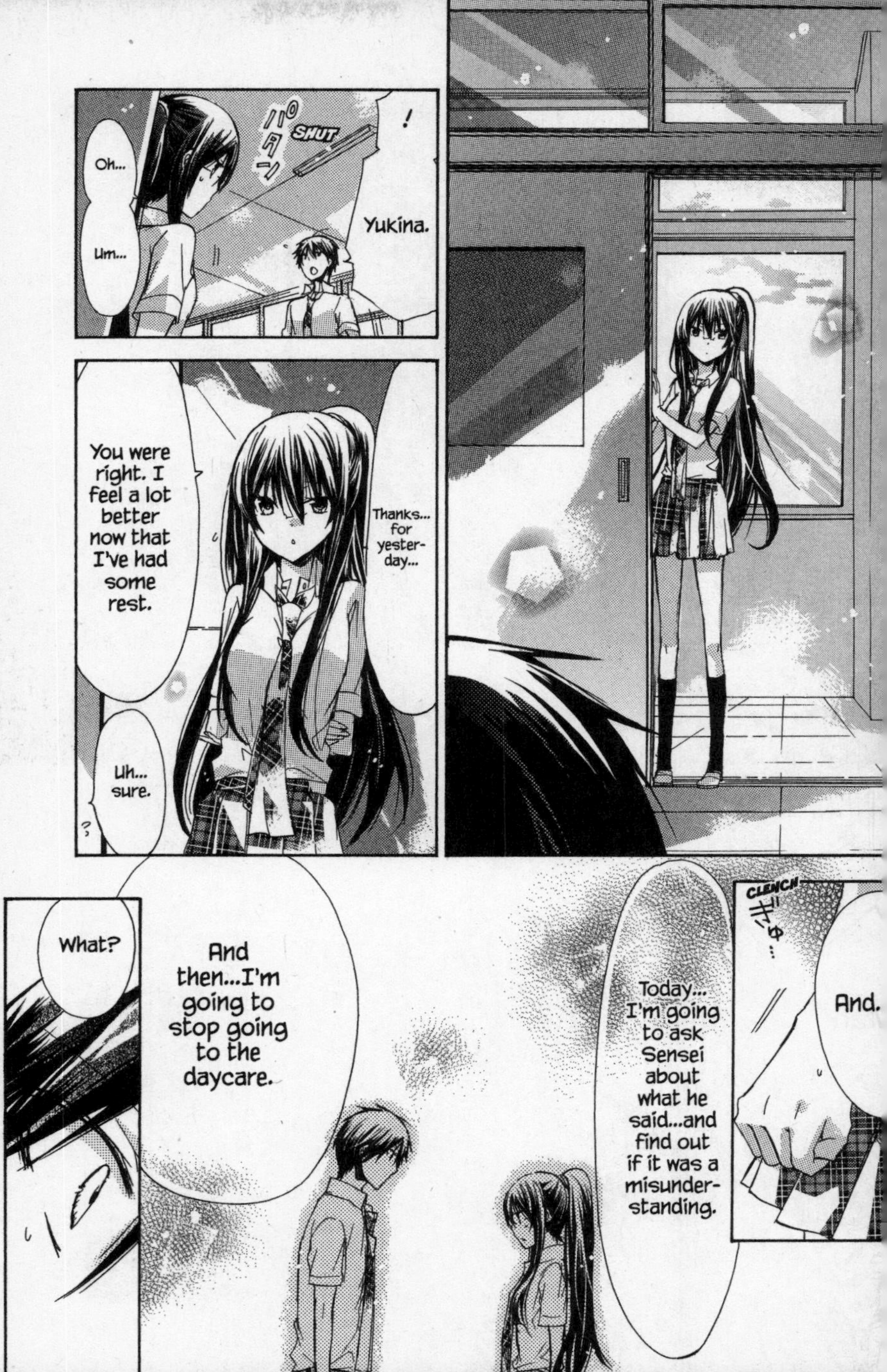
!
SHUT
パタン
Yukina.
Oh...
Um...
Thanks... for yester-day...
You were right. I feel a lot better now that I've had some rest.
Uh... sure.
CLENCH
ぎゅ...
And.
Today... I'm going to ask Sensei about what he said...and find out if it was a misunder-standing.
And then...I'm going to stop going to the daycare.
What?

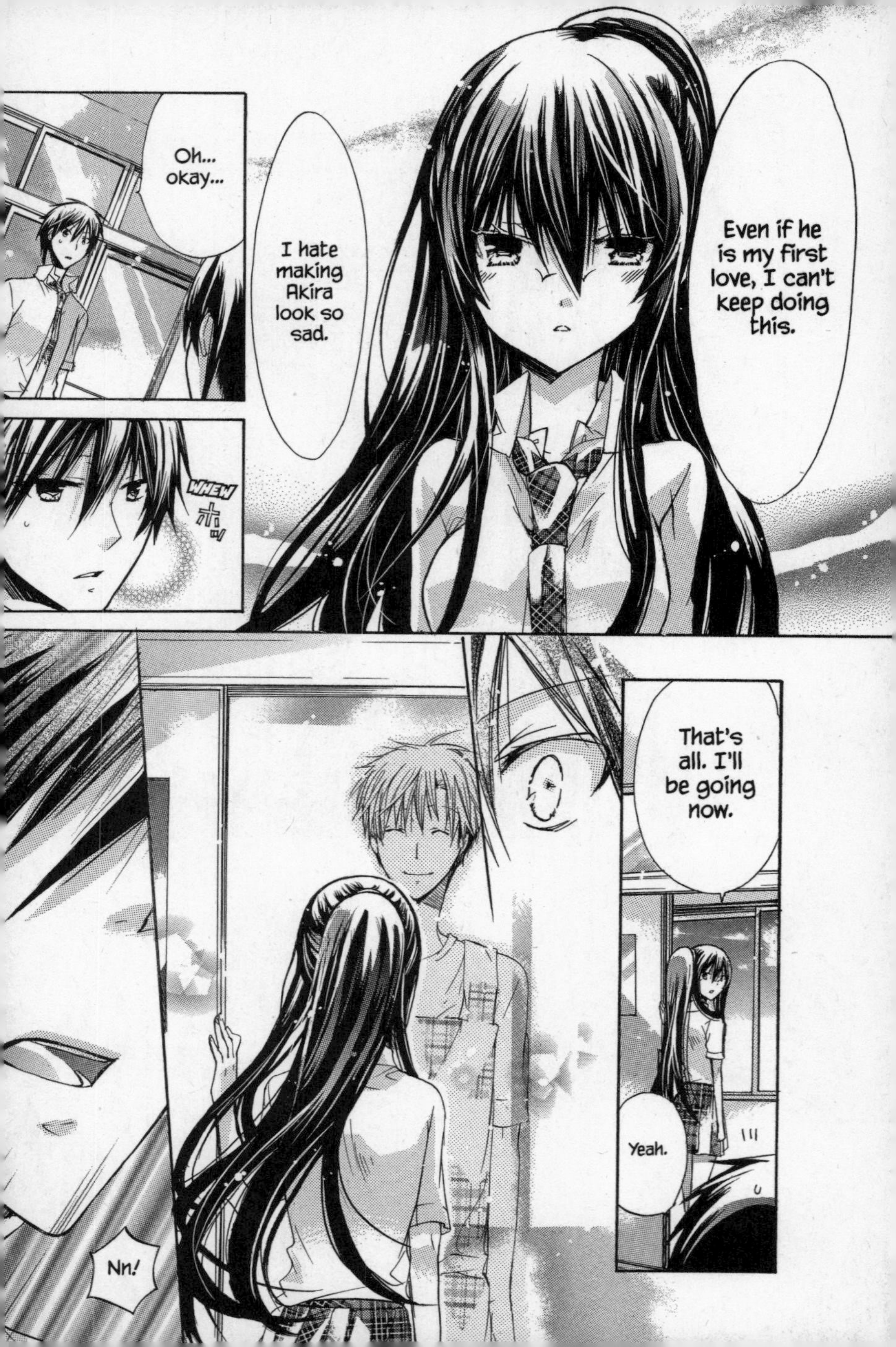
Even if he is my first love, I can't keep doing this.
I hate making Akira look so sad.
Oh... okay...
WHEW
ホッ
That's all. I'll be going now.
Yeah.
Nn!

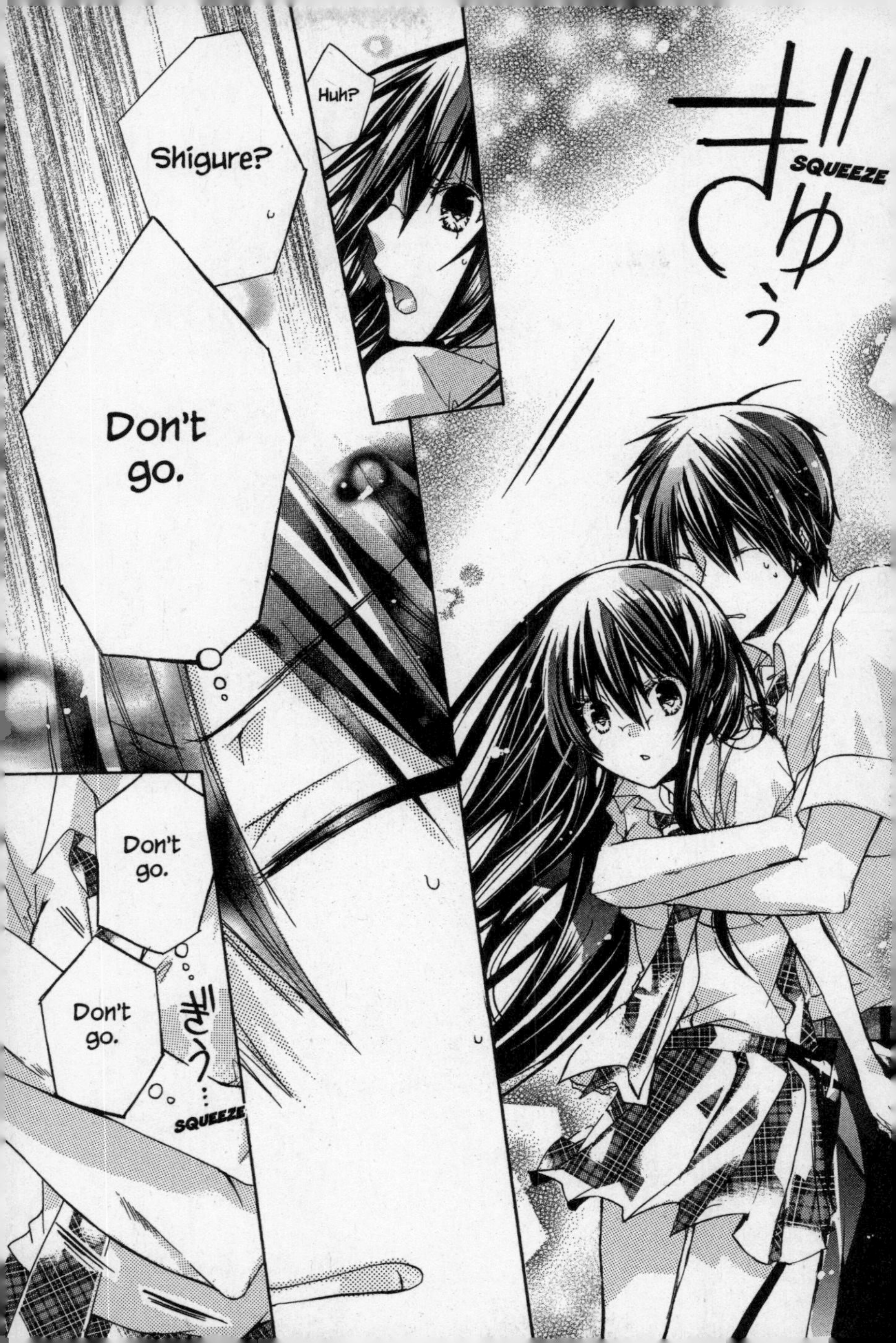

ぎゅう
SQUEEZE
Huh?
Shigure?
Don't go.
Don't go.
Don't go.
ぎゅう…
SQUEEZE

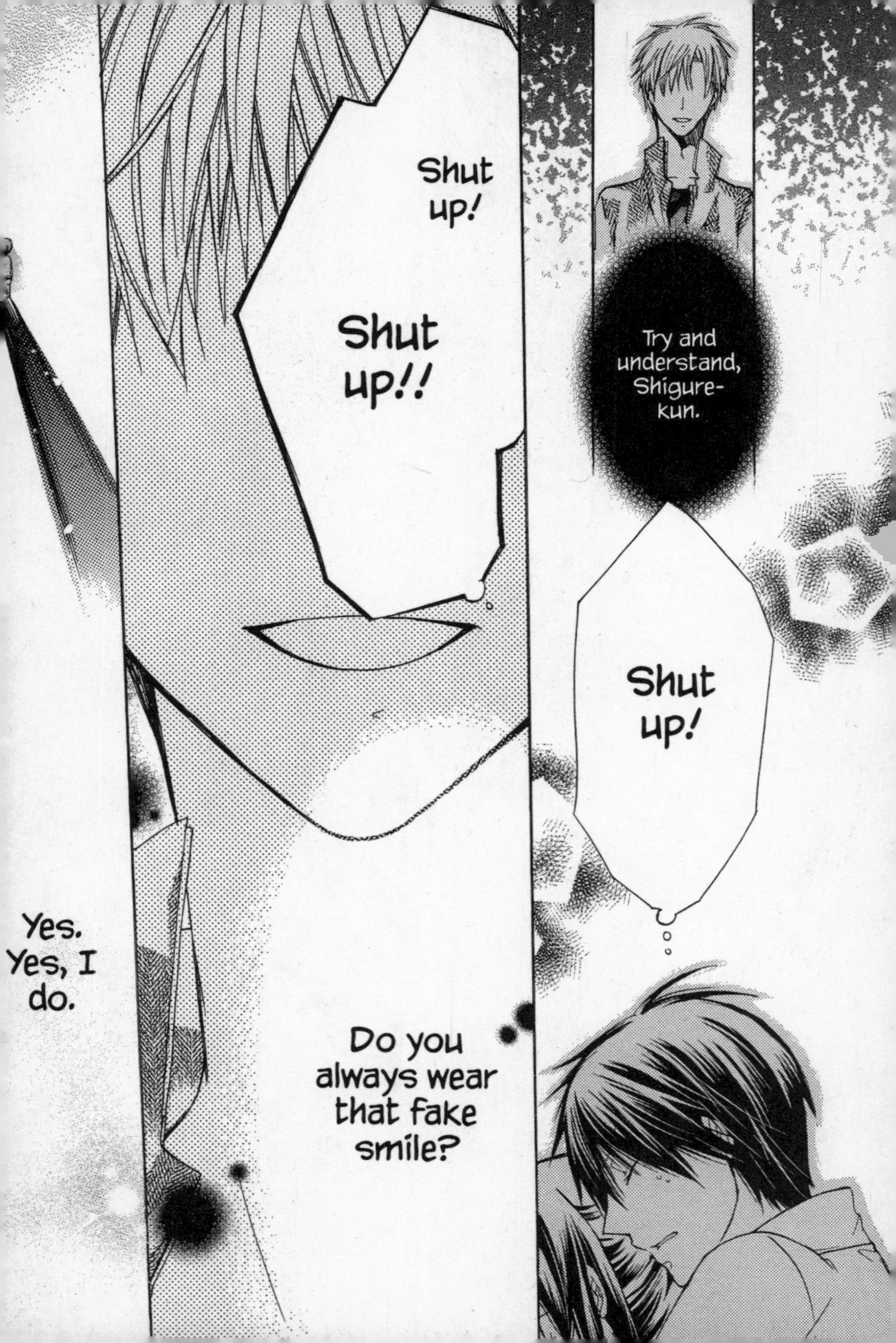
Try and understand, Shigure-kun.
Shut up!
Shut up!
Shut up!!
Do you always wear that fake smile?
Yes. Yes, I do.

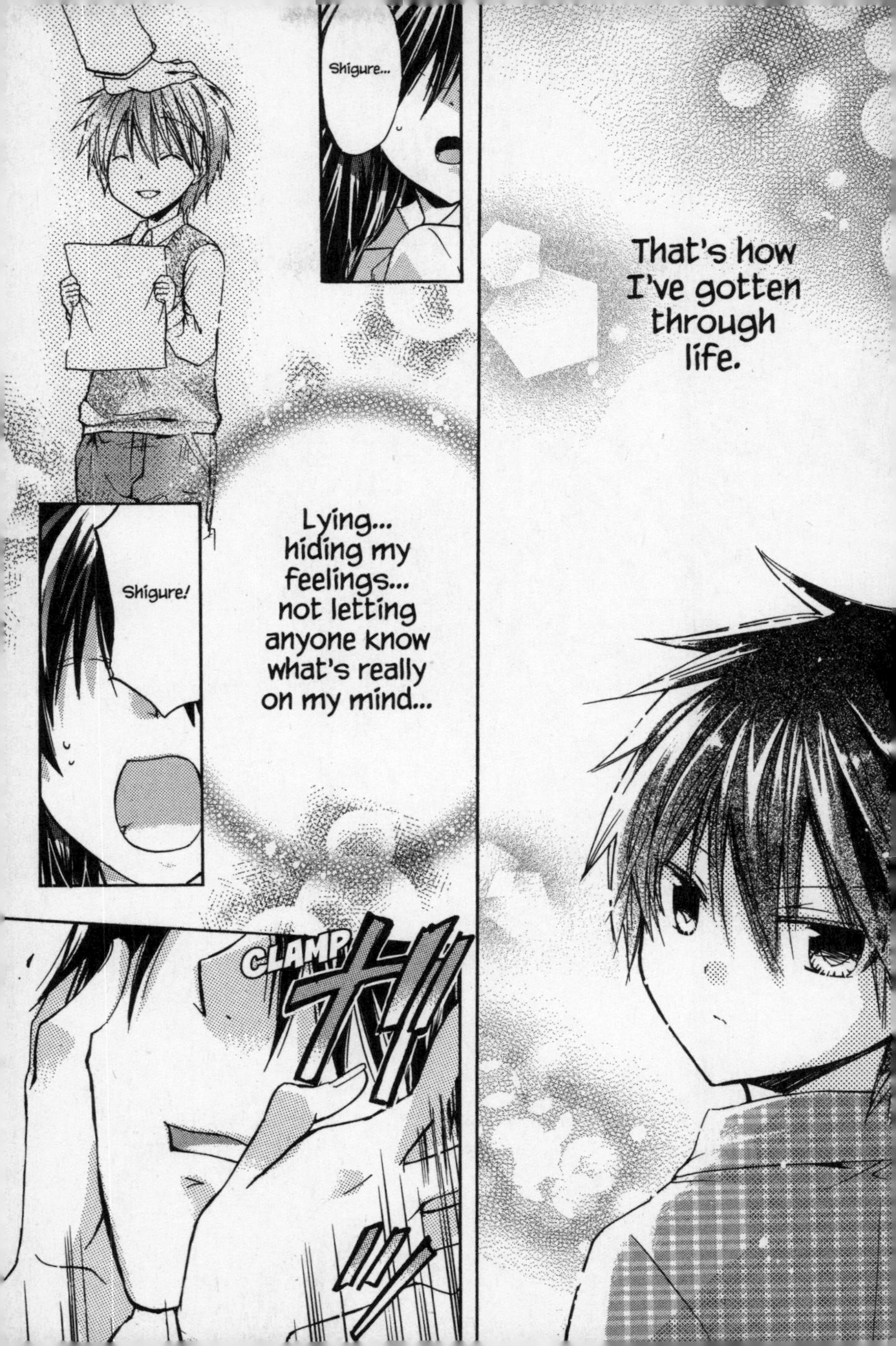
That's how I've gotten through life.
Shigure...
Lying... hiding my feelings... not letting anyone know what's really on my mind...
Shigure!
CLAMP

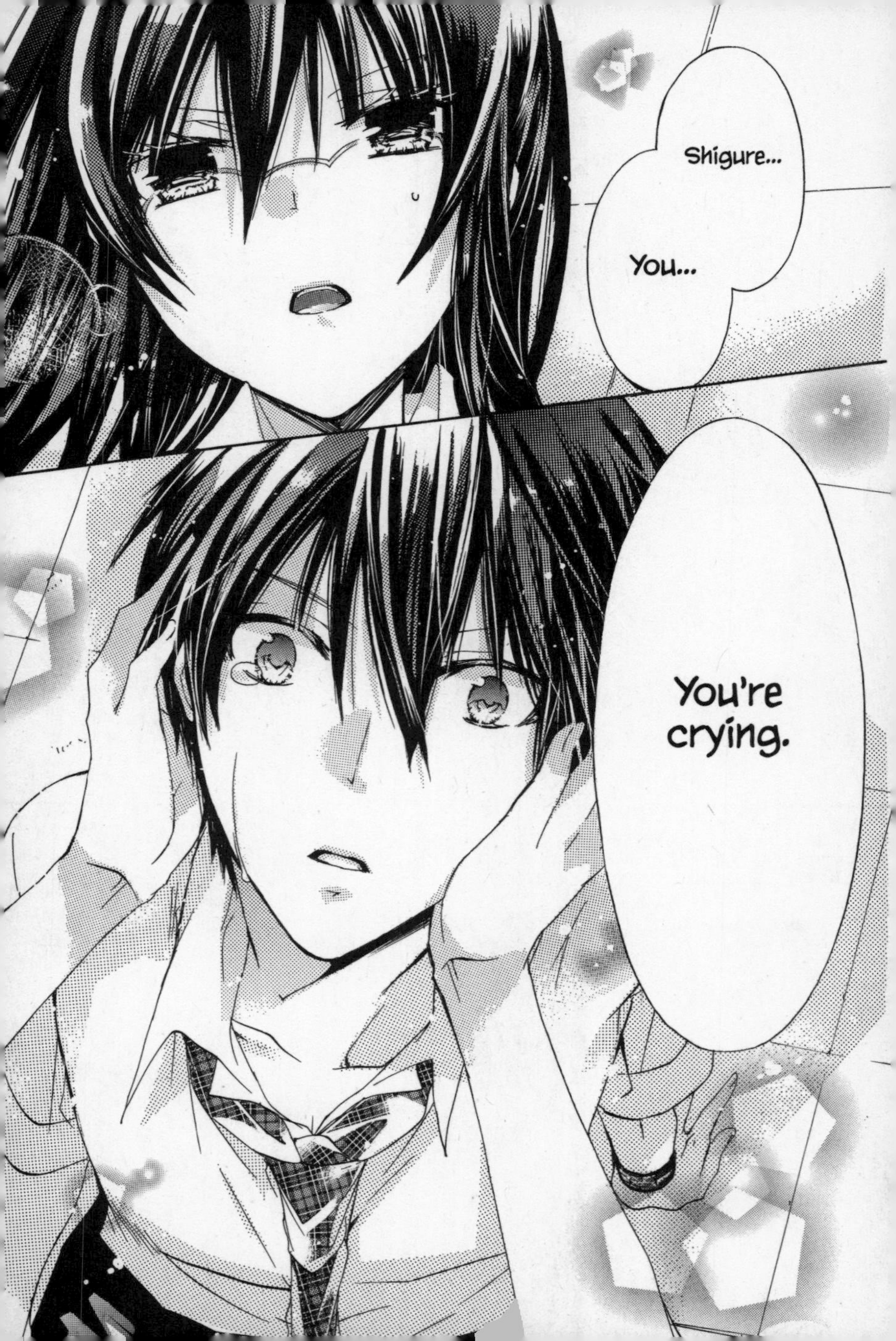
Shigure...
You...
You're crying.

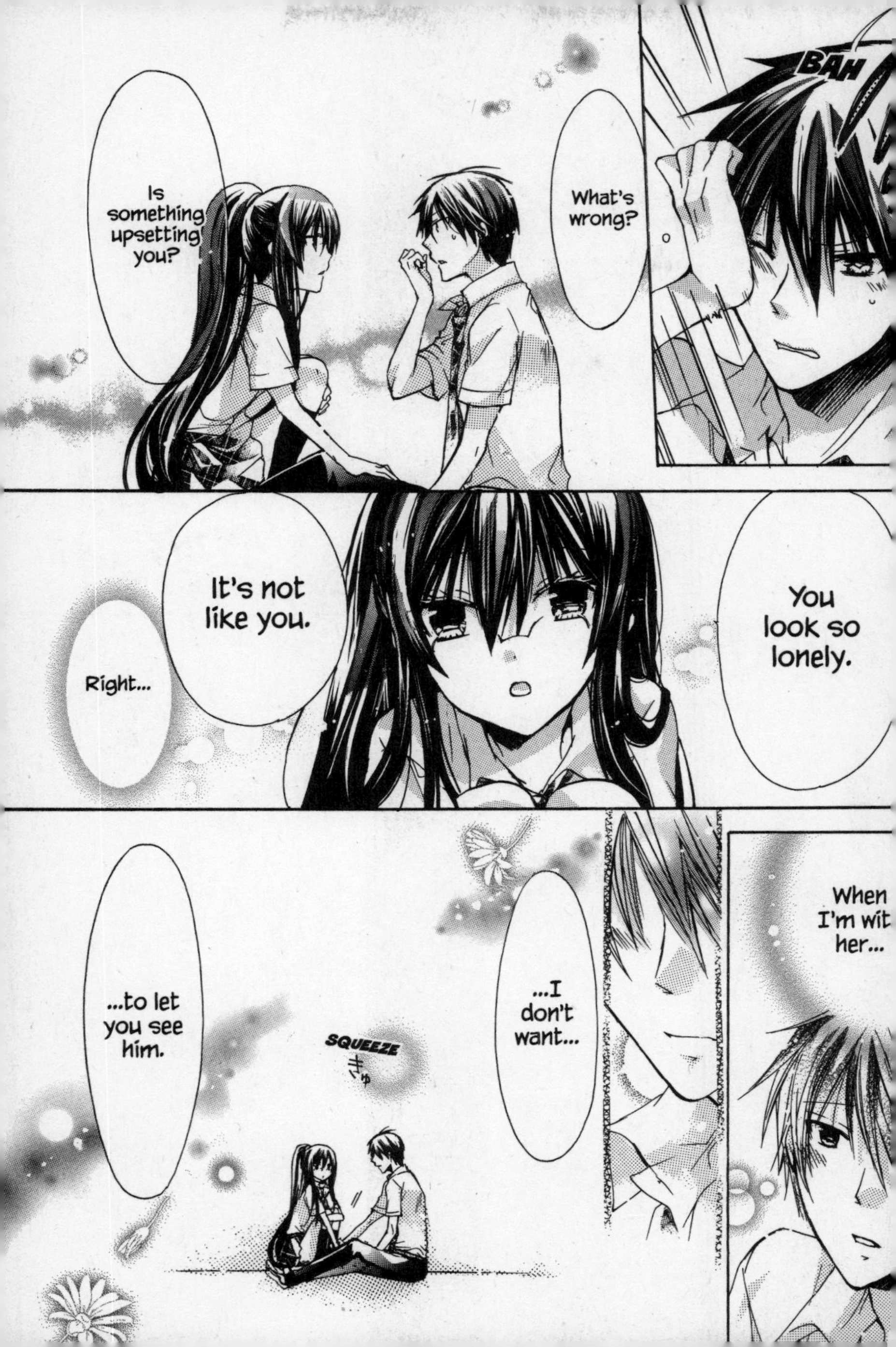
BAH
What's wrong?
Is something upsetting you?
You look so lonely.
It's not like you.
Right...
When I'm wit her...
...I don't want...
SQUEEZE
きゅ
...to let you see him.

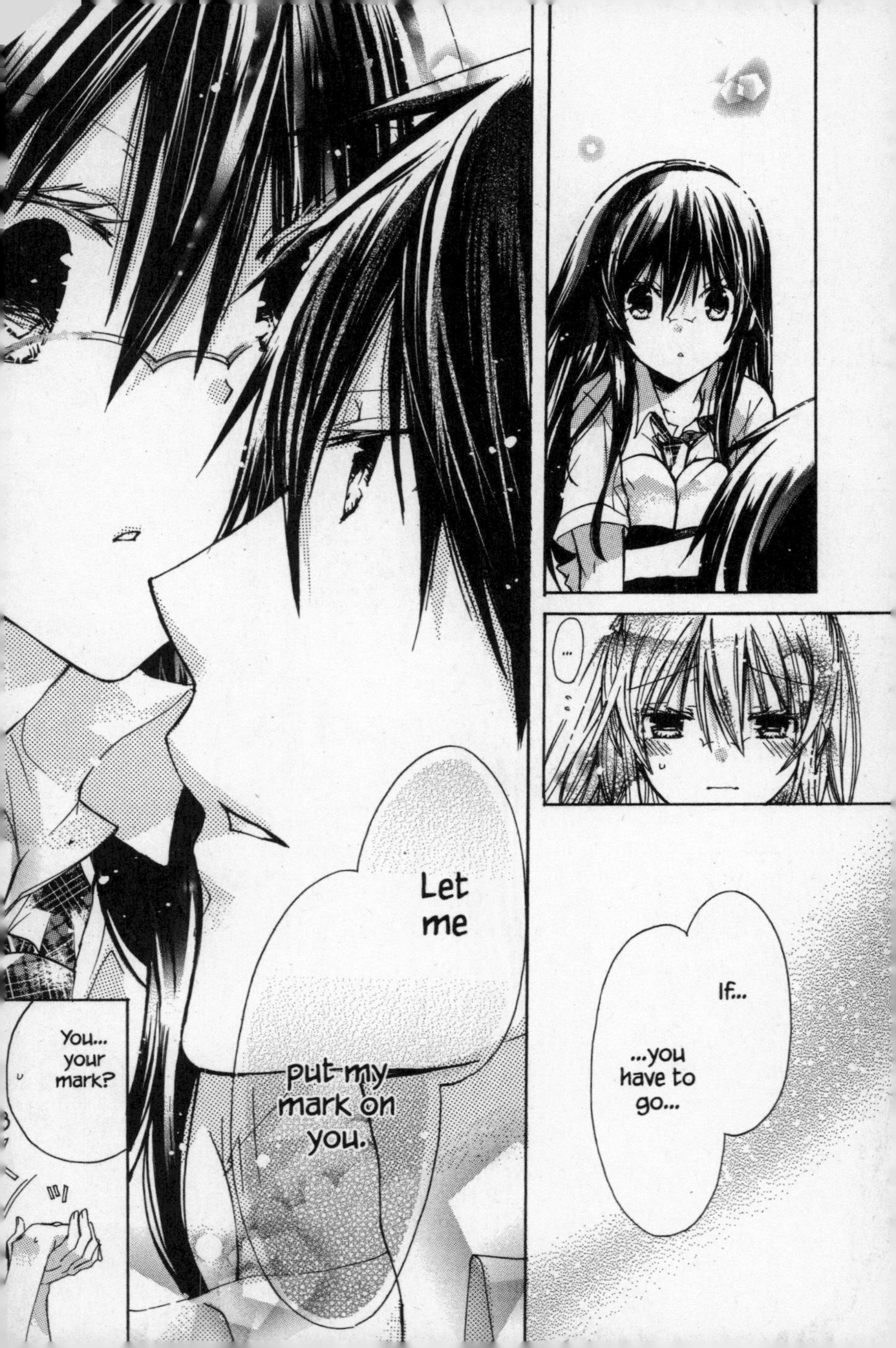
...
If...
...you have to go...
Let me
put my mark on you.
You... your mark?

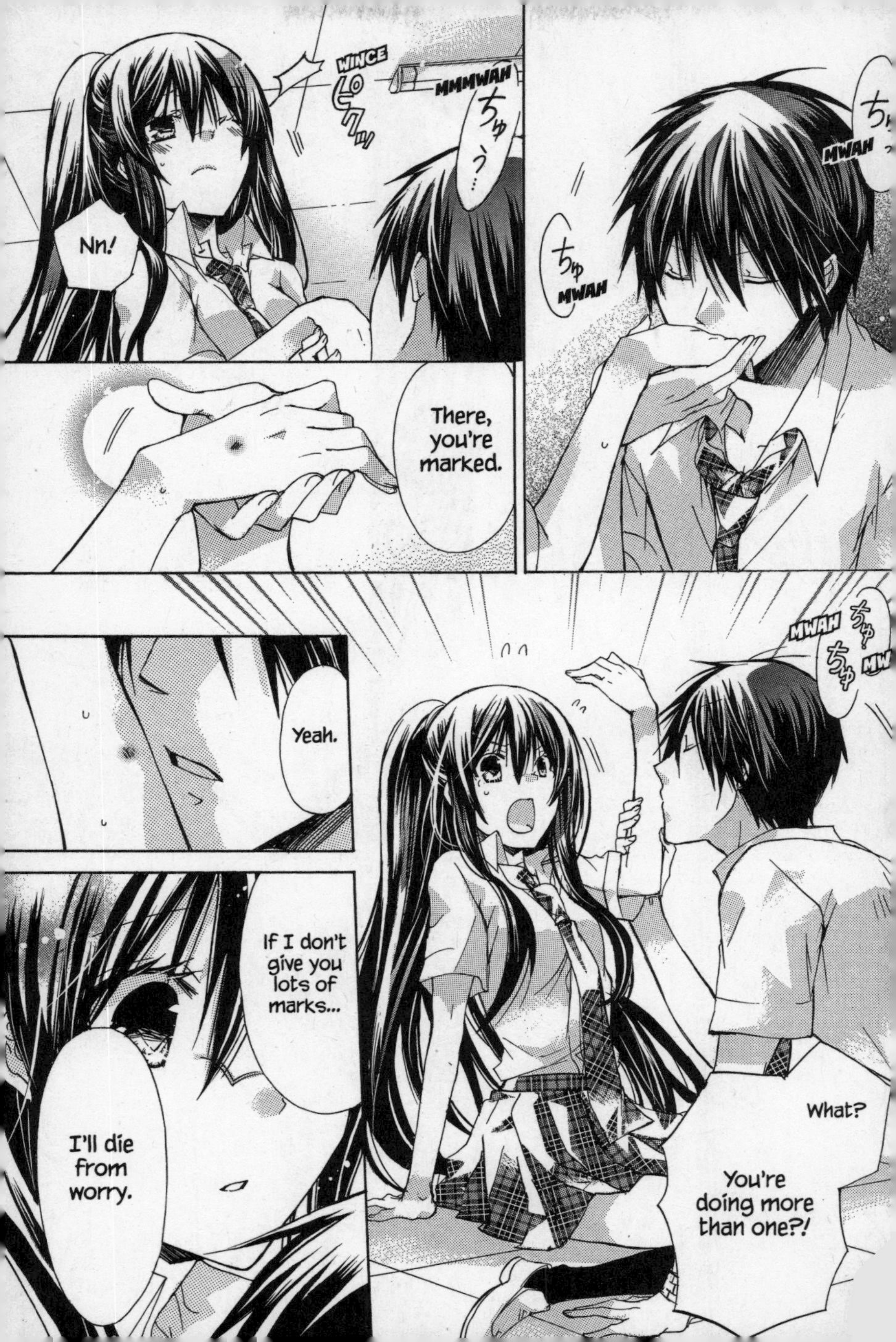
ち
MWAH
ちゅ
MWAH
WINCE
ピクッ
MMMWAH
ちゅう…
Nn!
There, you're marked.
MWAH
ちゅ
ちゅ
MW
What?
You're doing more than one?!
Yeah.
If I don't give you lots of marks...
I'll die from worry.

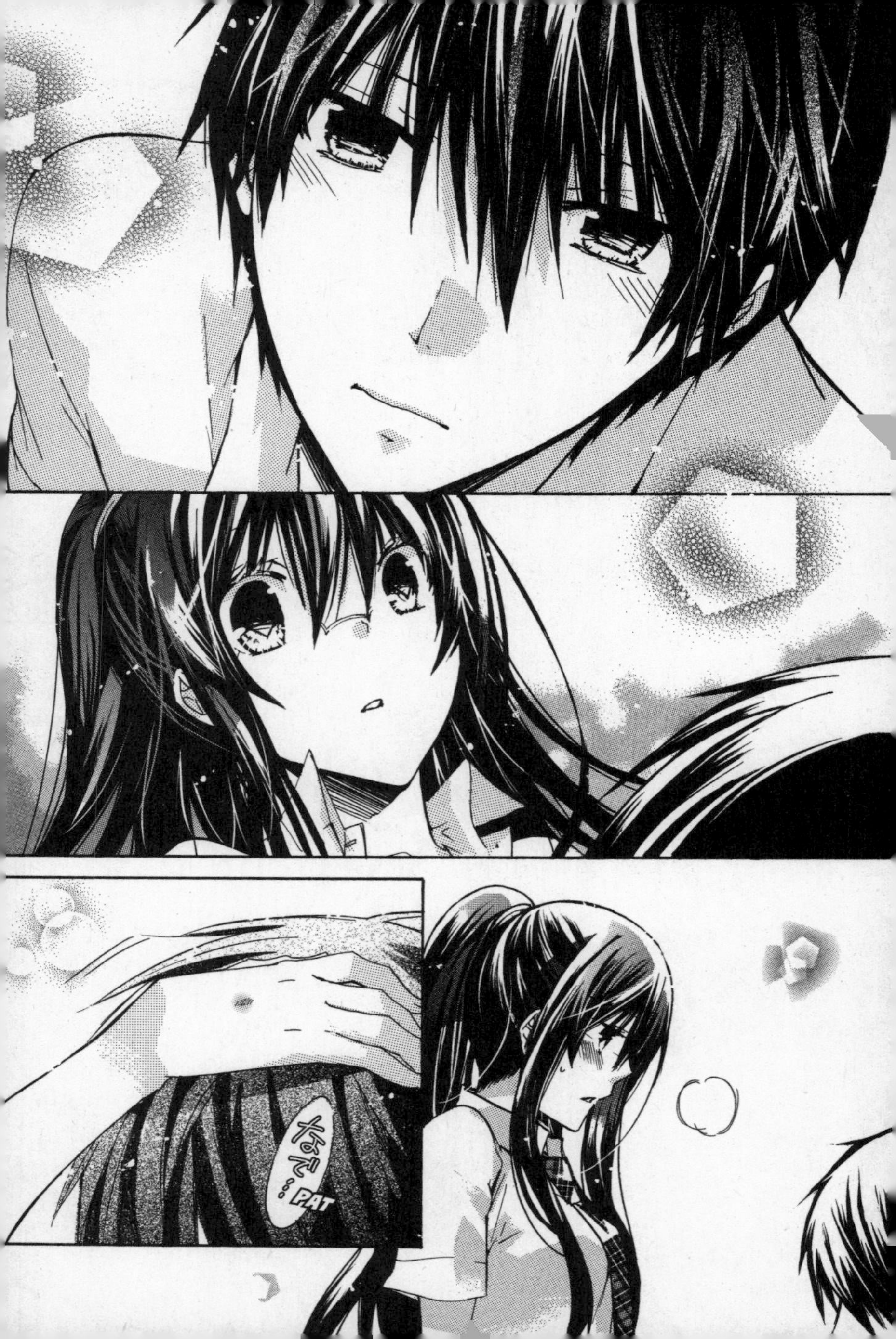
なで…
PAT

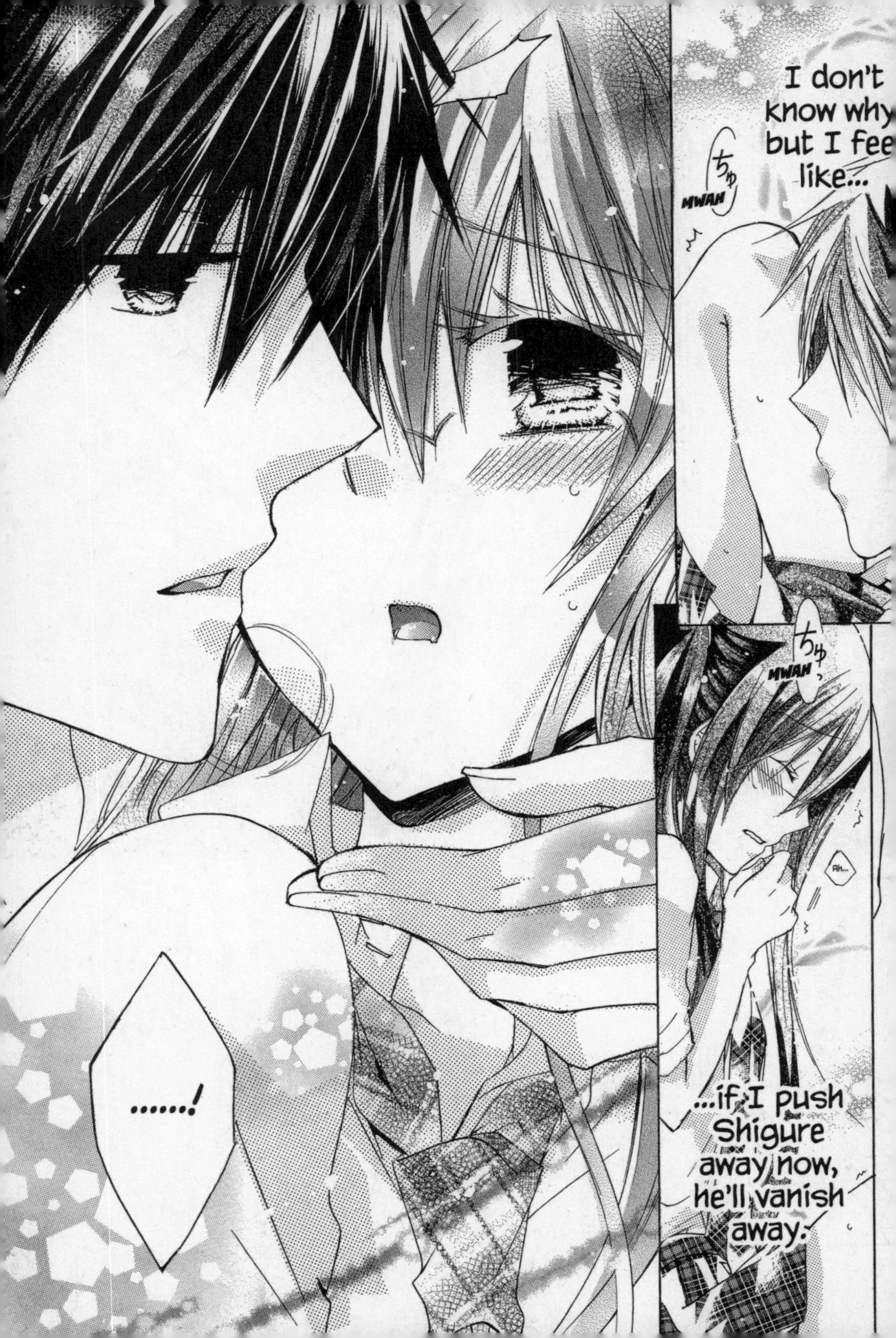
I don't know why but I fee like...
ちゅ
MWAH
ちゅ
MWAH
Ah...
...if I push Shigure away now, he'll vanish away.
......!

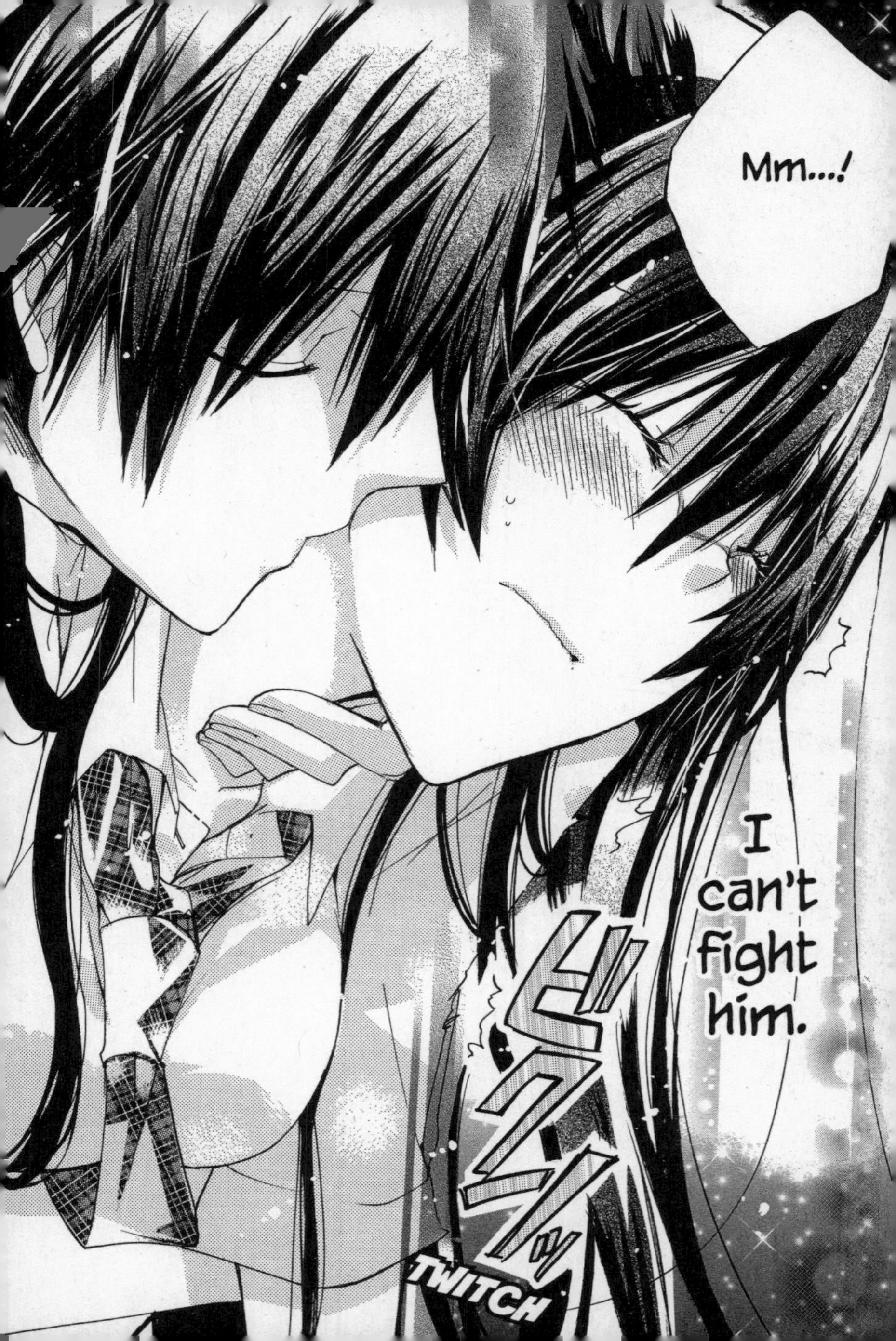
Mm...!
I can't fight him.
TWITCH

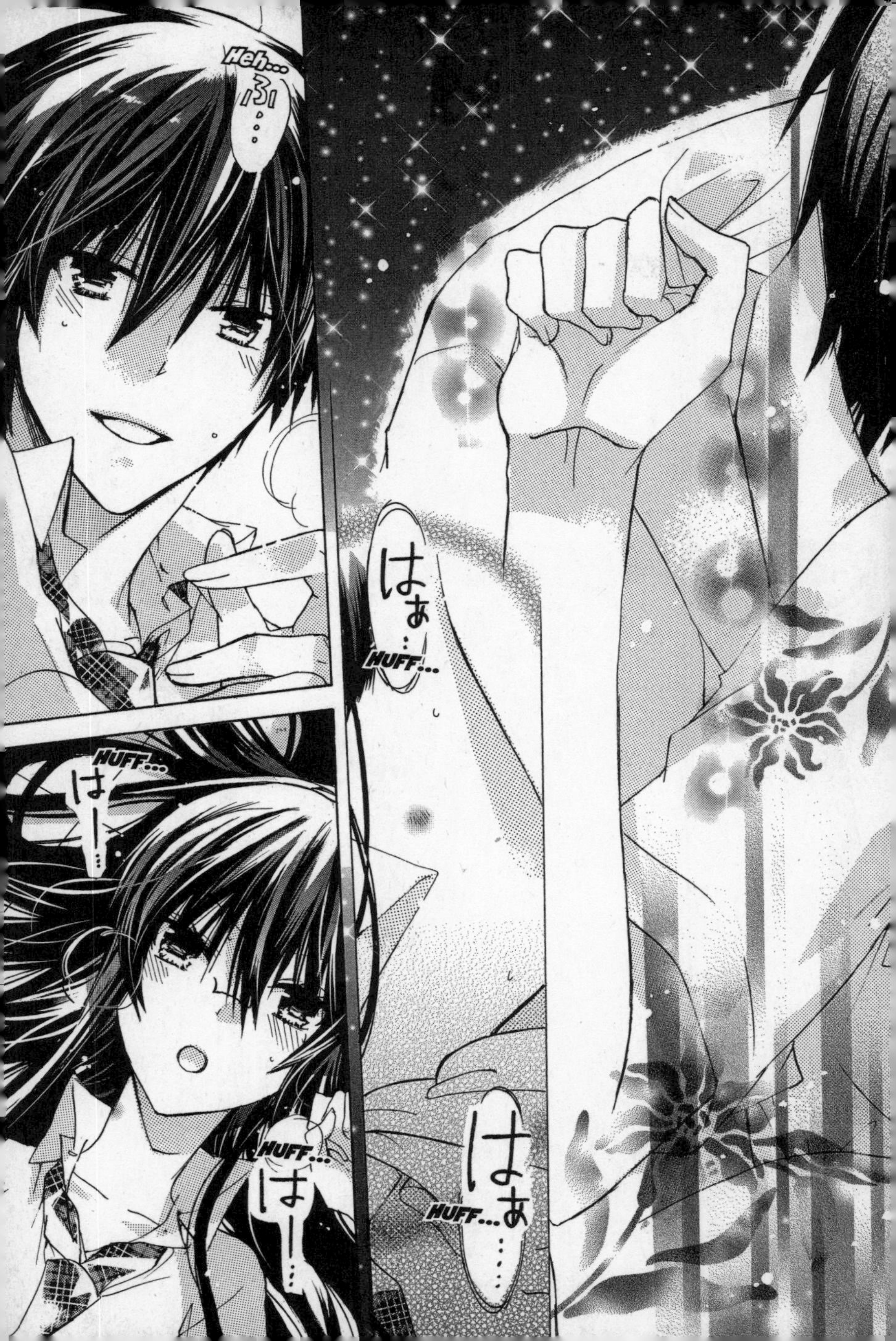
はぁ…
HUFF...
はぁ……
HUFF...
Heh...
ふ…
HUFF...
はー…
HUFF...
はー…

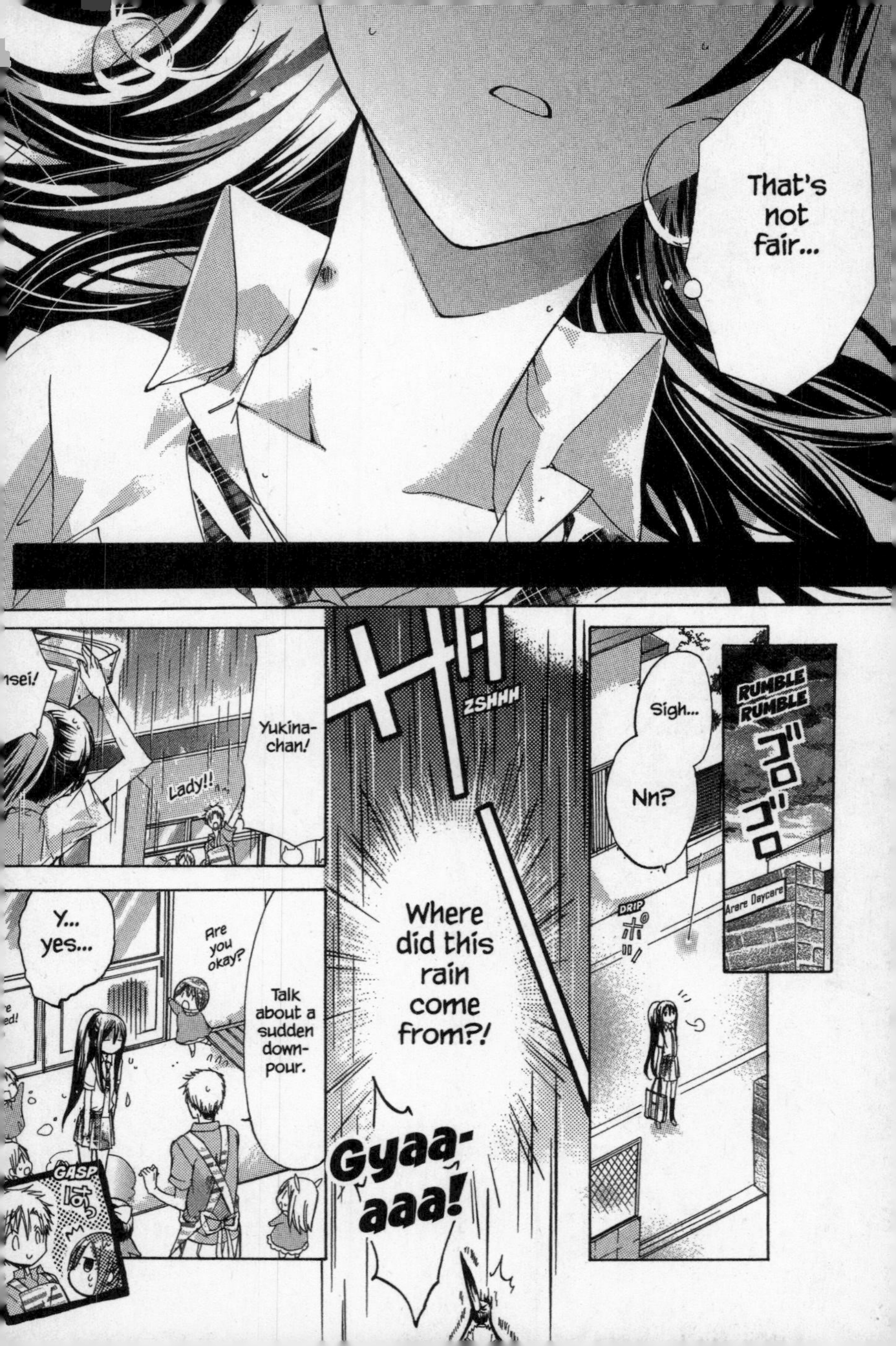
That's not fair...
RUMBLE RUMBLE
ゴロゴロ
Sigh...
Nn?
Arere Daycare
DRIP
ポツ
ZSHHH
Where did this rain come from?!
Gyaa-aaa!
Yukina-chan!
Lady!!
nsei!
Talk about a sudden down-pour.
Are you okay?
Y... yes...
GASP
はっ

ROANOKE
COUNTY VA
PUBLIC LIBRARY

Roanoke Valley Libraries

User name: RILES, CAYLA JANEE'

Title: Missions of love
Item ID: 0119708173982
Date due: 10/31/2020,23:59

Title: Missions of love
Item ID: 0119707512487
Date due: 10/31/2020,23:59

Title: Missions of love
Item ID: 0119707512495
Date due: 10/31/2020,23:59

Title: Missions of love
Item ID: 0119707512503
Date due: 10/31/2020,23:59

Title: Missions of love
Item ID: 0119707137145
Date due: 10/31/2020,23:59

Title: Missions of love
Item ID: 0119708174006
Date due: 10/31/2020,23:59

Title: Missions of love
Item ID: 0119708174014
Date due: 10/31/2020,23:59

Renew online at www.rvl.info

ROANOKE COUNTY VA PUBLIC LIBRARY

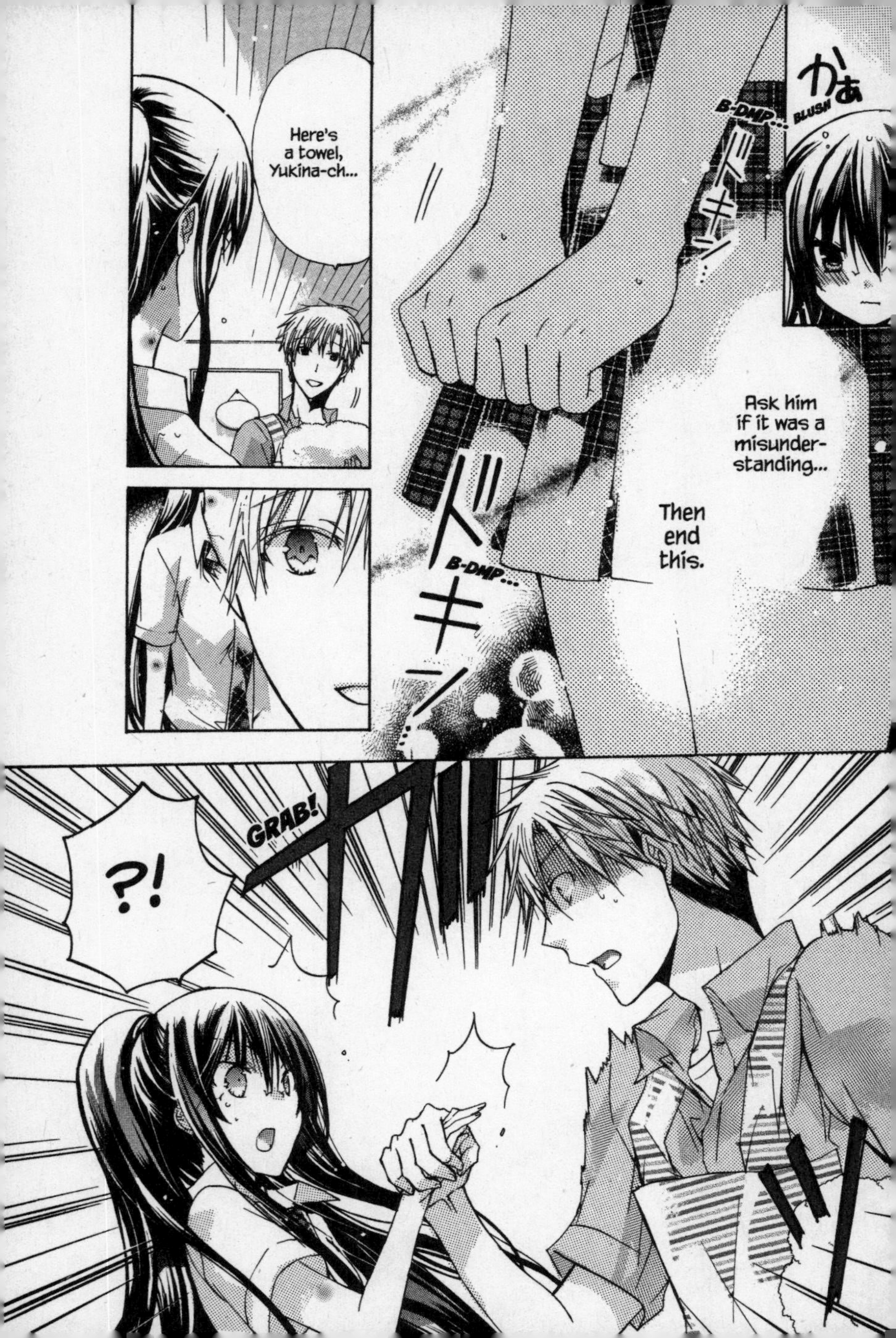
かぁ
BLUSH
B-DMP...
Ask him if it was a misunderstanding...
Then end this.
B-DMP...
ドキーン
Here's a towel, Yukina-ch...
GRAB!
?!

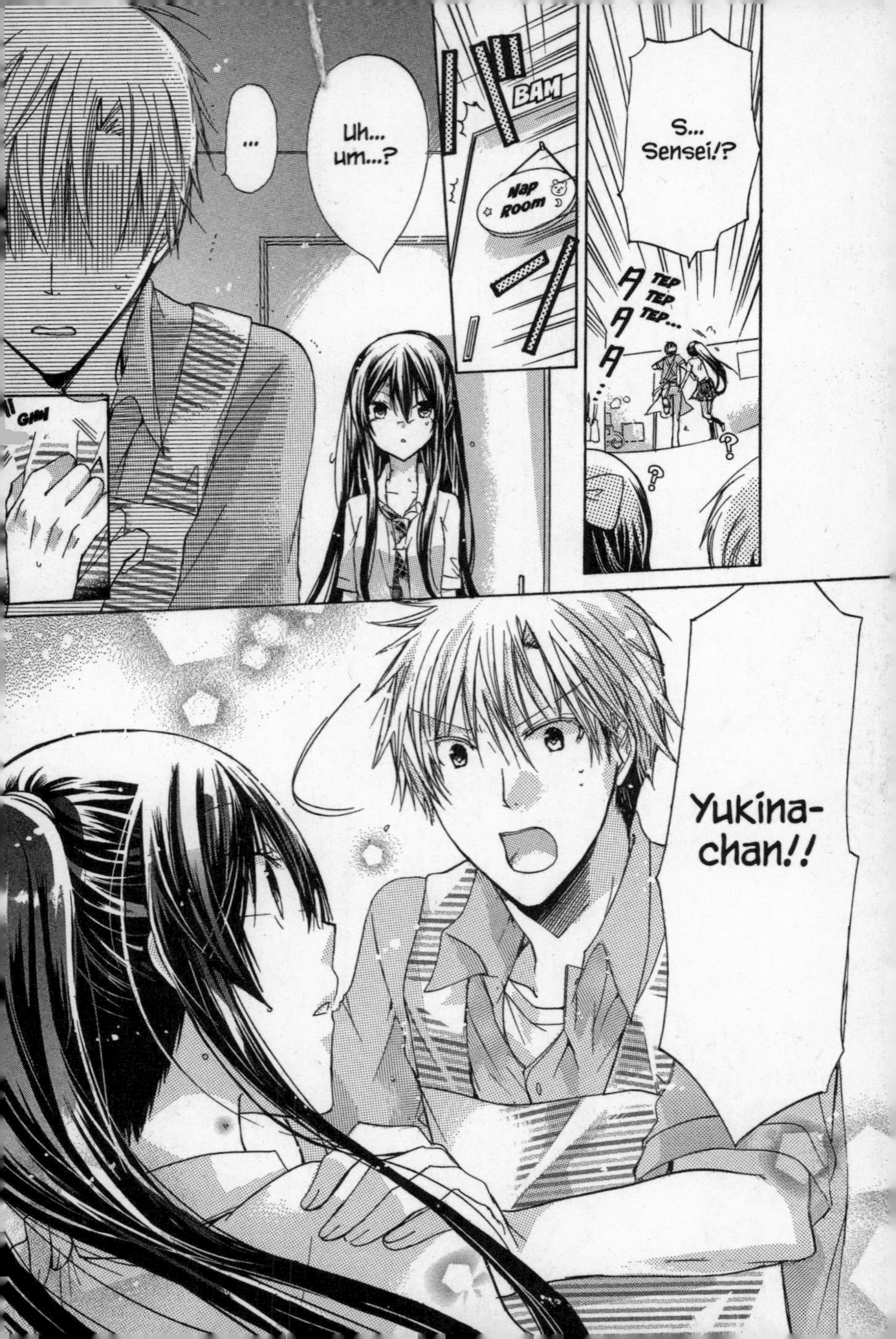
S... Sensei!?
TEP TEP TEP...
AAA...
BAM
Nap Room
Uh... um...?
...
GHN
Yukina-chan!!

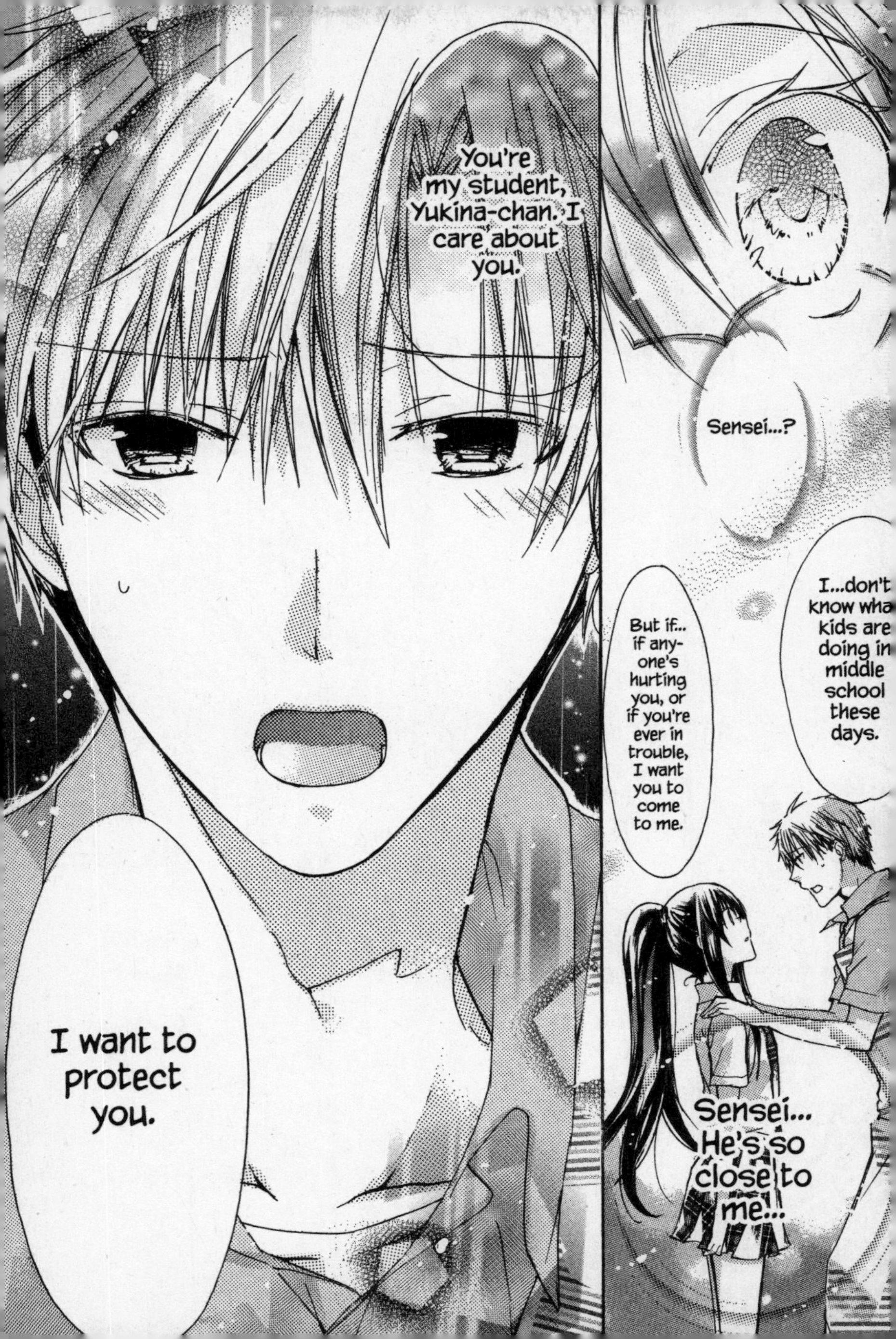
Sensei...?
I...don't know wha kids are doing in middle school these days.
But if... if any-one's hurting you, or if you're ever in trouble, I want you to come to me.
Sensei... He's so close to me...
You're my student, Yukina-chan. I care about you.
I want to protect you.

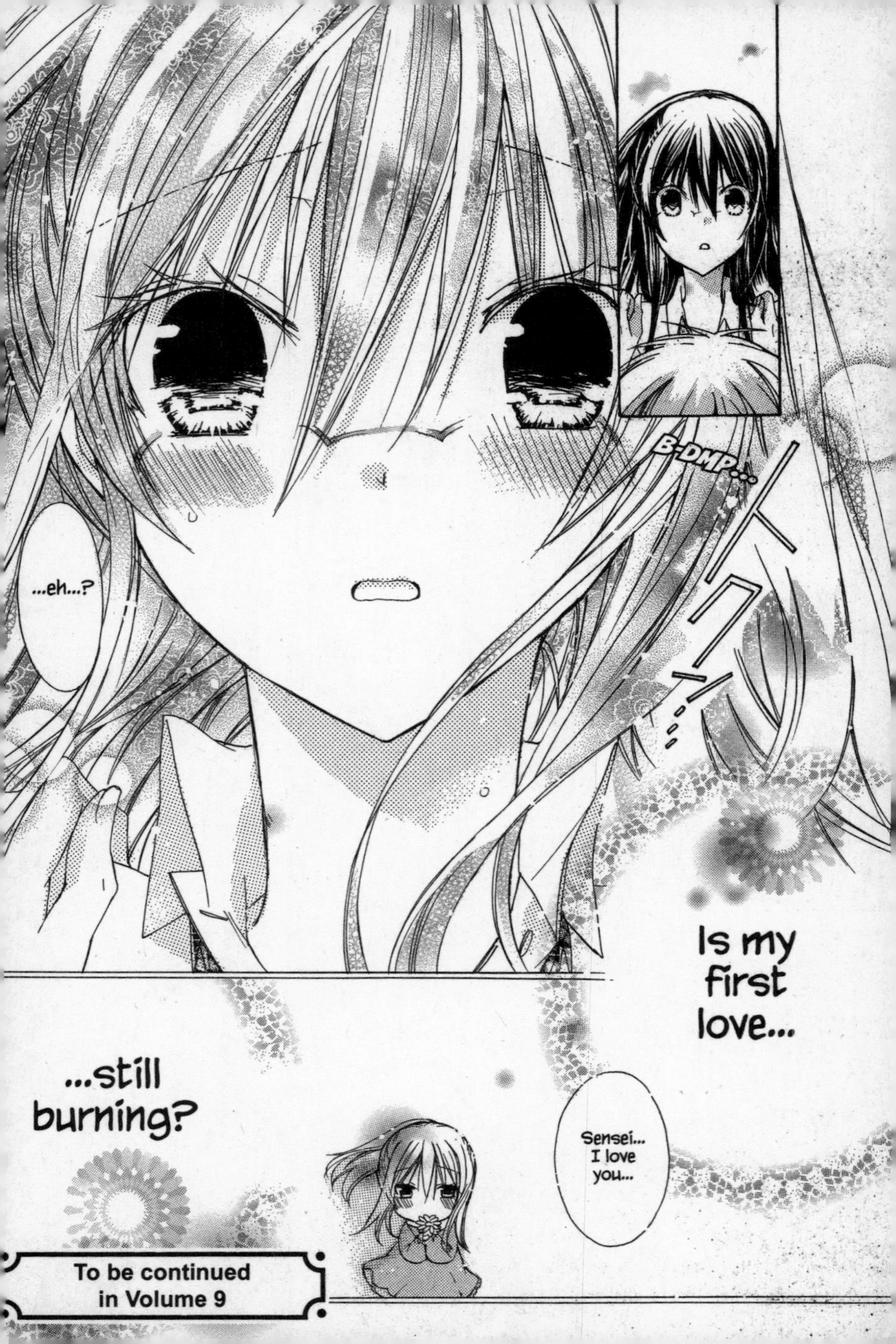
B-DMP...
...eh...?
Is my first love...
...still burning?
Sensei... I love you...
To be continued in Volume 9

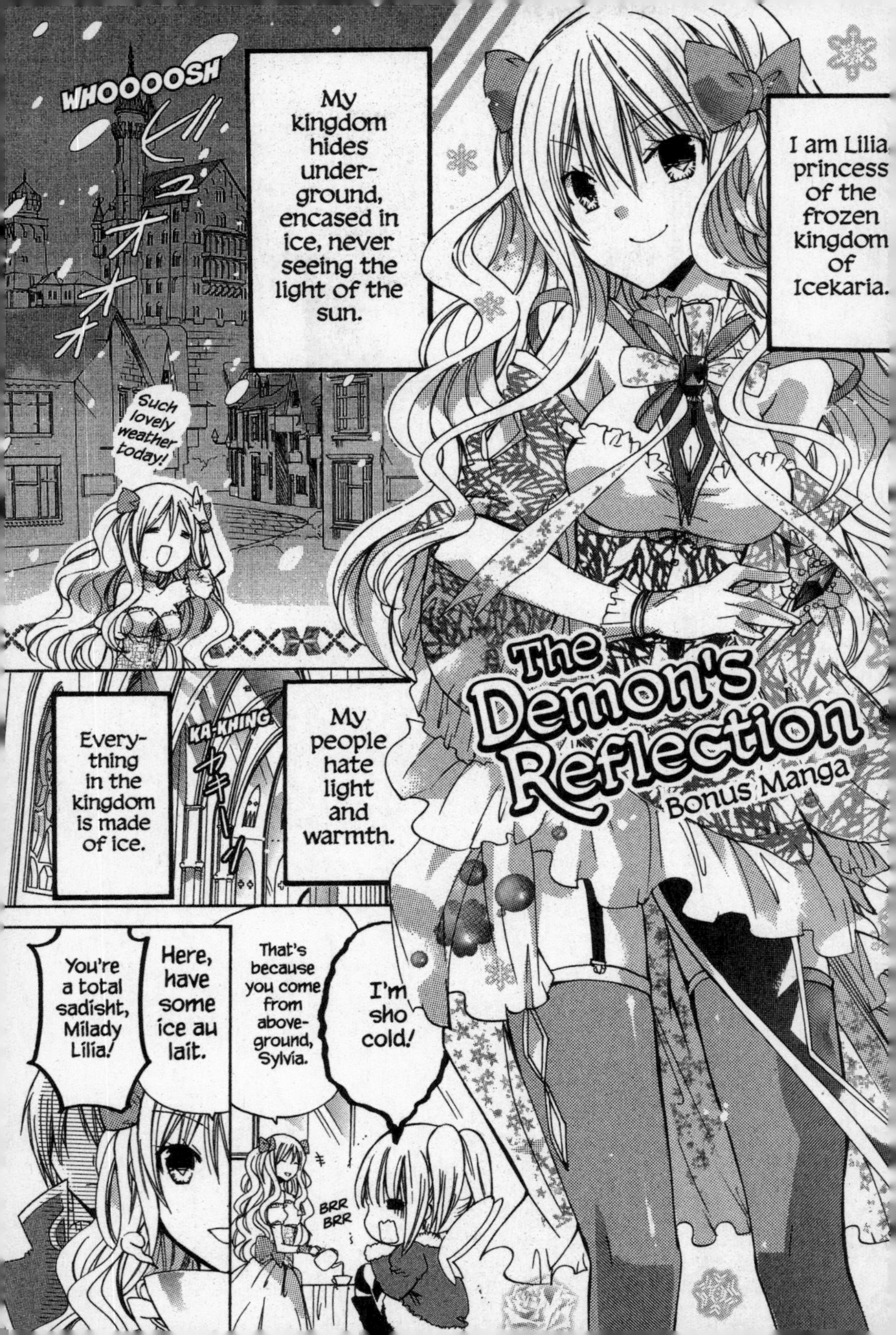
I am Lilia princess of the frozen kingdom of Icekaria.
The Demon's Reflection
Bonus Manga
My kingdom hides under-ground, encased in ice, never seeing the light of the sun.
WHOOOOSH
Such lovely weather today!
My people hate light and warmth.
KA-KHING
Every-thing in the kingdom is made of ice.
I'm sho cold!
BRR BRR
That's because you come from above-ground, Sylvia.
Here, have some ice au lait.
You're a total sadisht, Milady Lilia!

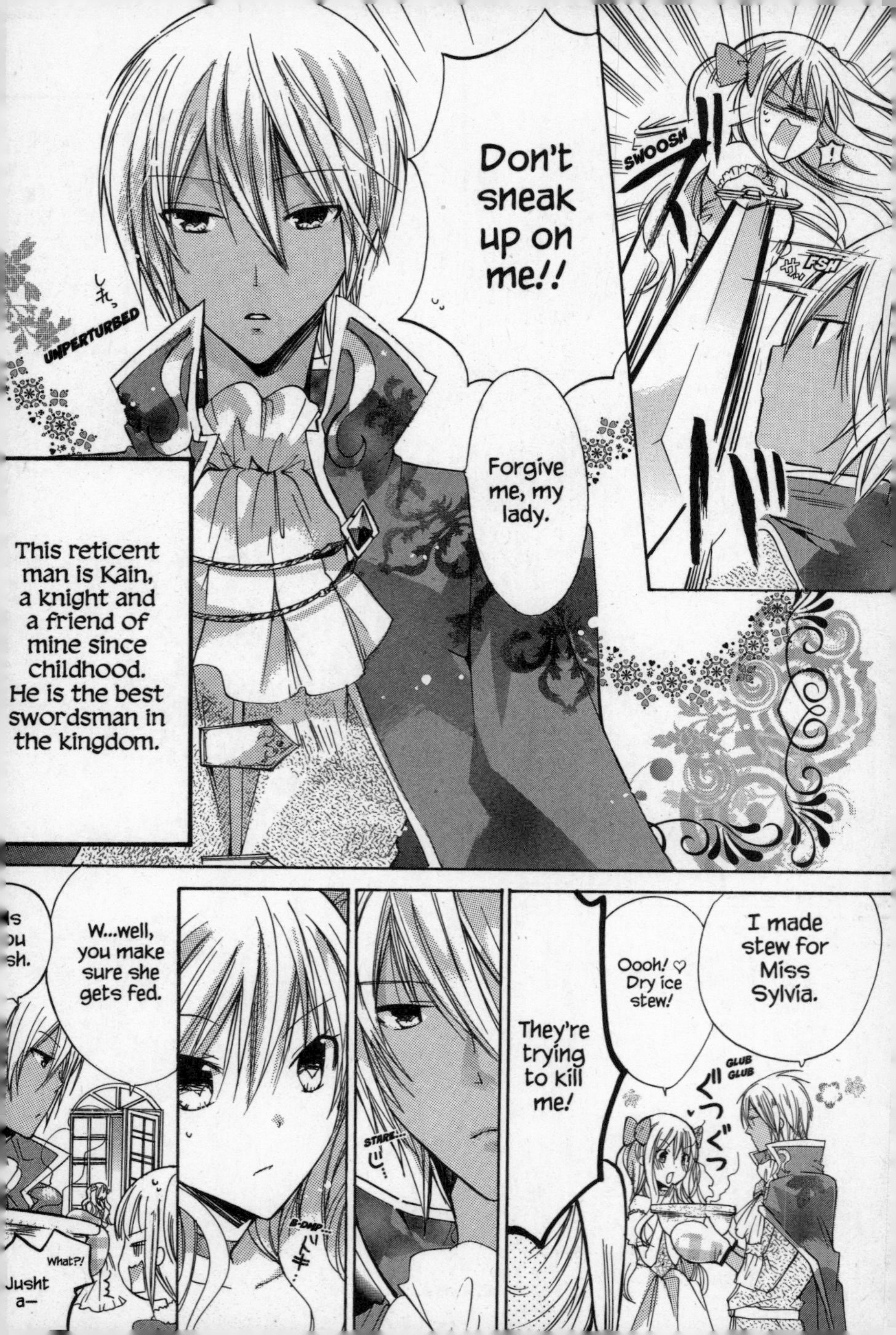
SWOOSH
!
FSH
Don't sneak up on me!!
Forgive me, my lady.
UNPERTURBED
This reticent man is Kain, a knight and a friend of mine since childhood. He is the best swordsman in the kingdom.
I made stew for Miss Sylvia.
Oooh! ♡ Dry ice stew!
They're trying to kill me!
GLUB GLUB
STARE...
B-DMP...
W...well, you make sure she gets fed.
What?!
Jusht a—

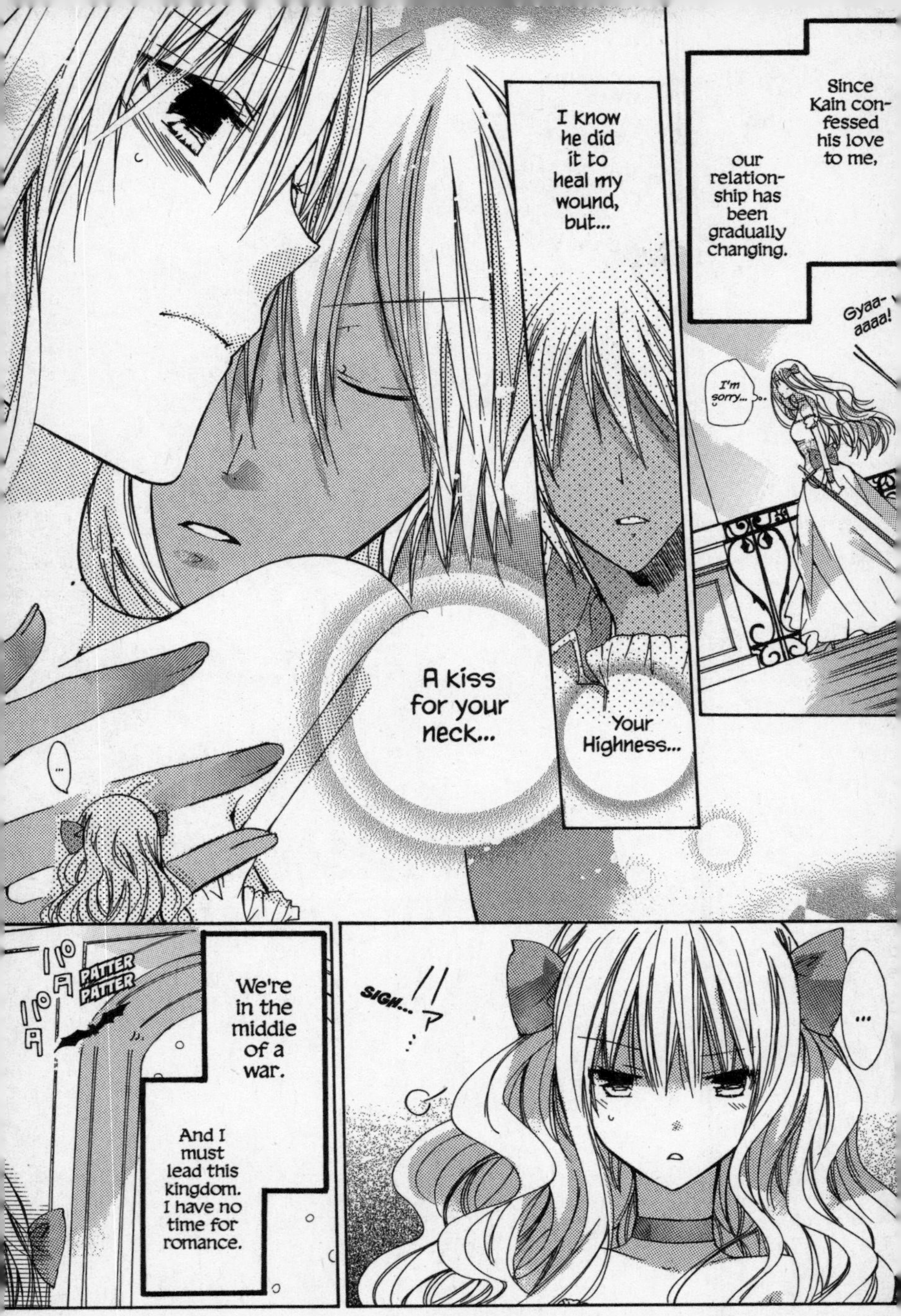
Since Kain confessed his love to me,
our relationship has been gradually changing.
Gyaa-aaaa!
I'm sorry...
I know he did it to heal my wound, but...
Your Highness...
A kiss for your neck...
...
...
SIGH...
We're in the middle of a war.
And I must lead this kingdom. I have no time for romance.
PATTER PATTER

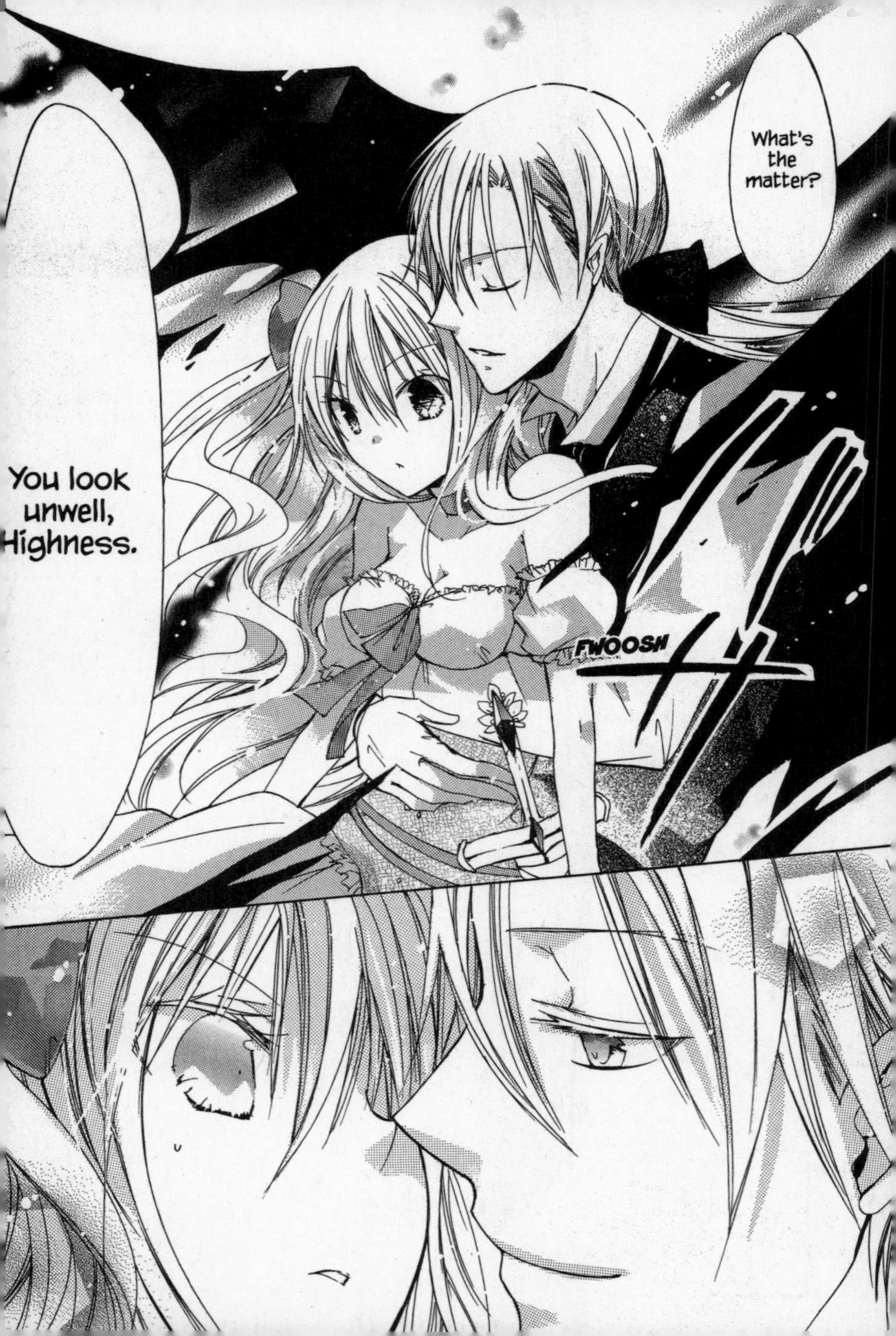
What's the matter?
You look unwell, Highness.
FWOOSH

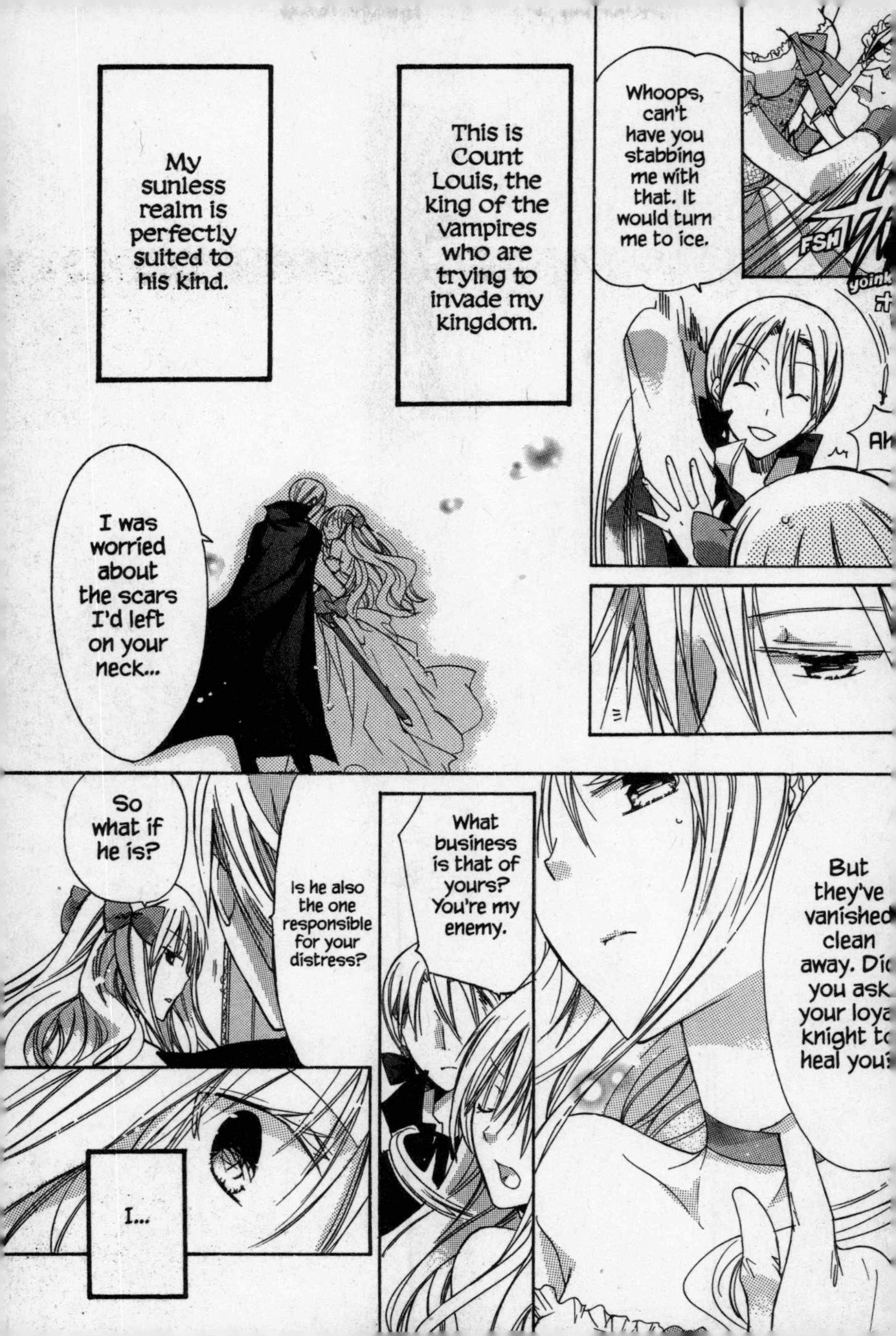
FSH
yoink
Whoops, can't have you stabbing me with that. It would turn me to ice.
Ah
This is Count Louis, the king of the vampires who are trying to invade my kingdom.
My sunless realm is perfectly suited to his kind.
I was worried about the scars I'd left on your neck...
But they've vanished clean away. Did you ask your loyal knight to heal you?
What business is that of yours? You're my enemy.
Is he also the one responsible for your distress?
So what if he is?
I...

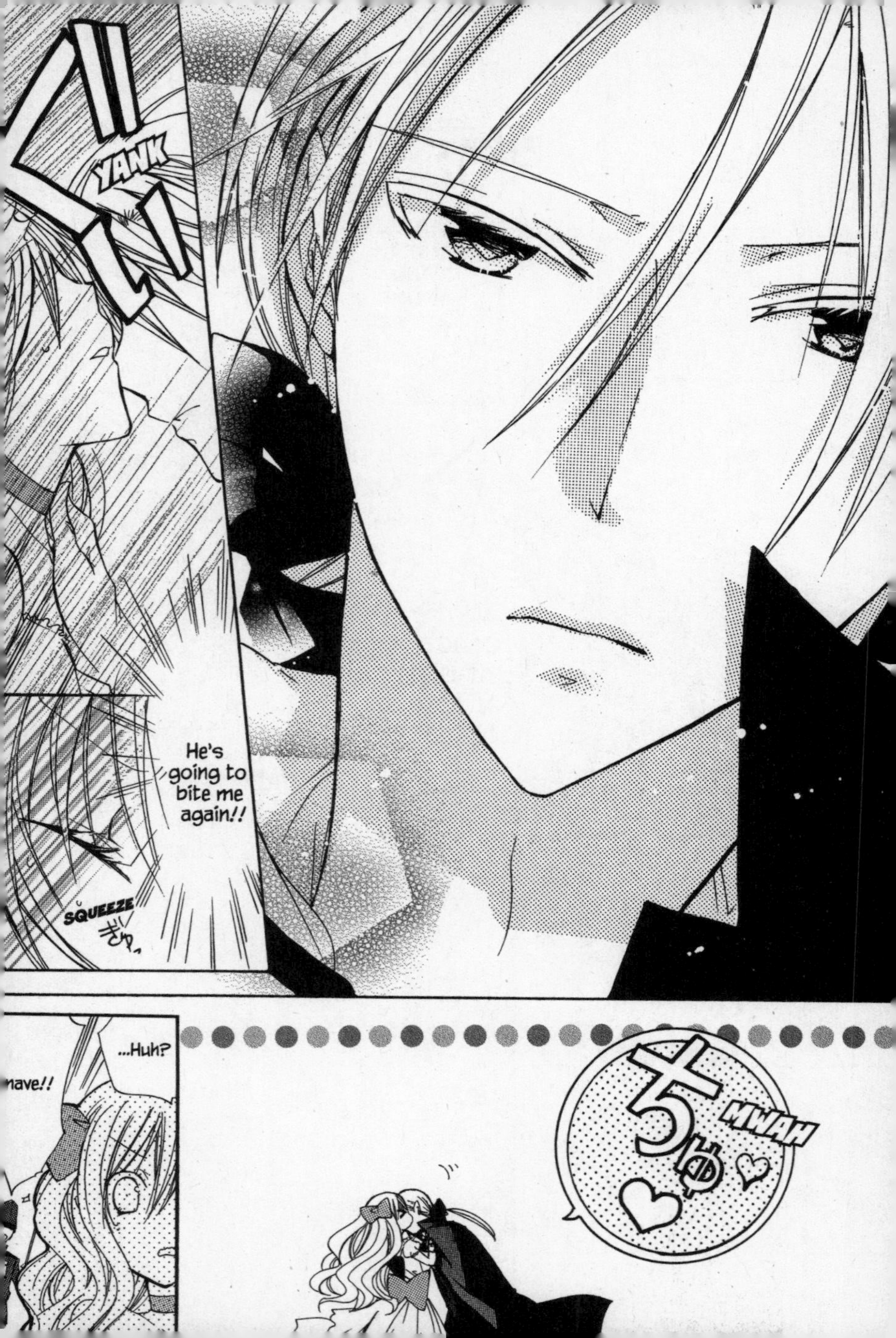
YANK
He's going to bite me again!!
SQUEEZE
MWAH
...Huh?

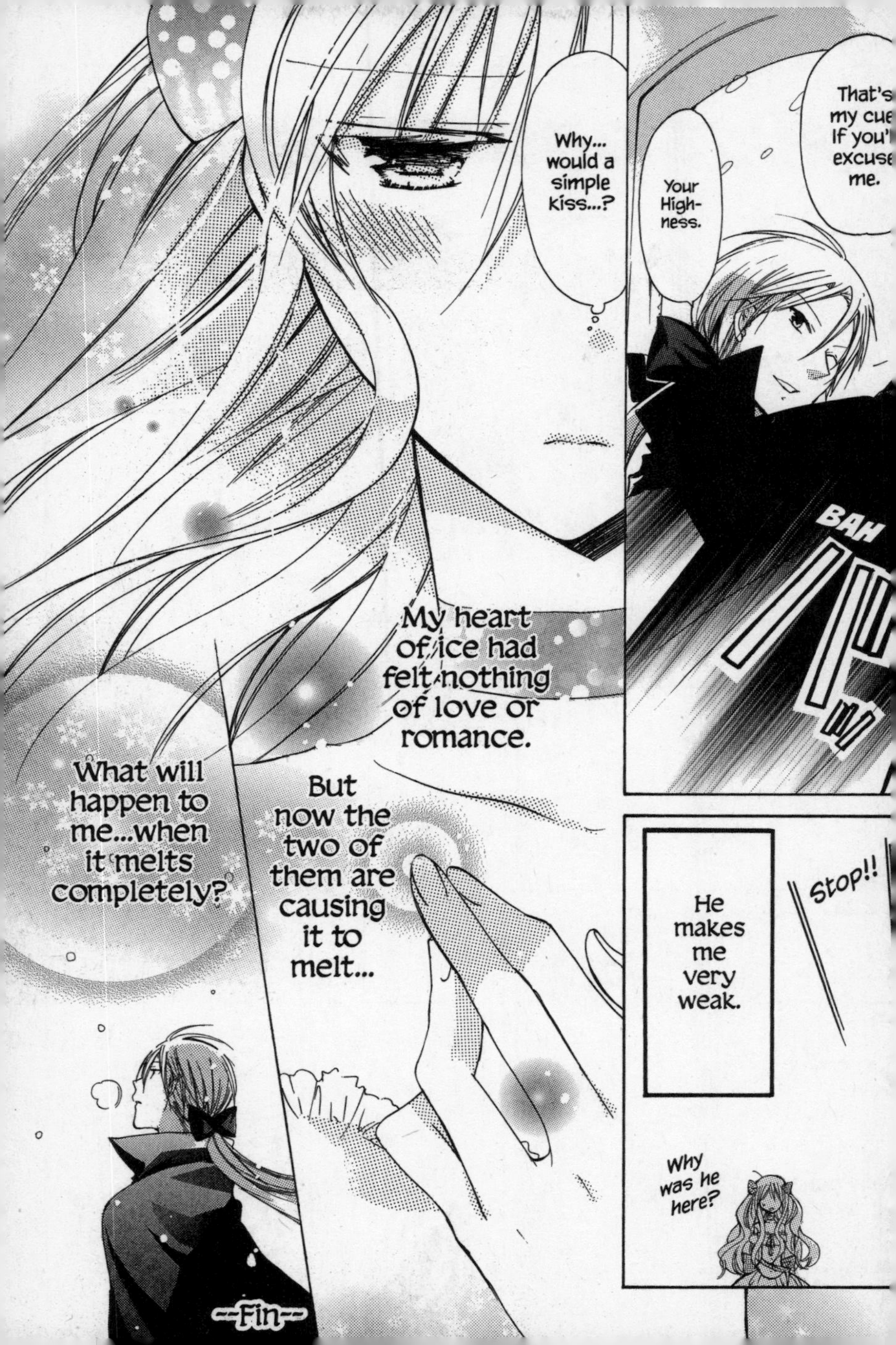
That's my cue If you' excuse me.
Your Highness.
BAH
Stop!!
He makes me very weak.
Why was he here?
Why... would a simple kiss...?
My heart of ice had felt nothing of love or romance.
But now the two of them are causing it to melt...
What will happen to me...when it melts completely?
--Fin--

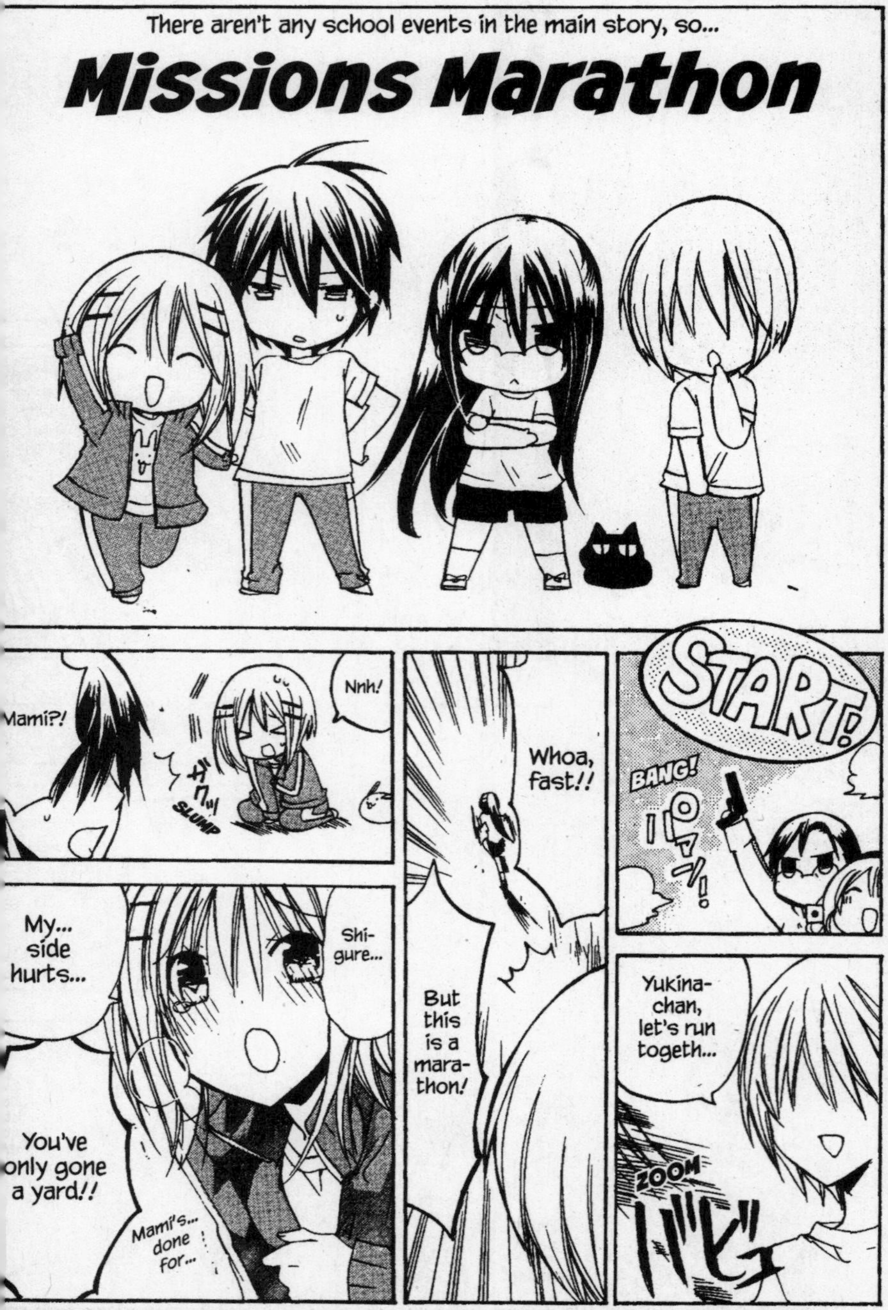
There aren't any school events in the main story, so...
Missions Marathon
START!
BANG!
Yukina-chan, let's run togeth...
ZOOM
Whoa, fast!!
But this is a marathon!
Nnh!
Mami?!
SLUMP
Shigure...
My... side hurts...
You've only gone a yard!!
Mami's... done for...

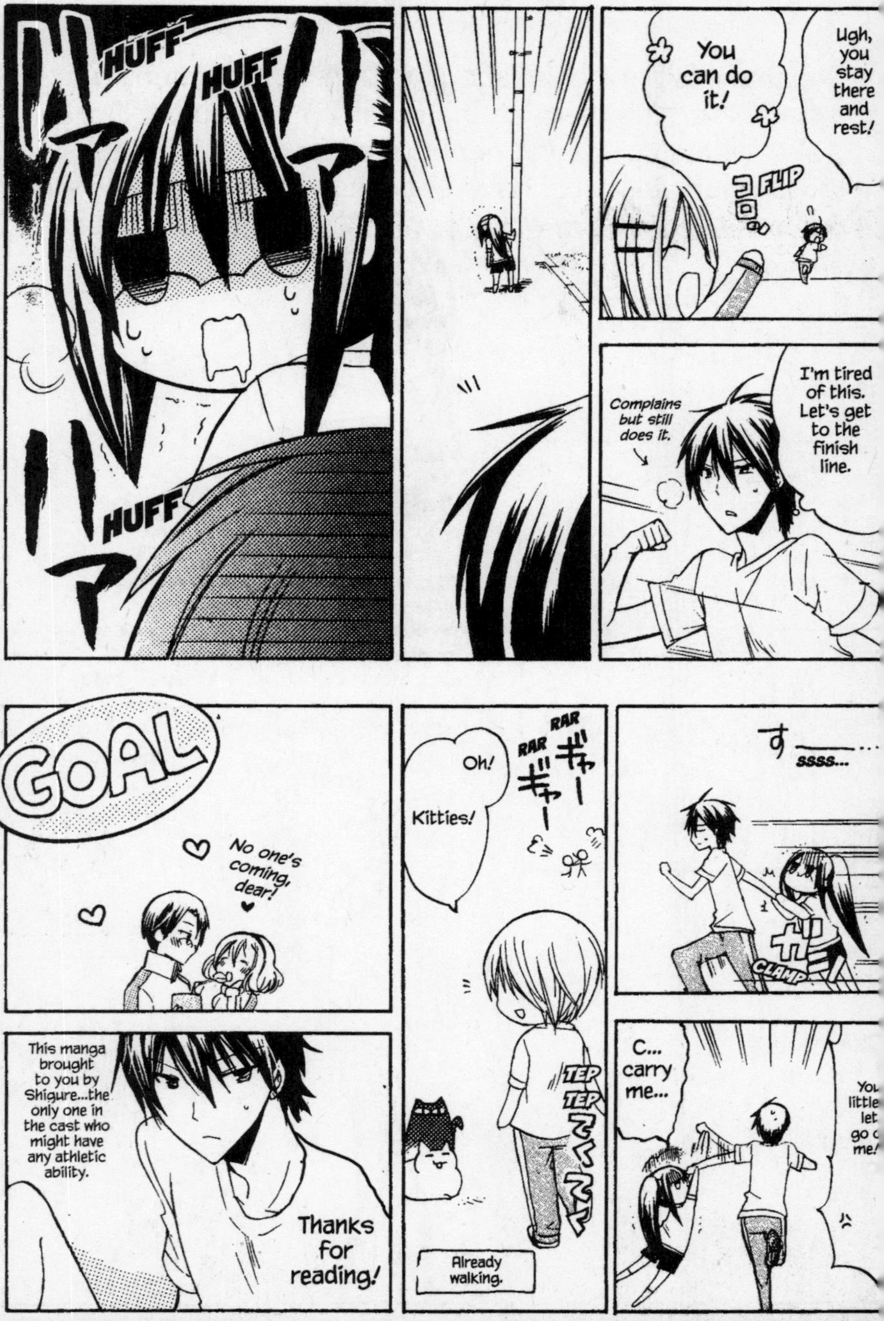
Ugh, you stay there and rest!
You can do it!
FLIP
I'm tired of this. Let's get to the finish line.
Complains but still does it.
HUFF
HUFF
HUFF
ssss...
CLAMP
You little let go o me!
C... carry me...
RAR
RAR
Oh!
Kitties!
TEP
TEP
Already walking.
GOAL
No one's coming, dear!
This manga brought to you by Shigure...the only one in the cast who might have any athletic ability.
Thanks for reading!

Translation Notes

Japanese is a tricky language for most Westerners, and translation is often more art than science. For you edification and reading pleasure, here are notes on some of the places where we could have gone in a different direction in our translation of the work, or where a Japanese cultural reference is used.

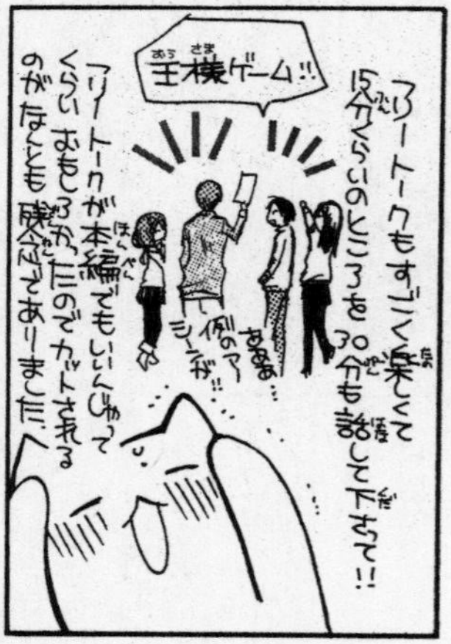

王様ゲーム!!
フリートークもすごく楽しくて15分くらいのところを20分も話して下さって!!
ああああ…
例のア〜シーンが!!
フリートークが本編でもいいんじゃってくらいおもしろかったのでカットされるのがなんとも残念でありました!

Ōsama Game, page 48

The Ōsama Game is a popular party game in Japan. An Ōsama, or king, is chosen at random, by drawing straws or some other method, and gives commands to all his or her subjects. It's sort of like the dare-only edition of "Truth or Dare." This game has a special connection to Missions of Love, because there is a real-life cell phone novel called *Ōsama Game* which was popular enough to be made into a movie.

Missions of Love volume 8 is a work of fiction. Names, characters, places, and incidents are the products of the author's imagination or are used fictitiously. Any resemblance to actual events, locales, or persons, living or dead, is entirely coincidental.

A Kodansha Comics Trade Paperback Original.

Published in the United States by Kodansha Comics, an imprint of Kodansha USA Publishing, LLC, New York.

Publication rights for this English edition arranged through Kodansha Ltd., Tokyo.

First published in Japan in 2012 by Kodansha Ltd., Tokyo as *Watashi ni xx shinasai!,* volume 8.

ISBN 978-1-61262-290-3

Printed in the United States of America.

www.kodanshacomics.com

9 8 7 6 5 4 3 2 1

Translator: Alethea Nibley and Athena Nibley
Lettering: Paige Pumphrey